Who Will Speak for the Victim?

A Practical Treatise on Plaintiff's Jury Argument

JIM M. PERDUE

WHO WILL SPEAK FOR THE VICTIM?

A Practical Treatise on Plaintiff's Jury Argument

Austin 1989

The State Bar of Texas, through its Books & Systems Department, publishes practice books prepared and edited by knowledgeable authors to give practicing lawyers and judges as much assistance as possible. The competence of the authors ensures outstanding professional products, but, of course, neither the State Bar of Texas, the editors, nor the authors make either express or implied warranties in regard to their use. Each lawyer must depend on his or her own knowledge of the law and expertise in the use or modification of these materials.

The use of the masculine gender in this publication is purely for literary convenience and should, of course, be understood to include the feminine gender as well.

International Standard Book Number: 0-938160-54-0
Library of Congress Catalog Card Number: 88-63945

The author and the State Bar of Texas gratefully acknowledge permission of the copyright holders and publishers to reprint the following selections from their publications: "It Couldn't Be Done" and "The Broken Wheel" (in chapter 11) and "To a Little Girl," "Lonely," "Father," and "Mother" (in chapter 27) from *Collected Poems of Edgar A. Guest* by Edgar A. Guest, © 1934 by Contemporary Books, Inc., Chicago, reprinted by permission of the publisher. Excerpts (in chapter 24) from *Lonesome Dove* by Larry McMurtry, © 1985 by Simon & Schuster, Inc., New York, reprinted by permission of the publisher. Facts and argument (in chapters 29 and 31) from *The Law of Texas Medical Malpractice* by Jim M. Perdue, © 1985 by Houston Law Review, Houston, reprinted by permission of the publisher.

Printed in the United States of America

First Printing, 1989
Second Printing, 1991

*To Jim, Joe, and Jeff, my sons,
who have always supported me
and understood the life of a trial lawyer.*

Contents

STATE BAR OF TEXAS

James B. Sales
President

1301 McKinney
Gulf Tower
Houston, Texas 77010
713/651-5151

The State Bar of Texas proudly presents *Who Will Speak for the Victim?* a multidimensional work that demonstrates how a case is effectively argued before a jury.

In these instructive and entertaining pages, author Jim Perdue distills a wealth of trial experience and presents a superbly crafted work that will benefit the novice and the seasoned trial lawyer alike.

The commitment of the State Bar of Texas to continuing legal education includes the important mission of providing publications that will help Texas lawyers improve their professional competency. We are deeply grateful to Mr. Perdue for so generously giving his time and sharing his knowledge in the furtherance of this mission.

James B. Sales

James B. Sales
President, State Bar of Texas

Preface

THERE are two kinds of law books. The most commonly encountered law books are used for reference and source material. No one really "reads" these books. (When was the last time you read from cover to cover a volume of the *Southwestern Reporter*, *Texas Jurisprudence*, or one of the fine treatises published by the State Bar?) The second kind of law book is for reading. Unfortunately, perhaps because there are few of these books on the market, most lawyers do very little general legal reading.

Who Will Speak for the Victim? is a book of the second type. It was written with the intent that it be read. While it may be used for reference—there are many sections to which a lawyer might refer in preparing a specific argument—it will best assist those who take the time to read it in its entirety.

Several considerations prompted this work. Although I have had the opportunity and privilege of authoring or coauthoring other books, supplements, chapters in legal and medical reference works, and numerous law review articles, all my previous writing has been primarily reference oriented. It was time to undertake a different kind of writing. The primary impetus for this work, however, was the realization that there was really no single source to which a lawyer—whether a novice or an experienced trial lawyer—could turn for help in improving the technique and content of jury argument. Indeed, few books even contain summations given in personal injury cases. Those that do, such as some of Moe Levine's fine works, are not really appropriate to our practice in Texas. Most other jurisdictions submit cases on a general charge with oral instructions from the judge. The Texas method of submission by questions and written instructions produces drastic differences in the approach and manner in which trial lawyers must address and argue their cases.

This is not a "law book" in the strictest sense. It contains very few legal references. Some readers may consider it a "how-to-do-it" book. In reality it is intended as a provocative writing, created to make the trial lawyer who is preparing for summation think about what he is doing and why he is doing it. The arguments in this book should trigger and excite the trial lawyer's mind toward thoughts, approaches, and arguments that are appropriate to his case. The examples, illustrations, and vignettes given here are not fictitious; each is a firsthand, personal experience. Most of the arguments used as illustrations were made either by me or by other lawyers involved in a case I tried.

I certainly do not consider myself an extremely gifted oral advocate for injured plaintiffs in this state. Texas is blessed with many great trial lawyers who have innate or natural oratorical ability. I doubt, however, that many lawyers have been privileged to enjoy the type of training and direction I have been afforded over the years. As a college debater and moot-court participant at the University of Houston, I enjoyed the tutelage of such recognized champions as our former Texas Supreme Court Justice William Kilgarlin. The first few years of my law practice were spent on the defense side. No one could ask for any better direction or training than that given me by Jerry Walker of Houston and the late Royce Till of Houston. If I have enjoyed any success as an oral advocate for injured plaintiffs, it should prove the point made throughout this book: any lawyer of reasonable intelligence who sincerely believes in the cause of the injured and oppressed can by self-discipline, preparation, and training become an effective advocate for his clients.

Acknowledgments

THE AUTHOR wishes to acknowledge the assistance of Kevin Dubose, professor of law at Bates College of Law at the University of Houston and of counsel with Perdue, Turner & Berry, and Mark Clore, an associate with Perdue, Turner & Berry, for their input, assistance, and support in writing this book.

Moreover, the author would particularly like to acknowledge the contributions of Susannah R. Mills, Director of Books and Systems of the State Bar of Texas. Her suggestions and comments and those of staff members Irene Aldrich and Dorothy Morse have proved invaluable in this effort. It is believed that their insight has improved not only the quality of this work but also the quality of arguments that lawyers who use this book may advance before juries of this state.

PART 1

The Concept of Forensic Argument

Discretion of speech is more than eloquence.

—Francis Bacon, "Of Discourse," No. 32 in *Essays*

1

Interrelation of Argument and the Case

The members of the jury panel stood along the wall of the courtroom like baffled suspects in a lineup. As the bailiff called their names, they shuffled uneasily to their seats on the long benches stretched across the back half of the courtroom. Each potential juror had been observing, in his own discreet way, the attorneys seated at the tables in front of the courtroom. None had failed to notice a significant difference in appearance and attitude between the two camps of lawyers. On one side sat two well-dressed, neatly groomed individuals; erect and attentive, they seemed to be studying the panel members' every move and gesture. On the other side, two lawyers seemed intently engrossed in some private joke. One slouched in his chair, a mischievous grin etched on his face. The other, leaning in his chair, had his hand cupped over his mouth as he whispered to his colleague between chuckles. Studying these two warring camps, the anonymous audience began to observe more differences.

Some days later, twenty-four eyes cautiously studied the lawyer standing before them. As he presented his final summation, his words were lost in the blur of impressions that had largely been formed during those first few moments at the beginning of the proceedings.

"Ladies and gentlemen of the jury, we have appreciated your service and attention as jurors. [Sure you have, that's why you've been joking with your co-counsel and client in the courtroom and hallways at every break or recess.] . . .

"We've tried to bring you this evidence in a straightforward manner. [When you could find the exhibit, when you could decide what question you wanted to ask, when you stopped rambling from point to point.] . . .

"My client [and that's all he is to you—just another fee] *demands strict justice.* [You'd better think again if you think you've got the right to demand anything from me for the way you've presented this case.] . . .

"We ask that you give my client the fifty thousand dollars in damages that we have asked for. [Who does he think we are, some Washington bureaucrat running a welfare program?] . . .

"We made a bond on the voir dire examination, and my client and I now call on you to live up to your part of that bargain. [Now he's going to try and shove down my throat some bargain that he claims we made, that I had nothing to do with formulating, and that he believes he advanced with his tricky lawyering.] . . .

"We have established the defendant's negligence. [What was the legal definition of that term the judge read a few minutes ago? What does all this legal jargon mean anyhow?] . . .

"You will recall that the first witness we called was my client, Bill Jones. Mr. Jones testified . . . [He's not going to go through each witness's testimony in chronological order!] . . .

"The next witness we called was the investigating officer, Patrolman Gilbert Holloway. [He's going to do it. He's going to summarize every witness's testimony in chronological order.] . . .

"The next witness was Dr. George Truman, the plaintiff's treating physician. [I think I'm getting sleepy. I'd better not eat at that hamburger joint tomorrow.] . . .

"In summary, ladies and gentlemen, we believe the evidence demands you give us your verdict." [What verdict? The judge read us a bunch of legal definitions and questions. What did it all mean? What are we supposed to do when we go back to the jury room? Maybe the defense lawyer will explain it so we can understand what's going on.]

Later, out in the hall during jury deliberations, the plaintiff's lawyer was asked how the case went. "Oh, I don't think the case went that well," he conceded, "but I think I pulled it out in final argument."

* * * * *

This is not a fantasy.

SCENES LIKE THIS are enacted daily in Texas courthouses. This vignette demonstrates some of the basic principles and concepts that will be explored as we consider the technique and strategy of forensic argument in personal injury cases. While our perspective is that of argument to advance the cause of the plaintiff or victim, many of the rules and principles apply with equal vigor to defense summation.

The first step in understanding the concepts of forensic argument begins with appreciating how argument interrelates with the entire case. While presentations are frequently made by our State Bar, local bar associations, and plaintiffs' and defense bar groups on such specific topics as argument, cross-examination, and use of demonstrative evidence, the experienced trial lawyers who make these presentations would agree that it is impossible to separate any particular phase in the trial of a personal injury case from any other phase. All aspects of trial are bound together, particularly with regard to final argument.

Most experienced trial lawyers agree that jurors generally do not make up their minds about their verdicts before the final summations. During the trial, however, jurors form impressions, and the verdict will be influenced greatly by the conceptions that crystallize before argument. The following principles, based on this premise, apply to closing argument:

1. The plaintiff in a personal injury action cannot win his case in argument in the face of unfavorable impressions the jurors have already formed during earlier stages of the case.
2. It is possible for a defendant to win his case in argument, particularly in multiparty litigation, if the impressions previously formed by the jury are not distinctly unfavorable or adverse.
3. The plaintiff's closing argument can dramatically affect the amount of damages recovered, particularly in cases involving significant injuries. Although the jurors may have formed impressions concerning the plaintiff's right to recover and the seriousness of his injury, it is not until argument that they begin to focus on any specific amount of damages.
4. The plaintiff can lose his case in argument, even though the jurors have previously formed favorable impressions about the plaintiff's case.

The more cases a lawyer tries, the more apparent the truth of these precepts will become. Underlying them all is a basic premise that must be understood and applied for the lawyer representing the injured victim to have any significant chance of consistent success: JURIES DECIDE CASES MORE ON IMPRESSIONS THAN ON CONTENT.

To state this principle is not to imply that content is unimportant. It is simply to emphasize that jurors are called on to make decisions in an unfamiliar arena and under conditions that are totally foreign to them. Throughout the trial their attention may be diverted for various reasons. Because they are functioning in an unfamiliar setting, it is difficult for them to retain all the pieces of evidence, even in a fairly simple trial. Hence, the victim's lawyer must strive not only to present a case containing sufficient bases, data, and facts to warrant a favorable verdict but also to create favorable impressions in the jurors' minds that will propel them toward a plaintiff's verdict.

As will be detailed in chapters 3 through 8, the physical or dynamic aspects of communication cannot be overemphasized. Throughout the trial, counsel representing the injured victim must present both a verbal and a nonverbal message designed to produce a favorable verdict. For this exercise to be successful, the attorney must start preparing his argument in the initial client conference. What jurors see as an extemporaneous effort at marshaling the evidence and other forms of persuasion on the client's behalf is really the product of a continuous, ongoing process.

The most essential element of an effective argument is consistency. The message or theme of the plaintiff's case must be consistent throughout the trial, so that the closing summation ties in with and reinforces the approach taken during the voir dire examination, the presentation of the plaintiff's case, and the cross-examination of the defense witnesses. To accomplish this end, three basic strategies are required: developing a case theme, projecting a favorable image, and understanding the jury's perspective.

Developing a Case Theme

Develop a case theme early and follow it throughout the trial.[1] A good theme is simple, unique, and easily understood as embracing the central facts and providing motivation for an adequate award to the plaintiff. A theme is a path of truth leading to affirmative liability findings and adequate damages. An effective case theme—

- is easy to remember,
- is something that the favorable juror can use during deliberation,
- makes sense and is consistent with the jurors' concepts of fairness and justice, and
- is consistent with and supported by the evidence.

Many competent, experienced trial lawyers restate the case theme to themselves at the close of proceedings each day. They ask themselves, "Did my presentation of the evidence, or my cross-examination of the defense witnesses, forward my case theme?"

Formulation of a case theme uses essentially three concepts: the "rule of three," parallel language, and anchoring.

The *rule of three* recognizes that most people can retain no more than three specific items of information. The communicator, whether giving a speech to professionals, students, or jurors, must be aware that no more than three items or specifics of information can be imprinted on the listeners' minds. Studies have demonstrated that most efforts to exceed that number fail.[2]

Parallelism, as it is embodied in the art of communication, simply recognizes that specifics that are forwarded must have parallel form in language context and structure.

Anchoring is the concept of fixing in the listener's mind the theme or statement presented. Anchoring may be accomplished both verbally and physically. For instance, it is effective to choose a spot in the courtroom where you intend to stand each time you present your case theme. Then stand in that spot each time you refer to the theme. Use that area to anchor the initial

---

1. For additional discussion on this concept, see L. SMITH & L. MALANDRO, COURTROOM COMMUNICATION STRATEGIES 316–20 (1985).
2. *Id.* at 318.

presentation of your theme in the voir dire examination, stand in approximately the same place when presenting it in opening statement, and stand in the same place and in the same manner when presenting the case theme during closing argument.[3]

Here is an example of a case theme that might be presented initially during the voir dire examination in a death case brought by the parents of a boy killed in an automobile-truck collision:

> It is our contention that the tragic collision of June 28, 1986, was needless, senseless, and endless.
>
> It was *needless* in the sense that Johnny Brown's death could have been avoided by the exercise of simple care and ordinary prudence on the part of the driver of the Gas-Tex truck in question.
>
> It was *senseless* in the sense that, as a result of this driver's negligence, these parents have lost their only son. They have sustained a substantial and tragic loss.
>
> It was *endless* in the sense that these parents must now face the twenty-five years of life that lie ahead of them without the comfort, aid, and protection that a loving son, like Johnny Brown, would have provided his parents.

This theme would be restated in the opening statement and then incorporated with the closing summations.

Projecting a Favorable Image

It is a hard lesson, but one that all plaintiffs' lawyers must learn: Jurors tend to decide cases on the basis of their perceptions of the plaintiff and plaintiff's counsel.

Helping jurors develop a positive perception of the plaintiff is an essential task for the plaintiff's lawyer. Spend enough time with the plaintiff to know and understand all aspects of the plaintiff's existence—how he hurts, when he hurts, and how the injury has affected his daily life. Jurors are often suspicious of plaintiffs, and understatement can help dilute this attitude. Jurors feel more compassion toward a plaintiff who is trying to cope with his problem instead of complaining profusely.

Counsel's attitude during the trial is equally critical. Because jurors wonder if they can trust lawyers, the image the victim's lawyer projects is vitally important. Jurors form an impression of the lawyer; if they like him, they will tend to help him. A lawyer perceived as sincere, straightforward, efficient, and competent will be persuasive. In short, the manner in which you

---

3. *Id.* at 405.

deliver final argument may be as important as substance and content: the cosmetic may prevail over the substantive. Artificial phrases and speech patterns are earmarks of insincerity. Later chapters will present in detail many of the concepts you can use to enhance a favorable image.

Understanding the Jury's Perspective

It is easy to forget that jurors are strangers to the case the lawyer has studied for months and years. The evidence is presented to the jury in a totality, over the span of several days, and the individual juror is then expected to separate the important elements from the unimportant. Most jurors are not uniquely equipped for this function. They cannot remember all the evidence; they will not remember all of the court's charge. It is important to instill in the jurors a favorable view of their verdict. The jurors must be made to feel that they are participating in a significant and substantial case and in an important cause. The jurors must understand that they are more than just twelve people; they constitute a body that can stand for something. Try to create an attitude that it is not an achievement to bring in a defense verdict. To this end, you must appreciate what the average juror finds compelling in an argument. Experience has demonstrated that the approaches suggested below find favor with most jurors.

Show Sincerity

Sincerity is projected in a number of ways. One of the most common failings of the inexperienced trial lawyer is to imitate or parrot arguments, mannerisms, and style he has seen more experienced and successful trial attorneys employ. Although imitation may be the sincerest form of flattery, it tends to project an insincere, counterfeit attitude most people find offensive. In the words from Shakespeare's *Hamlet*, "to thine own self be true." Employ the style and mannerisms that are basic and innate to your character.

Convey Honesty

Second in importance only to projecting sincerity is the need to convey an image of honesty and integrity. Despite some inherent distrust of the legal profession, the empirical data show that jurors will vigorously support a cause championed by an honest attorney. To convey honesty, be careful not to overstate your case at any stage of the proceedings. Be forthright and fair in dealings with adverse witnesses, and don't engage in argument or analysis that appears specious or "too clever."

Never Violate the Fundamentals of Etiquette

The failings within this category are many. Unjustifiably referring to the other side or their lawyers as crooks or suggesting fraud or fabrication of the facts will yield few rewards. Any suggestion of perjury is risky, particularly if there is no hard evidence to support it. It is extremely dangerous to call a witness or a party a liar. The advocate need not assume this burden: if the witness is mistaken, dead wrong, or confused, merely pointing out that fact will elicit favor enough from most jurors.

Likewise, blatant appeals to racial or ethnic prejudice are always inappropriate. Name-calling (for example, referring to the other side as "shysters," "pickpockets," or "thieves") will not enhance a cause. Improper argument (for example, testifying for absent witnesses or parties) will inevitably be seen for what it is. Similarly unproductive are arguments seeking to impose large damages because the defendant is wealthy and can afford to pay.

Face Up to the Case

No important point should be left unanswered. In most cases, time constraints make it impossible to answer *every* contention advanced by a skillful defense adversary, but try to answer the significant contentions and deal with them in a satisfactory manner.

Harmonize the Evidence

It is much more effective to take the defense witnesses' testimony and make it consistent with the plaintiff's theory of the case than it is to contend against all defense proof. Consider whether the testimony offered by the defense is truly inconsistent with the case theme being advanced. Don't try to argue every detail. Especially in a substantial and complex case, the evidence must be simplified. Argue and emphasize your strong points. Sing your sweetest song, and keep singing it.

Put the Opposition on the Defensive

The victim's lawyer cannot prevail by assuming a defensive posture. The lawyer who finds himself in closing argument spending most of his time responding to defense contentions has surely lost his cause. Keep in mind that the victim can prevail only by consistent presentation and support of his essential contentions.

In examining the relationship of argument to the whole case, it is appropriate to consider one crucial difference between the lawyer who represents the injured victim and those who defend these cases. As the victim's lawyer, we are given the opportunity and obligation of choosing the cases we prosecute. The cases we feel are not meritorious are simply not filed or not brought to trial. Defense lawyers, on the other hand, have no choice. They are simply told to defend the case regardless of the merits of the defense. This distinction is based on our principles of justice that every person, regardless of the merit of his position, deserves and is entitled to a defense. For obvious reasons, however, it becomes inexcusable for a victim's lawyer to rise to his feet and champion a cause in which he does not truly believe. Inevitably, the projection of faith and belief in a cause he finds just, coupled with professionalism and preparation, will yield a favorable plaintiff's verdict.

2

Preparing the Argument

The elderly gentleman rolled his high-backed chair away from the large oak desk and rose as he spoke to the two young lawyers seated in front of him. The judge's court reporter had already begun the mechanical exercise of disassembling the stenographic machine, which was now filled with incomprehensible notes and abbreviations.

"Counsel, now that your objections to the charge have been ruled on, how much time are you requesting for final argument?" After a brief debate, the lawyers agreed that, since the case had not been particularly long or complex, thirty minutes for each side would be reasonable.

"Very well, I would suggest that we take the rest of our noon recess and return at two o'clock. I will ask the bailiff to advise the jury that arguments will be heard at that time."

The young lawyer thought, Two o'clock. That gives me almost an hour to prepare for argument. *He walked briskly from the judge's office into the adjoining courtroom.* What parts of my file will I need to prepare for argument? Certainly, the doctor's deposition. I'd also better think about using the part of the defendant's deposition I introduced for impeachment. *After ruminating further, he settled on the two depositions and a legal pad full of notes he had made during the course of the trial.*

A frantic search of the courthouse facilities yielded an unoccupied jury room in an adjacent court. Finding his privacy secure, the lawyer spread his notes before him on the massive jury table. He mused thoughtfully, Perhaps my best approach on liability would be to stress the defendant's speed. On the other hand, didn't the investigating officer testify that the gouge marks on the highway indicated the defendant was on the wrong side of the road at the time of impact?

* * * * *

THIS UNFORTUNATE SCENARIO is the rule rather than the exception. Most victims' lawyers with little experience go about their preparation for argument much as depicted above, and results are predictably catastrophic.

It has been suggested that we no longer have great orators but, rather, great preparers. Certainly this axiom recognizes the evolution of oral advocacy over the past several decades. The type of jury argument formerly in vogue was essentially the same type that cost Socrates his life. He was so smart he made all the citizens of Athens angry, and he was the one who died, while Melitus, outwitted, lived.

Today, victims' advocates who find success embody three essential qualities or characteristics: preparation, flexibility, and identification of goals.

The first two characteristics go hand in hand. The lawyer who is prepared for argument can be flexible. The skilled advocate does not wait until the court's charge is completed to start preparing for argument; he begins with the initial client interview. He develops a notebook in the case. Even during initial discovery, he is compiling the section of the notebook tabbed "Argument." As the case is being tried, he inserts additional notes and thoughts. The dedicated advocate may find some of his most inspirational concepts occurring even as he rests. For that reason, he keeps a notepad at his bedside so he can preserve every thought for later reference. He keeps ideas and concepts segregated on separate pages in this section of the notebook, so he can easily discard arguments that become inappropriate.

It is this intense preparation that allows flexibility. The skilled advocate is constantly aware of the need to modify his argument based on the perceived action or reaction of the defense counsel, the judge, and the jury. Likewise, he is constantly aware of the shifting mosaic painted by the facts of the case as they are presented.

Constant vigilance and awareness of the aims and goals of argument are required.

Goals of Argument

The final argument is the time to accomplish these critical goals:

- Support the jurors and help them decide
- Give the jurors the reasons for blame
- Help make the jurors sure of their decision
- Give the jurors the information that will help them muster their best judgment based on the facts of the case and the law
- Make the jurors feel strong enough to judge and punish[1]

Opening should always set the tone for the argument. The victim's lawyer should open fully, remembering that first impressions are hard to erase.

Not only must the jurors understand what course you intend to follow; they also need to become involved in the reasons for the argument and to see that you know what they need to hear. They must also discover your

1. *See* S. HAMLIN, WHAT MAKES JURIES LISTEN 318–23 (1985).

approach to the process of persuading them. Do you see the jurors as capable, fair, responsible adults? They need to see how much room you will give them to make up their own minds. Will you deliver your argument manipulatively and oppressively, pushing them to your conclusion, as did Socrates? At the very beginning, they need to see your sincerity and commitment, as well as your structure and style.

Many lawyers spend time thanking the jurors for their service. While this may be appropriate, given in the absolute it may be offensive; after all, these citizens have given up their time because they considered it their civic duty. Hence, it is appropriate to recognize the difference between *thanking* and *complimenting* them. You compliment the jurors by commenting on how hard they worked. Tell them that you know, that you saw and appreciated how hard it was just to sit still and listen. If they've been especially attentive in a long, complex case, tell them how impressed everyone in the courtroom is with the level of their attention and concentration.

Construct a bond between your client and the jury. "Those of us who have heard the testimony have now shared this tragedy." "Only we in the courtroom know fully and completely how this tragedy occurred and how it affected these people."

Do not ask the jury to hold your excesses or omissions against you and not your client. If an attorney has done his job poorly, the jury will surely hold it against the client.

Never use the phrase "my client." Humanize your plaintiff. If the plaintiff is older than you and deserving of your respect, it may be appropriate to address the plaintiff as "Mr." or "Mrs." If the plaintiff is your age or younger, or if there is an indication of a strong bond, a more informal approach may be appropriate: "My friend Bob, who was crippled by this dangerous product, . . ."

Don't say to the jury, "This case is very simple." If it was so simple, why did it take weeks to tell it? Further, cases never seem simple to the juries who are considering them. From the jurors' standpoint, they have been barraged with legalese, evidence, arguments, cross-examination, bench conferences, objections, and other technical details that have led them to believe the case is far from simple. Saying a case is simple will distance you from the jury; doing so implies they are dumb if they don't think it's simple.

Don't argue that this is the most important decision the jurors will ever make. Most people would consider such a statement presumptuous. A victim's attorney simply cannot know enough about the jurors to be justified in saying that.

Describe the jury's task and your role. Describe in opening argument generally what you are going to do. Make it possible for the jury to join you in your conclusion. Use the rhetorical. In summation it is appropriate to *ask* the jurors, not just to *tell* them.

Show the jury you believe in your case and your cause. There must be passion, commitment, and zeal enough to convince the jury that you believe in your client and his cause with utmost faith and confidence. You must raise the jury to that level of conviction, and you cannot do so unless you believe in the case yourself.

Talking over the jury's head in abstract terms breeds resentment as well as boredom. The greatest danger in final argument, aside from disorganization, overstatement, and cliché-ridden presentation, is talking down to the jurors. Respect them. Talk straight, and talk about life as you and they know it.

Most articles about argument suggest that you should never attack opposing counsel. This principle is salutary when limited to exactly what it means: Do not attack the opposing counsel *as a person*. It is appropriate, however, to attack the *ideas*, *contentions*, and *presentation* of opposing counsel. Let the jurors dislike the defense for not being fair or forthright, for being overbearing, aggressive, or boring. Let them see by contrast with your superior style, wit, intellect, personality, and irreproachable behavior the differences between the two sides. Show them what is wrong with the defense's case. Show them what was not proved and where the mistakes lie. Attack the opposing issues and ideas presented, but do not attack the opposing counsel himself.[2]

Don't forget the virtue of silence. When you deliver your final line, you should let the jury think about it. Don't walk off. Stand still. By standing there, silently, you will compel the jury to consider what you have said.

Sometimes you can use repetition with great dramatic effect, particularly when you select a theme or phrase and continue it throughout the argument. For example, in a product liability case you might want to adopt the phrase "And then, in an instant, he was crippled."[3]

You could explain the details of the design of the product, establishing the imprudent nature by which the product was conceived. You could point out that this design was such that it placed into the stream of commerce a product that was likely to cause harm. ". . . And then, in an instant, he was crippled."

You may want to discuss the sale of the product to the user—and how the product was overpromoted and its benefits overstated. "When the Clark Company purchased this product, to be used by Bob, they did not know that shortly after he used it, in an instant, he would be crippled."

Go then to a description of what the plaintiff was doing when he was using the product. Explain how he was using it in conformity with his understanding of proper use as stated in the manufacturer's own directions. ". . . And then, in an instant, he was crippled."

Repetition gives a jury a sense of predictability. It also involves a creative use of language, rhythm, and reassurance.[4]

---

2. *Id.* at 343.
3. *Id.* at 171–73.
4. *Id.* at 172, 346–49.

Meeting Goals

The argument should be well prepared. The attorney should map out and outline in some detail exactly how he will approach the case. A major concern of all trial lawyers is the use of notes. Many lawyers who prepare their arguments, and prepare them well, lessen the effects of their presentations by overdependence on their notes. Your notes should be brief enough to give you an orderly progression of the argument. Make your outline so clear to yourself that you could write it on the board if you desired. However, do not read it. You must make eye contact with the jury and continue that during your delivery. The visual cues contained in your outline should be reference points or guidelines, not crutches. Try to talk directly to each juror, and especially to the leaders. Your approach should be straightforward, laden with logic and appealing to reason. Equip the jurors on your side with the intellectual ammunition to persuade the recalcitrant jurors to share your view.

Most skilled advocates have, over the years, developed the ability to conceive the "jury view." They have a concept of the questions that will be asked by jurors who may choose to champion the cause of the defense, and they can provide answers to those questions. These questions are not necessarily arguments that the defense will make. For example, in a product liability case you may see that a strong argument will be made (either by the defense or by defense-minded jurors) that the product met industry standards and was therefore not defective. Your argument might be,

> Well, let's see, who is industry? Industry is the varied corporations who manufactured and designed this dangerous product. *Those* are the people who manufactured and designed this dangerous product. *Those* are the people who have made these standards. According to this line of thinking, we should have no fear, because the fox is diligently guarding the henhouse.

Opening Argument

There is no legitimate excuse for the opening argument or summation not to proceed and flow smoothly. After all, the plaintiff has had months or even years to prepare for it. While the closing argument must depend largely on the approach and tactics used by the defense, the opening argument is not handicapped with such restrictions. Because the victim's attorney normally has the burden of proof with regard to the overall case, he would be entitled to open and close the argument.[5] In the opening argument counsel must argue, at least to some extent, his entire case.[6]

---

5. TEX. R. CIV. P. 269(a).
6. *Id.* 269(b).

Here is a suggested outline of essential matters to cover in the opening argument.

Introduce the Argument

Consider using some type of introductory statement designed to seize the jury's attention. This statement is usually brief, because counsel does not want to stray too early into deep waters. By the same token, using an attention-getter will show the jury, at the very beginning, that they are not in for a dull sing-song or recantation and summary of the evidence. The introduction might be designed to jerk the jurors to attention and provoke their anticipation. For example, refer to the case theme used for illustrative purposes in chapter 1. In that example, involving an automobile-truck collision and resulting death, the introductory comments might be as follows:

> On our voir dire examination and opening statement we told you that this tragedy of June 28, 1986, was needless, senseless, and endless insofar as these parents were concerned. It was needless in the sense that it was caused by the carelessness of the defendant's driver, who was operating the Gas-Tex eighteen-wheel tractor-trailer unit. It was senseless in that my friends, Mr. and Mrs. Brown, lost their only son. It was endless in the sense that they will carry the effects of this tragedy with them to their graves. Having now heard all the evidence, including the excuses and defenses offered by the defendant, we could add a fourth element. The insensitivity and lack of understanding of this defendant appear limitless. Despite their obvious responsibility for this tragic loss, they have remained hardened and impatient with any effort to appreciate the close and loving bond that existed between these fine people and their son, who has been snatched from them by this defendant's carelessness.

From that introductory comment, counsel would then proceed into the other aspects to be covered in his opening argument.

Thank the Jurors for Their Time and Attention

It is appropriate to thank the jurors for their attention, recognizing any particular sacrifice of which counsel may be aware. It is seldom appropriate (and is often considered demeaning) to thank the jurors for their service, which most citizens render voluntarily and with civic pride.

Outline Each Party's Function

While it may seem mundane or pedestrian, in most cases it is effective to outline briefly the role of the judge, the lawyer, and the jury. This enables the attorney to bring home the importance of the jury's decision.

Describe the Effect of the Verdict

Stating the fact that the jury's verdict is a final decision, which in itself is not appealable, is appropriate. Explaining to the jury that the judge will render the judgment based on the verdict clarifies the jury's role.

Discuss the Evidentiary Standard—Preponderance of the Evidence

Explaining the standard of proof is a significant argument in a civil case. It takes little time to explain to the jury the difference between preponderance of the evidence and the standard of proof in a criminal case. Yet failure to make this argument may well result in a defense verdict that could have been avoided.

Explain the Issues

When issues are complex or technical, the plaintiff's attorney must explain these issues and boil the matter down into simple terms. Indeed, there are few special issues[7] in the personal injury field that could not be considered complex or technical. A lawyer who tries a workers' compensation case and later talks with the jurors about their difficulty in understanding the concept of "total incapacity" will quickly understand this salient fact. Certainly the jurors must understand the question being submitted if they are to answer it properly. In opening argument it is crucial to the victim's cause that the jury fully understand the questions being submitted, rather than merely being bombarded with a recapitulation of the evidence.

Account for All Absent Parties and Absent Evidence

If there is any indication of culpability of a missing party (one who has not been named as a defendant), the plaintiff must somehow account for that party's absence from the case. Plaintiff's counsel must adopt a "jury view" and try to foresee the arguments that might be advanced regarding possible culpability of some entity who has not been named in the lawsuit. Some jurors delight at playing advocate and may go to great lengths to second-guess plaintiff's counsel. Likewise, if there is any missing evidence the jury might conclude is available, the plaintiff must account for its unavailability and his failure to bring it to the jury.

Consider Damages

There have always been (and probably will always be) two schools of thought regarding argument of dollar amounts of damages. Some attorneys strongly

---

7. TEX. R. CIV. P. 277 was amended effective Jan. 1, 1988, to delete references to "special issues" and to substitute the term *questions*.

believe that dollar amounts should be specifically urged; others, equally competent, believe it is inappropriate to suggest exact figures to the jury. The rule seems to be that there is no rule—the decision should be based on the specifics of each case. Flexibility is particularly important when dealing with damages.

There are also two schools of thought regarding argument of details of the injury. Many competent victims' attorneys believe it appropriate in opening argument to give a detailed account of the injuries sustained by the plaintiff; others understate the injuries and avoid a detailed description. Again, the better rule is to remain flexible, making the required judgment at the time of argument.

Principles of Closing Argument

Closing argument must be approached from a different perspective than is the opening summation. In traditional parlance, the opening summation is a speech to educate or inform; the closing argument is a speech to motivate or inspire. The closing argument will leave the jurors with the last impressions they will take with them to their deliberations. In motivating a jury to find liability and large damages, there are essentially three actuating factors: (1) empathy for your client, (2) anger at the defense, and (3) a personalized concern for the verdict.

The closing argument further differs from the opening in that some arguments, although ordinarily improper, are not considered improper if they are invited by opposing counsel's argument.[8] Closing argument provides an opportunity to rebut defense arguments. In many cases, this may indeed be the first time that the issues of the case are directly joined. It is particularly important that plaintiff's counsel be flexible in closing argument. Prepare in advance at least two approaches to close, and choose which one to use on the basis of the tactics and strategy employed by the defense. Essentially two

---

8. Word v. United States Coffee & Tea Co., 324 S.W.2d 258, 264 (Tex. Civ. App.—Amarillo 1959, writ ref'd n.r.e.). The concept that a jury argument, which would otherwise be improper and a basis for reversal, may be proper when invited or made in response to defense argument is illustrated in the recent case of Plains Ins. Co. v. Evans, 692 S.W.2d 952 (Tex. App.—Fort Worth 1985, no writ). The plaintiff argued: "This is the worst insurance company I have ever seen. . . . This is the worst insurance company I have ever done business with and I'm ashamed of them. I am ashamed that they're permitted to sell insurance in the State of Texas to people like [the plaintiff] and to you." *Id.* at 958. The court held that this argument, while improper, had been invited by the defense argument that the insurance company was "a good company" and that the attorney was "proud to be their lawyer." *Id.* Furthermore, the defendant had attacked the plaintiff by saying that he thought the plaintiff's attorneys owed the jury an apology for bringing them "such a weak and ridiculous and silly" case. *Id.*

approaches are used by the defense, the "Admiral Yamamoto" approach and the "Mother Teresa" approach.

Defense Approaches to Argument

The "Admiral Yamamoto" Approach

Many defense lawyers prefer the "Admiral Yamamoto" approach to argument and use it inflexibly in every case, regardless of the nature of the case, the personality or posture taken by plaintiff's counsel, and the impression the plaintiff has made. The basic concept of this approach is that, if the defendant can convince the jury that the plaintiff is opprobrious, his treating physician a fraud, and his lawyer a greedy shyster, there can be no basis for a plaintiff's verdict. This approach gives the victim's lawyer the opportunity to rise to heights of indignation, disgust, and anger; if he has not seemingly provoked such an attack, it gives him a serendipitous opportunity that should not be lost. In the minds of many jurors, it casts the victim and his lawyer in the role of the hero at a Saturday-night wrestling match. You and your friend have now been attacked and abused. The chair has been brought into the ring. Under these circumstances, few jurors will be appalled or offended by a vigorous, animated response. Indeed, most jurors will heartily support you, particularly when they find the defense approach excessive.

The "Mother Teresa" Approach

Many skilled defense lawyers are more subtle and use the "Mother Teresa" approach. They may extol the plaintiff's virtues and compliment you on your presentation of a difficult case. Some will even cry over the plaintiff's tragedy. This approach always ends with a plea that the jury not be influenced by any sympathy for the plaintiff and a reference to the hard, uncomfortable, but undeniable fact that the plaintiff has simply not proved his right to recover from the defendant.

Obviously, the diversity of these approaches dictates differences in types of reply that may be effectively made by counsel for the victim. It is invariably disastrous to close against "Mother Teresa" in the same way you would against "Admiral Yamamoto." Again, the rule is to be flexible.

With these concepts in mind it is appropriate now to consider arguments that may become pertinent to advance in your closing argument.

Closing Argument

Respond to the Defense's "Sympathy" Argument

In many cases, especially those involving significant injury, the defense will have spent a great deal of time stressing the court's instruction that the jury not consider sympathy in reaching its verdict. This argument must be answered, since the jury may take silence on the part of the victim's lawyer to mean assent to the proposition that is implicit in the argument—that a substantial verdict could be based only on sympathy. Among the arguments that can be advanced in reply are the following:

- Distinguish between improper sympathy and understanding of the victim's injuries.
- Emphasize how important understanding the injuries is in determining the issues.
- Point out that no appeal has been made to sympathy during presentation of the case.
- Stress that sympathy, like charity, is demeaning and inadequate.
- Distinguish between sympathy and facts.

The following type of argument might be made in reply to the defense argument:

> The argument advanced by the defense is one that I have heard many times before—in other cases, by other defense lawyers. The defense would have you equate adequate damages with sympathy. They say that the only basis for finding the damages we have proved and ask you to find for Mrs. Williams—the only explanation for such a verdict—would be that you were moved by sympathy.
>
> As often as I have heard this defense approach, I still find myself frightened every time I hear it. Frightened that some of us may be misled, deceived, or confused by that which has a simple appeal but can be distorted to produce a result that can only mirror injustice.
>
> There is a difference between sympathy and empathy. Sympathy means you hurt and I hurt with you. Empathy means you hurt and I understand. All we have asked for is understanding. The evidence we have brought about Mrs. Williams's injuries was brought so that you could understand just how substantial the impact of this defendant's carelessness has been on her life. How could we decide these questions about physical pain and mental anguish if we had no understanding of how these injuries have affected this fine lady? You have heard how, because of these injuries, Mrs. Williams will never be able to pick up her grandchildren. Her back injury will forever prevent her from doing the gardening she loves so much. She needs help now with even the simplest task, such as carrying in her groceries. These are facts. They were not offered for the purpose of invoking sympathy. Is this the type of evidence the defense has in mind when they make their

argument? Forget the pain. Forget the worry. Forget the frustration. The suggestion is that if we think about it, talk about it, or consider it, we are doing something improper. This defense argument confuses facts with sympathy.

We did not ask for sympathy in our opening statement or our presentation of the evidence. We do not ask for it now. Sympathy is a form of charity. Like charity, a verdict based on sympathy would be demeaning. Like charity, sympathy is always inadequate.

We have asked for substantial damages in this case because they have been proved by a preponderance of the evidence. This tragedy was not of Mrs. Williams's making. It was brought about because of the careless and irresponsible conduct of the defendant. If you find inadequate damages—less than has been proved and supported by the evidence—you will be rewarding irresponsibility. You will be taking from the victim and giving to this careless defendant.

The suggestion of the defense that substantial damages can be justified only by an appeal to sympathy is a blatant and not very clever effort to divert us from the real issues in the case. Would the defense have us decide this case without any reference to the pain and agony of a crippling injury that struck this gentle lady? Mrs. Williams has earned by blood, sweat, and tears the damages that are sought. Throughout this trial, as now, all we have sought is your understanding. Not your pity. Not your sympathy.

Run the Skunk Out of the Box

In very few cases will the victim's lawyer find himself in the enviable position of having no prejudicial evidence offered against his client. It may be that the plaintiff was drinking at the time of the accident, or that the deceased had at one time left his wife and children to later return; perhaps the plaintiff had been fired from a job some years ago. The list of possibilities is endless, and in most cases the defense will relish bringing forward any fact considered unsavory or damaging to the plaintiff's image. If you have properly prepared your case, these facts come as no surprise. You have probably been able to defuse the impact of such matters by mentioning them on voir dire and bringing them out yourself during the direct examination. An effective response simply points out to the jury that, while these facts are nothing to be proud of, the plaintiff did not try to conceal them from the jury. "He was honest with you about it." Suggest to the jury that of all the people who are in a position to criticize this individual, the least qualified would be this defendant, whose negligence has rendered the plaintiff a cripple. Catchy phrases may be effectively incorporated: "Since when does the fiddle pick the tune" and "Slander, like coal, will either dirty your hand or burn it."

Emphasize the Impact of the Verdict

While the closing argument gives the victim's counsel the opportunity to respond, the necessity of gaining the offensive should not be overlooked. It is catastrophic for the plaintiff to spend the entire time allotted for closing argument responding to the defense's contentions. Identify the arguments that must be answered—not only the arguments advanced by the defense but also those you believe will be advanced by a juror. Work these arguments into your presentation, but always with a view toward returning to the strong points of your case. In so doing, you may want to emphasize the effect of the jury's verdict on the defendant's future conduct and on the industry, as well as the effect of the defendant's conduct on the plaintiff.

The impact of the verdict on the defendant's future conduct. In malpractice cases, for example, it may be appropriate to ask, "Is this the type of medical care that we want to approve and salute as appropriate for all of us?" In an automobile case, plaintiffs might want to argue, "If we find this truck driver not responsible for this tragic injury, are we not saying that these drivers have the right to speed on our freeways with impunity?"

The impact of the verdict on the industry. In a product liability case, one argument that may bring home the real issues involved is that the jury's verdict will stand for safer cars, better warnings, more careful inspections, and less overpromotion of products. Likewise, in malpractice cases, an argument can inform the jurors that their verdict will tell the hospitals, "When we come into your hospitals, please be careful with us."

The impact of the defendant's conduct on the plaintiff. A moment of carelessness can visit upon another an eternity of pain, worry, and disability. In closing argument it is appropriate to return again to the nature and extent of the plaintiff's injuries and the terrible effect that the defendant's conduct has had not only on the plaintiff but on his family as well.

How a Jury Speaks as the Conscience of the Community

Many experienced trial lawyers appeal to the jury as the conscience of the community. Stress the importance of the jury's function, and suggest that the verdict requested by the plaintiff is in the interest of the entire community. The jurors are the "community's conscience." They speak for the community about the type of conduct they require on the part of drivers, industry, or medical professionals. What jurors determine in this case speaks not only to the way that the plaintiff was treated but also to that conduct which is approved and accepted as professional or prudent and that which is not. The jury is, in a very real sense, the last sentry on duty against irresponsibility.

How a Defense Verdict Encourages Repetition of the Same Conduct

The argument that a defense verdict encourages repetition of the same conduct is particularly useful in product liability and malpractice cases. If the jury finds that the defendant was not responsible for this injury or death, or if it finds inadequate damages, the only effect will be to encourage careless or substandard conduct. Such a verdict will say to the defendant, in essence, "Do it again."

The Plaintiff's Innocence

If there is no evidence or issue of the plaintiff's responsibility, an argument stressing the plaintiff's innocence must be advanced. This important argument is often overlooked when the victim's lawyer concentrates on the issues of liability against the defendant. It is particularly effective when correlated with the argument on damages.

> When some member of this jury suggests that you should find less damages than have been proved, less damages than we have sought, we would hope that our friends on this jury would ask the simple question: "Why?" Why should we reduce our damages in this case? Is it because the plaintiff contributed to his own tragedy? There is no suggestion of that even by these defendants. There has been no offer of proof, and the court's charge contains no issue suggesting that the plaintiff was responsible for his injury. Certainly, if the plaintiff had contributed to his injury, a reduction of his damages would be appropriate. But that is not the case here. This plaintiff was crippled solely because of the negligence of this defendant. The plaintiff was helpless. He was blameless. He is entitled to his full damages.

The Defendant's Callousness

In some cases the defense may choose to defend against your cause so vigorously that the defendant appears to the jurors to be callous. The evidence may reveal, for example, that after the incident in question the defendant continued to conduct business as usual. A company may have retained a driver in the same capacity; a physician may suggest that he has continued to do the procedure in exactly the same manner. In many instances, the victim's lawyer may be able to demonstrate that the company responsible for a death on the highway immediately directed its energies and efforts toward building a defense rather than addressing any concern for the lives it had ruined. Arguments of this nature are limited only by the attorney's imagination.

Damages

It is critical to address the matter of damages again in closing argument. In most cases it should constitute the final part of closing. Some successful advocates believe that in every case at least half the close should be directed to a discussion of damages; like all rules, this one is subject to exception. In at least three situations you may elect to spend less than half your close on damages:

- when the case is weak on damages,
- when liability is particularly strong, or
- when liability is particularly weak.

If your appraisal leads to the conclusion that your case is weak on the damages question, stress another aspect of the case. You may choose to emphasize the callousness of the defense or the egregious nature of the acts that brought about the victim's injuries. If you sense it is going to be a close call on liability, you may elect to bring all your energies and resources to bear on that issue; if the case is lost on liability, the findings on damages will be meaningless. Determining the amount of time that should be devoted to damages (realizing that correspondingly less time will be available for a discussion of liability) is one of the most agonizing decisions the victim's advocate is called on to make.

An effective closing argument adopts some common thread or theme, which is offered at the beginning and should run throughout the argument. This theme is the central thought of the advocate's case. Many skilled advocates try out their arguments on members of the office staff, lawyers in the office, or members of the family. This practice provides an objective appraisal and helps in avoiding arguments that are offensive or ineffective.

In the final analysis, the result achieved by the victim's lawyer is invariably and directly dependent on the extent and nature of his preparation. Without adequate preparation, no amount of oratorical skills can carry the lawyer to the successful conclusion he would otherwise have reached.

PART 2

Concepts of Persuasion

The true use of speech is not so much to express our wants as to conceal them.
—Oliver Goldsmith, *The Bee*, No. 3 (October 20, 1759)

3

Levels of Communication—Verbal, Vocal, and Physical

The lawyer gazed intently at the jury and studied each face. His weight was shifted slightly to the left, and his arms were at his sides. In his right hand he held the notes he was using for summation. The dark blue suit he wore gave him a somber appearance reminiscent of a pastor or a concerned friend. He had already addressed the liability issues in this closing argument, and now he would discuss damages.

"We must now consider the damages that are due to Mr. and Mrs. Brown as a result of the death of their son, Johnny. You have heard the evidence about this boy, who was in the prime of his life, eighteen years of age, when he was torn from his parents by the reckless conduct of this truck driver. [pause] *Before we review the evidence that has been presented by those who knew and loved Johnny, as to the kind of person and young man he was, it is appropriate that we consider what the death of a son means."*

The advocate took two slow, purposeful steps to his left and placed his hand on the court reporter's table. His voice became slower, his voice tone lower. He breathed more slowly. He paused and then continued: "The death of a son is one of the most tragic and significant losses we can experience. While we are all aware of the love that is shared between husband and wife and between brothers and sisters, it is still the loss of a child that for thousands of years has been recognized as the most significant loss one can experience. This is because the bond between parent and child is greater than any bond that can exist between other human beings. We may love and be devoted to our wives and husbands. We may love and support our parents. We may be close to our brothers and sisters. But the love a mother and father feel for a son is different. This mother carried that child and brought it into this world. This father nurtured that child from the time of his birth. In every son resides a part of the mother and the father. A son is God's way of giving us some sense of immortality on this earth. We know [pause] *that even after we are gone* [the voice lowers even more] *a part of us continues to live and contribute to mankind. That is why the "good books" speak so often and so favorably of the relationship between mother, father, and son. The Bible tells the story of the prodigal son. This boy wasted his fortune but was still taken back with open arms by his father."*

The lawyer paused and studied the jury. He continued: "And, when it became time for the good Lord to make the ultimate sacrifice, the Good Book tells us that he gave his only Son. This indicates the kind of sacrifice that for thousands of years we have felt goes with the loss of a son. When we speak of loss of comfort, aid, and society, we are speaking of the companionship, love, and comfort that a son bestows on his parents. When we speak of love, what do we mean? While I recognize that the philosophers and poets have eloquently stated its meaning in many passages, my best understanding of it came recently from a movie. It was a movie about an alien who came to earth. He did not understand the ways of humans. In one scene, he asked a young girl, 'What is love?' Her reply was, 'Love is when you care more about someone else than you care about yourself.' "

As he continued, the lawyer took two more slow, purposeful steps forward. "When you consider the damages that should be found in this case, there may be some among you who will suggest that, while the loss to these parents was great, it does not support the damages sought on behalf of these fine people. We would simply request our friends on the jury to ask those skeptics and cynics this simple question—"

The lawyer's voice was now lowered almost to a whisper. "What loss could have been greater?"

He paused and then continued: "If Mr. Robert Brown had been rendered blind as a result of this defendant's negligence, is there anyone who would not say the damages we have asked for are not adequate or sufficient? If Johnny's mother, Linda, had been rendered paralyzed, is there anyone who would not ask why we did not sue for more?

"Now that you know these parents and understand their loss, is there anyone who believes for a minute that Robert Brown would not accept blindness today if he could have Johnny back? Would not Linda condemn her body to a wheelchair if she could but have a healthy son able to enjoy all the blessings and rewards that lay ahead of him at the time of his death?"

The lawyer stepped backward and made purposeful eye contact with one of the jurors. "The simple realization is that the kind of feeling shared between these parents and their son helps us to understand the value of what has been referred to by the judge in this charge as the loss of 'love [pause] *support* [pause] *companionship* [pause] *and society.' "*

* * * * *

UNFORTUNATELY, READING TRANSCRIPTS OF SUMMATIONS gives the student of oral advocacy little guidance in developing communication techniques. Only verbal content is manifested in the manuscript; vocal and physical[1] messages

1. Some authorities in speech and communication prefer the use of the term *nonverbal* in lieu of the term *physical*. *See, e.g.*, S. HAMLIN, WHAT MAKES JURIES LISTEN (1985).

conveyed during argument cannot be revealed. The sublety of these messages may be even greater than previously suspected. Some years ago a noted advocate gave a summation to a group of hardened trial lawyers. At the conclusion of his summation there was not a dry eye in the house; yet those who later viewed the argument on videotape were not similarly affected.

These sophisticated communication techniques may be developed by most lawyers who are simply dedicated to learning the essentials and who don't mind continual practice. The first step is to understand the levels of communication a trial advocate may employ.

Three levels of communication occur during the trial: verbal, vocal, and physical. Most lawyers concentrate on the *verbal* aspects of communication—choosing the verbal content of the message. However, the other two areas, vocal and physical, are learned through a trial-and-error process during practice in the courtroom.

The *vocal* areas of communication include voice qualities such as pitch, rhythm, pause, rate of speech, and other vocal factors. All these factors affect both the jurors' perceptions of credibility and their abilities to retain information.

The *physical* area of communication involves factors that include eye contact and facial expression, movement, gestures, posture, touch, personal appearance, space and distance, and environment.

For effective communication that produces the desired result, a consistent message must be presented through all three channels. Jurors are greatly impressed by the vocal and physical messages presented by trial attorneys. As the ancient philosophers observed almost one thousand years ago, what you are may speak more loudly than what you say.[2] A strong courtroom image is established through three methods: consistency, repetition, and simplicity. A single method will not create a long-lasting or effective image; all three elements must be present for an image to work.

Projecting the desired image in the courtroom depends on properly influencing the jurors' perceptions of competency, trustworthiness, and dynamism.

Competency—Expertness. Does the lawyer seem competent, prepared, and knowledgeable about his case, courtroom procedure, and the applicable law?

Trustworthiness. Is the lawyer honest and forthright, or does he tend to exaggerate and overstate his case? Does he convey an impression of sincerity and believability? Is he the type of person we could depend on in a crisis?

---

2. *See, e.g.*, Publilius Syrus (fl. 1st cent. B.C.), in *Maxim 1073*: "Speech is a mirror of the soul: as a man speaks, so is he." In more recent times, John Morley, Viscount Morley of Blackburn, in *Recollections* (1917), vol. 1, bk. 5, ch. 4, echoed this thought with the following: "Success depends on three things: who says it, what he says, how he says it; and of these three things, what he says is the least important."

Dynamism. Is the lawyer animated, energetic, and dedicated to his cause? Does he move about the courtroom in a purposeful, confident manner, or does he seem shy, uncertain, and restricted?

For the lawyer to project the desired image, he must understand the basic means of communication.

Means of Communication

Over two thousand years ago, the Greek philosopher Aristotle considered the concept of persuasion and broke it down into three elements. *Ethos* embodied the establishment of the speaker's credibility, *pathos* appealed to the listener's emotions, and *logos* appealed to the listener's logic.

Today, psychologists and communicators recognize that there are three basic systems or means of communication: kinesthetic, visual, and auditory.

Kinesthetic (feeling)

The kinesthetic means of communication concerns the moods and visceral reactions jurors experience during argument. The lawyer may want to evoke anger or hostility on the part of the jury, or a feeling of sorrow, concern, or empathy may be the goal. Whatever the mood, it can be transferred to the jury only by using all three levels of communication—verbal, vocal, and physical.

Visual (seeing)

The visual aspect of communication is often inadequately employed. This aspect includes the nonverbal and nonvocal messages conveyed to the jury by the way the lawyer stands, moves, and handles exhibits. It also includes the incorporation of visual aids into the argument, a factor becoming more and more significant because of the time restrictions placed on oral argument by many trial judges today. "Grabber" charts are effective, not only because they appeal to the senses (the eyes and ears), but also because they shorten the time required for verbal communication. These charts can show the desired answers to issues, a breakdown of damages, brief summaries, highlights of witnesses' testimony, or other relevant information.

Auditory (hearing)

The auditory means of communication is the form best understood and most obvious, although many lawyers have failings in using even this basic technique. The style needed to present a case effectively to a jury is entirely different from the style that would be used to argue a case before an appellate court.

In verbal communication with a jury, it is important to remember not to impose your own language on the jury. Avoid legalese and heavy emphasis on legal phrases and terminology. Simplify the legal and factual concepts, and use words and phrases that are familiar to the jury. Do not be condescending to the jurors or convey that you are talking down to them. Do not insult their intelligence with such comments as "I know you probably don't understand this" or "I doubt you have followed this evidence."

Transferring a Feeling

Of the three systems of communication, kinesthetic is probably the most difficult to master. You can learn to transfer a feeling, however, if you understand the basic principles and concepts.

If you want jurors to experience a particular feeling as you present your argument, use those behaviors—vocal, verbal, and physical—that correspond with the particular drama you are trying to create. Too often, trial lawyers deliver a very emotional argument in terms of the verbal content, but they do not use the correct vocal and physical behaviors. If the verbal content is emotional but the vocal and physical behaviors are not, you will not be able to instill an emotional state in the jurors' minds. Whenever there is a contradiction between verbal content and vocal and physical behaviors, the jurors will ultimately believe the behaviors.

In general, verbal content and vocal and physical behaviors can be used in a personal injury case to convey feelings of tragedy and anger, to impart facts, and to paint a scene.

Tragedy

To convey a feeling of empathy for a tragic and emotional experience of your client, you might want to use these behaviors:

- a slower voice pace,
- a lower voice tone,
- extremes in vocal patterns from soft to loud,
- lowering of the eyes,
- slower body movements,
- a slower breathing pattern, and
- dramatic pauses.

When a person is experiencing a feeling of sadness, his voice pattern slows and his voice tone drops. This is the way we express concern to others. By using extreme vocal tones going from soft to loud, you can create the drama associated with a feeling. Remember, however, if you are not genuinely experiencing the feeling you want to create, it will be impossible for jurors to share it with you.

Next, make sure the jurors start to process the information on a kinesthetic, or feeling, level. To do this, simply use gestures that are low enough to cause the jurors to look down. An individual can best process kinesthetic information when his eyes are lowered to the right. You need to put jurors in the mood to process kinesthetic information when you deliver your most important and dramatic lines; therefore, gestures that direct the jurors' glances down and to the right should be saved for key points in your argument.

Anger

Different techniques are required to instill a feeling of anger in the jurors. To transfer or display anger, these behavioral patterns are appropriate:

- a fast vocal rate,
- higher vocal pitch,
- a louder vocal volume,
- eyes moving straight across,
- direct eye contact,
- gestures made from midwaist to the upper level of the body,
- gestures that are firm and definite,
- quicker movement patterns,
- decisive movement patterns, and
- dramatic pauses.

Don't be afraid to point, as long as you are pointing at opposing counsel or his client. Never point at the jury or at your client, because this will create an undesired, adverse reaction.

Factual Information

At times you may want to convey facts to the jury. To transfer factual material, these techniques are effective:

- keeping the eyes level,
- keeping the breathing pattern even,
- using a moderate rate of speaking,
- avoiding extremes in vocal tones, and
- keeping all behaviors in moderation.

When transmitting factual material, it is appropriate to adopt a low-key approach. Many skilled advocates suggest that this technique should be employed throughout argument. Unfortunately, such an approach overlooks the potential benefits of evoking other emotions and feelings on the part of the jury.

Painting a Scene

Sometimes you may want to paint a picture, scene, or event for the jurors. The techniques used to transfer visual information include—

- using quick vocal patterns,
- keeping eye movement up to the upper right or left,
- using expansive gestures that are above the waist,
- pointing up to a chart, and
- maintaining a fast pace.

When you want the jurors to visualize an event, never pass out material to them. When they are looking at the material, their eyes will be down, and you will not be able to transfer the appropriate feeling. Re-creating an event or painting a scene is best done by using blowups. They should be placed and used at a reasonably high level in the courtroom, so that the jurors are looking at the blowup with their eyes level or focused slightly upward.

Practicing these techniques will develop your ability to enlist all the levels and techniques of communication.[3] This ability is crucial and essential for the victim's lawyer, who is constantly challenged to overcome feelings of indifference, insensitivity, and cynicism.

---

3. For further reference on these techniques, see L. SMITH & L. MALANDRO, COURTROOM COMMUNICATION STRATEGIES (1985).

4

Subliminal Persuasion

The man in the black robe peered over the top of his spectacles at the jury. This judge had just finished reading the charge. He shifted his weight in the large leather chair and turned toward the group of lawyers seated haphazardly at the counsel table. "Ladies and gentlemen, you may now commence oral argument. We will hear first from counsel for the plaintiff."

A lawyer rose and walked confidently to the lectern, which stood some feet back from the jury railing. He placed his notes on the lectern, stepped to the side, and studied the twelve faces before him.

"May it please this honorable court. Ladies and gentlemen, as I was preparing my thoughts and attempting to outline the points I wanted to discuss with you in this very significant case, I could not help but remember an incident that happened in our family several years ago. It must have been about ten years ago when I went to one of those ice cream places that sells the imported ice cream. Some of you may have tried the ice cream from this kind of place. Anyway, I bought a pint of some of their peppermint ice cream. At that time my oldest boy was seven years old. My second son was still a toddler."

The lawyer shifted his weight slightly and placed his hand on the lectern. "I took the ice cream home and put it in the freezer. I told my boy that I had some other errands to run, but as soon as I returned we would get the ice cream out and I would give everyone a portion. As fate would have it, when I returned I found the empty container in the trash. I knew what had happened and confronted my son. He immediately denied the offense. 'What happened to the ice cream?' I asked. 'The dog ate it,' was his response. I explained to him that it was very unlikely that the dog opened the freezer and got the ice cream out. He then replied that he had *gotten the ice cream out and had taken a small portion but had left most of the ice cream on the counter. I explained to him that our dog was not big enough to reach up on the counter and get it. His response was, 'The cat must have knocked it off.' I then pointed out to him that the container was in the garbage, and it was very unlikely that the cat could have knocked it off and the dog then eaten it and put the container in the garbage. He ultimately confessed, explaining that he originally intended to eat only a small portion of the ice cream, but that it was so good he had eaten the whole pint."*

The lawyer smiled as he proceeded: "I told my son, 'Shakespeare once said that "oftentimes excusing of a fault doth make the fault the worse by the excuse." ' His cherubic response was, 'Who's Shakespeare?' "

The lawyer took a purposeful step toward the jury.

"Unfortunately this case deals with the most tragic of situations. The owners and operators of this apartment project had allowed this railing to become so defective that, when this innocent lady leaned against it, she fell to the concrete below and sustained the tragic and crippling injuries you have heard described. Unfortunately, these defendants seek to excuse their fault with a number of contentions—a number of excuses—that, in the words of Shakespeare, have made 'the fault the worse.' "

* * * * *

EVERY SKILLED ADVOCATE who has experienced any degree of success in the personal injury field knows the importance of subliminal persuasion. Juries are motivated and persuaded on the basis of impressions they have formed about the victim, the victim's attorney, the defendant, and defense counsel. Perceptions formed in the jurors' minds are organized and structured within a brief time. Psychologists and communicators recognize what is called the rule of primacy: in forming impressions of others, we tend to place the greatest emphasis on the information we receive first. Since the victim's lawyer is permitted under our rules to "go first" at virtually every stage of the case, it is imperative to understand the rule of primacy and use it to support the victim's cause. It is equally critical to recognize that the jury's decision-making process will be affected by many factors in addition to the verbal content of the evidence and argument.

Factors Affecting the Decision-Making Process

As jurors become familiar with their environment, the courtroom surroundings, where the judge and lawyers are seated, and the roles of the various participants, they begin to form impressions. They notice how the lawyers look, how they act, what they sound like, and of whom they remind the jurors. Jurors begin to ask themselves questions, both consciously and subconsciously, as a natural response to reduce the uncertainty they have about the attorneys.

Is the attorney married? Does he have children? How old is he? Is he trustworthy? Is he interesting? Is he honest? Is he likable? Is he someone I could approach and talk to on a one-to-one basis? Does he attend church? Is he arrogant? Is he experienced? What type of personal life does he have? Is he intelligent? Is he rich? What sorts of books does he read? What type of car does he drive? What hobbies does he have?[1]

---

1. *See* L. SMITH & L. MALANDRO, COURTROOM COMMUNICATION STRATEGIES 95-96 (1985).

The goal of the victim's lawyer is to instill in the jury feelings of confidence, comfort, and respect. Does the jury perceive him as a dependable family man, a responsible citizen, a qualified and competent professional doing his best for his client? Or do they perceive him as someone even his own dog doesn't like?

In making shortcut decisions, jurors tend to rely on single pieces of evidence to indicate a trend and to use stereotypes and generalizations to organize data.

A jury's verdict represents not only what jurors thought of the evidence but also what they thought of the individuals involved in the trial. If the jurors see a plaintiff as a complainer, an irresponsible citizen looking for a free ride, or someone willing to exaggerate to obtain a desired result, that plaintiff is not apt to be the beneficiary of a favorable verdict. Likewise, the plaintiff's lawyer who is perceived as unprofessional, tricky, devious, or insincere will have difficulty motivating a jury toward his cause.

Four important factors come into play when one considers the aspect of subliminal persuasion: the principle of obligation, the desire to be consistent, the importance of scarce information, and the incorporation of nonissues.

Jurors May Feel Obligated

Communicators and psychologists recognize that people feel obligated to repay others, regardless of whether they like the gift or the giver.[2] People often ask before agreeing to another's argument or suggestion, "Do I owe this person something?" If the answer is yes, they will frequently reply affirmatively to a request they would otherwise have declined. This fact is significant to the lawyer representing the victim in a personal injury action. If the jurors see the plaintiff as a person who has contributed to his community—who has contributed not only to his own betterment but also to that of the jurors—they may believe that the plaintiff is worthy and that something is owed him. This response may be totally subconscious.

Similarly, if they see the victim's lawyer as a responsible citizen who is contributing to the welfare and betterment of the community, they are apt to feel obligated to return a favorable verdict. Thus, it is vital to project an air of approachability, responsibility, and dependability. Preparedness in presenting the case strengthens this image. The lawyer who moves easily from witness to witness, from exhibit to exhibit, and who moves the case expeditiously along will be well received. Likewise, personal references showing the attorney has strong family ties, community responsibilities, and a professional dedication to his calling will garner support for his side.

---

2. *Id.* at 172–74.

Jurors Want To Be Consistent

People have a need to be consistent with their commitments, and lawyers can build on that need.[3]

Jurors need to be consistent with earlier comments they have made during the voir dire examination. An inexperienced lawyer may misjudge this need, which is not susceptible to a gross appeal. Here, for example, is a typical argument the novice might make:

> On the voir dire examination we made a contract or a bond. Each of you told me that, if we proved these injuries and damages, you could find the sums of money we seek. I now call on you to fulfill your part of that contract and that bargain. You promised me on the voir dire examination you would do that. We now demand your fulfillment of that contract.

Such an argument is offensive, at best. The same appeal may be made successfully by using an embedded command (see chapter 13), but a blatant approach will inevitably pay poor dividends. Although jurors want to be consistent, they naturally resent an appeal to one-sided bargains.

Similarly, jurors may not accept an argument, although it is based on sound proof, that otherwise does not appeal to their sense of justice, fairness, and square dealing. The lawyer who strives in his daily activities to understand where the ordinary citizen's anger lies, where his frustration is, and wherein dwell his fears, is better equipped to accurately pitch his cause. If the plaintiff's fears are shared by the jury, they will be received, understood, and acted upon.

If the defendant's conduct is perceived as a threat to all citizens, the jurors may seize the opportunity to castigate it. If the verdict the plaintiff seeks is consistent with the jury's notion of right and wrong, that verdict will probably be given; but if it is not consistent, no amount of proof may be adequate to propel the jury to give the verdict sought.

Scarce and Valuable Materials Influence Jurors

When jurors believe the information they have received is scarce and valuable, they may be more receptive than usual.[4] Argument can be used to convey this impression—"Only you know this." "This is the first time this information has been released." "We were able to bring you this information, which had previously not been known." When jurors believe they are dealing with scarce or valuable information, two things happen. First, they pay

---

3. *Id.* at 174–76.
4. *Id.* at 180–81.

attention to the information presented. Second, the information is anchored in their minds, so they will recall it more easily.

This concept is useful in complex, substantial cases involving drug liability or product malfunction, but it can also be used to good effect in even the most simple automobile case. Consider the following argument:

> You now know all the information about how this accident happened. Those of us who have been in accidents before have never had this opportunity. We may know what we perceive, but seldom do we have the opportunity to understand how the police officer goes about conducting his investigation. We do not have the benefit of the significance of these physical facts, such as what the skid marks mean or what the damage to the vehicles reveals.
>
> We have brought all this information to you. You are the first and only people who have had the benefit of all the facts about this dreadful collision. As you have heard, even the investigating officer, because of his pressing responsibilities, did not have the opportunity to discover all these facts. We brought you this evidence because this poor lady who was so tragically injured in this incident wanted to know. She knew she was stopped at the red light when she was hit from the rear, but she didn't know why the accident happened or how it occurred. She knew she was in extreme pain, and she is experiencing pain even today as a result of her injuries, but it was not until the trial of this case that the complete medical explanation was given. You now know all these facts. You have had an opportunity that few individuals have had. You have learned all about this accident, all about these injuries, and all about the consequences that a few seconds of neglect and carelessness can bring about.

Juries Decide Cases on Matters That Are Not Issues

Often a matter is established during the course of a trial that may be incorporated in argument and may profoundly affect the verdict. Such a matter may not be an issue in the true sense; it is an item of proof that will influence the jurors' perceptions of the parties or the case—some evidentiary matter that particularly appeals to the jury's sense of justice, fairness, or fair play. Incorporating such nonissues is a tactic successfully employed by many excellent defense attorneys. For example, the defendant may elicit from the plaintiff the innocuous statement that the injured victim never had a headache before the automobile collision in question. In argument this innocuous statement is made to appear as the main issue—everyone has had headaches and, if the plaintiff is not believable on this issue, he can't be believed on any other issues.

The victim's lawyer may also effectively incorporate these nonissues, as the following examples demonstrate.

About fifteen years ago, a case was tried in Harris County involving the toppling of a gantry crane. The trial was a lengthy one, lasting approximately four weeks. In the suit brought against the owner of the crane, which had leased it to the plaintiff's employer, a rather innocent piece of evidence showed the crane in question had been purchased by the company at the end of World War II for approximately 10 percent of the cost the government had incurred in building it. Obviously, the company that had purchased this gantry (as well as other government-owned equipment) had benefited greatly from such a transaction. It was the plaintiff's contention that the crane should have been equipped with certain safety features. In argument, this phrase became the plaintiff's rallying cry: "Don't let the Brown Company buy Jimmy Frank Thompson for ten cents on the dollar like they did that crane." The phrase incorporated in the victim's argument what might be strictly construed as a "nonissue," but it embodied a matter of significant importance in the jury's perception of the parties.

A workers' compensation case tried in Brazoria County further illustrates the principle. The plaintiff had sustained a back injury, and the evidence showed that following the incident he had held a job as a foreman at a hunting retreat owned by a large Houston corporation. This was the only job the plaintiff had held since his injury; and, by his own admission, he had quit that employment because his duties required his wife to serve alcoholic beverages to business executives when they came to the resort. The defense argued that the plaintiff could not be considered totally incapacitated or disabled since he had been able to get this job and keep it. In closing argument, the plaintiff's lawyer indignantly stressed that the only job the plaintiff had been able to find was one that required his wife to violate her religious principles.

> Can this insurance company seriously suggest that my friend Larry Gore is not disabled because he can find one job that will pay him wages? One job—that will require his wife to serve whiskey to a bunch of business executives while they are playing poker? Is that what the law is? Is that what this judge means by his definition of "total incapacity"?

The lesson to be learned is this: be constantly alert and on guard as to all items of proof, even those that seem innocuous or trivial. This is the discipline of attention to detail, which all successful advocates bring to jury argument.

Finally, remember that the subliminal factors that influence the jury's decision-making process do not all arise in the courtroom. Jurors see the lawyers and their conduct in hallways and at recesses. Jurors observe the plaintiff. They may even ask themselves, "Does the plaintiff move differently when he sees no one is watching?" "Does the lawyer have a different attitude when he is not before the court and jury?" In short, it is their entire perception of the victim and his lawyer on which the jurors may ultimately base a significant part of the decision-making process.

5

Technique Versus Style

It seemed as though the rafters of the courtroom ceiling were trembling. The elderly lawyer's voice had reached a deafening crescendo. His argument had been laced with biblical quotations and references to classical literature. Beads of perspiration appeared on his forehead. His rumpled shirt glistened with the moisture from his rotund body. He placed both hands on the jury railing and leaned forward. As he did so, the jurors on the front row immediately facing him leaned and twisted backward. He wheezed as he continued: "This insurance company is worse than the thieves of Bagdad. What they are trying to do is worse than what Joseph's brothers did to him. Worse than what Miriam and Aaron committed against Moses."

As the lawyer stood erect and leaned backward, the jurors shifted to a more comfortable position. "This insurance company would deny their rightful obligation in workers' compensation benefits to this man."

Extending his arm to its full length, he pointed at the sheepish-looking young man seated at the counsel table next to the lawyer's now-vacant chair. "This man gave his company the best years of his life. Every year this insurance company collected those premiums. Now they deny their obligation."

A sharp thud sounded as the lawyer hammered on the jury railing, and his voice rose another intolerable decibel. "They have the nerve to bring in this prostitute of a doctor to support their meretricious defense. That testimony was bought and paid for by this insurance company. That quack was no better than the ladies of the evening."

Now the advocate stopped pounding on the jury railing. Anxiety flashed across the jurors' faces as the man started to lean forward into the jury box to continue his argument.

* * * * *

THE PREFERRED STYLE OF ARGUMENT has changed considerably over the years. In recent years, shorter and more effective arguments have become the rule. Attorneys realized their arguments must be psychologically sound and must appeal to the instincts and experiences of the jurors. Many techniques that were successful decades ago fail today. As jurors became more sophisticated and knowledgeable, lawyers found themselves having to adapt and appeal to a more urbane constituency.

Today, style varies greatly among successful plaintiffs' attorneys, but they use essentially the same basic techniques. In working to develop your abilities as an oral advocate, it is helpful to bear in mind the difference between "technique" and "style."[1]

The difference between technique and style can best be understood by looking at the distinction between artists and their various works. Painters may use styles that are vastly different, yet they use the same technique to accomplish those styles; they use colors, brushes, and palette knives to place on canvas what becomes a picture. The same is true of trial lawyers. Their style of delivery is personal and unique to each of them, yet all great trial lawyers use the same techniques. To the successful victim's advocate, the techniques are a natural extension of personality. These lawyers use appropriate vocal cues and nonverbal messages. They employ subliminal persuasion. They have mastered the use of appropriate movement, gestures, and posture. The adroit application of various techniques is discussed elsewhere in this book. This chapter briefly considers the basic styles employed by successful advocates.

The Logical Delivery Style

The logical style of delivery is used effectively by many plaintiffs' lawyers. The delivery has some emotional content but not a great deal. This style of delivery is persuasive because it is so purely based on logic that one cannot help but believe it. It is simple and direct.

The proponents of the logical style couch their appeal exclusively in terms of the evidence and proof. Their arguments tend to be structured and to follow predictable organizational lines. Their opening consists of an outline of the intended summation. Invariably, the close essentially reviews or recapitulates the more salient points.

The delivery technique tends to be monotonic and low-key. Movement about the courtroom is fairly limited.

It is the goal of the lawyer employing this style to use the weight of the evidence to prod the jury toward a plaintiff's verdict. No real effort is made to employ kinesthetic communication.

The Emotional Delivery Style

The emotional style creates high emotional content and impact. This delivery style is used by many of the old-time orators. The bravado of the message

1. The analysis that follows may be found in L. SMITH & L. MALANDRO, COURTROOM COMMUNICATION STRATEGIES 795–97 (1985).

simply sweeps one away with its emotional content. Lawyers employing this style tend to use exaggerated gestures, great variances in volume and vocal pitch, and expanded movement throughout the courtroom. They seldom refer to the evidence, while they employ anecdotes, parables, poems, and fables liberally.

The difficulty with the emotional style is that its persuasiveness may be short-lived.

The Combination Delivery Style

The best style of delivery, for most victims' advocates, is a combination of the logical and the emotional delivery styles. Most good trial lawyers have characteristics suitable for both. The advocate employing the combination style fortifies his argument with direct references to the evidence; at the same time, he keeps his argument lively and entertaining with anecdotes, analogies, and stories of personal experiences. He is both technician and artist. He modifies his voice patterns to correspond to the nature of the message he wants to convey. He may move widely around the courtroom or limit his physical activities, depending on the type of communication he is undertaking.

First and foremost, the advocate using the combination style adheres to the cardinal rule of flexibility. He modifies his argument depending on his assessment of these essential variables: the jury, defense counsel, the injured plaintiff, and the defendant.

Using The Combination Style

Before your argument, assess the jury, particularly those members you perceive to be the leaders. Ask yourself this question: What is most likely to motivate these individuals? Sometimes you will perceive that a heavier hand on the logical presentation will be more successful; in other instances, the makeup of the jury will convince you that greater emphasis on emotional appeal may be successful. Be particularly aware of the technique and approach employed by defense counsel. If the defense makes an animated, imaginative argument employing emotional appeal, you may choose either to counter with a low-key, logical approach or to fight fire with fire. In assessing the injured plaintiff, consider such factors as whether the jurors perceive the victim as a member of a downtrodden or oppressed class or, conversely, as one who occupies a higher socioeconomic status than they do.

In determining how much logical style versus emotional style to incorporate in argument, be particularly conscious of the jurors' perceptions of the defendant. Obviously, an injury case brought against a large corporate manufacturer must be argued differently than a case in which an elderly schoolteacher is named as a defendant. In the former situation, efforts at inspiring anger, hostility, or frustration may be successful; in the latter case, it may be virtually impossible to create these feelings.

Whether you are engaged in a logical presentation or a more emotional effort, your argument represents but an extension of your own personality. It is with the force of your personality that you hope to mold a plaintiff's verdict.

PART 3

Physical and Vocal Principles of Argument

Language most shows a man: speak that I may see thee.

—Ben Jonson, "On the Use of Language," in *Timber*

6

The Trial Lawyer's Appearance

The jury had returned with its verdict. As the judge began to read their answers to the questions, the jurors continued to study the two lawyers seated before them. On one side of the counsel table sat a tall young man in his early thirties. His curly blond hair cascaded over his ears and neck onto the collar of his polyester suit. The suit's gray-green fabric glistened in the light of the courtroom as he shifted his weight in his chair. The kaleidoscope of colors in his tie seemed to make it literally explode away from his pale yellow shirt.

Seated across from this young man was a lady of neat appearance, dressed in a conservative business suit. The streaks of gray in her hair made judging her age difficult, but a reasonable guess would be early forties. Under her tidy blue jacket she wore a high-necked, white cotton blouse. Her features were enhanced by modest makeup. At her throat was a simple brooch; this and a wedding ring were the only jewelry she wore. While the young man sat slouched in his chair, this defense lawyer sat erect and attentive to the jury and judge as the verdict was read. As the jurors studied the lawyers' reactions to their findings, they consciously noted that their impressions of these lawyers had not changed since they had first seen them several days earlier.

* * * * *

THE TRIAL LAWYER'S APPEARANCE is an aspect of argument that is often overlooked. Appearance plays a significant role in the persuasion process. The victim's lawyer must remember that defense lawyers do not consider the effect of appearance lightly.

Victims' attorneys (both male and female) should aim for the most neutral look that will be acceptable to jurors. This is not to say, however, that the stereotypical image of the "Philadelphia lawyer" is appropriate. For example, in Texas few male lawyers on either side of the docket wear vests to trial because of the unfavorable subliminal message that this attire may convey to some jurors. Appropriate dress depends on the locality of the trial, the general makeup of the jury, and the lawyer's personality.

Attorneys representing victims in personal injury cases in Texas must often appear before juries in diverse areas. This state represents a wide geographical jurisdiction consisting of communities that differ vastly in ethnic structure, economic basis, and cultural heritage. In selecting clothes to wear while appearing before a jury, the attorney must consider the community in which the case is being tried. Rural jurors expect attorneys to be more approachable, down-to-earth, and informal. The attorney should not "affect" any particular type of appearance, however. Occasional news reports note the appearance of an urban lawyer, dressed in Western hat and boots, trying a case before a rural jury. A few attorneys can succeed with this type of affected appearance, but most juries see through it, and it detracts from the lawyer's sincerity. For the most part, the attorney should try to project by his appearance as much of his inner self, personality, and approach as possible.

Bearing in mind that the lawyer's appearance and dress must depend on an analysis of the community in which the case is being tried and the makeup of the jury, a few general rules are in order. While these rules are written literally for the male lawyer, they apply in spirit equally to the female trial lawyer.

If you want to project approachability and likability, a conservative sports jacket would be more appropriate than a suit. A suited look will give you a more formal appearance, while the sports jacket will give you a down-to-earth, country type of look. To enhance this look, you should wear more touchable fabrics, such as tweed—even a sweater vest if that is appropriate for the climate. "Pacing" your attire can also be effective. Consider beginning the trial in a sports jacket, moving to a gray suit, and then wearing a dark navy suit for your closing argument. This progression is particularly appropriate in death cases, where the dark suit can help convey the somber and serious nature of the undertaking the jury is about to begin.

Appearance affects jurors' perceptions. Are you seen as intimidating or friendly, trustworthy or untrustworthy? The ultimate blend for the attorney is to appear both approachable and credible.

With the jurors' first exposure to a lawyer during the voir dire process, they begin to form impressions based on stereotypes with which they are familiar. Does the lawyer appear neat, clean, professional, and organized? Does he "look like a lawyer," or does his initial appearance convey a different impression? The appearance and dress of some novice trial lawyers suggest a used-car salesman, a gambler, or a hard-hearted banker. These are extremes to avoid assiduously.

The lawyer who conveys an appearance of integrity and professionalism will find the jury readily accepts the verbal content of his argument. By the same token, it is difficult to overcome an unfavorable impression that has been formed on the basis of appearance, even with excellent verbal content. The victim's advocate should aim for the most positive, neutral appearance possible, bearing in mind that at least ten favorable juror responses must be achieved for a plaintiff's verdict. The defense is not faced with such constraints; after all, three jurors alone can produce a defense result.

The victim's lawyer should bring to choice of dress the same discipline used in preparing and presenting the case. Men's shirts should be neat, pressed, and subdued. Shoes should be cleaned and shined. Presenting an image of sartorial splendor, however, is not an advisable goal. For example, about twenty years ago, a very prominent West Coast lawyer tried a case in one of our most urban communities. He carried a velvet briefcase and wore monogrammed silk shirts. He was the epitome of fashion. Yet the jury's reaction to his appearance was unequivocally negative. While Texas is becoming more international in its racial and ethnic makeup, many of the traditional Texas values have been maintained. Ever since General Sam Houston's rag-tag army defeated General Santa Anna at San Jacinto, unique qualities have been the hallmark of Texans. Even today there persist remnants of the frontier attitude of suspicion toward the "dandy." This fact probably explains why, although the trial bar has produced many fine advocates on both sides of the docket who are trendy or fashion-conscious dressers, there are probably a greater number of accomplished advocates who assume a less-than-fashionable appearance.

The general rule is that the lawyer should strive to "look like a lawyer." But what kind of lawyer? Experience teaches us that the lawyer who conveys an image of the down-to-earth professional who is competent, friendly, and sincere will achieve the best overall result.

Adjustments in appearance during trial may convey subtle messages to the jury. Loosening a tie during argument suggests informality, vulnerability, and eagerness to engage in the intellectual struggle. Pushing up one's coat sleeves gives the impression of a lawyer hard at work on the critical issues. Likewise, an attorney who stuffs into his coat pocket a sheaf of papers containing his notes may project the image of the approachable, down-to-earth country lawyer. In short, the successful victim's advocate realizes that his appearance and dress must be used to promote the desired verdict in the same way that gestures and language are used.

In addition to dress, the attorney should be aware of personal habits that the jurors will observe during breaks and recesses. The experienced trial lawyer will not chew gum, smoke, or engage in other conduct that might be offensive to the jury. If, for example, you enjoy smoking a cigar or cigarette during the lunch hour, do it in the privacy of a jury room or conference room where it cannot be observed by members of the jury.

The experienced trial lawyer knows his client's appearance is as important as his own. The victim should be advised to dress neatly and properly for the occasion. What is appropriate for a courtroom appearance is generally the same attire that would be appropriate for attending a church service. When the victim is a working man and the case concerns workers' compensation or an automobile injury, a plain, neatly pressed white shirt with khaki pants may be appropriate. Both male and female victims should avoid the ostentatious display of jewelry. Obviously, jurors cannot be expected to award significant damages to a person displaying greater wealth than they possess. Both lawyer and client should remain aware that the jury will be observing them at every opportunity; the content of the jurors' impressions is not necessarily limited to those formed while court is in session.

A malpractice case tried some years ago in Jasper illustrates the effect that appearances may have on juries. The defendant-surgeon had been on the stand for approximately a day. At the conclusion of the examination, the doctor left the witness stand and returned to his chair at the counsel table. He was seated immediately in front of the jury. He proceeded to pull from his coat a long glass tube, which contained a large cigar. He carefully opened the tube, removed the cigar, and lit it. As he sat smoking this monstrous stogie (smoking was permitted in this particular court), the expressions on the jurors' faces unmistakably revealed the unfavorable impressions being formed. The ensuing verdict dramatized in a pellucid manner how much impressions can affect a jury verdict.[1]

---

1. For additional information and assistance in this area, see L. SMITH & L. MALANDRO, COURTROOM COMMUNICATION STRATEGIES 29–43 (1985).

7

Posture, Gestures, and Movement

The issue being addressed by the lawyer was simple and straightforward. As a part of its verdict, the jury had been asked to determine whether a nurse employed by a hospital had become the "borrowed servant" of the codefendant-physician. The lawyer who stood in the center of the courtroom cast a magnetic image. His tall stature, the patch over his eye, and his immaculate appearance brought to mind the Hathaway Shirt Man. He was now incorporating into his discussion of the court's definition of "borrowed servant" the evidence the jury had heard over the past week and a half. He recounted it in a deliberate and careful fashion.

"You will recall that Dr. Jones, as he began to administer anesthetic to Rocky Smith, asked Nurse Green to obtain for him some Inapsine. She left the operating room and went down that short hall to the supply room. In there she obtained a vial of Levophed. You have heard of the disastrous results that occurred when Dr. Jones administered this drug to Rocky. The hospital contends that when this nurse went into the supply room to obtain that vial she was acting as the 'borrowed servant' of Dr. Jones. What did she do wrong in there? She misread the label."

The lawyer was now walking slowly and deliberately toward the jury room door, which was situated to the immediate right of the jury box. He continued, "Recall that the court's definition of borrowed employee is one who is subject to the right of another to control the details of the particular work involved. How would this doctor have controlled the nurse in the details of the way she went about reading a label?"

The tall, gray-haired lawyer now stood to the far right of the jury box with his hand on the doorknob of the jury deliberation room. "How could the doctor have controlled this nurse in the details of what she did in that supply room?"

The lawyer opened the jury deliberation room door, stepped inside, and closed the door behind him. The jury gazed around in wonderment. The judge smiled. The minute or two that elapsed seemed like an eternity. Finally, the door opened and the lawyer walked back into the courtroom, closing the door behind him. He now stood before the jury. "How could anyone control another so that he or she would be a 'borrowed servant' under these circumstances?"[1]

* * * * *

THE MOMENT A LAWYER rises and faces the jurors, he is telling them about himself. He may shuffle, stride belligerently, move about with jerky motions, or walk in a quiet and purposeful manner to his position in front of the jury box. The jury can sense at once the meaning conveyed by this approach. Those who study speech and communication have learned that the audience—the jury—tends to imitate the speaker's movements. This is true even though jurors seldom may outwardly change their posture. The inner pull is there. They are always inwardly imitating what they see.

Therefore, the trial advocate's bodily action will do one of three things to those who listen:

1. If you use no action, or almost none, the jurors will relax too much or even become drowsy. They will not pay close attention to what you say.
2. If you fidget and fumble, or if you constantly meander back and forth, the jurors will inwardly fidget and fumble with you. These actions will make some jurors outright nervous or irritated and will distract everyone from what you are saying.
3. If you use controlled and purposeful action, and enough of it, the jurors will be kept aroused and alert. They will find it easier to pay attention to what you say.

We talk to the jury with our bodies. Many lawyers underestimate the significance and effect of this type of communication. The way you stand before a jury tells them whether you are trying to shrink from them, are indifferent or self-conscious about your case, are cocksure and arrogant, angry and defiant, or are eager to tell them something. This nonverbal communication—accomplished by appropriate posture, gestures, and movement—transmits messages that are hard to ignore.

---

1. The various anecdotes and vignettes used throughout this book are based on true experiences. For obvious reasons, in most instances the identities of the lawyers have not been revealed, and the characters are thus "anonymous." However, the author does not believe that the trial advocate par excellence, Dick Cullen of Victoria, Texas, would object to being identified as the author of this colorful argument and effective use of movement and gestures.

Posture

An expression commonly used in political parlance is that someone "stood tall." This expression has significance for every trial advocate, regardless of his physical stature. The lawyer should ordinarily stand erect while addressing the jury and should not assume a hunchback or defensive posture.

Standing with your weight equally distributed makes you look strong—as though you're on solid ground. However, it can also make you look stubborn, too powerful, and sometimes challenging. It is not a very conversational look.

Standing with more weight on one foot is very disarming. It is a more relaxed posture. It makes you look off-balance (and indeed you are). It makes you look softer, more vulnerable. You may want to assume this posture from time to time, depending on the images you are trying to present. A relaxed body posture increases likability and approachability.

You want your posture to look as natural and easy as possible. You don't want to appear stiff and awkward, nor do you want to slouch. These extremes are difficult to avoid, and two suggestions may help:

- *Keep your weight chiefly on one foot at a time.* Notice the rule says *chiefly*, not wholly. This posture keeps you from getting in a split-legged position. It also saves you from the irritating mannerisms of rocking up and down on the toes and swaying from side to side.
- *Keep your center of alertness in the chest.* Not only should the weight of your body be properly distributed; good posture also requires a feeling of buoyancy, alertness, and easy strength throughout the whole body.

Gestures

Gestures should be made with the whole body. Even the simplest action of the hand or arm, if gracefully done, is supported by the whole body. The novice trial lawyer who gestures with his arms while his body is tense and frozen is unconsciously being as funny as the comedian who does so deliberately. Cultivate your entire body action. Support the slightest movement of your hands by balancing your whole body, moving your head, or coordinating your hips, knees, or ankles. In short, give each gesture with abandon, yet with vigor.

The stroke of a gesture should be properly timed with the emphasized word or syllable. Emphasizing the statement "This is significant" is never done by spreading the gesture over the entire sentence in one wild, awkward jab. Nor is it done by spreading the gesture over the whole emphasized word. The voice emphasizes only one syllable of the word—sig*nif*icant. Coordinate the stroke of the gesture with vocal emphasis on the syllable, to gesture only at the time the emphasized syllable is spoken.

As a rule, avoid gesturing at the beginning and ending of an argument. A car that starts too abruptly jerks the necks of its passengers; a speaker who leaps into the first sentence at a high rate of speed, with vigorous gestures, affects the audience in the same way. Subtle and small movements—a nod, a smile, a movement of the shoulders—are more effective in starting. Withhold more vigorous gestures or comments until both you and the audience are in the mood.

Gestures should fit the expression of ideas. Incredibly, most sign languages of the peoples in this world are strangely alike. (When Columbus discovered the New World he found that the copper-skinned natives nodded their heads for assent and shook them for dissent, just as the the white-skinned Europeans had always done.) Hand movements may be classified into the following five groups.

The Hand Supine: Palm Upward

Gesturing with the palm upward indicates in general an idea of which we approve. "We ask for justice." "We ask that this jury answer 'Yes' to Question 2." People are more easily influenced by people they like. Keeping the palms up while gesturing, as contrasted with speaking with the palms down, conveys approachability. Holding palms up tends to project such nonverbal messages as "I want your help" and "I want to work with you."

The Hand Prone: Palm Downward

Keeping the palm downward represents dislike, disapproval, and opposition. "We cannot accept this argument advanced by the defendant." "The suggestion that this victim's injuries are trivial must be rejected."

The Hand Adverse: Palm Outward (away from the body)

Holding the palm outward expresses a feeling stronger than mere dislike and suggests complete rejection or repulsion. "We cannot base our verdict in this case on the testimony of an expert who owes his livelihood to this corporation."

The Hand Index: The First Finger Extended As If Pointing

Extending the index finger points out an idea, fact, place, or person. But always remember that finger pointing is an intimidating gesture. Never point at jurors. If you need to make a point in the direction of the jury, use a pencil or your glasses. Pointing your finger may be an effective gesture to focus negative attention on opposing counsel or his client.

The Clenched Fist

Clenching the fist expresses great earnestness or intensity of feeling. "Let the defense come with their proof if they will make such a contention." "We have proved this defendant's responsibility the hard way, by hard work developing this evidence you have heard."

Many lawyers have difficulty with gestures. They seem acutely conscious of what they are doing with their hands during the course of the entire argument. Some basic textbooks on public speaking advocate that a speaker should never put his hands in his pockets while speaking. Most experienced trial lawyers do not subscribe to this theory. Putting your hands in your pockets can renew images of the country lawyer—a kind of rumpled Spencer Tracy. It establishes an easy, relaxed format. It can make the jury feel more secure with you as an individual. This stance is particularly effective when you are engaged in argument designed to appeal exclusively to reason, logic, or explanation. This posture, combined with a shrug of the shoulders, can effectively communicate that you are perplexed by the testimony or contentions of the defense.

It is not wise to clasp your hands behind your back, because this is a tense gesture. It is rather militaristic and suggests that something is being repressed.

Movement

Movement during argument may involve a myriad of aspects ranging from simply smiling at the jury, to deciding how much of the courtroom to use, to determining whether and how to touch your client. To properly use movement during argument, you must understand the principles of physical communication. These basic concepts include:

- using good eye contact,
- using animated facial gestures,
- displaying sincere interest in others,
- keeping normal to close distances from the jurors,
- using excessive vocal cues, and
- appearing relaxed and confident.[2]

A speaker cannot give an effective summation while standing in one spot, rigid and stiff. On the other hand, too much uncontrolled movement is distracting. The speaker who paces back and forth uncontrollably, like a tiger in a cage, actually distracts the jurors with his movements and gestures.

---

2. *See* L. Smith & L. Malandro, Courtroom Communication Strategies 300 (1985); S. Hamlin, What Makes Juries Listen 428–31 (1985).

Generally, most of the advocate's movements during summation should be restricted to the upper torso. He can move from side to side but generally should be stationary for many moments at a time, never appearing to be nervously pacing. No good speaker keeps the same posture long; he adds meaning and interest to his words by changing position.

Movement may be fairly restricted in area. For example, a step forward may emphasize "therefore," "also," or "furthermore." A step sideways may say "in the next place" or "nevertheless." A step backward can be "but" or "yet." A turn of the body can say, "I want you all to see this." Obviously, no single movement is limited to any single definite meaning, for different speakers will use different movements; and even the same speaker in a different mood will use different movements.

How much should you move? That question depends on three things:

- your personality;
- what you are talking about—whether you are attempting to educate, inform, motivate, elicit feeling, and so forth; and
- the extent to which you refer to visual aids.

Chapter 5 draws the distinction between style and technique. It is the style of some trial advocates to talk fast, move fast, and move often. They do this in everyday conversation, and naturally they will do this before a jury. Other people move more slowly and deliberately. They use less movement in everyday life, and therefore they will use less in their summations.

Next, consider how movement is related to what you are discussing with the jury. Do you remember Hamlet's soliloquy? It begins:

> To be, or not to be: that is the question:
> Whether 'tis nobler in the mind to suffer
> The slings and arrows of outrageous fortune,
> Or to take arms against a sea of troubles,
> And by opposing end them?

In this scene, Hamlet is perplexed. He is trying to grope his way through a problem. He speaks slowly, deliberately, and uses only very little movement.

But consider the same Hamlet in act 3, scene 2, which follows almost immediately after the soliloquy quoted above. Now he is instructing the players. He is alert and active, and he moves about a great deal:

> Speak the speech, I pray you,
> As I pronounced it to you, trippingly on the tongue.

Movement always depends partly on what you are talking about. If you want to convey feeling to the jury, such as pain and suffering, death, or the lack of ability to enjoy life, you may be relatively quiet and use relatively little movement. But in discussing the liability aspects of an accident, in deploring the flagrant carelessness that caused a death or injury, you may demonstrate your deep concern by ferreting out the facts and using a great amount of movement.

Deciding how much to move also requires an appreciation of the principle of controlling space. Most of us equate the accumulation of space with status and dominance. The bigger your house, the larger your car or office, the more responsibility, power, and authority people will perceive you to have. In the courtroom as well, status and space correlate. Lawyers who are seen as more powerful and confident have a greater control and ownership of space in the courtroom. Four factors project confidence with regard to space:

- learning how to own and express ownership of space,
- learning how to use gestures to control space,
- avoiding invasion of territory that belongs to the jurors or the judge, and
- staying physically exposed to the jurors.

It is important that you own the space you occupy: when you walk into a courtroom there should be no surprises. You should know the territory.

The use of gestures controls space. Gestures in the courtroom should be natural. Expansive gestures—those that move away from the body—will create a larger personal territory and control more space. The more space you control, the greater will be your dominance as perceived by the jurors.

In projecting confidence, however, you must avoid invading the jurors' territory. You never want to lean on the jurors' box, because that is their territory. That box becomes their personal space in the courtroom. The same is true of the judge's territory.

One of the most significant ways of controlling space is to act as if you belong where you are.

In preparing for argument, it is important to consider the spatial relationships involved. Look at the courtroom in which you are trying the case. Try to determine the best sight lines. Where should you stand in the room to best be seen? Is there a glare from the windows? How does it vary at different times of the day?

Where are the places that the jury will see you but will not see much activity behind you? Locate and avoid the doors through which the bailiff, the clerk, or other people arrive and depart. Find places in the courtroom that will allow attention to remain fixed on you.[3]

Because the center of your space in front of the jury is the most important place, save it for your really key points. Likewise, as discussed in chapter 1, it is important to address the essential theme of your case from a specific place

---

3. *See* S. HAMLIN, *supra* note 2, at 163.

you have previously "anchored." Take the center ground at the beginning of your argument. Take it at the end. There may be several times when you will want to emphasize what you have said by moving to the center.

Visualize where you will deliver the first, second, and third parts of your statement. Then, in argument, go to those three different places; this puts you in a new spatial relationship to the jury and your material each time. This sequential spacing will be inherently logical to the jury. Finally, go back to those places every time you want to reinforce those points.

The experienced trial lawyer can project likability with his movements and actions. Most jurors find an attorney unapproachable when he remains stoic, grim, or angry throughout the trial. Respond in accordance with the jurors' reactions to events they find interesting. Smile with the jurors or nod in agreement with them to comments you want them to support.

Your voice can also project likability and approachability. Credibility increases with a deeper resonance. Likability and trustworthiness tend to increase with a softer voice tone or one that is easy to listen to.

Smiling is another desirable characteristic for projecting likability. Smiling is considered a highly rewarding behavior. When you smile, people generally tend to smile with you and to like you more.

Eye contact with the jury is very significant. It says, "I see you, I notice you, and I care about you." It is important to look from one person to another. As you make eye contact with each one, you link them together as a group, and each feels equally important. This contact may develop an energy level of its own. It reaches out and includes everyone.

Think of the jurors as friends from next door with whom you want to talk on a conversational level: you will find that talking to jurors is not only much easier, but much different than you might otherwise envision. Your movements, gestures, and posture become more relaxed and natural.

Some basic movements during argument involve handling objects and touching the victim. When you read important information from a book or document, handle it carefully, hold it for a second longer than usual, and then place it slowly and easily on the table as though it were the most valuable object in the courtroom.

On the other hand, if you want to show disdain for information contained in a document, hold it away from your body and put it down as soon as possible. This behavior is a nonverbal display of dismissal.

Avoid passing exhibits to the jury during the main body of your argument. Jurors are apt to become engrossed in the exhibits and become distracted from what you are saying. If you have a critical exhibit to show at this time, use a blowup, which allows you to command the jury's attention while the visual aid is discussed. If you must pass exhibits to the jury, save this maneuver for the closing portion of your summation.

The attorney representing the victim in a personal injury case may appropriately physically touch his client during the course of an argument, because touching is interpreted as a sign of affection. Touching projects that the attorney, like the juror, has feelings and empathy for human beings and their suffering.

Certain important principles govern touching another person during trial. Generally, it is always appropriate to touch a client of the same sex. Touching that client on the shoulder or on the elbow shows that you are not afraid to have contact and that this person is important to you; it demonstrates closeness between lawyer and client. On the other hand, be careful when dealing with a member of the opposite sex, particularly an attractive one.

An older, fatherly type of attorney may appropriately put his arm around or touch a client of either sex. An older female attorney may be seen as mothering a younger client by her touch. The touching of older clients by young attorneys, regardless of their sex, is usually permissible as long as the touch can be interpreted as indicating, "I believe in this client" or "I have feelings for this client."

Many lawyers come to the trial bar without any formal education in the mechanics of speech. The mastery of posture, gestures, and movement, however, may be easily attained through attention to the principles that have been discussed, coupled with repetition and practice.

8

Demeanor

The two jurors peered through the small window in the door into the courtroom in which they had spent the better part of their waking hours for the past two weeks. Their deliberations on the questions presented by this case had been proceeding slowly. The noon break was almost over. The diverse group was assembling in the hall, and deliberations would begin again as soon as all their number returned to the appointed place.

Inside the courtroom, the warring camps gathered around the plaintiff's counsel table. All the lawyers were laughing riotously; one seemed to be engaging the others with some private joke or story.

One of the faces at the window turned to the other with a quizzical look. "I don't see how those fellows could be very sincere about this case. This morning, in argument, it seemed they were at each other's throat. Now, just look at them. They're laughing and joking as though each was the other's lost brother."

The man to whom the remark had been directed continued to stare through the small window and simply replied under his breath, "Hypocrisy certainly seems to have its place in the legal profession."

* * * * *

THE LAWYER'S DEMEANOR may have a significant, although subtle, influence on the jury verdict. As discussed in earlier chapters, these aspects of physical communication are often turning points in a jury's assessment and determination of the case. Your demeanor, as well as that of your client, must be consistent throughout the trial. You cannot on the one hand attempt to project anger or disgust with the defense, and on the other convey closeness and camaraderie. You need not be "standoffish," but remember that your demeanor will be assessed by the jury at all times. For example, while opposing counsel is addressing the jury, it is important to convey a neutral but attentive behavior. Sit upright in your chair to reflect courtesy and respect for opposing counsel.

Likewise, jurors are intently aware of the victim's demeanor during the proceedings, particularly during argument. Instruct your client not to display any outward reaction either approving or disapproving statements made by counsel. Additionally, the client should appear courteous, attentive, and interested in the proceedings.

Consider carefully where to seat the victim during closing arguments. The options are—

- seating the client at the counsel table,
- seating the client in front of the railing but back from the counsel table,
- seating the client in the audience, or
- keeping the client out of the courtroom.

The choice will depend on the facts of the particular case. Many good trial advocates routinely seat their clients with them at the counsel table, to remain there during the entire proceedings, including jury argument. In some instances, however, this practice is not only inappropriate but probably disadvantageous. Often, the defense may have its corporate representative seated at its counsel table. If the defendant or the business representative is seated at the counsel table, the victim may be presented to some advantage in a different position. If the injured victim is a worker and the case is brought against a large corporation, it may be effective to seat the client in the first row on the other side of the railing. This position identifies the client with the jurors. He is "one of them"; they sat on those same benches days before.

If the arguments may be particularly personal and if the victim is very young, impressionable, or easily affected by such arguments, consider keeping the client out of the courtroom altogether during summation. This simply evinces your sensitivity and concern.

If you decide to seat the client in the courtroom during summation, it is vital to advise the client about the importance of his physical behavior. Remind the client to assume an attentive and interested position and caution him against unduly feigning discomfort or displaying effects of the injury.

In projecting a favorable demeanor, the victim's lawyer must adopt facial expressions, physical patterns, and mannerisms that display confidence but do not project arrogance. Also, the trial lawyer must adequately deal with nonverbal responses from the jury.

Projecting Confidence

There is a difference between *being* confident and *portraying* confidence in the courtroom. Sometimes one's level of confidence is lower than at other times, but the effective trial lawyer must portray confidence throughout every phase of the trial. The skilled advocate has learned that, regardless of how poorly the case may be going, he must never show this concern to the jury. Even when a witness's response is particularly damaging, the skilled trial advocate will normally smile and continue, his words and mannerisms projecting an attitude of unconcern.

One of the most common stereotypes in our country is that of "winners" and "losers." If you were to ask someone to describe a winner, he would say that person has good posture, keeps his shoulders back, holds his head high, maintains direct eye contact, breathes deeply and evenly, uses expansive gestures rather than gestures close to the body, takes large steps when walking, and appropriately controls his space. Winners act as if they know what they are doing even when they do not. Winners also have lower voice tones. Their voices project confidence. They control their voices by using pauses effectively. They never seem to be rushing because of nervous energy or to be talking too slowly. Winners use powerful speech and definite word choices.

Losers, on the other hand, have poor posture, avoid eye contact, angle their heads downward, move slowly or haltingly, appear to be in a confused state, do not speak fluently, and use impotent speech. Powerless or impotent speech includes hedging words, such as "like," "kind of," "perhaps," and "maybe," as well as frequent pauses with "ah," "and," and "you know."[1]

The experienced plaintiff's lawyer projects not only confidence but also approachability, friendliness, and competence. The jury is convinced not only that the trial advocate believes in his cause and that he has proved his case but also that he is confident and friendly enough to be the kind of person who would be willing to discuss the case in privacy with the jurors following the conclusion of the proceedings. In short, the lawyer's demeanor should convey an impression and feeling of comfort and ease.

Avoiding Projection of Arrogance

The natural style of many trial attorneys, on both sides of the docket, is combative, truculent, or pugnacious. This demeanor, in and of itself, is not faulty, but it can be disastrous when coupled with the projection of arrogance. Behavior that projects arrogance should be avoided at all costs. The arrogant attorney speaks down to the jurors, forces his contentions on them, and displays the attitude of an elitist who does not consider jurors his equals but merely the pawns in his masterful plan. Many jurors initially perceive attorneys as arrogant; when the lawyer contributes to this perception, he loses his ability to communicate, inspire, and motivate.

The behavioral cues that indicate arrogance are head tilt, speech patterns, and emphasis on key words. The lawyer who speaks or addresses the jury with his head tilted upward, so that his chin is up and his eyes are looking

---

1. For further discussion see L. Smith & L. Malandro, Courtroom Communication Strategies 68–70 (1985).

down, appears arrogant. Speech that is drawn out or enunciated in a peculiar or particular way conveys the same negative impression.

Projecting insensitivity and aloofness may be similarly disastrous to the victim's lawyer. These characteristics are manifested by leaning away from another person, avoiding extended eye contact, and dropping one's voice at the end of sentences.

Jurors admire tenacious fighters. They expect this quality and instinctively hope their champion would adopt such an attitude toward their cause. In short, it is not the quality of being combative, forceful, or angry that may produce a negative reaction. Indeed, all these contentious characteristics may endear the advocate in the minds of the jurors, provided that arrogance plays no role in the lawyer's image.

Dealing with Responses

One of the most difficult tasks the victim's advocate faces is dealing with negative or inappropriate responses from jurors. When an attorney perceives what he feels is a negative reaction from a juror, the attorney needs to be particularly careful that this reaction does not lead him into casting negative images. He must remain calm and self-assured. He may want to pay particular attention to that individual juror by using more eye contact, being more heedful, and talking directly to the juror whenever possible.

Reading body movements can be particularly dangerous. Eye movement and facial behavior of jurors are extremely difficult to evaluate and may produce unreliable information. A juror may cross his arms, and it may not mean anything; it may simply be a more comfortable position for the juror at that particular time. Likewise, jurors who nod their heads, smile, and appear to be in agreement with you may not necessarily be on your side.

Many accomplished advocates have been misled by jurors' reactions. Even though the trained advocate may be aware of a particular juror's response, he should consider the totality of perceived reaction from all jurors and recognize that he must modify his argument if necessary. If, for example, the attorney forms the impression that most of the jurors are either uninterested or are rejecting a certain argument, he must consider whether he should move on to more appropriate matters.

Again, flexibility is the key.

Out-of-Session Demeanor

Finally, consideration must be given to the conduct of the victim's lawyer when court is not in session. Jurors are constantly forming impressions and resorting to stereotypical images in formulating their opinions. If the victim's lawyer is trying a case against one of his good friends on the defense side of the docket and he believes the case will be tried by both sides in a straightforward, courteous manner, his conduct toward opposing counsel during breaks and recesses will be different than if the fight is intensely waged. Many successful advocates have a natural, friendly style and display it not only toward the jury but toward opposing counsel as well. Even in these circumstances, however, undue friendliness and association with the opposing side may be viewed with distrust by the jurors. You must refrain from evidencing a lack of concern and of complete dedication to your client's cause. This is not to say that if something humorous occurs in the course of the proceedings, you cannot enjoy the experience. But remember that jurors will develop a distrust for the lawyer who proceeds with verisimilitude to castigate and criticize the defense counsel for suggesting that the victim is a fraud, a malingerer, or incapable of telling the truth but who later acts as if that defense counsel were his closest friend.

The most effective demeanor to adopt is courteous respect. Defense counsel is an officer of the court and is charged with presenting his client's cause in its most favorable light. Thus, as the victim's lawyer you should avoid, for example, unduly interrupting the defense's final summation. Be attentive and respectful during the defense argument. At breaks and recesses, be pleasant, courteous, and helpful. But never engage in any activity that could conceivably convey to the jury that you are not completely and unalterably the victim's champion who believes absolutely in the righteousness of your client's cause.

The victim's advocate must always be aware that the jury is constantly analyzing and evaluating the demeanor of counsel as well as that of his client. The behavior of lawyer and client is but another form of nonverbal communication that may have a telling effect on the jury's verdict.

9

Mechanics of Speech

The young female defense lawyer who had addressed the jury on behalf of the insurance company was particularly effective. The plaintiff was a middle-aged Hispanic woman, who now sat in the front row of the courtroom beyond the three-foot oak partition that separated the audience from the participants. She shifted the weight of her huge body to a more comfortable position as her lawyer continued to address the jury. The defense had argued that the plaintiff would have made a better recovery from her back injury if she had lost the weight the doctors told her to lose. That argument, with additional points regarding the plaintiff's preexisting arthritic condition and other medical maladies, had been effectively delivered.

The plaintiff did not understand these arguments. She did not speak English. Her testimony had been given through an interpreter.

The victim's lawyer had now recounted the medical evidence. The doctors' divergent findings were discussed and explained. As the argument progressed toward the inevitable conclusion, the lawyer tried to visualize in his own mind the hurt, agony, and frustration he knew this injury had brought to his client.

He changed his position before the jury. He was now standing immediately in front of his client. His voice lowered, and his eyes dropped.

"The unwillingness to understand another's tragedy or injury, or the failure to be concerned about it, can only be called insensitivity. [pause] *Insensitivity is a narcotic that deadens the heart as well as the soul. We become addicted to it, as we do to any narcotic. We demand more insensitivity and intolerance to wall ourselves off from the tragedies with which we may become involved."*

The lawyer now raised the volume of his voice. He studied each juror as he carefully measured each word.

"The tough thing about insensitivity is that before long in order to function we need the hard stuff—prejudice. Now instead of simply being uncaring and compassionless, we justify our attitude toward others with disclaimers such as, 'Well, if this lady weren't so heavy she would have gotten over the injury sooner,' or 'If this lady spoke English we could better understand her problems.' "

The victim's lawyer paused for several seconds before he continued: "As you have heard from the evidence, it isn't as though Mrs. Rodriguez has not tried. Three times she got a job. Three times she lost it. She lost it because the only work she knows how to do requires a good and healthy back."

* * * * *

EARLIER CHAPTERS examine the concepts and principles of the physical aspects of nonverbal communication. Now it is appropriate to turn to more familiar and basic principles that apply to the mechanics of verbal persuasion. Vocal mechanics involve the manipulation of three basic variables: vocal pitch, vocal tone (volume), and vocal rate (cadence or rate of speech). The skilled advocate uses these variables to achieve maximum effect of the verbal content of his message. The manner in which these variables are orchestrated depends on the nature of the message being conveyed, its content, and the purpose to be achieved.

Vocal Pitch

The pitch—the highness or lowness of a vocal tone—is a good indicator of emotionality. By changing pitch levels appropriately, you can attract the jurors' attention, generate interest, and make your point in a manner the jurors will more likely remember. Many people's voices are pitched a little too high; women advocates worry about this, for example. It *is* easier to listen to a lower-pitched voice, and it is worth some effort to develop this pitch. We all remember with admiration the melodious tone of voice of the late Senator Everett Dirkson. A lower pitch sounds more credible and important, and it makes listening easier for the long haul of the trial.

Emotions (anger, sympathy, solemnity) can also be expressed through changes in pitch. The voice can be used as a behavior indicator of various moods and emotional states. One way to do this is to visualize what you are talking about. Imagine the scene you are actually describing. Imagine the story as it is happening. Imagine the person you are talking about. Imagine the sorrow and shock the plaintiffs experienced when they were told of the death of their son. Imagine the client's reaction when he was told by the doctor that his eye had to be removed and could not be saved. This type of imagining helps create color and nuance in your voice. You will find yourself altering the pitch and tone almost subconsciously, and that makes your delivery much more interesting.

Vocal Tone

Loudness is another vocal cue attorneys can use effectively. Volume can be used to create an appropriate atmosphere for your presentation. By dramatically lowering your voice, you can work to create a warm, friendly, almost private-club-like atmosphere. When voice tones are lowered, jurors typically respond by leaning forward and increasing their attention to hear what is being said.

Loudness—though not to the extreme of screaming and shouting at maximum decibel level—is related positively to perceived credibility. Perceived credibility increases with volume that influences the jurors to believe the attorney is in control, is confident, and knows what he is doing.

Nuance in the voice is very important. You can enlarge your voice to make it forceful and compelling, then soften it to become more intimate and more personal. Tone depends on what you are talking about: you can sound insincere if you talk about sad or touching subjects while using exactly the same tone you used in describing the number of feet the defendant had within which to stop his eighteen-wheeler before he collided with the plaintiff. It is vital to make your voice reflect what you are saying.

Consider the following arguments:

- The defendant laid down one hundred and eighty feet of skid marks before the initial impact. This truck, which was estimated by the defendant-driver to weigh in the neighborhood of twenty tons, collided with another vehicle before it struck the car being operated by my young friend Billy Brown. We all recall the testimony of the investigating officer that it was his opinion, based on the length of the skid marks and the amount of damage done to the vehicles, that the driver was operating this truck at approximately seventy miles per hour. The posted speed limit was fifty-five miles per hour. The impact to Billy's car caved in the rear end in the manner that is depicted in Plaintiff's Exhibits 10 and 11.
- In this tragic collision of June 18, 1984, our neighbor Billy Brown sustained these injuries to his neck, which you have heard described by the doctors. It certainly is true, and Billy has not tried to conceal it, that with the aid of his physicians he was able to make good initial recovery. However, it is the nature of this type of injury that while the initial recovery may be good, it is the long-range prognosis that is so difficult. After a while, the improvement comes slowly. It is agonizingly difficult. It may not come at all. His condition now is probably as good as it will ever be.

The first example consists of content of an exclusively factual nature. That argument would be made with little change in volume or cadence. The second example illustrates a more kinesthetic approach. Consider the inflections that occur during the course of the last four sentences. The following chart depicts variations in volume that would be incorporated for emphasis. The scale ranges from the loudest a lawyer could speak without being offensive (10) to the quietest he could speak and still be heard and understood by the jury (1).

10			
9			
8			
7			
6			
5	After a while, the improvement comes		
4		slow	
3			ly.
2			
1			

10						
9						
8						
7			difficult.			
6		agonizingly		It		
5	It is				may not come	
4						
3						
2						at all.
1						

10					
9					
8					
7					
6		now			
5	His condition		is probably as good as it		
4				will ever	
3					
2					
1					be.

Vocal Rate

The rate of delivery the attorney uses in the courtroom affects the impression he makes on the jury. Communicators have noted that a person who talks faster is generally regarded more favorably by his listeners—and the listener tends to learn from the fast talker. A speaker with a faster rate of delivery is more persuasive and is also seen as more intelligent, knowledgeable, and objective. A brisker, faster delivery leaves the juror with the impression that the attorney is confident, capable, and in control.

Experience teaches us that people tend to talk longer to those they like. Similarly, people are more attentive to speakers whose delivery is consistent with the listeners' conception of confidence and reliability.

You can use pauses effectively during argument to highlight important points in presentation of the case. Pauses help jurors to refocus their attention back to the case. The pause should be a purposeful interval of silence, giving the jury time to digest the information or concept they just heard; never fill a pause with distracting vernacular such as "ah," "um," and the like. Effective speakers use pauses to punctuate what they are saying. A controlled, deliberate pause can have a significant effect by jarring the listener's attention. You must practice to become effective in using pauses; for many people, pausing is not natural.

Unfortunately, some trial advocates use the style of the college debater. The 300-word-a-minute rat-a-tat-tat bombards the jury with ideas, concepts, and evidence.[1] You can avoid offensive impressions formed by this delivery style by slowing the rate of delivery and effectively using pauses. Remember, though, that the unfilled pause, if not used at a logical point, reduces your credibility; used at an opportune moment, it greatly increases credibility. Use a pause to create a moment of silence that sets the dramatic stage before an anchoring sentence. Use it, too, as you reach the close of the summation to establish a moment of great emotional impact.

Assume the printed page represents the normal rate of speech most trial advocates use. The following paragraph would depict the rate of speech or cadence you might use in delivering the argument illustrated above:

> After - a - while - the - improvement --- comes -- s-l-o-w-l-y. --- It - is - agonizingly - difficult. --- It - may - not - come - at - all. --- His - condition - n-o-w -- is - probably - as - good - as - it - will -- ever -- be.

To make your argument animated and interesting, remember to vary the pitch and volume of your voice and your rate of delivery.

---

1. The average rate at which people generally speak is approximately 150 words per minute. M. JONES, SPEAK, LOOK, COMMUNICATE! 1, 85 (1978). Speeches by many famous politicians, in contrast, are often given at a slightly faster rate. *Id.* Some of the outstanding trial advocates in Texas have very different speech rates, which are accentuated by their inherent use of voice inflection and cadence. For instance, a speech by the excellent defense lawyer James B. Sales usually contains about 161 words per minute (calculated from a June 1985 recording of "Current Status of Tort Law in Texas," audiotape, Professional Development Program, State Bar of Texas), with frequent pauses and inflection; without such pauses, his vocal rate would approximate 200 or more words per minute. Conversely, one who was known as a champion college debater and excellent trial advocate and who formerly sat on our supreme court, William W. Kilgarlin, speaks a more methodical 134 words per minute (calculated from a June 1985 recording of "Strategies in Personal Injury/Wrongful Death," audiotape, Professional Development Program, State Bar of Texas) in rhythmic fashion.

PART 4

Verbal Principles of Argument

Choice word and measured phrase, above the reach of ordinary man.

—William Wordsworth, "Resolution and Independence"

10

Selection and Use of Words

The jurors looked bored. The plaintiff's lawyer was discussing the damages aspect of the case. What should have been the high point of argument was turning into a catastrophe. The victim presented a compelling and pitiful sight. The right side of this middle-aged man's face was etched with grotesque scars—a hideous reminder of the automobile-truck collision that occurred three years earlier. His right arm was also mangled in that collision and now hung limply in his lap.

The lawyer's words evoked little response from the jurors. "We ask that you answer Question 12—four hundred thousand dollars. My client, Larry Taylor, is entitled to be given that for his pain and suffering. If you don't believe he is entitled to that sum of money, then you just didn't listen to the evidence."

The discussion of medical evidence that followed was lost in the negative impressions now indelibly engraved in the jurors' minds.

* * * * *

SUCCESSFUL ADVOCACY depends on the proper selection of words and communication of ideas. This concept is often ignored or violated by the inexperienced advocate. In selecting words, you are trying to accomplish a number of goals or purposes that include—

- enhancing your credibility,
- educating and informing the jury, and
- motivating the jury toward a plaintiff's verdict.

Attorney Credibility

Credibility is a multidimensional concept. Experts in communication say credibility is influenced by the perception of competence, trustworthiness, and dynamism.

In a trial setting, competence is the lawyer's skill and knowledge. Trustworthiness means the advocate presents information without bias; he is fair, ethical, and just. Finally, dynamism is measured by how forceful, bold, or active the lawyer appears to be. As with the general concept of credibility, the importance lies in the jurors' perceptions of each of these factors.

Word choice and language affect a person's credibility. Powerful speech enhances credibility: an attorney who uses powerful speech is more likely to be perceived as intelligent, likable, and believable. Using powerful speech and language techniques, such as repetition, metaphors, similes, analogies, and rhetorical questions, can build credence in jurors' minds.

It is impossible to transfer a mood to the jurors unless they trust you. To have the jurors' trust, one of the most important things you must do is reciprocate their trust. Questions that affect a juror's perception of credibility include:

- Is the attorney well prepared?
- Is the message consistent, easily remembered, and well delivered?

Jurors will not see you as more intelligent because your message is complex; in fact, they will likely see you as less intelligent and as incapable of communicating a clear and simple thought if you complicate your message. Likewise, jurors must be able to identify with you before they can view you as a credible source. The degree to which a juror can identify with you and see you as he sees himself largely determines whether that juror will reach a positive evaluation of you and your case. Sincerity, honesty, and fairness are three of the most important and admired traits that people look for in another individual. Be conscious of the effect of your message and the jurors' perceptions of your objectivity during the trial.

Common Mistakes of Plaintiffs' Advocates

Several aspects in arguing the personal injury case on behalf of the victim constitute common pitfalls for the beginning advocate. For example, in arguing the desired answers to special issues or questions, you might say, "We ask you to answer this question . . ." While you may use this phrase occasionally, it should not be your flagship terminology. Instead, rely on such statements as:

> We have proved this aspect to you by a preponderance of the evidence . . .
>
> Justice and the evidence presented require that this question be answered . . .
>
> A terrible injustice will be done and Bob Jones's tragedy will be compounded if you do not find this question, as established by the evidence, to be . . .

Obviously, there are other phrases that may be used to indicate the same thing. The important point is that the jurors must understand that the judge is bound by their answers and that it is not merely plaintiff's "wish" that a question be answered in a certain way; they must realize that the desired answer to the question is supported by the evidence and is *critical* to the outcome of the case.

Likewise, many inexperienced advocates constantly make references such as "my client" or "my client, Larry Taylor." This is ineffective advocacy, at best. It conveys to the jury a notion that this fellow is simply someone the lawyer is representing with no real feeling. Avoid the term *client*; in its place use references like the following:

> My *friend* Larry Taylor . . .
> This *man we are privileged to represent*, Larry Taylor, . . .
> This *good man whom we have gotten to know so well* . . .

Another common mistake occurs when the attorney adopts a condescending attitude toward the jury. "You just didn't listen to the evidence if you didn't get that point." "You weren't paying attention if you don't recall that evidence." Arguments like these portray a condescending attitude that must be avoided at all cost. It is vital that each of your actions, words, and deeds convey to the jury the following concepts:

- that you have faith in the jurors to arrive at an appropriate verdict;
- that you know they have listened to the evidence and understand it; and
- that you and they are one in sharing the same attitudes, beliefs, and desires for justice.

Here is a more appropriate argument:

> We have proved by a preponderance of the evidence that this company didn't care. Does the defendant think we will ignore this evidence? Do they think we were asleep or were not paying attention when we heard it? Do they think we will look the other way and forget it? Of course not.

Finally, the beginning advocate may fall into the trap of using language like this: "We believe that you should give Mr. Taylor $400,000 in damages." Here again is a phrase to avoid—it says the damages awarded are to be *given*, and it thereby implies charity. Instead stress that the damages found by the jury are part of a verdict that is demanded and supported by the evidence. Thus, it is much more effective to make a statement similar to the following: "The preponderance of the evidence demonstrates and supports a finding of $400,000 for this element of damages."

More significantly, in arguing damages it may be important to remind the jury that the defense required proof, as the law permits it to do. "We have proved these damages at no small expense to our friend Mr. Taylor." "We have brought you evidence from doctors, medical records, and other sources that establishes these damages, while the defendant's sole attitude is that, somehow, this evidence should not be believed, followed, or accepted."

Self-Deprecation

Another technique you may use effectively is self-deprecation. The experienced trial advocate never makes fun of opposing parties or defense counsel. Likewise, it is important that the trial lawyer not emphasize "I" and "me" too much in his argument. While the victim's lawyer is certainly one of the central figures in any trial cast, the injured victim is the critically and principally involved person. A good advocate bears these principles in mind and chooses words that do not tend to cast him as a principal character; rather, the advocate's status is similar to that of the jury. The following argument illustrates these principles:

> We are faced with a difficult and ponderous responsibility in this case. We must decide the damages that are due our friends Mr. and Mrs. Jones as a result of this tragedy—a tragedy that was not of their own making. The evidence is clear and compelling that the death of their child, Johnny, was brought about by the negligence of these defendants. Neither these parents nor young Johnny did anything that contributed to or caused his death—
>
> —Most of us have never been called on to deal with and handle a personal crisis of this magnitude. I seriously doubt that if any of us were thrust into this midnight of madness we could handle it any better than these people have. Our responsibility is attempting to understand, to feel, and to know the loss involved—
>
> —Interestingly enough, the defense's attitude toward these people serves to reinforce the image that most people have of lawyers. In *Luke*, chapter 11, verse 46, it is said, "Woe unto you also, ye lawyers! for ye lade men with burdens grievous to be borne, and ye yourselves touch not the burdens with one of your fingers." Unfortunately, this biblical concept is all too accurate in many cases—
>
> I would try to affect the burden carried by these people in the only way I know how, by a fair and effective presentation of evidence to a jury that, by its oath, is committed to justice. One person does not have the strength, fortitude, or ability to right this wrong. But twelve of you, standing tall, armed with your oath and charged with your responsibility, can do exactly that. The verdict

we render becomes a public emolument forever stored in the archives of this courthouse. It is as important a legal instrument as any deed or will. It is protected, preserved, and recorded in the same manner. Your children and grandchildren can see what you did on August 5, 1988.

Powerful Language

In a personal injury case, it is particularly important to select language—specific words and terms—that will conjure the strongest impressions within the jurors' minds. Unfortunately, the words and phrases victims' lawyers often use have little impact. Before argument, conscientiously select words, terms, and phrases to use during summation. The following chart contrasts inappropriate or impotent terminology with other words that could be successfully employed to provoke a desired visual image.

Impotent Words	Power Terms and Phrases
Accident (This word connotes an incident that occurred without fault.)	• Tragic and avoidable collision • Impacting of steel and iron • Crashing impact of tons of metal • Recipe for disaster
Disabling injury	• A tragedy that maimed my friend • Crippling injuries involved • The tearing of muscles and nerves • This painful and agonizing disruption of flesh
Effects of injury	• Struggle for independence • Catastrophic consequences • Nightmare of tragedy • Maiming misfortune

Impotent Words	Power Terms and Phrases
My client	• My friend • This good citizen • This innocent victim • Our neighbor
Defective product	• This deadly defective device • This apparition of an appliance • This device of deceit • This contraption of contempt • This sinister instrument
This negligent defendant	• This careless driver • This irresponsible corporation • This reckless apartment operator
Young child	• Frail baby • Defenseless infant • Fragile human being in its infancy

The list above briefly illustrates this idiomatic concept. Given the specifics of your case and the particular terms or phrases that may be in question, you can use a dictionary or thesaurus to formulate more powerful words and phrases.

Above all, use language that is natural to you. Some trial lawyers are more at home with flowery language and flashy prose than others. Choose sentence structure, phraseology, and words you can use much as you would wear an old pair of loafers. "Power" words can be effective, but only if they are a part of your natural eloquence. Chapter 2 refers to the example of Socrates, who by his own eloquence lost his case. Socrates was the most eloquent of those who spoke at this trial, but he offended the judges. Many times one can review an argument given by another lawyer and be impressed with the other's use of vocabulary and eloquence. However, if the language seems stilted, contrived, unnatural, or insincere, it is not likely to provoke the jury to a victim's verdict. In short, eloquence comes in various sizes, colors, and shapes. Some of the most eloquent jury summations given by victims' lawyers consist of simple, short, and direct words and terms. The essential rule is to select words that produce the maximum desired effect of credibility, communication, and motivation.

11

Use of Anecdotes and Poetry

The victim's lawyer had been discussing various aspects of the evidence as it related to the defense's contentions. He took a powerful step backward, slid his hands easily into the pockets of his trousers, and, after a slight pause, continued:

"As I considered the arguments that the defendant has advanced in this case, I couldn't help but recall a fellow I grew up with. His name was Roland, but it could have been Tom or Bob. All of us grew up with a fellow like Roland. Roland, you see, was the most gullible fellow who had ever been born."

The trial advocate smiled.

"In the small community where we grew up, we had these carnivals that would come to town on a regular basis. A part of the carnival was the "shell game." For the investment of a dime you had the chance to win a dollar. You would win the dollar if you could pick out which of the three shells the pea was under. Now, most of us boys knew that the barker was palming the pea. Even though we were only eleven or twelve years old, we had been able to figure that out. But not Roland. He would bet dime after dime in an effort to get that dollar. As a result, Roland never got any cotton candy at the carnival or rode the roller coaster or the Ferris wheel. He would always use up his dimes trying to win that dollar."

A couple of steps to his left brought the lawyer to the court reporter's table. He picked up an exhibit and proceeded, "I have the impression that the defense thinks that we are all a bunch of Rolands."

* * * * *

A DECISION about using personal or historical anecdotes or poetry first requires consideration of the legal rules of argument. A common and notorious objection is that such references constitute "arguing outside the record." Unfortunately, the rule of law forbidding such argument is misunderstood even by some experienced advocates and trial judges.

As the Preface to this volume states, this book is not intended to be a "law book" in the strict sense. However, since an understanding of the proper use of anecdotes and poetry in argument is so intertwined with an understanding of the legal principles regarding such argument, a brief analysis is appropriate.

The general rule is that counsel must confine his argument to matters within the record; hence, argument must be related to the facts and circumstances in evidence as well as to deductions that can be fairly made from them.[1] The two most common examples of arguing outside the record are (1) advising the jury of the effect of its answers or causing the jury to agree on the result to be accomplished and then to conform the answers to accomplish that result[2] and (2) improperly injecting the matter of insurance.[3] The rule also prohibits offering imaginary testimony.[4]

Proper use of anecdotes and poetry, however, will not extend advocacy into the forbidden zone. "It is well-settled law in Texas that the facts of a case may in argument be related to history, fiction, personal experience, anecdotes, Bible stories, or jokes."[5] Further, our supreme court has recognized the appropriateness of hyperbole and has encouraged imaginative advocacy.[6] Colorful prose or poetry may also be used.[7] It has been suggested that if the law were otherwise, a multitude of eloquent arguments and analogies would be discounted as improper and juries would be reduced to the "answering of factual questions in a vacuum . . . . [T]hus emotional argument is proper within limits because the jury is not, and has never been intended to be, a mere factual computer."[8]

---

1. Warren Petroleum Corp. v. Pyeatt, 275 S.W.2d 216, 219 (Tex. Civ. App.—Texarkana 1955, writ ref'd n.r.e.) (citing 41-B TEX. JUR. 281, § 237).

2. Texas & N.O.R.R. v. McGinnis, 109 S.W.2d 160, 164 (Tex. Comm'n App. 1937, opinion adopted).

3. Sutton Motor Co. v. Crysel, 289 S.W.2d 631, 638-39 (Tex. Civ. App.—Beaumont 1956, no writ).

4. Plains Creamery v. Denny, 277 S.W.2d 755, 764 (Tex. Civ. App.—Amarillo 1954, writ ref'd n.r.e.) (plaintiff's attorney argued to the jury what the decedent would have testified had he been there to speak).

5. Sheffield v. Lewis, 287 S.W.2d 531, 539 (Tex. Civ. App.—Texarkana 1956, no writ); *see also* 56 TEX. JUR. 2d § 242, at 576 (citing Louisiana & Ark. Ry. v. Mullins, 326 S.W.2d 263 (Tex. Civ. App.—Texarkana 1959, writ ref'd n.r.e.), *cert. denied*, 361 U.S. 966 (1969); A.B.C. Storage & Moving Co. v. Herron, 138 S.W.2d 211 (Tex. Civ. App.—Galveston 1940, writ dism'd judgmt cor.); Classen v. Benfer, 144 S.W.2d 633 (Tex. Civ. App.—San Antonio 1940, writ dism'd judgmt cor.); Fort Worth Hotel Co. v. Waggoman, 126 S.W.2d 578 (Tex. Civ. App.—Fort Worth 1939, writ dism'd judgmt cor.); Ford Motor Co. v. Whitt, 81 S.W.2d 1032 (Tex. Civ. App.—Amarillo 1935, writ ref'd); Missouri, K. & T. R.R. v. O'Hare, 39 S.W.2d 939 (Tex. Civ. App.—Waco 1931, writ dism'd); Gulf Ref. Co. v. Youngblood, 23 S.W.2d 522 (Tex. Civ. App.—Fort Worth 1929, writ dism'd); Texas Indem. Ins. Co. v. Pemberton, 9 S.W.2d 65 (Tex. Civ. App.—Amarillo 1928, no writ); Hewitt v. Buchanan, 4 S.W.2d 169 (Tex. Civ. App.—Eastland 1927, no writ); Winnsboro Cotton Oil Co. v. Carson, 185 S.W. 1002 (Tex. Civ. App.—Dallas 1916, no writ); Beaumont Traction Co. v. Dilworth, 94 S.W. 352 (Tex. Civ. App. 1906, no writ)).

6. Standard Fire Ins. Co. v. Reese, 584 S.W.2d 835, 838 (Tex. 1979).

7. Beaumont Traction Co. v. Dilworth, 94 S.W. 352, 355 (Tex. Civ. App. 1906, no writ); *see also* Standard Fire Ins. Co. v. Reese, 584 S.W.2d 835, 838-39 (Tex. 1979).

8. Crump, *The Function and Limits of Prosecution Jury Argument*, 28 SW. L.J. 505, 508 (1974).

Anecdotes and poetry may serve several functions in jury argument. They are dissimilar in style, function, and content.

Anecdotes

An anecdote is a short narrative of an interesting, amusing, or biographical incident. Anecdotes are usually used in much the same way as analogies, which are discussed in detail in chapter 12. Like analogies, anecdotes must be used with caution. An effective anecdote usually embodies these characteristics:

- It is short.
- It is interesting.
- It illustrates a pertinent and critical point in issue.
- Where biographical, it involves a historical personality who is not controversial or offensive.

The anecdote is an effective tool of argument because it allows the jurors to relax—to realize that the advocate is now stepping away from a pedantic recitation of the evidence and court's charge. Abraham Lincoln, for example, was noted for his use of anecdotes.

The skilled trial lawyers who use biographical anecdotes are careful to choose subjects who are beyond reproach. Many a political, military, or entertainment personality has certain facets of his reputation that disqualify him for anecdotal purposes; but what juror could be offended by a reference to Abraham Lincoln, Billy Graham, or Clarence Darrow? The following examples illustrate the effective use of anecdotes.

In a case involving the death of an adopted child, the victim's advocate must consider the prospect that some jurors may believe the parents' loss to be less because the child was adopted.

> I know that some of you, when you think of these parents' loss, may want to consider that young Danny Johnson was an adopted son. He had been brought to these fine people a few days following his birth. They had come to know him and love him as their own—as if he were the flesh of their bodies. I cannot help but recall the story that Reverend Billy Graham tells of his discussion with Roy Rogers and Dale Evans regarding their adopted children. Roy and Dale had adopted a number of children from varying ethnic, cultural, and racial backgrounds. Reverend Graham asked them whether they gave their adopted children the same rights and privileges that they gave to their real children. They were shocked and said, "Of course we do. They are ours as much as the ones who were born to us." Reverend Graham was interested in their answer and inquired

> whether they loved the children as much as their own. Roy and Dale replied, "Of course we do; after all we chose to be their parents, and they chose to be our children."

A more remote historical anecdote is often used to illustrate the independence of a jury:

> You were chosen to decide this case because you are not beholden to anyone, including a corporation as eminent and powerful as the Gas-Tex Company. In considering your independence and the significance of your jury verdict, I could not help but recall an incident that occurred in the late 1600s. At that time, in England, where the jury system came from, the king had the power to tell a jury that he wanted someone convicted. When he did that, the person was convicted. In about 1680 a young man was brought in for rabble-rousing and charged with the crime. A trial was held, and the king made his wish clear. The jury heard the case. In the instructions the court said, "It is the king's wish that this man be convicted." The jury went out, and they were out two days before they came back. The judge asked the foreman, "Do you have a verdict?" The foreman answered, "I do." The foreman stood up and looked at him, and the judge asked, "What is your verdict?" The foreman replied, "The verdict is not guilty." The judge said, "I don't think you understand. It is the king's wish that there be a conviction in this case. Go back out and stay. . ."
>
> They went back out. They stayed two more days, and then they came back in. The judge asked, "What is your verdict?" The foreman stood and looked at him—*this is a true story*—and said, "Not guilty." Again out, again back. The circumstances the jury lived in were not good. Several of them became ill. Finally, they were brought back in. For all they knew, they were going to be killed by the king. An exasperated judge asked, "What is your verdict?" The foreman said, "Not guilty."
>
> And then the words were exchanged that—out of the contribution of those jurors who sat there, where you now sit—have made you what you are today. The judge asked, "When will your verdict be guilty?" The foreman replied, "Never."[9]

In some cases the defense will strain in its interpretation and construction of the court's charge. They may argue the meanings of legal definitions that are farfetched or do not mesh with the facts of the case or the terms of the

---

9. Recounted in S. HAMLIN, WHAT MAKES JURIES LISTEN 368 (1985).

court's charge. In such instances the following anecdote might be used to illustrate the fallaciousness of the defense:

> As I listened to the defense argument and analysis of the court's instruction on "total incapacity," I could not help but recall that children's story we all read and loved so much—*Through the Looking-glass*. You remember reading the part where Alice points out to Humpty Dumpty that he has taken a word and given it the wrong meaning.
>
> "When I use a word," Humpty Dumpty said in a rather scornful tone, "it means just what I choose it to mean, no more and no less." To which Alice replied, "The question is whether you can make words mean so many different things." "No," said Humpty Dumpty, "the question is who is to be the master?"[10]

Many years ago, when oratory was considered an art and public speaking was studied more assiduously than today, there existed a number of fine works cataloging and containing useful historical anecdotes. Unfortunately, few of these books remain in print.[11] A few of today's skilled advocates keep notebooks containing anecdotes and may use them to illustrate various points, morals, or principles.

Poetry

Poetry has long been employed by many excellent trial lawyers. Like analogies and anecdotes, poetry must be used with great care. A poem that does not fit the case or otherwise appears to be a feigned effort to elicit jury sympathy may produce disastrous consequences. Generally, to be successfully used, poetry must have the following characteristics:

- The passage must be short.
- The language and words of the poet must be common, everyday language and not stilted.
- The passage must directly relate to the issues in the case.

The works of many poets—Shelley and Keats, for example—simply do not lend themselves for use before a Texas jury. America's legendary poet, Edgar A. Guest, on the other hand, wrote about people and used a style that is

---

10. *See id.* at 335.

11. An excellent work that has recently been published is THE LITTLE, BROWN BOOK OF ANECDOTES (C. Fadiman ed. 1985).

particularly appealing. The following examples represent the use of poetry in argument:

> The lawyer for National Presses has suggested that it was simply not possible or feasible for them to design this machine in such a way that it would protect and guard against the type of tragedy that we are talking about. They say there was no way to design this machine so that Robert Lee Landcaster's hand would not become caught in that machine and traumatically amputated. By contrast, you have heard from our expert, Dr. Stevenson, that such a design was not only possible and feasible but should have been employed. In considering the defense and the testimony of these experts, I couldn't help but be reminded of a poem. It went something like this:
>
> Somebody said it couldn't be done,
> But he with a chuckle replied
> That maybe it couldn't, but he would be one
> Who wouldn't say so till he tried.
> So he buckled right in with a trace of a grin
> On his face. If he worried, he hid it.
> He started to sing as he tackled the thing
> That couldn't be done, and he did it.[12]

In a case involving injury to an elderly woman, the following might be used:

> As I was pondering what I would say to you today in argument about the damages that should be recovered by Mrs. Henry, I ran across an old poem by Mary Dow Brine. The poem was about a lady. A lady like Mrs. Henry. The poem tells the story of a woman who was attempting to cross the street. School had let out down the street, and the boys were running by. One of the boys stopped to help the lady.
>
> He guided the trembling feet along,
> Proud that his own were firm and strong.
> Then back again to his friends, he went,
> His young heart happy and well content.
> "She's somebody's mother, boys, you know,
> For all she's aged and poor and slow,
> And I hope some fellow will lend a hand
> To help my mother, you understand,

---

12. E.A. GUEST, *It Couldn't Be Done*, in COLLECTED VERSE OF EDGAR A. GUEST 285 (1934).

> If ever she's poor and old and gray,
> When her own dear boy is far away."
> And "somebody's mother" bowed low her head
> In her home that night, and the prayer she said
> Was, "God be kind to the noble boy,
> Who is somebody's son, and pride and joy!"[13]

The following excerpt has been used in a product liability case involving a defective tie-rod:

> When we consider this tragedy and the legal issues that have been submitted by the court, it is easy to overlook and forget that this defective tie-rod was designed by someone, was manufactured by someone, and was put on the car by someone. Many years ago one of America's great poets had occasion to consider a similar situation. He said,
>
> "We found the car beneath the tree.
> The steering knuckle broke," said he;
> "The driver's dead; they say his wife
> Will be an invalid for life."
> I wonder how the man must feel
> Who made that faulty steering wheel.
> Perhaps the workman never saw
> An indication of the flaw;
> Or seeing it, he fancied it
> Would not affect his work a bit,
> And said: "It's good enough to go—
> I'll pass it on. They'll never know.
> It's not exactly to my best
> But it may pass the final test;
> And should it break no man can know
> It was my hand that made it so.
> The thing is faulty, but perhaps
> We'll never hear it when it snaps."[14]

Anecdotes and poetry provide an opportunity to make an argument entertaining and lively. These communicative techniques, properly used, may bring home to the jury thoughts and concepts that could not have been effectively conveyed in any other manner.

---

13. *Somebody's Mother,* in THE BEST LOVED POEMS OF THE AMERICAN PEOPLE 373, 374-75 (H. Felleman comp. 1936).

14. E.A. GUEST, *The Broken Wheel, supra* note 12, at 418.

12

Use of Similes, Metaphors, and Analogies

The tall, thin lawyer stood before the jury, a copy of the court's charge in his hand. He had just read the definition of circumstantial evidence to the jury. The timbre of his voice conveyed ease and comfort.

"In considering how best to illustrate and explain the legal concept of circumstantial evidence, I could not help but recall the story of Robinson Crusoe. Most of us have read this book or studied it in high school."

Each juror's face betrayed a flash of recognition as the lawyer continued: "Robinson Crusoe found himself marooned on a desert isle. He lived completely by himself for a long time. He was extremely lonely and believed that he would never see another human being. One morning when he was walking on the beach, he saw a set of footprints. He knew that he had not left these footprints, because he had not been previously walking on that part of the beach. He concluded that he was not alone, and he immediately began to search for the person who ultimately became his friend, Friday."

Pausing purposefully, the advocate studied each face.

"When Robinson Crusoe found those footprints on the beach, he did not see a man. He did not know a man was there. He based his conclusion that he was no longer alone on 'circumstantial evidence.' It was a conclusion that could be fairly and reasonably inferred, in the words of the court, from other facts. The inference Robinson Crusoe made was that since there were footprints on the beach and he did not leave them and since footprints like those could be made only by a man, he was thus not alone."[1]

* * * * *

AKIN TO THE USE OF ANECDOTES AND POETRY is the use of similes, metaphors, and analogies, which serve a number of purposes. Similes and metaphors make the lawyer's communication more lively and forceful. Analogies, like anecdotes, make his presentation more entertaining and enjoyable for the jury.

---

1. This effective use of analogy to explain the concept of "circumstantial evidence" is attributed to the accomplished trial advocate Stan Binion of Houston, Texas.

Similes

A simile is a rhetorical device that uses the word *like, as,* or *than* to make an explicit comparison. By creating images in the listener's mind, a simile makes speaking more vivid and conveys the message more effectively. Some common examples of similes are—

tough as nails,
quick as a cat,
cagey as a fox,
welcome as a skunk,
quiet as a church mouse,
like shooting fish in a barrel, and
slower than molasses.

Similes like these are not particularly effective, because they are basically clichés. Many experienced trial lawyers, both for plaintiff and for defendant, have developed more colorful similes:

Like being named the fattest horse in the glue factory.
The argument (contention) unravels like a cheap sweater.
As disadvantaged as a one-legged man in a soccer game.
They used as much thought in designing this product as a baby uses when he wets his diaper.
When the defense says they stand tall on this issue, it's like Tatu lording it over Tom Thumb.
As conscientious as an intoxicated adolescent.
Like going to McDonald's for dinner. You know you are not getting the gourmet stuff, but it's easy and safe.

Metaphors

A metaphor is a figure of speech that uses a word or phrase to denote literally an object or thought in place of another. It suggests an unexpected likeness or analogy between them. Thus, a metaphor can be described as a word or phrase that implies a comparison. Juries listen very carefully to metaphors, which can be presented in stories or examples that often remind adults of childhood stories and fairy tales. The noted children's author of the Dr. Seuss series uses many metaphors in his stories, which are basically parables. His stories convey such morals as the willingness to accept others who are different from us, the failings of individuals who show no tolerance, and the foolishness of resistance to trying new things. By the same token, Aesop's fables contain many appropriate morals that may be effectively used during the trial of the case.

A metaphor communicates to the subconscious mind because it relates to a subject that does not put the listener at risk. A metaphorical story used in argument describes an event that is removed from the trial itself; therefore, jurors can relax and listen to the story.

Metaphors may lend themselves particularly well to arguments of the personal injury case. For example, in a case involving an injury to an elderly man, the following argument might be made:

> Mr. William Wadsworth was playing in the fourth quarter of his game of life. He had done well. He had scored a few touchdowns, and sometimes he had been stopped on the goal line. But he had always played the game by the rules—honestly and fairly. He was running in the open field on his way to another long-gainer when the Valley Verde bus came off a sideline and blind-sided him. They didn't just keep him from making the long-gainer. They took him out of the game. Mr. Wadsworth is now limited to watching his game from the sidelines, waiting and hoping that the fourth quarter will soon be over.

Another example of a metaphorlike argument was given several years ago in a Harris County case. The plaintiff, his wife, and their children were all injured when their car was struck by a switch engine. The defense was that the lights at the railroad crossing were flashing when the plaintiff pulled onto the railroad tracks. Other evidence, however, established that for many months it had been a common occurrence for those lights to be flashing even when there was no train traffic in the area. The plaintiff's argument went something like this:

> The Pasadena Belt and Terminal Railroad suggests that Harvey Henry was negligent because he didn't stop his car at this crossing on June 7, 1978. The railroad says that he was negligent because, after all, the lights were flashing. Yet we have all heard the evidence of the many times that my good friend Harvey had passed this way when the lights would be flashing. He would stop and wait, and there would be no train. The fact that these lights had been malfunctioning for many months before this unfortunate tragedy is beyond dispute. This situation reminds me of one of Aesop's fables. We all remember the story told to us as children, of the boy who cried wolf. The young shepherd boy was charged with guarding a small flock of sheep. This wasn't a very interesting job. Nothing ever happened. Day after day he would watch the sheep graze on the hillside just outside the village. And then one day, while he was in a mischievous mood, he decided to run into town and tell the townsfolk that a wolf was in the area. Of course, the men immediately rushed out of town to the hillside to protect the flock. But there was

no wolf. After a few days the mischievous boy decided to play his prank again. Again, the men of the town came out to slay the wolf. Again, there was no wolf. According to Aesop this happened three or four times. Finally, the boy was awakened from his twilight slumber by the growling of a wolf. He could see that the wolf was going to attack the flock. He ran into town to tell the townspeople. Unfortunately, this time they refused to come because the boy had told them so many other times of a wolf when none was in the vicinity. This railroad's defense seems a lot like Aesop's story. They "cried wolf" so many times that the people who regularly used that crossing, like Harvey, had come to the point where they could not believe the railroad.

Analogies

Analogy is another form of comparison, which seeks to make something clear by comparing it to something else or to an idea that may be difficult to express. The relationship between items in an analogy and items in your argument can best be demonstrated by the ratio A:B::C:D. Thus, if in argument the evidence establishes a relationship between items *A* and *B*, in the analogy you should find the same type of relationship between items *C* and *D*.

Analogies always provide a change of pace in the argument. By turning away from the case and finding a story that suits the basic principles, you can cause the jury to transcend a particular issue of the trial in quest of a more familiar basis for its decision. This technique bolsters your argument and amuses the jury, as well.

The analogy's best feature lies in the jurors' recognition of the analogy's ending, when you connect the points of your analogy with the points you wish to make about the case. At that moment, the light goes on and your meaning becomes clear to the jury. Analogies clarify meaning most effectively because they can extract the basic truth from a seemingly lighthearted moment. Analogies may be based on personal experience or on some imagined event.

Analogy is a powerful tool to use in summation. Parables are used in the Bible to make a point, but analogies may be used for many aspects of the case, including illustrating injuries, helping the jurors comprehend liability, or interpreting points of law.

In deciding whether to use an analogy in your argument, examine it cautiously. How truly apt is it to the case? Does it create the right kind of instant image? Does it clarify the issues? Can everyone on the jury get the meaning? Does it convey only what you mean and nothing more?

Many attorneys hesitate to use analogies because the analogy may be construed against them. This legitimate concern dictates that the use of any analogy should be undertaken only after careful thought.

The following analogy might be used in a case in which the impact of a collision was slight and the property damage modest. The plaintiff received a cervical injury that was superimposed on an arthritic condition. As a result of that injury, the victim had experienced extensive pain and suffering, limitations in her work, and medical expenses.

> The defense has stressed that the property damage sustained by Lois Brown in this rear-end collision was not significant. According to them, since the damage to her automobile was only two hundred and fifty dollars, her injuries cannot be great. This is not surprising and only reinforces our belief that it is only property, profit, and the balance sheet that these people understand.
>
> Forget for a moment that we are dealing with a case that involves a rear-end collision between the plaintiff's car and the defendant's eighteen-wheeler, which occurred on the streets of Houston.
>
> Imagine instead that this same truck driver, while backing into a loading dock, misjudged his stopping distance as he contends here. He bumped the dock. On the dock were stacked some priceless pieces of crystal. The crystal was knocked off the dock, onto the ground, and broken. In that case these company lawyers would argue that the crystal should not have been on the dock. Instead, they would argue that cartons of groceries, like those the defendants were delivering, should have been on the dock. That way the cases of cans and boxes could have been picked up off the ground and sent on their way without any problem.
>
> Your response to such an argument would be that it is absurd and ridiculous. Yet, that is the defense that is being presented in this case. They are saying that Lois's neck should have been resilient. It should have been like cartons of groceries, boxes of soap, cans of stewed tomatoes. That neck should not have been fragile with any preexisting arthritic condition. But that is not what the judge tells you in this charge.

Analogies are often effectively argued in workers' compensation cases. Many times there will be evidence that the plaintiff suffered only a 10 or 20 percent disability. Yet, if the plaintiff has a back injury and earns his living by doing heavy labor, that degree of disability may constitute sufficient impairment to establish the legal requirements of total and permanent disability. In that situation, you might use this analogy:

> The defendant has argued that Joe Johnson, according to his doctor as well as the insurance company's doctor, suffered only a ten or twenty percent impairment in the function of his spine. There is a difference between impairment and disability. A person can suffer a small impairment and still be totally and permanently disabled.

> That's because of the type of impairment combined with the nature of the man's work.
>
> Let's assume you have a pickup truck with one bad tire. It is not totally flat, but it won't hold air for an extended period of time and will go flat if you put any kind of load on it. If you were trying to assess the impairment of that pickup truck with the bad tire, you could not give it a twenty-five percent impairment since it can still function to some extent. So you might say that the truck is ten or twenty percent impaired. But it cannot do the work. You cannot use it in your business.
>
> Joe's employability in the construction business was like the requirements for the pickup. He had to be able to do the job. He had to be able to do the job under all conditions. Employed as a construction worker, he would be about as effective as that truck would be.

Many times the defense may argue in injury cases that the victim's problem or disability is a result not so much of the injury as of some preexisting condition, such as osteoarthritis, obesity, or old age. In those cases, this analogy might be effective:

> When I hear this kind of argument, I cannot help but remember the story about the farmer who was on his way to town to sell the products of his trade. This man happened to be a poultry farmer. His truck was loaded down with fresh eggs. He intended to sell them to the wholesaler, who would then sell the eggs to the stores, who, in turn, would sell them to the people who lived in that town. People like you and me. The farmer's truck was hit from the rear by another truck. His cartons of eggs flew off his truck and crashed onto the ground. The cartons that managed to stay on the truck were crushed. The result was that he lost all his egg production for that run.
>
> He felt that he should recover his damages from the person responsible for that accident. He didn't ask for the retail price paid by the shopper in the grocery store. He didn't even want the wholesale price that the stores would have paid to the middleman. He simply wanted the value of the eggs that he would have received had they not been destroyed.
>
> The defense's contention was that if the farmer had been carrying crates of ping-pong balls there would have been no harm done. They contended that while the crates might have been knocked off the truck, the ping-pong balls would have bounced harmlessly on the highway and could have been gathered and restocked in the cartons.

> Of course, if any of you sat on a jury involving that type of case, your reaction to such a defense contention would be predictable. The same principle applies here. As in our story, some of us sell eggs and others sell ping-pong balls. It is no defense when an injury such as this occurs to suggest, "Well, the poultry farmer should have sold ping-pong balls instead of eggs." Likewise, it is no defense to argue, "Well, if you hadn't been obese, you wouldn't have had so much trouble." "If you hadn't been older and had some arthritic changes in your spine, the results of our negligence would have been less."

In summary, the use of analogies is interesting not only to the jury but to the victim's advocate as well. It is an entertaining challenge to devise valid, effective analogies. It is also a uniquely rewarding experience to learn after the jury's verdict that it was your analogy that most helped the jury understand the questions presented by the case.

13

Use of Rhetorical Questions and Embedded Commands

The advocate's argument was in the form of an inquiry rather than a statement: "Who will speak for the victim? Mary Bryant was a devoted mother and a loving wife. She was the kind of neighbor and citizen we would all be proud to know. She invested her energies in the betterment of her family and community. She was active in her church. She supported the school her children attended. Every day she obeyed our laws. She and her husband, Bob Bryant, paid their taxes; they maintained their home in a way that both their children and their neighbors could be proud of.

"We hear so much today of the rights of the criminally accused. It is appropriate that those charged with crimes have rights, but when do we say, 'It is time that we did something right by you, madame'?"

The lawyer adjusted his position before the jury and continued: "Before you were chosen to serve on this jury, we told you the evidence would demonstrate that the loss of Mary had been particularly tragic and catastrophic to Bob and the children, Bob Junior and Betty. I know you were wondering, during the voir dire and opening statements, why this death was so tragic and catastrophic. The death of a mother and wife is always so. I knew then what you know now. I knew then of the sleepless nights that evidence would demonstrate that Bob has experienced since the loss of his wife. I knew then of the agony and frustration that this loss had brought to this family. I knew then of the trials, tribulations, and torment that these young children had experienced since the loss of their mother." The lawyer paused.

"You know now what I knew then. The look on the faces of these innocent children when they come home to that empty house. The loneliness in Bob's voice as he has explained to you how he tries to comfort these troubled children and explain why their mother cannot be with them."

* * * * *

RHETORICAL QUESTIONS AND EMBEDDED COMMANDS are particularly effective forensic techniques.[1] Instead of assertively restating your conclusions to the

---

1. *See* L. SMITH & L. MALANDRO, COURTROOM COMMUNICATION STRATEGIES 366–73 (1985).

jury, you can use these techniques to allow the jurors to move on their own toward the inexorable conclusion—to give them intellectual space. The jurors will believe that you have confidence and faith in their ability to reason for themselves.

Rhetorical Questions

Rhetorical questions can be particularly effective with the jury. Many eminent trial lawyers[2] have employed this technique, which lends itself to all personal injury cases.

The effective rhetorical question embodies these elements:

- It is short.
- It directs the jury's attention to a critical issue in the case.
- The answer is self-evident.

Here are some examples of rhetorical questions commonly used in personal injury trials.

Workers' Compensation

- Where could this man get a job?
- How could he do the work?
- If he *could* get a job, how could he keep it?
- If you had to base the future of your medical care on the findings of a doctor, would you choose the doctor who had followed you through the course of your treatment or the doctor who had seen you for only a brief period at the request of the insurance company?

Automobile Cases

- Is it asking too much that these truck drivers obey our laws?
- When we must come safely to a stop on the freeway because of traffic conditions, do we not have the right to expect that those who are following us will do likewise?
- When my friend Janet Lindsey pulled out from the stop sign, was she required to anticipate and foresee that the car approaching that intersection would be speeding at sixty miles per hour?

---

2. The well-known New York trial attorney Moe Levine is perhaps most notable for his use of this type of argument. *See* M. LEVINE, SUMMATIONS: THE BEST OF MOE (1967); M. LEVINE, SURGICAL MALPRACTICE: SURGICAL ERRORS AND ACCIDENTS AND PROFESSIONAL LIABILITY TO THE INJURED (1970).

Product Liability

- When the defendant designed this high-pressure gauge, what did he think would happen to the men who would be using the gauge if it failed and exploded?
- What was the worker thinking when he attached this defective tie-rod to the automobile?
- Didn't the engineer who drafted these instructions realize that those who would use this product might not have his expertise?

Malpractice

- Who was caring for the patient during this time?
- What kind of medical care do you want the doctors of this community to render?
- Couldn't the defendant have at least picked up the telephone and talked with a consultant?

Embedded Commands

Embedded commands start with phrases like these: "I know you were wondering . . . " "I know that you have been thinking . . . " "This must be on your mind . . . " Embedded commands in summations can tie the jurors' previously formed conceptions to specific pieces of evidence. The expression "I knew then what you know now" can be used to emphasize what the evidence has established. For example, in a burn case where the plaintiff is arguing substantial damages for pain and suffering, you might use embedded commands in this way:

> During the voir dire examination, most of you were wondering why we asked whether any of you had any reservation about or objection to awarding substantial damages for conscious pain and mental anguish. We asked whether you could be fair and return a verdict of a substantial sum of money for this element of damage. You know now what I knew then, that the agony, the mutilation, the pain, and the mental torment that John Jones lived through following this needless tragedy were indescribable. The burns he sustained to his arms and legs were what the doctors call third-degree burns. All the layers of the skin were mutilated. He was literally cooked down to the muscle and underlying tissues. You know now what I knew then, that this burning and searing of skin causes agonizing pain. It is a pain that cannot be controlled by the strongest drug known to medical science. In order to cleanse these wounds and prevent infection, it is necessary to place the victim in a special bath. The dead skin is literally peeled off. You know now

> what I knew then, that the pain, agony, and torment a person undergoes during this medical process caused this man to cry out and pray for death. You know now that the treatment and rehabilitation caused John to be in almost constant pain. It was agony to turn. It was torture to move. Even though I am sure that most of you were wondering why at the time of voir dire we had to ask whether you could return a verdict for such a substantial sum of money for this element of damage—you now know why.

Many novices misapply the embedded-command concept, producing argument that is ineffective at best and disastrous at worst. Here is a common example (mentioned earlier, in chapter 4) of such an inappropriate argument:

> During the voir dire we asked whether you could find a substantial verdict if we proved the defendant was negligent and his negligence had caused substantial injuries. All of you indicated that you could. We have now proved our case. We kept our part of the bargain. You made a pact with us, no less sacred than a sworn contract. We now call on you to live up to your end of that pact. That bond we entered into on the voir dire examination is now due. If you knew you were not going to fulfill your end of this bargain, you should have raised your hand during the voir dire examination. We have relied on the promises that you made at that time, and we expect that the terms and conditions will be fulfilled like those of any other bond, contract, or agreement.

This type of argument has been made by both plaintiffs and defendants in personal injury cases all over Texas.

How much more effective is the following approach in attempting to use the embedded-command principle:

> During the voir dire examination and opening statements, we asked if there was anyone who would have any reservation about finding this trucking company negligent or careless—if the evidence demonstrated that. We knew when we made that statement that we would produce not one or two, but three witnesses who would testify about the speed of the Gas-Tex truck.
>
> You know now what we knew then, that Joe Johnson saw this truck some miles back from the collision site when it passed him. It was going seventy to seventy-five miles per hour on the freeway at that time.
>
> You know now what we knew then, that Peter Palmer saw this truck as it crested the Fourteenth Street overpass at seventy or seventy-five miles per hour. The driver was then racing pell-mell toward this catastrophic collision.

> You know now what we knew then, that Georgette Thomas, whose automobile barely avoided this collision, saw the truck in her rear-view mirror as it came over the overpass traveling in that middle lane. The driver was going seventy to seventy-five miles per hour when he finally applied his brakes. It was too late.
>
> You know now what we knew then, that because of this speed, the collision between the twenty-ton truck and Johnny Jones's compact vehicle was an awesome one. The truck hit Johnny's vehicle and drove it completely off the freeway.
>
> We knew when we asked you these questions on the voir dire examination that the photographs would demonstrate the magnitude and force of that collision. You know now what we knew then, that the impact of that mass of steel and metal demolished Johnny's car. You know now that the injuries that Johnny sustained are crippling, devastating, and permanent.

By using the embedded command, you can tie in your summation with the theme you first advanced during the voir dire examination, allowing each juror to forge in his own mind the conclusions and impressions that have been formulated by the evidence throughout the trial.

PART 5

Argument Strategies

Don't quote Latin; say what you have to say and then sit down.

—The Duke of Wellington, in advice to a new member of Parliament

14

Content of Argument

The victim's lawyer stood before the twelve expressionless faces. His notes were spread on the lectern, which appeared to be a silent monument separating him from those whom he now addressed. As the words flowed from his mouth, he was agonizing in his mind: If I could only know what they are thinking; if only there were some way I could get into their heads to understand the questions they have.

The lawyer proceeded with his introductory comments, but even as he did, the private, personal imponderables continued to haunt him. If only I knew what they were thinking.

* * * * *

MOST ARTICLES CONCERNING ARGUMENT that have been written by the many fine trial advocates of Texas, on both sides of the docket, have dealt exclusively with the subject of this chapter. The content of argument—the words, substance, and thoughts conveyed—is a subject both simple and notoriously complex. All advocates recognize that it is not enough for the jury merely to listen to the testimony presented: counsel must weave the facts of the case into a unified and logical pattern that the jury can both understand and believe.

During the trial, evidence is presented piecemeal to the jury in accordance with a master plan that many jurors will not follow. At the end of the case, it is the task of the victim's lawyer to reiterate the essential theory of his client's cause—both by marshaling the plaintiff's evidence to support his theory *and* by showing the weakness of the defendant's proof.

Probably your most important task as the victim's advocate is to arouse in the jury a sense of identification with the plight of the plaintiff. Because you are the vibrant link between the relatively mute plaintiff and the jury, your objective is accomplished by advocacy. In other words, through the sincerity of your expressed feelings for your client, you can make the jury feel the plaintiff's sufferings. Pay particular attention to statements made by prospective jurors on their voir dire examination: these statements often serve as a lightning rod to the jurors' thoughts and may significantly indicate the direction the summation should take.

To ensure that all important testimony is included in the summation, make daily notes about what each witness said. About each witness's testimony, ask, "What was the outstanding feature or aspect of this testimony?" Exceptionally favorable testimony you expect to use should be obtained from the court reporter and read verbatim to the jury during summation. A verbatim recitation of such testimony is far more effective than an attempt to paraphrase it, since paraphrasing the testimony will often cause the jury to speculate on the accuracy of your recollections. (For obvious reasons, however, avoid long recitals, readings, or statements.)

As the trial progresses, prepare notes regarding every person who had knowledge of facts in the case and was under the defense's control but who was not called by the defense to testify, particularly if the absence of the witness is not explained. You may wish to point out that such witness would ordinarily have been called by the defense to testify, and the jury may conclude that since the witness was not called, his testimony would not have been favorable to the defense.

Your goal in summation should be to present the facts so persuasively that the jurors' desire to be reasonable will be fired by a spirit of indignation stemming from their perception of the need for justice. In short, strive not only to argue clearly and logically but to present lively and challenging argument as well. Remember that an appeal to logic differs from boring, uninteresting, or dry argument.

Many fine articles on jury argument suggest that the attorney's argument should be pragmatic and based on "plain common sense" or "good horse sense." With the advent of modern technology, however, such an approach is often unrealistic or impractical. Many problems submitted to today's juries require analysis and discriminating thought far above the "horse sense" level. Scientific evidence, for example, although necessarily stripped of overly technical terminology, demands that the jury exercise the highest degree of intelligence. In making their decision on such matters, jurors are aided by the fact that modern means of communication have given them a far greater insight into the realm of science than has ever before been possible.

During the trial of a case, particularly a long one, attentiveness to summation varies among individual jurors. Therefore, it is crucial to make important points more than once, camouflaging the repetition in a number of ways. It is too much to expect that the untrained minds of the jurors will always appreciate the full significance of an important piece of evidence noted in a single statement.

In determining the content of argument, consider the various purposes you seek to achieve. In opening, you are trying to obtain the jurors' attention, allocate time for their minds to focus on what will be said, and allow them to become familiar with your personality and style. Accordingly, you must interlace your argument with statements that are factual, descriptive, and true.

Many attorneys begin with a focusing statement in their opening or closing argument: they tell the jurors what they are going to explain to them. This is fine, except that such statements should only follow the opening. The purpose of the focusing statement is to direct the jurors' attention to your case theme.

Never speak *to* the jurors; rather, speak *with* them. The only way you can truly speak with the jurors is to relate to the way in which they think. Means of relating to an audience may include using such phrases as "What this means to you is . . ." or "This is important to you because . . ." A relating statement involves the jurors directly in what you are going to say.

Jurors' Questions

All the considerations discussed above dictate that one of the most effective schemes for determining the content of argument is to identify the questions that are festering in the jurors' minds. Identifying these questions not only helps you in preparing content but also governs your general approach to argument. Here are some of the most common questions that jurors have.

Why Should We Listen?

Many jurors consciously wonder why they should listen to argument. After hearing the evidence, some individuals tend to resist argument because they believe it must be designed to manipulate them. Others may initially resist argument because they perceive it as sermonlike pedantry that will add nothing to their deliberations. Thus the victim's advocate often faces jurors' questions like these when he begins argument:

> *Will the lawyer's argument be interesting?*
> *Will it help us understand our role and function?*
> *Will he try to impose his concepts on us?*
> *Does he trust us?*
> *Does he consider us reliable and responsible adults?*
> *Will the argument assist us in organizing the information?*
> *Will we be able to identify the critical issues and proof?*

In the opening it is vital to address each of these concerns. Demonstrate to the jury that your argument will not consist of a mere chronological recapitulation of the evidence. Likewise, show at an early stage that your goal is to assist the jurors in understanding their role and function in arriving at an appropriate verdict.

What Are We Deciding?

The second prominent question in a juror's mind concerns a natural curiosity, *What exactly does the verdict mean?* You must be consciously aware that jurors are untrained in our legal procedures. They are not aware of what occurs after the rendition of their verdict. In most instances they have received no information on this subject from the lawyers or the trial judge. Hence, some of the more common matters they initially ponder are—*What are the issues of the case? Why is this case important? What does our verdict mean to the parties?* To answer these questions, you must explain the issues in the case. Not only must you expound on the submitted questions, you must also identify the "real" issues. The meaning and importance of the case in regard to the plaintiff's future, the defendant's future conduct, and other similar considerations must all be addressed. Many experienced advocates attempt to make the issues bigger than the case.[1]

In the injury case, it is particularly significant to stress that this is the plaintiff's only day in court. If the jury were to make a mistake, it would not be possible for the trial judge or some appellate court to "rewrite" the verdict and make everything turn out right and just.

By the same token, it is vital to dispel the notion held by some jurors that they are only making a "recommendation" or "suggestion" to the judge. They are not reaching a "settlement" on behalf of the parties; they are *deciding* the case. The judge will be bound to enter a judgment *based on their verdict*.

How Do We Go About Reaching a Verdict?

While the court's charge contains explicit instructions and directions about how the jury is to reach its verdict, the practicalities are often lost in the initial reading by the court. No extensive explanation has usually been given the jurors regarding the mechanics of their deliberations. Thus common questions that arise in jurors' minds include—

> *What is required of us during the deliberation phase?*
> *How do we vote?*
> *How should we conduct our discussions?*
> *How do we resolve conflicts in the testimony?*

The lawyer who spends a few minutes addressing the jurors' concerns not only enhances the likelihood of a victim's verdict but also casts himself in a

---

1. Clarence Darrow was noted for this approach. Although he tried primarily criminal and labor cases, a study of his summations is certainly helpful to any trial lawyer. The specific example of this type of argument was used when he defended Thomas Kid on criminal conspiracy charges. *See generally* I. STONE, CLARENCE DARROW FOR THE DEFENSE (1941 & reprint 1971): "I do not appeal for him; that cause is too narrow for me, much as I love him and long as I have worked by his side. I appeal to you not for Thomas Kid, but I appeal to you for the long line—the long, long line reaching back through the ages and forward to the years to come—the long line of despoiled and downtrodden people of the earth." *Id.* at 134.

more comfortable light. During the final summation, it is crucial to explain in a pellucid manner the standard by which the jury is to determine the case. Consider explaining the concept of "preponderance of the evidence" with the rhetorical questions one of the jurors might ask: *On what basis do we decide the case? How do we reject one witness's testimony and accept the other's?* Then you might follow with this argument:

> You will see from the court's charge, which you will have with you in the jury room, that the law does not require any injured person to prove anything beyond all doubt. We all know that few decisions in life, even the most vital, could ever be made if every element of doubt about them had to be removed. Life is not like that. Whether you should attend this college or that, whether you should go to work for this company, whether you should marry this person or that one or even marry at all—these types of decisions are rarely free from all doubt. There are pros and cons to be balanced in each decision that we make. So, too, in this case there are pros and cons that must be considered. The judge has given you the tools and measures by which to make these decisions that are so vital and crucial in this case. His Honor, Judge Brown, has instructed you regarding "preponderance of the evidence." This is sometimes referred to as the "rule of the scales." If you were to imagine scales in balance, much as you have seen Lady Justice holding them, you can envision the concept employed by the judge in this charge. How does the law determine that justice shall be weighed on these scales? What is weighed in a court of justice is the quality of the testimony of the witnesses—not the number of witnesses. What you are to do is to place the evidence on the scales after determining what makes sense to you. All Mrs. Jones has to do to establish the elements of her case is to tip the scales ever so slightly.

In malpractice, product liability, and airline disaster cases, the plaintiff's proof may often be based on circumstantial evidence. In these instances, the summation should emphasize that the defendant undertook to care for the plaintiff, perhaps while he or she was unconscious and under the effects of anesthetics; that the plaintiff had no control over the design and malfunction of the product; or that the airline undertook to carry the decedent safely to his destination. A plaintiff who was under anesthesia, using a defective product, or on a faulty plane did not know what was wrong when he was injured. The victim's attorney could therefore inquire of the jury whether it is not patently ridiculous for the defendant to ask that the plaintiff or the decedent's survivors tell the doctor, the manufacturer, or the airline company just what went wrong in the operation, or why the product malfunctioned, or why the plane crashed.

In certain cases it may be advisable to spend some time explaining the exact mechanism by which ten jurors may reach a verdict, particularly if broad-form negligence questions[2] are submitted:

> You have heard testimony to the effect that the defendant was negligent in a number of ways. [*Then list and go over the various acts of negligence established.*] As we have already discussed, any ten of you can reach a verdict. This does not mean that all ten of you who agree on the verdict must agree on the act of negligence committed. The court submits negligence in a broad form, realizing that some of you may believe the defendant was negligent in one way, while others of you believe the defendant was negligent in another way. As long as you believe that the defendant was negligent in one or more of the respects that have been established by the evidence, then you should support a "yes" vote on this question. Others of you may disagree on the respect in which the defendant was negligent but nevertheless believe that the defendant was negligent in *some* respect. In short, to reach a verdict of negligence against the defendant, each of you does not have to agree on the exact respect in which the defendant was negligent.

What Does the Court's Charge Mean?

Many novice lawyers mistakenly assume that the jurors understand and grasp the significance of the court's charge after the initial reading. This is simply not so. After days of testimony, the jury is given, usually within a few minutes, technical and legal definitions as well as complex questions they are asked to resolve. It is understandable that jurors ask themselves—

> *Why are the answers to the questions important?*
> *How do the legal definitions tie in?*
> *What do our answers to the questions mean to the parties?*
> *How does the evidence tie together?*
> *What is the big picture?*

Your primary function in opening argument is to help the jurors understand the legal concepts involved in the case and comprehend the meaning of the questions submitted for their determination. An explanation of the "big picture" of the case must be tied in with an analysis and explanation of the questions. How can the jurors be expected to return a victim's verdict if they do not know or understand what answers to the questions are desired or how those answers are supported by the evidence, reason, and legal concepts?

---

2. *See* TEX. R. CIV. P. 292.

Whom Should We Blame?

Wondering whom to blame may appear simplistic or naive; time and again, however, this inquiry is a cornerstone of most jurors' analytical processes. Blame or fault is a concept all jurors understand and appreciate. The concept of negligence, malpractice, or product defect must be interwoven with the jurors' basic understanding of responsibility or blame. No matter what the evidence demonstrates or what questions are submitted to the jurors, if their basic reaction is that the defendant was "blameless," the victim is not apt to receive a favorable verdict.

Is There Anyone Else To Blame?

Consider carefully whether there is any unnamed party the jury could identify as equally or more responsible for the victim's tragedy than the defendant. Never assume that the jurors will limit their discussion and analysis to the parties before the court. Not only must you demonstrate that the defendant is to blame for the plaintiff's tragedy, that the jury has good and sufficient basis to cast that blame, and that the jury is strong enough to place that blame on the defendant; you must also demonstrate that there is no other culprit in the case. Skilled defense attorneys are extremely imaginative when using the "Perry Mason" defense: "It was, after all, not our responsibility but really that of another."

Is the Victim Worthy?

Jurors help those whom they admire and respect. (This principle was discussed in earlier chapters.) Whether you choose to argue the victim's worth or not, that factor will play a significant role in the jury's decision-making process. It is advisable to meet the matter "head on." If the plaintiff is a good, responsible, and worthy citizen, stress these facts in a direct and straightforward fashion. If there is any aspect of the victim's character or reputation that is questionable, however, you must dispel the jurors' doubts. By the same token, stress that there can be no compromise on issues of liability:

> Mary Jo Brown has demonstrated that she doesn't deserve to be compromised. She spent her life being a good wife, mother, schoolteacher, and member of her community. She has proved her case against the ABC Trucking Company. How can we require more proof from this kind of citizen?

How Do We Feel About the Lawyers?

Few jurors decide cases on the basis of what they think about the lawyers as persons. On the other hand, few cases are decided without reference to how the case has been presented by the attorneys. Few juries will decide a case based on *who* you are, but many cases will be decided based on *how* you conducted yourself. Accordingly, it is appropriate to demonstrate during argument that the case has been professionally, competently, and fairly presented. Many defense lawyers thrive on the prospect of trying plaintiff's counsel as well as the case; when this tactic is employed, it must be recognized, met, and defeated. When the victim's advocate has carefully prepared his case, has not been guilty of any overstatement, and has been professional in his demeanor and attitude, this defense tactic usually produces disastrous consequences for those who employ it.

What Evidence Can Be Used To Support the Blame?

A common thread that runs throughout the questions posed by jurors concerns what they may rely on to support a finding of legal responsibility: *To what extent can we use our personal experiences in answering the questions? What are we permitted to discuss? What may we not discuss?* To clarify these points, it may be appropriate to talk in some detail about the various instructions regarding deliberations. If you are particularly concerned about the potential for jury misconduct, you should dissuade the jury from any such activities. This argument is usually effective: "If you limit your discussion to the evidence, you will have plenty of material for discussion."

Is the Plaintiff To Blame?

Whether or not the question of the plaintiff's conduct or responsibility is submitted to the jury by way of defense, the concept of plaintiff-blame must be considered. "Blame" in this context does not necessarily mean contributory negligence in the legal sense: it may be a visceral belief of the jurors that the plaintiff seized on an unfortunate moment to capitalize and benefit from it. Did the plaintiff "jump" at the chance to be in this lawsuit, or was he "compelled" to seek his just redress? Is the plaintiff's proof consistent? Have the witnesses told essentially the same story, or are there significant inconsistencies?

In many instances the defense may make the victim's lawyer a target for abuse and derogatory statements. If you face such a situation, you must carefully consider your response. You may choose to ignore the statements altogether, or you may determine that a reply is appropriate. If you choose the latter option, the following argument may be helpful:

> The defense has selected me as the target for their abuse and would suggest that, after all, I am somehow responsible for Johnny Jones's continued problems. Everything that has been said has been caused by frantic desire to save the defendant from liability.
>
> In the course of the defense's argument, it has become apparent to all of us that, just as self-preservation is the first law of nature, self-justification is the first law of litigation—even to the extent of

> making carelessness assume the guise of innocence. I asked for no protection at the time of the defense's attack on me. I ask for no protection now. I would like to discuss the issues presented by this case with you, as if I were speaking to you personally in your living rooms. I would like to discuss a matter of mutual interest to us as parents and as members of this community.

Is There Evidence Missing?

Jurors may contemplate whether all the proof necessary to form the basis for their verdict has been presented. This very natural concern can be particularly disastrous to the injured victim, who assumes the burden of proof under our procedures. For this reason it is sometimes imperative to dispel any reservations the jurors may have regarding absent or missing evidence:

> We have proved our case to you by a preponderance of the evidence. We have brought the critical and salient witnesses, exhibits, and documentation on the elements required of our case. The matter to be determined by you is simply whether a preponderance of the evidence establishes our contentions. The issue is not whether there is other evidence that someone can imagine or speculate about or that might have been brought. The defense has the same subpoena power that we have. If there were any evidence available that would tend to disprove our case, you can rest assured they would have brought it.
>
> In every case there are bits and pieces of evidence that are not brought by the plaintiff simply because they are not essential to the proof of the case. If we had brought you every conceivable piece of evidence, your time here might have been multiplied many times over. During our presentation of the case, we have tried to be conscious of the sacrifice and inconvenience that jury service has meant for you. We have proved our case. If someone during jury deliberation suggests that you should not find for us on these issues because there is some imagined bit or piece of evidence that we did not bring, inquire of them simply: "Well, if it would have helped the defense—why didn't they bring it?"

How Do We Approach the Determination of Damages?

How to determine damages is always troublesome for jurors. In personal injury cases, they are called on to quantify intangibles and evaluate that which is literally imponderable.

> How do you evaluate pain and suffering? You can't go into the grocery store and find it on the shelf. There is no way to hire

> someone else to experience it for you. There is no table or chart to consult. It is because the agony of a human being defies the drafting of any formula that these matters are decided by people. People who understand the torment of pain. People who understand the value of good health.

Since pain and mental anguish cannot be seen, it is only natural that many jurors view these elements with suspicion. Common jurors' questions include—

> *How do we know the plaintiff is really hurting as he says he is?*
> *How do we know how much he is hurting?*
> *How do we go about evaluating the hurt that we believe he has experienced?*
> *Doesn't the plaintiff usually sue for two or three times more than he hopes to get?*
> *How do we know what the deceased would have made of himself if he had not died?*
> *How has the injury affected the plaintiff's life?*
> *How has the injury affected the plaintiff's employability?*
> *How has the injury affected the plaintiff's enjoyment of his life—his ability to care for his wife and children?*

In response to these questions, the obvious argument is that damages cannot restore the plaintiff, but they are the only remedy we have to compensate him. You may further desire to stress the preciousness with which we all view good health:

> The victim did not ask to be in this lawsuit. If we go broke, we can pick up the pieces and start over. Not so with a crippled and maimed body.

Many times the victim's counsel may weave his specific evidence into a theme on damages that he has carefully developed:

> In considering what, in the words of the court, would be "that sum of money that would reasonably compensate the plaintiff" for these various elements of damage that are set out in the court's charge, it has occurred to me that the first question that anyone would ask in attempting to make such a determination would be: "Well, what should we consider?"
>
> You have now heard all the evidence from both sides as to what happened; you have seen the presentation of the plaintiff's case and the defendants' answers or reply to our evidence, and you have heard how this tragedy affected these fine people. I have

attempted to consider every element or aspect that would bear on this determination. While there are a number of factors that would obviously affect your judgment and verdict, the basic considerations appear to fall under three categories: the conduct of the parties, the attitude of the parties, and the losses the plaintiff has sustained.

Obviously, the conduct of the parties is a significant consideration in determining damages. We would consider the conduct of the defendants as well as that of the plaintiff. Let's discuss the plaintiff's conduct first. He was blameless in this accident. There has been no suggestion or contention that he did anything to contribute to his injuries. Undoubtedly, it would be proper for you to consider his conduct and reduce the damages you would find in this case *if he had contributed to or in any way caused this unfortunate tragedy.*

When we consider the conduct of the defendants, it is significant to ponder whether this injury was caused by some momentary inadvertence or whether the evidence demonstrates an indifferent, careless type of recklessness that not only must be disapproved of and reproached in this case but also would be the type of conduct about which we as a community would say, "We will not tolerate this under any circumstances or under any conditions, at this time or in the future." [*At this point discuss the defendants' conduct.*]

The second aspect that would be significant in determining damages is the attitude of the parties. Do you feel that we have been fair with you in our presentation of the case? Have we brought you the evidence that you as a juror feel should have been brought? Have we represented these people in the way you hope someone would represent you in similar circumstances? Have we been honorable? Have we been professional? Have we been thorough? Has the plaintiff been honest with you? Has he attempted to conceal any relevant facts or information? Has he indicated that he is attempting to gain an unfair advantage by this case, or is he merely seeking that which every citizen is guaranteed by our laws—the right to full and complete justice when he has been the victim of a needless tragedy?

We would ask the same questions about the defendants. Following this needless tragedy, did they evidence any concern toward Ted Johnson, or did they immediately direct their energies and attention toward developing evidence they could use to their advantage or distort? Did they begin looking around for other people to blame or drag into their distasteful recipe of reckless and heedless conduct?

Have the defendants, through their lawyers, been candid with you in their presentation of the evidence? Have they brought you appropriate evidence, or have they attempted to inject matters into

> the case that could not have any reasonable bearing on the questions to be decided by you, in an obvious effort to somehow prejudice you or distract you from a full, fair, and reasonable determination of this tragedy?
>
> Finally, in determining damages we would obviously want to consider the loss that this plaintiff has sustained. In considering that aspect, it would seem to me that three elements would play a vital role: the permanency of the loss, the type of person who sustained the loss, and the substantial nature of the loss.

The victim's lawyer would then want to discuss the evidence, including the medical proof, as it tied in and supported these various elements.

In arguing damages, the victim's advocate is often called on to deal with the "sympathy" argument. The defense, during its summation, will emphasize the portion of the charge that instructs the jurors not to allow bias, sympathy, or prejudice to enter into their verdict. Various responses may be considered. When the defense has used this argument as its "flagship premise," you may want your reply to be the theme of your closing summation:

> The defense, on the voir dire examination, obtained the assurance from each of you that you would not be swayed in your determination of this case and the evidence by any consideration of sympathy for the minor victim, Johnny Jones. Counsel was entitled to receive this assurance from each of you, and you all gave it. But let the defense remember that, when their attorneys obtained that assurance from you, they also assumed the corresponding obligation that they would not say or do anything that would in any way prejudice this young boy—like offering misleading issues or creating confusion about the testimony given by the witnesses. The assurance that you gave to follow the court's instructions and evidence meant that these defendants gave you similar assurances and that they would not evade, confuse, or obscure the issues of the case. For the defense to mouth justice and, at the same time, attempt to create bias and warped judgment is the highest form of hypocrisy. Was the defense dealing fairly with you when they attempted to direct your attention to the prior medical maladies of this young boy, when such problems have nothing to do with the questions in this case? Were they dealing fairly with you when they brought out the marital discord of Johnny's parents?

Here is another reply to the "sympathy" argument:

> The defense has suggested that in my closing remarks I may attempt to appeal to your sympathy for Johnny Jones's sake. Like so much of what the defense has done throughout this case, such a statement

represents a clever mixture of part-right and part-wrong. I certainly do intend to appeal to you on behalf of Johnny. If I did otherwise, I would not be discharging this very serious responsibility that I owe to him, you, and the court, but I would be neglecting and forsaking the oath that I took when I was admitted to practice. All lawyers who are worth their salt appeal for their clients. We began appealing for Johnny during the voir dire examination several weeks ago when you were selected to hear this case. Every shred of evidence that we have offered to support his cause was an appeal.

Our appeal now to you is for justice under the evidence. In order for us to accomplish that, all of us must appeal to what is inside us that says that we, and not the beast of the field, were made in the image of our maker. The appeal we must make to ourselves is not one for sympathy. This would mean that our verdict would be based on the fact that we feel sorry for Johnny. Sympathy is a form of charity; it is demeaning and insulting. Johnny has never asked for that, nor would he ask for anything like that from his friends, parents, or neighbors—like us.

But all of us have a right to appeal to that part of ourselves that is strong, proud, and noble—that part of us that causes us to take a given day in each week and turn from our labors to contemplate and meditate and worship about how we can better ourselves, why we should be thankful for what we have, and the lessons that we can learn from others who had the strength to be concerned not only with themselves but also with their neighbors. It is that aspect of human character that offers the only hope for the world—hope that we may avoid a nuclear holocaust—hope that the strife that exists in so many parts of the world may come to an end—hope that we may someday learn to live in peace together. It is that same strength of character that causes the black man to stop by the road to give the white man a hand when his car is broken down. It causes the teenager to assist the elderly lady down the stairs. It causes the Jew to work on Christmas Day in the place of his Christian friend and the Christian to work for his friend on Yom Kippur.

It will not be easy for us to arrive at a verdict that represents full justice for Johnny. Just as there is that quality of man which directs him to go to the heavens, there is also that within all of us which feeds on and grows with prejudice, pettiness, bitterness, envy, and distrust. That is the part of all of us that cheapens us and makes us small. If I felt that I had to appeal to that part of human character to prevail for Johnny, I would be heartbroken. I could not do it, nor would Johnny ask me to.

Thus, I hope you will see that our argument, while it may constitute, in the words of the defense, "an appeal," is a proper one. It is an appeal for a verdict based on the evidence, the law, common sense, and an understanding of and appreciation for the dignity of man.

The Final Five Minutes

The closing thought of final summation has been called the "final five minutes." This term is not intended literally; it describes a *concept*—the salient thought the advocate wants to leave with the jury, which may require minutes or merely seconds to deliver.

There can be no doubt about the importance of the "final five minutes." This is the point in summation where you should use a slower rate of speech and a lower voice tone. Dramatic pauses can be particularly effective here, as well. Each closing line, in terms of emotional content, must be in balance with the nature of the case. For example, in a whiplash case, too much emotional content—content that is out of proportion to the nature of the inquiry—will cause a loss of credibility and, therefore, a definite drop in the persuasiveness of your message. On the other hand, if you are dealing with a catastrophic injury, disability, death, or disfigurement, the emotional content of your closing lines can be proportionally increased.

Before giving your final summation, consider what aspect of the case is most likely to provoke the desired verdict on behalf of the victim. Many articles on jury argument suggest that the lawyer should never return to the liability questions once a discussion of damages has begun. Like all good rules, this one has exceptions; in a particular case, it may be advisable to return to the liability aspects of the case in the closing thought. Regardless of the tack you take, recognize that it is your closing lines that the jurors will remember best: of all your argument, this is the part they will take with them to the jury room.

In presenting your closing thought, you do not want to seem to end "in midstream." Thus, your closing thought should be the high point of summation. It should be a concept or idea that ties the case together and brings it to its logical and strongest conclusion.

After presenting the final thought of your summation, do not immediately begin to gather up your notes and return to your seat. Rather, stand for a few seconds and study the jury. Give the jurors an opportunity to think and to consider your thought-provoking and incisive argument.

15

How Juries Deliberate

As the door shut with a thud, the jury room filled with the cacophony of voices and movements of twelve individuals who now inhabited the stark room. The sound of the wooden chairs being dragged across the tiled floor created a further stridulous note. One of the female jurors left for a few moments through the door to the women's restroom, which, like its counterpart, opened directly into the jury room. A middle-aged gentleman and a slim lady in her sixties busied themselves by arranging their personal effects—coats, books, and newspapers—on the window ledge. This particular jury room had an advantage over many other such rooms in the courthouse: it had an outside view. The window overlooked the courthouse lawn and the downtown business district.

A male voice rose above the others: "Which end of the table is going to be the smoking section?" Some muffled and disorganized discussion followed. Finally, all twelve participants were seated around the large oak table on which had been piled the numerous exhibits in the case. Materials were distinctly diverse in their size, shape, and content. The large stack of hospital records was bound together so that they appeared to be the composite notes assembled by some student over a four-year undergraduate course. The color photographs varied in size: the smaller snapshots lay cluttered on top of the eight-by-tens. The mass of papers included letters, manufacturer's literature and specifications, and other miscellaneous documents. Against the wall next to the jury room door rested a number of mounted blowups. The one lying faceup on top was a color photograph of the accident scene, but all twelve jurors recalled that beneath it lay less colorful, but equally interesting, documentation relating to the question they were about to discuss—whether this accident, which had resulted in the serious injuries sustained by the plaintiff, had been caused by a defective tire on a company vehicle he had been driving.

The young man who taught computer science at the local university spoke first: "According to our instructions, the first thing we should do is select a presiding juror. I would suggest Mr. McKenzie." The middle-aged executive smiled and nodded at this recognition. There was a note of diffidence in his reply: "John, I would rather not be the presiding juror. This is my first time to serve, and I would really prefer that one of the others who have had jury service tackle that responsibility." A brief discussion among the jurors resulted in unanimous support for Mrs. Emma Lou Harris. Not only had Mrs. Harris had previous jury duty, she was also a legal secretary for one of the large corporations headquartered in the city. Mrs. Harris presented a rather striking image in her stylish business suit. Her gray-blonde hair was brushed back in a neat coiffure. She read the court's charge with alacrity. Her legal experience and familiarity with many of the terms contained in the court's charge enabled her to accomplish this function with ease.

The initial question to be determined by the jury went to the heart of the case. Rita Gonzales, a junior high school counselor, asked that the question be reread. Mrs. Harris complied, this time taking great pains to stress each individual word: "Was the tire defective at the time it was sold by American Tire Company to Johnson Oil Field Supply?"

The ensuing discussion was discordant. This was to be expected: after all, the expert testimony on this question had been diverse and conflicting, and it ran together in the jurors' minds. The exchanges between the experts and the lawyers had been marked by asperity. Finally, someone called for a vote. The raising of hands revealed that nine of the jurors were in favor of a "no" answer to the first question.

L. Thomas Hanson had remained relatively quiet during this initial deliberation phase. Not particularly striking in physical appearance, he was of average height and rather muscular, and his face failed to betray his fifty years of life experience. Over his open-necked shirt he wore a light brown sweater. The years he had spent in the oil fields were now long behind him. He had spent the last fifteen years in the real estate business, but his outward appearance effectively concealed the financial success that he enjoyed. "Tommy," as he was known by his friends, could be stubborn and patient. His voice and mannerisms were similar to those of a high school teacher or college professor. To his surprise, however, he found a note of emotion in his voice as he spoke: "I don't think we have considered this question seriously enough. There are a lot of aspects to this case no one has talked about."

Walking to the wall, he thumbed through the large exhibits stacked against it. Finding the photograph he desired, he carefully lifted it from the stack and began pinning it up on the corkboard. Tommy was comfortable now. The points he wanted to make were mutely supported by the black-and-white blowup that now hung by his side. As he continued speaking, he found his earlier sense of timorousness disappearing. None of the twelve minds that were hard at work in the crowded, smoke-filled room could have conceivably foreseen that two days later they would announce in open court a jury verdict that would support a judgment for the plaintiff in a substantial amount.

* * * * *

THE MOVIE *Twelve Angry Men* illustrates a fascination with the jury deliberation process that has captured the minds of writers, moviemakers, lawyers, and judges during the past few decades. To be an effective advocate for the client, the victim's lawyer must have a thorough understanding of the jury deliberation process. Few of us have ever experienced this process firsthand. It is understanding this process and the principles inherent in it that enables the victim's lawyer to succeed consistently. There are no set rules or patterns: each jury has its own collective, unique personality. However, experience has shown that certain fundamentals in the deliberation process must be appreciated, understood, and woven into the presentation of the case.[1]

Presiding Juror Influences the Outcome

Almost invariably the presiding juror will assert considerable influence over the outcome of the case, often working to translate his own viewpoint into the verdict instead of acting as an impartial chairman of the deliberations. For this reason you should seek to identify, at the earliest possible stage, the likely candidates for this position. Juries tend to select people who have had previous jury experience, those who occupy professional positions of some authority, those with the more assertive or confident personalities, and those perceived to be organized and disciplined. In some instances a person nominated as presiding juror may decline to serve,[2] but this is probably the exception rather than the rule.

Leaders Determine the Outcome

Lawyers have always recognized that some jurors are more important than others. Some people, by virtue of their personalities, are simply not going to play a significant role in the outcome; they are followers who will generally shift their votes depending on what they perceive to be the "prevailing wind." The jury's leaders are those individuals who will be outspoken and firm and will assert their views of the evidence and the case. For this reason it is critical to identify those jurors who are perceived to be the leaders. Speak to those particular individuals, and use illustrations that appeal to them. Bear in mind, however, that some statements and arguments may constitute such a direct appeal as to be improper or reversible.[3]

---

1. For an excellent review of the jury deliberation process, see Hittner, *A Judge's View of Jury Service: A Personal Perspective*, 47 TEX. B.J. 227 (1984); *see also* Call, *The Psychology of Jury Deliberations*, 50 TEX. B.J. 590 (1987).
2. Hittner, *supra* note 1, at 230.
3. While the general rule is that it is not reversible error to refer to the jurors by name, as long as personal appeal is not made, Wallace v. Liberty Mut. Ins. Co., 413 S.W.2d 787, 788 (Tex. Civ. App.—Houston 1967, writ ref'd n.r.e.), such personal appeals are, at best, risky and should be avoided. *See* Thaxton v. Reed, 339 S.W.2d 241, 246 (Tex. Civ. App.—Dallas 1960, writ ref'd n.r.e.); Metropolitan Life Ins. Co. v. Moss, 109 S.W.2d 1035, 1038 (Tex. Civ. App.—Amarillo 1937, writ dism'd).

Remember that there are no rules of evidence in the jury room. The strong, tough jurors win. The "street fighter" may prevail. Hence, one of the primary goals of argument (discussed in chapter 2) is to equip your jurors with arguments, ideas, and evidence they can use to marshal and harbor support among their peers.

Most Jurors Are Conscientious

Most jurors strongly desire to follow what they consider to be the established facts and the law. Many may question the justice of certain legal rules but will nevertheless follow them in arriving at a verdict. When a juror fails to follow the law, it is usually the result of a communication failure on the part of the court or counsel. Simply put, juries that fail to follow legal instructions usually do so because the advocate failed to make the meaning of the instructions clear.

Jurors Decide Cases Based on Their Concept of Justice

Jurors will use their personal lives, experiences, and value concepts as bases for their verdict. They will naturally reject evidence or arguments that are inconsistent with these bases. Any juror will tend to fight harder for a cause with which he can identify; hence, it is crucial to attempt to define the aspect of your case that may have some particular appeal and to identify those jurors who will be motivated by that appeal.

Jurors Make Shortcut Decisions

Sometimes the jurors take shortcuts by skipping over the many exhibits and charges given to them. You cannot assume that, because the jurors were out long enough to examine the exhibits and engage in a normal discussion of the case, they actually *did* examine the exhibits in detail.[4] If you wish to rely on an exhibit, show it carefully to the jurors in the courtroom. If the exhibit is particularly important or critical, use blowups. If written documents are offered into evidence, read or develop the important parts in some way during trial and argument. You simply cannot expect the jury to ferret out proof that has not been made apparent.

Additionally, remember that exhibits are often used as a crutch or support during deliberation. Jurors are generally not as articulate as lawyers, nor do they have the same kind of training. Jurors are more comfortable with a "show-and-tell" approach. They can be more persuasive in communicating

---

4. *See* Hittner, *supra* note 1, at 232.

their ideas when they are equipped with some type of visual aid. For this reason many skilled advocates mount even letter-size exhibits, such as automobile accident reports, on a larger piece of cardboard. These aids enable a juror to use the exhibit to strengthen and support his argument. The juror who has in his possession such an exhibit—

- will usually have the "floor" and, thus, the attention of other jurors,
- is more comfortable with his argument and presentation, and
- bolsters his argument with proper and appropriate evidence.

The principle on which these suggestions are based may be learned from watching small children. All of us recall our school days, when those of us who were reticent, shy, and afraid of public speaking could flourish when it came time for "show-and-tell."

Jurors Need Guidance on Damages

The two schools of thought about whether the victim's lawyer should argue specific amounts of damages were mentioned in chapter 2. Although this decision must be based on the circumstances of each case, the better rule is that some specific figure must be suggested and argued by the plaintiff: without any guidance whatsoever, a jury left to its own devices may arrive at a totally inappropriate figure. Indeed, those who have studied the process have suggested that it is wise for both plaintiff and defense to argue specific figures.[5]

Damages, unlike questions on liability, can be readily compromised. When the liability question calls for either a "yes" or "no" answer, little room is left for any trading. Damages, on the other hand, are dealt with in an entirely different fashion; they may be assessed at the tyranny of a lone juror. It is for this reason that strong jurors play such a significant role in determining damages. One or two strong jurors can make literally millions of dollars' worth of difference in a significant case. Litigation experience indicates that certain fundamental tenets govern most jurors' deliberations regarding damages.

Jurors Seem To Be More Impressed with and Conscious of Economic Damages

The typical Texas citizen is more concerned with the projected costs of necessary future medical care, the loss of past earnings, and the loss of future earning capacity than with such imponderables as pain and suffering.

---

5. *See id.* at 229.

The Average Juror Is Impressed with the Uncertainties of the Future

If the plaintiff's injuries are obviously disabling, permanent, and substantial, the average juror is conscious of the unfortunate implications for the victim's life. An uncertain future in which a person would be unemployable and unable to support a family is the type of tragedy that most people secretly dread in their own lives. Hence, jurors may particularly identify with this type of damage.

Jurors Bring Various Factors into Their Formulation of Damages

Some jurors consider the concept of investment income and the interest that may be realized from an award. In addition, most lay people are aware of the expense associated with obtaining just redress in the courts, including lawyer's fees.

Legal Instructions Are an Impelling Influence

It is a rare advocate who has not seen a case take an unexpected turn because of some misunderstanding of the court's instructions. Although jurors will not ordinarily ignore the legal instructions, the legal concepts embodied in the court's charge are foreign to them; if the attorneys have not taken the time and effort to explain the meanings of the legal definitions and instructions, the jurors may formulate their own meanings.

In most instances the jurors will assiduously follow the court's instructions. Most jurors take their service quite seriously and are impressed with their obligation to apply the law as given to them by the trial judge. Thus, a significant portion of the jury's deliberation time may be spent in considering the exact meanings of legal definitions and instructions. While few jurors will consciously ignore the court's charge, they may misinterpret or misapply its contents. In most instances this unfortunate result arises from the advocate's failure to tie the legal instructions in with his theory of the case.

Jurors Try To Reconcile Conflicts

The jurors spend most of their deliberation time attempting to reconstruct the events in question. During deliberation many scenarios may be advanced: one juror may suggest that the events occurred in one fashion, while another juror will suggest another formulation of events. In this process, each juror is attempting to reconcile perceived conflicts in the testimony and to resolve in his own mind what the likely chain of events was.[6]

6. For an excellent discussion regarding this concept, see Call, *supra* note 1, at 590.

Many deliberations quickly evolve to this stage. The jury attempts to formulate a consensus on the "facts"—how the accident happened, what made it happen, what motivated the actors—in short, the story as the jury sees it. Once a consensus has been reached about the probable scenario, the collective mind can then deal with the specific questions presented by the court's charge. For this reason it is important to understand the necessity of harmonizing the evidence with the victim's theory of the case and the court's charge. If you do not undertake this task, the deliberations will almost certainly focus on conflicts.

A Harmonious Group Is Required To Reach a Victim's Verdict

Finally, you must be aware of the nature and composition of the group that constitutes the jury. Is it harmonious or discordant? A fractionalized jury will inevitably produce a defense result of either negative findings on liability or modest damages. When you observe the jurors at recesses and breaks, try to determine whether the individual jurors are being amalgamated into a cohesive unit. Jurors who develop a feeling of camaraderie to the extent that they take breaks together and share rides are far more likely to be able to return a victim's verdict than jurors who are splintered and fractionalized. Do all within your power to select a jury that is a harmonious one.

PART 6

Specific Arguments on Liability

There is no such thing as an accident. What we call by that name is the effect of some cause that we do not see.

—Voltaire, *Lettres de Memmius III*

16

Arguing Liability—Generally

ARGUING LIABILITY is the process by which the victim's lawyer attempts to obtain jury findings that will support legal responsibility. Whether the question is one of compensable injury, such as in a workers' compensation case, or of professional negligence, such as in a malpractice action, the goal is essentially the same. Although the methods and tactics used to achieve that goal may be colored by the lawyer's personality, certain basic characteristics of an effective liability argument may be recognized:

- It is based on the evidence that is before the jury.
- It is organized and easy to follow.
- It is persuasive.

In preparing for the argument, the victim's attorney must select from the hours of testimony and multitudes of exhibits those matters that are most salient and significant; then he must present the argument in an organized and pellucid manner. For the argument to be meaningful, the jurors must understand the questions that are being submitted to them on liability, as well as the desired answers to those questions. Hence, an effective argument on liability combines the evidence and proof with an explanation of the legal concepts and principles contained in the questions. Most effective liability arguments are generally organized according to one of two approaches:

- The questions may be discussed separately, with the evidence that supports the desired answer being discussed in connection with each question.
- The questions may be discussed in their entirety, with argument and evidentiary support following such discussion.

Even under the first approach, some of the liability questions may be grouped in order to place particular emphasis on specific questions.

To illustrate the distinction between the two basic approaches, consider an argument in a premises liability case. Under the first approach, the argument would be organized along the following lines:

> Ladies and gentlemen, Question 1 asks whether on the occasion in question the railing on the second-floor balcony of the apartment project was rotten. Young Theresa and her parents would ask that

> you answer that question "yes." You will recall the testimony and the evidence. After Theresa's tragic fall it was discovered that this railing had pulled from the column on which it was nailed. Billy Johnson, who called the ambulance for Theresa, saw that the wood was rotten, soft, and splintered where it had parted from the column. Mr. Thompson, Theresa's father, looked at the part of the railing that was still on the ground when he returned from the hospital the same night. He saw that it was rotten. Plaintiff's Exhibits 7 and 8 are the photographs taken by Mr. Thompson. Anyone looking at those photographs would have to be blind not to see that the wood of that railing was rotten and deteriorated. Even the manager of the apartment project, Mr. Clark, admitted on cross-examination that when he looked at the railing that was lying in the yard where Theresa had fallen, the wood "didn't look any good." The defendant offered the testimony of only one witness to contradict this evidence. Mr. Theron Street, the owner of the project, indicated that he looked at the railing some days later and it looked fine. His explanation was that this young girl, who weighed sixty-five pounds, had pushed a good railing loose from the column. That testimony is simply not credible in view of the other evidence that has been produced. We submit that a preponderance of the evidence, the greater weight of the evidence, requires a "yes" answer to Question 1.
>
> The next question submitted by the court is Question 2 and is based on a "yes" answer to Question 1. It asks essentially whether the owners of the apartment project knew or should have known that the railing was defective. [*At this point, argue the evidence that would support the "yes" answer.*]

The alternative approach to organizing the liability argument is simply to outline the questions and suggested answers before proceeding to an argument on the evidence. Essentially, such an argument groups all the liability questions and then follows with the evidentiary argument. This alternative approach is illustrated by the following argument:

> Ladies and gentlemen, the first four questions that are submitted to you involve the legal responsibility of the owners of this apartment project. On behalf of young Theresa and her parents, we ask that you answer each of these questions "yes." The first question submitted to you is whether the railing on the second-floor balcony of this apartment project was rotten at the time of Theresa's fall. The second question asks whether the owners knew or, in the exercise of ordinary care, should have known that the railing was rotten. The third question asks whether the owners' failure to repair the railing

was negligence, and the final question inquires whether such negligence was a proximate cause of the occurrence in question. We submit that a preponderance of the evidence requires each of those questions be answered "yes." [*If there are other questions, such as negligence questions as to other defendants or the plaintiff, the desired answers should likewise be given at this time. Then present the evidentiary basis for the proposed jury findings.*]

These illustrations of the ways a liability argument can be organized underscore one significant fact: before the jurors can relate the evidence to the verdict in a meaningful way, they must understand and appreciate the significance of the questions they are called on to answer. Once that goal is achieved, you can consider the most effective manner to present and argue the evidence. Again, this approach will vary from lawyer to lawyer, depending on personality and temperament. Some fundamental rules are observed by all good advocates.

Do not argue the evidence in chronological order. In other words, do not attempt to simply summarize the testimony of each witness in the order in which the witness testified. Rather, attempt to correlate your evidence, whether it is oral testimony, documentary evidence, or exhibits, in a meaningful and persuasive fashion.

Do not overstate the evidence. The successful trial lawyer does not attempt to take his case beyond the point that has been proved.

Do not attempt to argue all the evidence. Instead, stress the strongest pieces of evidence that tend to support the desired answers to the questions. Particularly strong or favorable evidence may even be repeated.

Incorporate visual aids when they are practicable. Remember that a photograph, a document, or a blueprint, if properly used, can be more persuasive and effective than a million words.

Attempt to harmonize the evidence. Do not assume that simply because certain proof has been offered by the defense, that proof is necessarily adverse to the victim's cause. Often a little thought will reveal that such evidence is not necessarily in conflict with the plaintiff's theory.

To effectively present a liability argument, you must interrelate and incorporate many, if not all, of the concepts and principles that have been discussed earlier in this book in more detail. The argument must be interrelated with the case and well prepared, as discussed in chapters 1 and 2. The concepts of subliminal persuasion and nonverbal communication, discussed in chapters 3 through 5, will be employed. Your demeanor, gestures, posture, and voice must be appropriate; these principles are discussed in chapters 6 through 9. You may select the right words and employ anecdotes, analogies, rhetorical questions, and embedded commands in advancing the liability theories, as explored in chapters 10 through 13. The remainder of this chapter concerns a few of the many concepts and tactics that play a role in the effective argument of liability.

Setting the Stage

In some instances you may wish to put the jury at ease before beginning your discussion of the evidence that supports affirmative findings on liability. You can reassure the jurors and reinforce the importance of their role, setting the stage for the jury to recollect the strongest evidence in support of the victim and the tenuousness of the evidence that supports the defense theory. The following argument illustrates this principle:

> Ladies and gentlemen, as this trial has progressed I'm sure you've all noticed how formal the atmosphere is. Formalities are required in the courtroom, and I'd like to compliment you all on your attentiveness during this case when I'm sure you've felt uncomfortable at times. I could not help but notice that the witnesses seemed a little tense or uptight because of the formalities as well. And that's perfectly natural—that is to be expected, because in everyday life we do not come to the courtroom to testify about another person's conduct. Yet I think there's a tendency to lose perspective of the questions of liability because of the formal setting in which all this testimony has been given.
>
> Let's get out of the courtroom for a minute. Imagine that we're at your house having coffee and trying to resolve the liability questions in this case. We have talked about the evidence and the questions, and now you must determine whether the defendant's negligence caused Pam Johnson's injuries. In making this determination, you will have to use the facts, the law that His Honor gives you, and most importantly, your own common sense.
>
> We have found from experience that no computer or machine—not even an expert board of select citizens—can replace a jury. Juries are used to decide these cases because they reflect the attitude and conscience of the community. It is the common, ordinary citizens who have personally felt the pain that a lie can bring, who know the agony of tragedy, who have had someone try to make them eat the fine print of an insurance policy, who are best able to make the critical decisions like those presented by this case. It takes street sense to judge credibility. Even though matters may be technical or scientific, it takes a person who has done some living to ferret out that which is good and sound from that which simply "sounds good."

Painting a Picture of Your Case

Before discussing the evidence that supports the liability questions, you may want to take a few minutes to paint a picture for the jurors so that they can understand the nature of the cause of action the plaintiff has brought. This technique can be used in virtually every type of injury case; this example is from a case that might be asserted under a deceptive trade practices or breach-of-warranty product theory:

> Some of you, ladies and gentlemen, have lived in Houston as long as I have. You may remember the old building that used to sit at the corner of Travis and Jefferson. In that building people took wrecked and damaged cars and then rebuilt them. About a block from that building was a used-car lot. All the cars that were sold off that lot were cars that had been wrecked and damaged. This wasn't the only building in Houston that did this. It wasn't the only place in this state that did it. Wrecked and damaged cars were rebuilt and then sold as good used ones. The purchasers were never told that the cars had been wrecked and damaged. In practically every instance, after driving the car a short distance, the buyer discovered that the car was no good. It couldn't be repaired, because the frame was bent and had been straightened. It didn't steer right. It was dangerous. Laws were passed, because it was believed to be wrong to let the unscrupulous profit at the cost of honest, law-abiding, hardworking citizens. Today you cannot sell a damaged car as a good used car. You have to tell the person who buys the car about that material fact. Likewise, in this case, the law does not permit someone to sell a trailer house as a safe, comfortable, sound place to live when they know that the trailer house is built of materials that will emit noxious and dangerous fumes. Yet that is exactly what the evidence shows happened in this case.

Killing the Defense with Kindness

Sometimes the defense will present its case in such a straightforward and professional manner that you will recognize that this sincerity and professionalism have affected the jury. If the defense uses such a tactic, you must mitigate its effects. In such instances it is appropriate to attempt to separate, in the jurors' minds, the defense attorney from the defense cause:

> The ABC Company in this case chose as its lawyer Mr. Jones, one of the most eminent spokesmen for the defense bar. As I believe has been demonstrated throughout this trial, Mr. Jones is an extremely effective advocate and champion for his cause. He is in all respects a gentleman.
>
> He has defended his client in a straightforward and professional manner. As we have all observed, he has at all times been courteous and respectful of the court, the parties, and you—the

jury. Unfortunately, he has chosen to champion the wrong cause. Incompetence, carelessness, recklessness, and irresponsible conduct are just as reprehensible no matter who may choose to champion them or what they may be called in an effort to veil their true appearance.

I cannot help but remember the story that has been recounted so many times about General Robert E. Lee. Although Lee was from the state of Virginia, he did not believe in slavery. Likewise, he believed with all his heart in the Union. Thus, the greatest American general of his time chose to fight on the side that championed two causes in which he did not believe. Many historians have asked how much sooner the war might have been over if Lee had commanded the Union army from the inception rather than siding with the Confederacy.

The respect that even the Union soldiers had for Lee is demonstrated by the fact that at the ceremonies at the Appomattox courthouse all the Union soldiers who were in attendance (very few Confederate soldiers were allowed) tipped their hats to Lee and saluted him. Today, who can doubt that Lee championed the wrong cause? There is no one within the sound of my voice who does not consider slavery an abomination that had to be abolished even at the cost of so much blood, sweat, and tears. Yet, even though Lee was in effect fighting for the institution of slavery—an abominable concept—those who opposed him respected the vigor and imagination he used in mustering his forces.

To the same extent, we may admire Mr. Jones for his advocacy but still believe with all our hearts that he has chosen to champion the wrong cause.

Distinguishing Between Negligent and Intentional Wrongdoing

In most injury cases, although the defendant's conduct may have been negligent, it will not have been intentional or malicious. For that reason, be careful not to insinuate or imply that the defendant is somehow a bad person or that he should be condemned because of his conduct. Unless the evidence warrants ostracism or chastisement, remember to point out that the trial is not a test of character:

> Let me make one thing perfectly clear. You do not have to find that the defendant is a bad person or that he deliberately injured Gordon Johnson. Almost no one is so inhuman as to intentionally injure another, and the law does not require this in order for Gordon to recover the damages he seeks. If our laws were otherwise, victims like Gordon would hardly ever be compensated for their injuries.

If a surgeon performs an operation and carelessly strikes a major artery, he can be found liable in damages for the injuries he has caused. By the same token, if a person drives recklessly or at an excessive rate of speed on our highways and injures another, he will be liable as well. Both carelessness and recklessness are types of conduct that are not intentional, yet they often have tragic consequences for those around us.

In this case the test is simply whether the defendant was careless or reckless in causing these injuries to Gordon Johnson. From the evidence, I'm sure you all know what the answer to that question is.

Explaining Responsibility for Failure To Act

Many injury cases involve allegations of what must be considered, in a strict legal sense, errors of *omission* as opposed to *commission*: the proof will simply establish that the defendant failed to act, rather than that the defendant acted improperly. A nurse, seeing that a patient is developing complications, simply fails to call and notify the doctor. A truck driver who is given a truck with bad brakes just doesn't complain or try to get them fixed. A product is inspected but is passed in spite of the fact that it is defective. In these types of cases, the following argument may be used with some effect:

The defendants' silent stand is one that the centuries have seen. Their faces have gazed from other crowds. When a man was unduly tried before a mob and ordered to carry a cross for his crucifixion, people like the defendant stood in silence.

When innocent girls were pilloried and burned at the stake by the pious, bystanders watched and spoke not.

When the sailing ships unloaded their ungodly cargoes of black men, women, and children for sale to the highest bidder, men and women like the defendants watched. They did not own the slaves; they did not buy the slaves; they did not use the slaves. They witnessed the injustice and stood silently by.

When their friends and neighbors, who happened to be Jewish, were dragged from their homes in the middle of the night to be transported to concentration camps, these people merely peered from their windows. No protest, no words of outrage.

The list goes on and on. Abraham Lincoln spoke of this attitude. When Mr. Lincoln was in New Orleans, he saw a slave being brutally beaten by his master. A small crowd had gathered at the scene, but most people just went about their business. An aide of Mr. Lincoln's, who was transfixed by the sight of the beating, said, "Mr. Lincoln, isn't it terrible the way that slave is being beaten?" And Abe Lincoln responded, "Yes it is, but the real tragedy is the people who can watch passively or merely ignore the torture."[1]

Discussing Comparative Responsibility

Since the adoption in Texas of the concept of comparative negligence—amended in 1987 and renamed "comparative responsibility"—the duty of apportioning responsibility between the negligent parties has rested with the jury. The effect of the adoption of the comparative negligence doctrine was to abandon the "all or nothing" approach that had been ingrained in tort law in this state for over a century. Of course comparative responsibility is not a significant issue for the victim's lawyer in the absence of jury findings that the plaintiff's negligence was a proximate cause of the injury.[2] Hence, your first goal is to secure jury findings establishing either that the plaintiff was not negligent or that such negligence was not a "proximate cause" of the injury.[3] The specific facts of a case will often lead to the conclusion that an effective argument can be made in the victim's behalf on the question of causation.

If this tactic fails, your goal is twofold:

- To obtain jury findings that the responsibility of the plaintiff does not exceed the percentage permitted under the statute.[4]
- To have the jury ascribe the lowest possible percentage of responsibility to the victim.

---

1. The source of this colorful anecdote, which may be apocryphal, is the noted trial lawyer Bill Allen of Houston, who has often embodied it in his persuasive summations.

2. Because of the so-called tort reform legislation enacted by the legislature in 1987, the substantive law in this area is now unsettled. The old concepts of comparative negligence embodied in TEX. REV. CIV. STAT. ANN. art. 2212 (repealed and codified at TEX. CIV. PRAC. & REM. CODE ANN. §§ 33.001 and 33.011) have now been replaced with the concept of "percentage of responsibility." Act of June 16, 1987, ch. 2, § 2.07, 1987 Tex. Sess. Law Serv. (1st Called Sess.) 79 (Vernon), *codified at* TEX. CIV. PRAC. & REM. CODE ANN. § 33.011 (Vernon Supp. 1988). A discussion of these substantive changes is beyond the scope of this work. Hence, some of the concepts and arguments discussed in this section may appropriately be subject to modification, depending on subsequent court interpretations of the 1987 Act.

3. Of note is the fact that the concept of "proximate cause" is not embodied in the 1987 Act. See discussion in *supra* note 2.

4. Under TEX. CIV. PRAC. & REM. CODE ANN. § 33.001 (Vernon Supp. 1988), the plaintiff in a negligence action may recover damages only if his percentage of responsibility is 50 percent or less. *Id.* § 33.001(a), (c). If at least one defendant is found liable on the basis of strict tort liability, strict products liability, or breach of warranty under chapter 2 of the Texas Business & Commerce Code, the plaintiff may recover damages only if his percentage of responsibility is less than 60 percent. *Id.* § 33.001(b). These rules do not apply to exemplary damages, which are limited by other rules. *Id.* § 33.002(a), ch. 41.

Most advocates realize that the initial reaction of lay people is simply to declare that both parties were equally at fault; your initial task is to dispel this misconception. Additionally, the jury must understand the nature of the comparative responsibility question. For example, point out that the only conduct to be considered in answering this question is that of the plaintiff, the defendants, and any settling persons whose negligence is found to be a cause of the injury. Although the jurors may believe that other entities or individuals have in some way been responsible for the injury, those considerations can play no role in their answer to this specific question. In short, whatever percentages are ascribed to the plaintiff, the defendants, and any settling persons must add up to 100 percent.[5]

To weaken the initial conception that, if two parties' negligence[6] cause the injury, they are "equally at fault," consider those factors that can be offered to contrast the negligence of the victim with that of the defendant. Some factors are inappropriate for this purpose.[7] The following factors may, depending on the facts of the case, be appropriate to illustrate and stress the disparate nature of the negligent acts committed by the plaintiff and the defendant.

The Nature of the Conduct

In many cases involving comparative responsibility, the evidence will demonstrate great disparity between the nature of the conduct of the victim and that of the responsible defendants. Perhaps the plaintiff pleads and proves that the defendant was operating his vehicle while under the influence of alcohol or drugs; the defendant's act should not be viewed in the same way as allegations and proof by the defense that the victim should have kept a better lookout for the defendant's errant vehicle. Perhaps it is shown that the owner of premises knew of a dangerous condition, such as a slippery floor or a rotted step, and failed to correct this condition to protect those who came on his property; his conduct should not be considered equal to the victim's conduct in failing to avoid and discover the defect. Perhaps the proof in the malpractice case demonstrates that the physician improperly performed surgery and that the plaintiff continued to have problems following the surgery. The defense may contend either that the plaintiff did not complain vigorously enough to the doctor or that he did not request more detailed follow-up in the office. Again, these acts are far from similar in nature to those of the defendant.

---

5. *See* 1 State Bar of Texas, Texas Pattern Jury Charges PJC 4.03 (2d ed. 1987 & Supp. 1989).

6. Note that the 1987 Act has substituted the concept of "responsibility" for that of negligence. See discussion in *supra* note 2.

7. For example, it would be error to argue that the percentage of responsibility attributable to a party is measured by the number of acts or omissions found against each party. *See* 1 State Bar of Texas, *supra* note 5.

The Time Element of the Parties' Negligence

In many instances you can contrast the length of time involved in the negligence of the injured plaintiff with that of the defendant. For example, in a premises liability case where the defendant has created a dangerous condition, such as a defectively designed step, a poorly attached railing, or the absence of guard railings in a dangerous area, you can effectively contrast the length of time involved in the plaintiff's negligence with that involved in the defendant's negligence. The defendant may argue, for example, that the plaintiff should have exercised more care in making his step or more care as he walked along an unguarded balcony or walkway. The plaintiff's negligence in this regard usually occurs in the space of split seconds: he takes a misstep; he fails to negotiate a dangerous curve on a bicycle. Although the plaintiff's decision about his conduct must be made in a matter of seconds, the defendant's decision was made under no such conditions of urgency. The defendant had ample time—several hours, if not even days—to consider the safety of the design, the manner in which a guard railing would be attached, the design of the pathway. If each party's negligence is measured in time, then the victim's negligence can represent only a small fraction of the total.

You can use the same basic approach when there is evidence that the defendant was intoxicated. The time that was required for the defendant-driver to become intoxicated can usually be shown to be quite extensive. In these types of cases, the defense will argue that the plaintiff was negligent during the split seconds that were available to him to avoid the catastrophe. Again, you can argue whether there is any reasonable comparison between the victim, who was faced with a critical decision that had to be made in a matter of split seconds, and the defendant, whose decision to become intoxicated was made over a period of hours.

Differences in Duty and Circumstances

Many times a consideration of the position of the parties will reveal salient and critical differences. The defendant may occupy some professional status, while the victim is cast in the posture of the ordinary citizen or layperson. For example, should the conduct of the professional truck driver who is operating his eighteen-wheeler on the highways on a daily basis, covering literally hundreds of thousands of miles a year, be measured in the same way as that of the homemaker who rarely travels the freeways? Should this professional driver, who is operating a large and dangerous truck as an occupation, be viewed the same as the lady who happened to be on the freeway after taking her children to school?

The professional position of the defense may be emphasized even more in product and malpractice cases. Perhaps it is proved in a product case that the designer of a high-pressure gauge was negligent in failing to equip the gauge with safety glass that would prevent injury in case of an overload. The defense contends that the oilfield worker-plaintiff was negligent because he was not wearing his safety glasses on the occasion in question. Is the designer of this gauge to be viewed, with respect to the care required of him, in the same manner as the oilfield worker? In a malpractice case, the defense may argue that the patient was negligent in not following the doctor's instructions for treating an infection at home. However, is the patient to be viewed from the same perspective as the trained physician? Can it be said that the patient's appreciation of the risks of not following the doctor's instructions was as great as the physician's appreciation of the risks he understood were associated with the treatment of the infection?

Control of the Instrumentality

A corollary to some of the considerations discussed above is control of the offending instrumentality. In a premises case, for example, you can show that the owner had control of the premises for an extended period before the occurrence of the incident that brought about the harm. The injured plaintiff had no control of the premises. He had no ability to perceive the danger and take appropriate steps to correct it. The allegations of negligence against the plaintiff are simply that he should somehow have avoided the dangerous condition by keeping a better lookout. Likewise, in many product cases you can demonstrate that the plaintiff never had any control over the product. The offending product was, at all times material to the case, under the control of either the manufacturer or the individual who purchased and used the product.

Differences in Degree of Care Required

Finally, the facts of a given case may lend themselves to an effective argument that stresses differences in degree of care that may be required. (In this context, the degree of care required is an extension of the court's instruction that the parties' conduct is to be judged by the circumstances; the comparison does not necessarily involve a higher duty imposed by law on either party, such as the higher duty owed by a common carrier.)

Should not the driver of an eighteen-wheel truck with a gross weight of fifty thousand pounds be more careful on the freeway than an individual who is driving a passenger car? The passenger car, if it collides with another vehicle, is capable of producing less harm and damage, merely because of its lesser weight and size. The truck, because it is massive, is capable of inflicting tragic consequences if it is negligently used. The patient who delays in returning to the hospital with complaints of a draining infection may be negligent in the strict sense. But can such negligence be equated with the negligence of the doctor who failed to give adequate instructions to the patient when he was discharged from the hospital? The doctor, because of his superior knowledge, understands and appreciates the tragic consequences that can ensue from delay in treatment. Although the layperson may admit that his complaints should have brought him back to the doctor earlier, is the degree of care to be exercised by these two individuals to be judged the same? Again, these are critical differences in circumstances.

A specific example will illustrate the actual implementation of the foregoing principles. Assume that the defendant stops by a garage for some minor work on his vehicle during the day. While waiting for his car to be repaired, he consumes almost a half-pint of bourbon and a couple of beers. Later that evening, while operating his car, he loses control of it; the car is stopped sideways in the middle of a busy freeway. Within a short time, the plaintiff's automobile approaches the defendant's stalled vehicle. The plaintiff is an accountant, who has been working late at the office. The evidence establishes that, given the area where the impact occurred and the configuration of the freeway, the plaintiff traveled a significant distance in his vehicle with an unobstructed view of the defendant's car before the impact occurred. Thus, the defense contends that the plaintiff was negligent in failing to see the stalled vehicle in time to avoid the collision and in failing to swerve to the right or left and go around the immobilized automobile. Within this framework of the evidence, the following argument might be used:

> Ladies and gentlemen, Question 10 submitted to you by the court asks you to attribute a percentage of responsibility to my friend Paul Vinson and the defendant, Harry Black. You realize that under the court's instructions, you do not get to this question unless you have found both Paul and Mr. Black responsible for negligence that proximately caused this tragic collision. We would hope that you will not reach this question. A preponderance of the evidence just does not demonstrate that the defendant has proved that my friend Paul could have reasonably avoided this collision. The evidence is that he had only split seconds to make what were literally life-and-death decisions for him.
>
> However, since the question is submitted to you and on the chance that ten or more of you may disagree with us in this respect, I must address it.
>
> This question asks you to compare the responsibility of these two parties—Mr. Paul Vinson and the defendant, Mr. Black. We all understand that negligence is essentially a concept of responsibility. The law wisely says that we are all responsible for our acts. We are all legally responsible for the effects of our negligence. This question asks you to apportion negligence between Mr. Vinson and the defendant with the understanding that theirs is the only conduct to be considered. In other words, the court tells you that the percentages "should add up to 100 percent."

I would begin my consideration of this most significant question with you with the realization that there are many of you who would initially suggest, "Well, since both men were at fault, why not simply answer the question fifty-fifty?" That is an easy answer, a quick approach. But, as you have heard the evidence, you have realized that the conduct of these individuals that brought about this tragedy was far from equal. It simply was not equal by any measurement, by any standard, by any approach.

Philosophers, legal scholars, judges, and other great minds have struggled for literally centuries with the concept of responsibility. Who should face the responsibility, who should bear the burden of loss, who should be held legally accountable for any given incident? The fact that this concept has given the scholars so much difficulty over the years only underscores the fact that there are many instances in which the easy answer of "fifty-fifty" simply does not apply.

If a twenty-five-year-old man gets a fourteen-year-old girl pregnant, there are those who might suggest that they are both equally responsible. But does society view it that way?

When the drug dealer, preying on young and vulnerable minds, introduces them to dangerous substances, again it could be suggested that they are equally responsible. After all, the young teenager voluntarily takes the drug that is given or sold to him by the peddler.

The lady who is raped can be said to be responsible because she did not lock her door.

The man who is robbed may be said to be responsible because he had money in his pocket.

Those of you who are old enough recall that when war broke out in Europe, many great minds suggested that the war was the responsibility of Hitler's Germany and of England and France. The reason given was that, if England and France had been less tolerant of Hitler and more aggressive in their reaction when he remilitarized the Rhineland, he never would have proceeded so far.

The point is that we can all refer to examples in history and in our personal lives where it might be suggested that two parties were at fault, but clearly we would not, for a moment, consider that the responsibility was equal. In this case, we have a man who loses control of his car and causes it to be parked in the middle of a freeway at night across the middle lanes. It is sideways. The man lost control of his vehicle because he was intoxicated. He didn't become intoxicated in the minute, or the five minutes, or even the thirty minutes before the collision. The evidence is that he embarked on that misadventure some hours before. He was negligent when he took the first drink, realizing that he was going to drink more. His negligence continued through those approximately two hours when he consumed a half-pint of bourbon while visiting with his friends at the garage. No one would quarrel with the fact that driving while intoxicated constitutes legal negligence. None of us would speak out on behalf of drunk driving. If we were to put this type of negligence on a scale measuring human conduct, it would be at the very worst level of conduct. If we were to view that negligence in terms of degree and time, and place it on a chart, it would look something like this. [*Here, display a visual aid or chart to illustrate this point.*] Conduct that none of us would approve of under any circumstances. Conduct that lasted over an extended period of time.

Mere inattentiveness and slow reaction, on the other hand, would rank much better on the scale of human conduct.

As we demonstrated on this diagram, Harry Black's negligence was of the worst sort. It continued over an extended period of time. Paul Vinson's negligence, on the other hand, in simply making the wrong decision—a decision he was required to make in a matter of split seconds—is viewed differently. If we visualize the negligence of the parties in this way, we can see that Paul's negligence represents a very small percentage of the total responsibility. Maybe one or two percent—at most.

But the defense suggests that you should put my friend Paul Vinson in the same category as a drunk driver.

We would submit that the questions in this case go beyond simply comparing the negligence of these two parties. They go to whether or not we, as a community, are going to condemn by our verdict the irresponsibility, callousness, and carelessness of a drunk driver.

There are those who will get behind the wheel of four thousand pounds of steel and metal and force that automobile out into our public highways and streets where our spouses and children travel, where our friends and neighbors drive to church, and where people like Paul Vinson have to spend a few hours each week getting back and forth to work to provide their families a living.

Yet the defense would suggest that the negligence of these two individuals can be compared. The lawyers would change the question submitted by the court by changing the test. Do they really suggest that so many feet of stopping distance is equal to so many cans of beer? Is there an equation for so many feet, reaction time, and stopping distance that translates into a fifth of bourbon? If these things are equal and whiskey equals seconds and beer equals feet, then we have all been here in vain. Because from this time forward, every time a drunk injures someone, every time an intoxicated driver cripples someone, the question will be, "Why didn't

> you avoid me?" If the drunk hits your car, the question will be, "Why didn't you get out of the way?" If you fail to avoid his car, which has been left sideways in the freeway imperiling all approaching traffic, the question will be, "Why didn't you avoid the collision?"
>
> These acts of negligence are not the same. The momentary inattention and slow reaction of Paul Vinson cannot be compared to the negligence of Harry Black. If there is any comparison at all to the negligence—the responsibility—my friend Paul Vinson's part is an insignificant amount.[8]

Recognizing the various concepts in this chapter does not necessarily imply that each is always appropriate. In a particular type of litigation, it may be more effective if you use some of these techniques but discard the others. The following five chapters explore the liability aspects of argument in different kinds of personal injury cases.

---

8. This discussion of comparative responsibility (pp. 140-47) was first published under the title "Arguing Comparative Negligence for the Plaintiff" in the *Texas Bar Journal*, December 1987.

17

Workers' Compensation

TWENTY-FIVE YEARS AGO, when many of today's skilled advocates began practicing law, the trial of the workers' compensation case was a staple to the lawyer who had aspirations in trial advocacy. Many gifted lawyers who now represent victims, as well as most members of the experienced and talented defense bar, began their practices defending insurance companies in compensation cases. Changes in the policies of the Industrial Accident Board over the last quarter century have significantly reduced the number of workers' compensation cases that are tried but have not eliminated these cases from the arena of trial advocacy. Many skilled and accomplished trial lawyers have spent the better part of their careers representing either victims or insurance companies in compensation cases.

As suggested in the previous chapter, the approach to arguing the liability issues in a compensation case is significantly different from the approach that must be used in other types of injury litigation. The principal difference is that, in the workers' compensation case, the jury is really not presented with concepts of fault, responsibility, pain and suffering, or specific money damages. Rather, the jurors are called on to answer some specific inquiries by the court, although the significance of their answers may be forever concealed from them.

In most instances the evidence in a compensation case will come from essentially five sources:

- *The injured worker* (the plaintiff).
- *The plaintiff's physician.* This witness is usually the medical expert who treated the worker and followed his medical condition for some time.
- *Lay witnesses called on behalf of the plaintiff.* Affectionately referred to as "grunt-and-groaners," these witnesses are usually relatives, friends, and coworkers who testify about their observations of the plaintiff's physical condition before and after the injury.
- *The insurance company doctor.* This witness is usually a physician who was retained for the purpose of doing a single examination.
- *Miscellaneous lay and expert witnesses on behalf of the defense.* Included in this catchall category are such individuals as representatives of the employer and rehabilitation specialists.

The victim's advocate and the insurance company's attorney have conflicting goals. The worker's representative is attempting to obtain jury findings of total and permanent incapacity, unless he is dealing with a case that involves only a specific injury. On the other hand, the insurance company's lawyer is attempting to obtain findings of partial disability and then limit the period of incapacity or disability. These general objectives provide a background for this chapter's consideration of specific arguments that are commonly used on behalf of the victim in compensation cases.

Explain That the Answer to Each Question Is Important

Jurors have less appreciation for the effect of their answers in compensation cases than in any other type of personal injury case. Jurors generally understand that the effect of finding a professional negligent in his professional activities, a driver negligent in the operation of an automobile, or a product inherently dangerous is, in essence, a finding of legal responsibility on the part of the defendant. Likewise, jurors appreciate that the money damages they find will bear a significant relationship to the actual amount the plaintiff recovers; indeed, they often realize that such findings determine the plaintiff's recovery.

The compensation charge is very different from the charge in the usual personal injury case. Inquiries are made concerning "disability," "length of disability," and "weekly wage." Not only are these legal concepts foreign to the jurors; the effect of their findings in terms of the plaintiff's recovery remains unclear to them as well. For this reason it is imperative to stress to the jury the fact that every answer to the questions submitted is important.[1]

Probably no Texas lawyer ever tried more compensation cases than the late Ray McDermott of Houston. In his arguments to the jury, he never neglected to incorporate a dramatic reference to the importance of the answer to each question:

> Ladies and gentlemen, the court tells you in Instruction 3 that every answer to these questions the court has submitted for your determination is important. When some member of the jury suggests to you that a question is not really important, that any answer will do, or that the judge could always correct the answer if it is wrong, I hope some of you will remind him or her of the judge's instructions in this regard. I can assure you that your answers to these questions are significant and that my friend Bob Swanson's future depends on your verdict. Please remember this and, when a juror suggests the contrary, simply ask [*at this point Ray would lower his voice to*

1. *See* TEX. R. CIV. P. 226a, pt. III, instruction 3.

almost a whisper], "Well, if that question was not important, why did the judge put it in the charge?"

Explain the Legal Concepts Involved

Explaining the legal concepts involved in the case is the cornerstone, the essential element, the sine qua non of the argument on behalf of the plaintiff in a compensation case. The most common error committed by novice trial advocates is failing to realize that most jurors do not readily understand the legal concepts of "injury," "total and partial disability," and "permanent and temporary." Indeed, most jurors have an understanding of these terms that is different from, and inconsistent with, their legal definitions. For this reason you must begin, during the voir dire, the process of educating the jury about the legal meanings and significance of the vital terms and words. Because the jury's understanding of these legal terms is fundamental to any opportunity for a plaintiff's verdict, it is appropriate to use much of your opening argument explaining the questions submitted to the jury and indicating the desired answers to these questions. When explaining the concepts of "injury" and "total disability," you may effectively use anecdotes, analogies, and visual aids. You may incorporate brief references to the evidence, but save any detailed discussion for later portions of the argument, after you have fully developed and explained the basic legal concepts.

There are essentially four legal concepts that are commonly pivotal in a compensation trial—injury, producing cause, incapacity, and temporary versus permanent incapacity. In some cases, all these issues are hotly contested by the defense; in other situations, the evidence may have narrowed the case to one salient issue. In any event, the following considerations may help you communicate the legal meanings of these concepts.

Injury

The concept of legal injury as it applies to workers' compensation can develop into a complex issue. A discussion of the legal principles governing "occupational disease," subsequent injuries, and other technical aspects would be beyond the scope of this book and is left to the many fine works dealing with the substantive law of workers' compensation.

Generally, "injury" in the compensation case means damage or harm to the physical structure of the body, such diseases or infections as naturally result therefrom, and the incitement and aggravation of any previously or subsequently existing condition.[2] For a recovery to be had, the injury must

2. TEX. REV. CIV. STAT. ANN. art. 8306, § 20 (Vernon Supp. 1988); *see* Gill v. Transamerica Ins. Co., 417 S.W.2d 720 (Tex. Civ. App.—Dallas 1967, no writ).

have been received by an employee in the course of his employment.[3]

The basic concept of injury becomes troublesome for the jury when the defense offers evidence of a preexisting illness or injury similar to the one that is the basis of the claim. Likewise, confusion can arise if the plaintiff's injury is one that could have been sustained for any of a variety of reasons. For instance, in a case in which the victim sustained a back injury, the defense may argue that the ruptured disc could have resulted from one of several causes—mowing the lawn, getting up in the morning, stooping over to tie one's shoes, and so forth. As the victim's lawyer, you must devote some time to explaining the concept of injury and "course of employment." Argue with vigor the precise mechanism that caused the victim's injury; stress, for example, that while the plaintiff may have had some evidence of advanced arteriosclerotic heart disease or some evidence of a weakened intervertebral disc, it was the incident that occurred on the job that produced the incapacitating "injury."

Producing Cause

The legal concept of producing cause that is used in Texas embodies the concept that the on-the-job injury, either independently or together with one or more other injuries or conditions, results in incapacity and that, without the injury, such incapacity would not have occurred.[4] If you fail to explain the concept of producing cause, you run the risk of having the jury confuse causation in the compensation case with the generally understood concept of sole cause. In other words, if you do not stress the meaning of the legal concept of producing cause, the jury may be swayed by the defense evidence about the role that other conditions played in producing the incapacity.

Incapacity (disability)

In practically every compensation case, the plaintiff's advocate is faced with the problem of whether to organize the argument so that the victim rises or falls on the determination of total incapacity. Even when there is evidence of partial incapacity and the defense argues this as an alternative, many skilled advocates lean toward the theory that it is not strategically advisable for the victim's lawyer even to address the concept of partial incapacity. The rationale is that an argument for total incapacity and partial incapacity in the alternative weakens the plaintiff's position in the perception of the jury.

The lay understanding of total incapacity differs greatly from the legal concept that is the cornerstone of compensation law. For this reason it is imperative both in the voir dire examination and in final argument to energize

---

3. TEX. REV. CIV. STAT. ANN. art. 8306, § 3b (Vernon 1967).

4. *See* 2 STATE BAR OF TEXAS, TEXAS PATTERN JURY CHARGES PJC 20.01 (2d ed. forthcoming). (If necessary, see PJC 22.01 of the 1970 edition.)

the legal meaning of total incapacity. Total incapacity does not imply an absolute inability to perform any kind of labor.[5] One is totally disabled when he cannot perform the usual tasks of a worker to such an extent that he cannot get and keep employment.[6]

Stress the two factors that, if present from the evidence, demonstrate total disability—first, the plaintiff cannot *get* a job, and, second, the plaintiff cannot *keep* a job. In many instances it may even be appropriate to contrast the legal concept of total incapacity with the common meaning of that term. Most people would initially believe that an individual is totally incapacitated only if he has been catastrophically injured so that he is paralyzed or brain damaged. The jury must understand that what most people might call a partial incapacity is, in terms of law, a total one. In many cases, either the plaintiff's physician or the insurance company's physician will have assessed the plaintiff's injury in terms of percentages of disability. The impact of such an assessment may be lessened by various arguments and analogies:

> A watch with a ten percent disability will lose two and four-tenths hours a day. A watch that loses two and one-half hours a day is not worth anything. A one-hundred-dollar watch that loses this amount of time is not worth ninety dollars.
>
> The critical difference that ten percent can make can be measured in athletic contests. No one in history ever ran a mile in less than four minutes until a couple of decades ago. But if anyone could reduce that time by ten percent, he would run a mile in just over three and one-half minutes, a figure that needs no elaboration. There are a hundred golfers on the professional circuit who can shoot the average course in seventy-two any day. But a sixty-five is the score of a champion at his best. Take your average professional basketball player who is six feet seven inches tall. Add ten percent and you have a star, seven feet three inches tall.
>
> We are not merely juggling figures. These are practical, objective computations of physical differences that ten to fifteen percent can make in performance, function, and ability to compete. The injured plaintiff must be employed and employable. He must compete to get a job and to hold it. A loss of ten to fifteen percent can handicap a worker for the rest of his life to a serious and important extent. Doctors who examine applicants for employment and the people who hire them often turn a ten to fifteen percent physical handicap into a one hundred percent disability to land a job. When the company finds an applicant ten percent disabled, the employer

5. *Id.* PJC 20.02. (If necessary, see PJC 22.02 of the 1970 edition.)
6. *Id.*

> does not hire him at ninety percent of the wages or ninety percent of the time. The employer simply does not hire him at all, and he remains one hundred percent out of a job.

The dual requirement for total incapacity must be borne in mind when there is evidence that the plaintiff worked at some job after the injury. In such an instance the victim's advocate will want to stress that the injured workman did what we all respect and admire—he tried. But, when he tried to work, his physical incapacity prevented him from keeping that employment. Again, stress that the concept of total incapacity requires that a worker be able both to get and to keep a job. If a worker, for whatever reason, can obtain employment but his physical condition does not permit him to do the work in such a way that he can keep the job, he is totally incapacitated.

Temporary Versus Permanent Incapacity

If you choose to stress the concept of total incapacity, you must carry the theme forward into the determinations of temporary versus permanent incapacity. A number of factors must be incorporated into a consideration of these concepts—the amount of education the plaintiff has, the type of work he is trained to do, any language limitations he may have, and his age. All these factors, when taken individually or collectively, can lead to the conclusion of total and permanent incapacity. For example, if the victim is a person of limited education whose only work experience has been manual labor, can it seriously be suggested that he is not totally incapacitated, because his back injury would not prevent him from doing office work or retail sales or that such incapacity is not permanent? Again, review and stress the wording of the question with regard to temporary or permanent incapacity.

Likewise, if the injured worker is approaching middle age, this factor may have great significance on the question of employability. Most jurors understand and appreciate the argument that a forty-five-year-old man with a history of a back injury or previous heart attacks is not employable in today's labor market. Good, healthy, whole men of forty-five years of age have a hard time getting a job, simply because the Texas labor market is constantly being supplied with new, younger, more robust workers. In this connection, the old adage that the middle-aged person is "the first to be fired and the last to be hired" is all too true.

Deal with Prior Injuries

Evidence of the existence of prior injuries can be significant in the trial of the compensation case. In some instances the defense may choose to argue that the employer would not have initially hired the plaintiff if it had known of the plaintiff's preexisting injury. Strangely enough, in these types of cases the defense will argue essentially a "catch-22" proposition: that although the plaintiff was not "employable" before the time he was hired and his on-the-job injury occurred, he is not now totally and permanently incapacitated. In this situation you might consider the following argument:

> Ladies and gentlemen, as I listen to the defense argument I realize that this case, like so many, in the final analysis has probably boiled down to one or two basic issues. If you resolve those issues, then all the questions submitted to you by the court fall into place. This is not unusual. Most lawsuits eventually come down to this point.
>
> Is Mrs. Stoddard totally disabled? If she is, then that condition—if it exists today—is certainly permanent. The defense states that if Mrs. Stoddard had told the ABC Company the full details of her back injury they would never have hired her in the first place. Bear in mind there has been no suggestion that she tried to conceal these facts. The defense argument simply seems to be that if they had had the benefit of more medical information, including these medical records, they would not have hired her. We can accept that. Indeed, all of us recognize that a person who has a serious back injury is virtually unemployable in today's job market. The evidence has demonstrated that. The ABC Company certainly wouldn't hire her today. Nor would virtually any other employer. As you have heard from the evidence, the only way that she has been able to get and keep a job is through the kindness and support of her friends. But that's not the court's definition. The fact that you might have a brother-in-law or neighbor who would give you some job does not mean that you are not totally incapacitated. We don't penalize people because they try. We don't take from them their legal rights because they are the kind of persons who have caring friends and relatives.
>
> We can accept the fact that this insurance company, which sold this workers' compensation policy to the ABC Company, has the knowledge and authority to state that ABC would never have hired her in the first place if they had known the full extent of her back condition. What does that tell you about how we must address the question of total incapacity? How can this defense lawyer on the one hand argue that she was not employable before this injury because of her previous back problems, but that following this injury and surgery she is now employable and not disabled?
>
> We would submit that these facts and this statement by the defense establish beyond any debate that Mrs. Stoddard is totally disabled as defined by the law and the terms of the insurance policy in question. That disability is permanent.
>
> That being so, doesn't the case boil down to the simple question of whether the injury at the ABC Company contributed to that disability?

Ask Whether Honesty Should Be Penalized

As has been indicated above, the existence of a serious on-the-job injury may affect a person's employability. In this type of situation, it may be appropriate to remind the jury that the injury has, in effect, placed the victim in a personal dilemma. Most jurors know from personal experience that when a job application is taken, one of the first pieces of information solicited from them concerns prior injuries. Not only does the written job application inquire whether the worker has ever received an injury before, the application further inquires whether that injury occurred on the job and, if so, the nature of the injury. The reason for this inquiry is obvious. A person who has sustained an on-the-job injury, whether in the form of a back injury, a broken hip, or a heart attack, is more likely to be injured in the future; if he is, the effects of the injury in terms of incapacity are likely to be greater. Thus, the injured worker who attempts to obtain reemployment is forced into the dilemma of having either to tell the truth about his previous injury or to lie about it to get the job. This consideration may lead to the following argument:

> Does this insurance company seriously suggest that Joe Black is not totally incapacitated because he will be hired if he simply lies on his future job applications about what has happened to him? You have heard from the evidence that while Joe did not have much education and supported his family with his back, muscle, and brawn, he was still a man of principle. He was raised by a working father and mother who taught him the virtues of honesty and the vices of deceit. He learned in church the commandments by which we measure others' and our own conduct. His work, though menial, was done with pride and honesty. The evidence and common sense now tell us that if Joe informs prospective employers of this prior injury, he will not be hired. Does the defense imply that he should not be completely truthful, candid, and honest with prospective employers? If this insurance company would imply that Joe is not totally incapacitated because he could lie and get a job, then what perspective does that give us about the evidence and arguments that this defendant has brought for our consideration?

Explain That the Plaintiff Is Not Claim-Conscious

In most compensation cases, the injured victim is making his or her first legal claim. Indeed, proof, if properly developed by the plaintiff's attorney, will often show that the injured worker had sustained other injuries on the job, had been treated by physicians and lost time from work, but had never made any type of formal or legal claim for compensation. In some instances the evidence may indicate that the plaintiff had, in fact, been injured several years previously. The plaintiff may have received some small compensation benefits but nonetheless returned to work. In either situation it is appropriate to dispel the idea that the injured victim is "claim-conscious":

> It never ceases to amaze me how an insurance company will try to tell you that the plaintiff is too claim-conscious and he just wants "something for nothing." From the evidence we have brought you, you know now that Debbie Matlock has had prior injuries while working for the ABC Company and she hasn't made any claim for those injuries.
>
> It is only now, when her family has been so affected by her injuries and her inability to work, that she has brought a claim. She had no choice. Debbie didn't bring this claim looking to get something for nothing. She brought this claim because she, as well as her family, has suffered tragic consequences from her injury.
>
> You might ask yourselves why the insurance company didn't quarrel with Debbie when she was hurt on the job before now. The insurance people didn't ask her, "Won't you make a claim? Why won't you make a claim for your injuries?"
>
> But now, when Debbie cannot do anything for herself or her family *but* make a claim, they tell her, "You're too claim-conscious."

Paint a Picture of the Case

As discussed in chapter 16, you may elect to paint a picture of the plaintiff's case so that the evidence and questions submitted by the court have some perspective in the jurors' minds. This tactic may be used in the compensation case:

> Gary Anton worked for the Zanadu Corporation for ten years before this accident occurred. During that time, he was protected against the effects of on-the-job injuries by the workers' compensation policy that was issued by the defendant, the Republish Insurance Company. During the ten years that Gary worked for Zanadu, the premiums for his protection were paid by his company. The Republish Insurance Company had no disagreement with that arrangement. They collected Gary's premiums, invested them, and made a profit.
>
> It was only when Gary was injured on the job on September 17, 1986, that the Republish Insurance Company decided there was something wrong with the deal. Until that seven-hundred-pound

> pipe swung loose and struck Gary in the head, the insurance company was happy. Collect Gary's premiums, invest them, and write another policy. Now Gary needs the benefits that he and his employer paid for. He cannot get and keep a job. He cannot support his family. The only thing that stands between Gary and his family and poverty are the weekly benefits that were provided by that policy. But the insurance company doesn't want Gary to have even that. The ten years of hard work, the sweat, and the agony that Gary put into that job are to be ignored. This case involves the rights that Gary and his family have under the terms of that policy. The same terms that are included in this court's charge were included in the protection that was provided to Gary by that policy.

Stress the Thoroughness of the Defense's Preparation

A unique characteristic of the compensation case is that it represents a direct action against an insurance company. While an insurance company may be the entity that will respond in damages in other types of personal injury cases, such as malpractice, product liability, premises injuries, and automobile collisions, Texas law normally prevents direct actions against the insurance carrier. You should not overlook this unique feature of the compensation case, since it presents an opportunity to allude to the financial resources of the defendant. For example, you may reason with the jury that, because of these resources, the compensation carrier would have been able to introduce evidence that contradicted the victim's injury, if such evidence existed; since the carrier has not offered any evidence or otherwise disproved the victim's injury, the logical conclusion is that the existence of the injury and disability has been corroborated.

> I am sure that you have been impressed throughout the trial of this case, as I have, with the preparation and organization exhibited by Mr. Dawson Cloud, the attorney for the ABC Insurance Company. This company is to be complimented for hiring such a skilled and dedicated advocate on its behalf. Also, it should be obvious to you that the ABC Insurance Company has been faced with no limitations, either financial or time, that have in any way constrained its efforts in the defense of this case.
>
> We have brought to you the facts that have established by a preponderance of the evidence that Barbara Keagan cannot work and that she has pains and certain limitations. This is all a result of being struck on the back with a box while she was working in the storeroom of the Poole Auto Supply Store.
>
> Don't you know, with all their resources, with their skilled investigators, and with the various sources that they can turn to for information, if the insurance company had any evidence that

would disprove Mrs. Keagan's injury and disability, they would have brought it to you? The evidence has shown that the insurance company has visited with Mrs. Keagan's neighbors. They have talked to her coworkers.

However, the defense contention now seems to be that somehow we had the obligation to ensure that, when Mrs. Keagan was injured, someone was there to witness it. Their argument seems to be that if there were no witnesses, then Mrs. Keagan is not entitled to recover. But we all know that most of these types of accidents occur without a witness. Even when someone was present, by the time the case is tried that person may have moved away and is unavailable to testify. The injured victim in cases of this type is always placed in the lonely and frightening position of establishing his right to these limited benefits for injury, before an unpredictable jury, under unfamiliar rules and procedures. The law recognizes this. That is why the law says that a person can establish the existence of an injury without a witness. If the law were otherwise, then all this insurance company would ever have to say is, "We don't care how badly you are hurt, we don't care what you told the doctors, we don't care what the doctors have found, we don't care how soon after the accident you may have told your supervisor—since no one saw your accident, we owe you nothing by way of workers' compensation benefits."

But our law goes further. It gives the injured victim the right and opportunity under our procedures to send questions to the insurance company. If you are injured on the job, you can then ask the insurance company, which has the access and right to all the information and cooperation from the employer who purchased that policy, to state under oath whether they have any information that indicates that the incident did not occur. This insurance company can investigate, they can interview witnesses, they can look at the accident site. They have the resources and means to check medical records and conduct a medical investigation. If there is any indication that the plaintiff is feigning the incident or not being truthful about it, they can state that under oath and give the plaintiff the opportunity to respond. Common sense tells you that this investigation was done in this case. And, after all their investigation, analysis, discovery, research, and legwork, this insurance company must be said to have concluded that they had no basis to say that this incident did not occur exactly like this lady has described it to you. The simple fact is, if they had had any proof to the contrary, they would have certainly brought it to you.

Stress the Differences Between the Physicians

Often, the workers' compensation carrier will request that the plaintiff be examined by a physician of the carrier's choosing. When the defendant elects to base its defense on the findings of the "insurance company doctor," you should stress the differences between the bases for the opinions expressed by the treating physician and for the opinions given by the insurance company's expert witness. In many instances you can effectively argue that the insurance company doctor was not familiar with the patient and, in fact, examined the plaintiff on only one occasion—an examination that lasted only a brief period. In contrast, you can describe the consultations with the plaintiff's treating physician who has often seen the patient over a number of years and who is intimately familiar with the patient's physical condition and limitations:

> On cross-examination, the insurance company's witness, Dr. Black, told you that the examination he performed on Frank Jackson lasted less than thirty minutes. And this doctor told you that the results of his examination could vary because it was done only once. Depending on the time of day, what type of activities Frank had done before the examination, whether he had had a good night's sleep, whether he had to make a long drive to get to the doctor's office, whether he had taken the medication that Dr. White had been prescribing—these, as well as a number of other factors, could affect the results of that examination.
>
> On the other hand, Dr. White, who treated Frank over the seven years before his injury, testified that he examined Mr. Jackson the day after his injury. Dr. White has continued to treat Frank over the past three years. He has seen Frank many times. He has seen him at different times of the day. He has seen him on different days of the week. He has seen Frank on his "good" and his "bad" days. His opinion is that this man has suffered a serious and permanent back injury.
>
> You are now called on to resolve the differences between these two physicians. On the one hand, the insurance company doctor tells you that Frank is not disabled and is not entitled to workers' compensation benefits. This doctor bases his opinion on a thirty-minute examination that was bought and paid for by the ABC Insurance Company. On the other hand, Dr. White bases his opinion on his knowledge of Frank both before and after the accident. Dr. White bases his opinion on his having treated this man for three years leading up to the trial of this case.
>
> If you had to make a life-or-death decision about some significant medical matter that affected you, who would you choose? Would you rely on the doctor who had seen you for thirty minutes,

> who regularly testifies for insurance companies, and whose testimony is being paid for by the ABC Insurance Company in this case? Or would you rely, in making such a significant medical decision, on the testimony of a doctor who had treated you the last ten years and who was intimately familiar with your medical and physical situation?

The compensation case presents a number of unique opportunities and problems for the victim's lawyer, who must use a different approach in the compensation case from the one he would use in a premises liability case, an automobile collision case, or a malpractice case. However, the trial advocate who incorporates the concepts explored in this chapter and the forensic tactics discussed in part 1 of this book should consistently win favorable compensation verdicts.

18

Automobile Cases

NO MATTER HOW SPECIALIZED a plaintiff's personal injury law firm may become, personal injury automobile cases seem to remain its "bread and butter." One obvious reason is that so many personal injury cases arise from automobile collisions. Further, the typical automobile case does not involve extensive financial investments, such as expensive expert witness fees, numerous depositions, or elaborate demonstrative evidence. For these reasons, many personal injury law firms and solo practitioners depend on automobile cases.

Although automobile cases enjoy some generic similarities, arguments vary depending on the differing facts in each case. The key to effectively arguing the evidence in the automobile case is flexibility. For instance, in one case the plaintiff may have been patiently awaiting a green light when the defendant rear-ended him; the plaintiff's argument would focus almost exclusively on the defendant's negligence. In contrast, if the plaintiff was drinking or failing to keep a proper lookout, his argument must address the issue of contributory negligence. In adapting the argument to meet the issues that are peculiar to each case, the victim's lawyer must paint a picture of his case for the jury. There must be no question in the minds of the jurors about the sequence of events leading to and surrounding the collision.[1] Furthermore, the attorney must retrace with the jurors the steps that constitute a prima facie case.

Duty and Responsibility

Unfortunately, the duty that the defendant owed the plaintiff is often overlooked in the plaintiff's argument. In an automobile case, the concepts of duty and responsibility can be easily conveyed to the jurors, because these duties and responsibilities are common to us all. Whenever a driver uses a freeway, road, or street in a particular community, the safety of those around him depends on the responsibility and care with which he operates his vehicle. Jurors can certainly envision the severe consequences associated with a dangerous, careless, or reckless driver. The purpose of such argument is, of

---

1. This technique is described in detail in ch. 16.

course, to highlight for the jurors the necessity of automobile safety by causing them to relate their own personal experiences to those of the plaintiff.[2] The following arguments are offered with that thought in mind:

> In determining the liability issues of an automobile case, we are in essence determining how responsible we will make the drivers who use our highways and freeways. It is a sobering thought to realize how dependent each of us is, every day, on our fellow citizens. When we drive the streets, whether it be in downtown Houston, our shopping centers, neighborhoods, or highways, we are at the mercy of other drivers. We depend on them to operate their vehicles in accordance with our laws and in a responsible manner. When we stop at our stop signs or bring our automobiles to a stop on the freeway, we are completely at the mercy of those who are behind us to operate their vehicles in a responsible manner. This case illustrates in a dramatic and graphic way just how dependent each of us is on the conduct of others.

. . . . .

> Ladies and gentlemen, the types of duties that we owe others depend on the types of activities in which we are engaged. For example, if I were to toss a glass into the air and fail to catch it, I might have acted carelessly. But the only possible harm is that the glass might break. If that glass were instead a stick of dynamite, we might all be blown up. Everyone would agree that my conduct would be irresponsible. By the same token, when the defendant drove his four-thousand-pound automobile down the highway, with only a few feet of space spelling the difference between safety and disaster—and he saw an automobile approaching him but turned his head to speak to his wife—his conduct was irresponsible, reckless, and careless.

. . . . .

> By way of defense, the trucking company has offered evidence that when Billy was seventeen years old, he was considered "irresponsible" and "not dependable." No one agrees more with the principle that we must all be responsible citizens. These parents, in their own way, attempted to instill responsibility in Billy. But of all people

---

2. Obviously, a direct invitation to the jurors to base the verdict on their own personal experiences would be improper. *See generally* 1 STATE BAR OF TEXAS, TEXAS PATTERN JURY CHARGES PJC 1.03 (2d ed. 1987 & Supp. 1989).

who could be talking about responsibility as a virtue, this trucking company is the least qualified.

What credentials of responsibility do they bring to this courtroom? They turn their drivers out on the road in lethal machinery and, through their business arrangements, encourage them to speed. Their drivers operate such lethal equipment from Port Arthur to Houston at what are observed to be not only unreasonable rates of speed but also reckless rates. One of their drivers comes over an overpass at seventy miles per hour into congested traffic and continues for some distance before he attempts to apply his brakes. The hundreds of tons of steel that he is sitting on are propelled into traffic so far that seven other vehicles are damaged. Billy's car is crushed and mangled, and it explodes.

When Billy dies and these parents look to the company to recognize their responsibility, their answer is that it was not their fault. Rather than recognizing their responsibility, they attempt to shift it to the construction company. And if this were not enough, they further attempt to avoid the responsibility by attacking the character, reputation, and memory of Billy and his parents.

Negligence

Liability of the Defendant-Driver

Unlike many cases in which evidence of negligence shows conduct that may not be too reprehensible, the automobile driver's negligence will give the jurors something to "sink their teeth into." Remember to embellish your argument with evidence of the defendant's negligent acts, as illustrated in the following arguments.

Speed and lookout.

The defendant may say that, according to the evidence, he was only speeding for the few seconds immediately before this collision. It is true that this is the only time we know of and can establish that this driver was speeding. We do not know how long he had been speeding prior to the tragic collision. We do not know on how many other occasions he might have imprudently operated his vehicle. But we do know that he was speeding on the occasion in question, and that fact has been established by a preponderance of the evidence.

. . . . .

What caused this collision? Speed caused the injuries sustained by John Palmer. It is common knowledge, something we hear repeated constantly on television and read in the newspapers and magazines, that speed is the big factor in most traffic deaths and injuries. You know from your own experience and general knowledge that most of the serious injuries and deaths do not take place downtown around this courthouse or in the business district. The traffic that you see on your noon breaks does not allow anyone to get up enough speed to seriously injure anyone or kill him. Likewise, the traffic congestion around our shopping centers and malls prevents anyone from getting up enough speed to cause serious injury. Where do people get killed or maimed in automobile collisions? These tragedies occur where the roads are wide open and where there is plenty of room and opportunity to push an automobile up to unsafe speeds.

You will recall that the defendant's excuse was, "I didn't have much time." He didn't have much time. When you are traveling at seventy to eighty miles per hour, you don't have much time. Things happen fast. But if the defendant had not been violating the law and if he had been going forty-five miles per hour—the posted speed limit—he would have had a lot more time. He would have had plenty of time to have avoided this wreck. He would not have crashed into the side of Mr. Palmer's automobile, causing these grave, serious, and crippling injuries you have heard about. If he had been observing the posted speed limit, we would not be here engaging in this morbid accounting of the worth of an individual.

. . . . .

Ladies and gentlemen, you may remember when we made our opening remarks to you—when I was standing right here next to the court reporter. When I spoke with you at that time, I told you that there would be a considerable amount of controversy about whether the defendant was driving too fast on the night in question. We all know from the evidence that the defendant's vehicle was traveling more or less at the posted rate of speed. The defense has been quick to point out this fact. They tell you that since the defendant was not speeding faster than the maximum speed limit, he could not have been negligent. When you return to the jury room to begin your deliberations, you will see from the court's questions that a person may be negligent by driving too fast even though he is not exceeding the posted speed limit.[3] This is because the posted speed limit states the *maximum* speed limit at which a person can drive. Under certain

3. If the questions submitted to the jury pertain to common-law negligence, rather than statutory negligence, such a question and/or instruction is appropriate. *See, e.g.*, Adams v. Morris, 584 S.W.2d 712, 717 (Tex. Civ. App.—Tyler 1979, no writ) ("Speed may be excessive even though it does not exceed the posted speed limit.").

circumstances, a reasonable person does not drive as fast as the speed limit. For instance, if the road is icy, a reasonable driver compensates for those conditions and may well drive much slower than the posted rate of speed. And so it is in this case: you now know that at nighttime on a long stretch of highway, with a severe thunderstorm making driving virtually impossible, the defendant was driving too fast. Even though the speed limit was fifty-five miles per hour and the defendant was approaching that rate of speed, he was still negligent because he was driving much faster than a reasonably prudent person would.

Braking.

Well, we have heard the defense's version of how this traffic collision occurred. According to the defendant's testimony, he had slowed down before the intersection to about twenty miles per hour. He then told you that upon approaching the stop sign he came to a complete halt. This defendant then went on to tell you how the plaintiff darted out in front of him at the four-way intersection.

Many of you have already recognized the fatal flaw in this defense. You know from the testimony of Karen Linton, the only eyewitness to this wreck, that she saw Jerry McCormick make a complete stop at the intersection. Karen told you the truth—exactly what she saw—that the defendant's truck slowed down and seemed to pause momentarily but still rolled into the intersection. Only when the defendant's truck careened into Johnny's car did it come to a complete halt. We have all seen drivers make those kinds of stops. Police officers have a nickname for them—"Hollywood stops." This is because when people visit Hollywood, few of them can afford to stay very long. They make a brief visit, a temporary delay. This type of stop may be fine out in California, but I've got news for the defendant: Jerry McCormick couldn't afford that Hollywood stop.

Yielding the right-of-way.

A preponderance of the evidence has established that Jimmy Green had the right-of-way on Martha Street. He had stopped at the stop sign facing him and proceeded through the intersection when it was his turn. But before he got through that intersection, the defendant crashed into him, crippling him forever. The defense's excuse is that Jimmy Green was going too slow, waiting too long at the stop sign. We do not know exactly how many seconds Jimmy was stopped at that stop sign. Was five seconds too long? Ten seconds? If Jimmy were stopped at that sign for fifteen seconds, would the defendant have been justified in peeling out as he did? Was he reasonable in burning the rubber from the tires of his car in an effort to gain the right-of-way? Perhaps Jimmy could tell him how much time is too long when you are forever trapped in a crippled body.

Liability of the Employer

An employer's vicarious or direct liability for his driver's negligence is best exemplified by the professional truck driver. The following capsulized arguments therefore focus primarily on a defendant-trucking company, although many apply equally to other defendant-employers.

Respondeat superior. In dealing with vicarious liability, it is essential to explain the concept of "course and scope" of employment to the jurors. An effective argument will simply convey to the jurors this message: the employer is responsible for its employee's negligence when the employee is driving on the job for the employer's benefit. Although this concept must be presented during the opening statement (and sometimes as early as voir dire), it should be reiterated in closing argument if course and scope is at issue. Blend evidence of the employee's compensation, route of travel, time of travel, purpose of travel, and final destination sequentially with the incidents that gave rise to the collision. Further, to the extent necessary, make the jurors aware that return trips, minor detours, and similar accommodations short of a deviation are included within the concept of course and scope of employment.

The defendant-employer will often stipulate that the defendant-employee was within his course and scope of employment. One commonly encountered defense in the course-and-scope area, however, is deviation. The defendant-employer will contend that the employee-driver had deviated from his course and scope of employment at the time of his collision with the plaintiff. In the typical scenario, the employee has been furnished a motor vehicle by his employer and has a wreck, but the company defends its case on the grounds of deviation. Consider the following argument in the situation where deviation is the only issue regarding scope of employment:

> When you retire to the jury room to decide the questions that are given to you by Her Honor, you will have to decide whether or not the defendant was acting within the scope of his employment at the time his eighteen-wheeler demolished Joe Brown's car. When you read the definition that goes along with that question, you will realize that this issue all boils down to just one thing: Was the defendant driving on the job for the Morton Truck Company? The defense has argued long and hard about how Mr. Flint deviated from his employment because he had driven some fifteen minutes out of the way to stop by his sister's house when this tragedy occurred.
>
> The defense has focused on fifteen minutes of Mr. Flint's trip, but they have failed to talk about the other ten days of his journey.

When Mr. Flint left Dallas on July 1, he was employed by the Morton Truck Company. You now know from the evidence that Mr. Flint was to drive from Dallas to California, pick up a load of computer equipment, and bring it back to Dallas. He drove a Morton Company truck on this haul, a truck that was owned by Morton Truck Company and was furnished by Morton Truck Company. For every night's lodging, Mr. Flint was reimbursed by the Morton Truck Company. He was also reimbursed for his traveling expenses, including his gasoline and his meals. The particular route he drove to California and back was one that had been assigned to him by the Morton Truck Company. In essence, the entire venture was for the benefit of Morton Truck Company.

But when Mr. Flint was nearing Dallas on his return trip, he decided to stop by his sister's house in order to sleep an hour or two. He exited the freeway and drove for about ten minutes along Farm-to-Market Road 501. You know from the evidence that Mr. Flint was very tired. He had a long layover in Los Angeles while waiting for the computer equipment to be loaded onto the truck. And so he had driven nonstop, without sleep, for almost twenty hours. You have also heard that Mr. Flint had made up that time, and he was still on schedule—still expecting to arrive in Dallas later that afternoon on July 10th. A few miles away from his sister's house, Mr. Flint fell asleep at the wheel and ended Joe Brown's life forever.

Mr. Flint's detour cost Joe Brown his life. But that's all it was—a *detour*. Sure, he took a break to catch a nap at his sister's house. A few hours of sleep would have enabled him to finish his haul for the Morton Company that day, would have served his employer. But could he really have been deviating from his job, as the defense suggests to you, when he was still loaded down with computer equipment, still tired from not having slept for almost two days in order to arrive on time in Dallas? How can the defense actually say that this truck driver, whose last ten days had been spent almost entirely behind a steering wheel, was not driving for their company at the time the Morton truck swerved into the opposite lane and crushed Joe Brown's car in a head-on collision? How can they suggest that fifteen minutes—for their ultimate benefit—out of a ten-day journey equals a deviation?

Notwithstanding the issue of deviation, when other elements of the scope-of-employment question are at issue, modify the argument accordingly. For instance, in addition to deviation, the defendant may assert that its employee was not acting in furtherance of his employer's objectives or was not accomplishing a work-related objective. Once again, using rhetorical questions is particularly appropriate for these types of issues.

You now know from the evidence that when Allen Banks was hired by the Parker Company he was assigned a company car. The car was furnished to him with the understanding that he would drive it only to and from work and to his various on-site job locations. You now know from the evidence that Mr. Banks was permitted to use this car only as long as he worked for the Parker Company. During his employment, he also had an expense account. The Parker Company would reimburse Mr. Banks at the end of each month for the gasoline he purchased, as well as any maintenance the car required.

How can the Parker Company now say that he was not within the scope of his employment on the day he rear-ended Sarah Smith's car? It is true that Mr. Banks was on his lunch hour at the time this tragedy occurred. But did the Parker Company actually think that when Mr. Banks was on a job site, his breaks would not be part of the scope of his employment? Mr. Banks was paid on a salaried basis, not by the hour. So he was paid for the time he spent on breaks, including lunch. In order to work the long hours that the Parker Company demanded of him, Mr. Banks had to eat. And the company knew this. They know that an employee doesn't work well on an empty stomach. It was to their *benefit* that employees like Mr. Banks would stop and eat lunch.

Did the Parker Company really expect Mr. Banks to leave his car at the job site and flag down a taxicab or bus, or hitchhike to a nearby restaurant? You now know from the evidence that these job sites were located on the outskirts of the city, several miles from any place to eat lunch. Are the defendants suggesting that Mr. Banks departed from his scope of employment simply because he did not bring his lunch with him on the day this tragedy occurred?

Negligent Hiring. In a negligent hiring case, the plaintiff's lawyer often possesses evidence that can be used to further the victim's cause. All of us who drive on freeways or highways know the danger presented by an incompetent trucker. We are concerned because we can appreciate the grave consequences associated with a careless driver encased within twenty tons of moving metal. The jurors will therefore realize that an employer should investigate and determine the competency of its drivers. Moreover, the victim's attorney can effectively transfer blame in the jurors' minds from the incompetent truck driver to his employer—the one that negligently sanctioned his work. Evidence of the driver's negligence, when combined with rhetorical questions and embedded commands, constitutes a powerful weapon.

When these steel and metal monsters come thundering down our roads and highways, don't we have the right to expect that their drivers are qualified? Does the responsibility lie only with the trucker, or should the company that furnishes the driver with its truck also have to be responsible? The Zane Trucklines would have you believe that it does not. This trucking company has told you that its employment application forms ask about a driver's previous employment and prior tickets. But what good is the form if no use is made of it? If the form is merely tossed into a file along with several hundreds of other papers, is it of any use?

You now know from the evidence that Zane Trucklines never called this truck driver's previous employers, never even sent a letter. What steps did they take to ensure that their drivers were competent and safety-conscious? "Look at the employment application. If it looks okay, toss it in a file cabinet. Check and make sure the person has a valid Texas commercial driver's license. And, then, give him a one-week training course."

How could Zane have been acting as a reasonable trucking company in this case? They never spoke with the four previous employers that Mr. Grange had over the last two years. The fact that he had driven for four different trucking companies in the last two years *alone* should have alerted Zane. What effort would it have taken to check out Mr. Grange's credentials? A couple of ten-minute phone calls? A letter or two with a twenty-five-cent postage stamp? It was only during the investigation of this lawsuit that Zane realized for the first time that "hey, this man may not be a competent driver." Only at the time of this case did Zane wake up and smell the coffee. Their attitude before now was, "Don't worry about it." Don't worry about this driver who has had four tickets and caused three wrecks over the past two years. "We will only worry about it if he hurts someone."

Ladies and gentlemen, if we yield and accept the arguments and contentions made by Zane Trucklines in this case, we will be doing nothing but making our freeways sanctuaries for the irresponsible and reckless. Our highways will then become safe harbors for those who insist that they have a special privilege not to obey our laws, to use less than appropriate care in operating these dinosaurs that roam our streets. We, on the other hand, will find that our freeways are jungles and that we, the prey, travel them at our own risk.

Negligent entrustment. A beneficial argument in the negligent entrustment case closely parallels that of the negligent hiring situation. The main difference, of course, is that in the negligent entrustment case the employer's actual or constructive knowledge may be more easily proved. The theory is simply that since the driver is already an employee, his employer should be conscious of, and familiar with, his skills and abilities. In such a case, focus your argument more heavily on the relationship between the employer and the employee. Many times, you may effectively convey the notion that the driver's conduct merely reflects the attitudes of his employer.

Of all the drivers who should be careful, safe, and law-abiding, it should be the professional truck driver. After all, he operates a rig that dwarfs our vehicles by its massive size and, by its sheer weight and bulk, represents a unique threat to everyone's safety. These mobile mountains of steel pull chemicals that can explode, steel that can tumble off and crush victims, and hazardous waste products that can destroy the human lung by merely being inhaled. For this reason, the professional truck driver is supposed to be uniquely qualified to operate his company's truck. He is given special permits and special licenses and is supposed to be examined and tested carefully by his employer before he is released to operate these modern-day dinosaurs on the highway. In this case, ladies and gentlemen, we have seen that, because of the unique relationship among the owners of a trucking company, its supervisory personnel, and its driver, the driver of a truck is not merely one individual. He does not represent one person; he represents many. He reflects the attitude of the owners of the company toward public responsibility and safety. In short, he reflects the attitude of his supervisors toward public welfare.

You now know what happens when a trucking company does not respect the safety of the citizens who drive on our highways. When the trucking company will not maintain proper supervision over its drivers, the relationship between the two damages our society. In this case, when the Alpha Truck Company would not review the performance of its drivers or their safety skills, both company and driver became a menace to society. Several excuses have been offered in this case why Alpha did not know of Mr. Stone's three previous wrecks in the past year. One of the excuses was that Mr. Stone was hiding these facts from Alpha and that Alpha did not know or have reason to know of Mr. Stone's record of careless driving. How difficult would it have been for someone at Alpha to have periodically checked with the Department of Public Safety on any tickets given to its drivers? How hard would it have been to have made periodic checks of its drivers' records? After all, is this not part of a trucking company's primary function?

We have seen from the evidence in this case a change from the traditional image of the trucker. Years ago he was considered a "knight of the road." The attitude that trucking companies had, that their supervisors promoted, and that their drivers carried out led us to believe that most of these people were kind, considerate, helpful, and law-abiding. That image has been tarnished and polluted. Our view today is no longer of knights of the road but, rather, of modern-day highwaymen. But unlike the highwaymen of old who, by pistol and at sword point, took our watches, wallets, and purses, these modern-day highwaymen take that which is beyond value and

> measure. They hurtle by us at excessive speeds, masked behind their iron, steel, and rubber. They are faceless, nameless, formless individuals who sit nine and ten feet in the air, who block out the sun when they pass us, and who insist on their privileges but refuse to recognize our rights. By their conduct they demonstrate that it is their belief that they have the right to the whole road. If they could do so today, David and Susan Thomas would tell Alpha and Mr. Stone, "You can have the whole road, you can have the whole freeway, you can even have the right-of-way at a red light; just please give us our son back."

Negligent maintenance and repair. If the employer's negligent upkeep of its vehicle has caused or contributed to the plaintiff's injuries, you will once again have the opportunity to castigate the employer's conduct. If you emphasize that the cost of such maintenance or repair is an integral part of the employer's business, the issue of responsibility should pose no problem. A litany of analogies can be created for this situation. For instance, the following analogy depicts the jury as a "brake" on irresponsible conduct:

> Our system of justice envisions a jury serving as a brake on the excesses of irresponsibility, whether they be those of an individual, a corporation, or an industry. This brake is much like the brakes of a truck. It is to maintain order and to control the speed and safety at which business activities are carried out. How many times have we seen what we feel are excesses in the trucking industry? Trucks that are operated unsafely because of defective tires and equipment. Trucks that are overloaded. Trucks that are not properly maintained, so that their cargo spills over highways, endangering our motorists. This jury serves as a brake on that type of conduct. We can certainly slow it down by your verdict, if not stop it altogether. What a shame it would be if we did not use our brakes and committed the same error that this trucking company did in negligently repairing the brakes on the truck it placed on our highways and roads.

Negligence Per Se

In a case in which the defendant-driver has run a stop sign or red light or has driven on the wrong side of the road, the defense will usually either stipulate liability and try the damages issues or argue that the plaintiff was also responsible. Damages are treated in subsequent chapters of this book, and comparative responsibility is discussed in chapter 16. A few comments regarding comparative responsibility are appropriate here.

The plaintiff's conduct must be distinguished from the defendant's egregious negligence. Pointing out that it was the defendant and not the plaintiff who "broke the law" will naturally shift the target of blame in the jurors' minds to the defendant. You can also argue that the defense realizes this fact and that its only hope is to try to have the jurors apportion some percentage of negligence to the plaintiff; by properly making this argument, you may help the jurors to recognize that assigning a percentage of responsibility may affect the plaintiff's overall recovery, without actually telling the jurors the effect of their answers.

> When the court submits the questions of fault in this case, His Honor does not inquire whether the defendant was negligent, careless, or reckless. That is because if the defendant ran the red light (and by that we mean either did not stop for the red light or, having stopped, still proceeded into the intersection when the light was red) he is at fault. The reason for that is that we have a statute, a law governing such conduct. No one can seriously argue that if he ran the red light it was not a proximate cause of this collision. The defendant's only hope is to try to pin some of the responsibility for this tragedy on the plaintiff. Make her responsible for a part of the damages. Ten percent, twenty percent, thirty percent—we don't care. Just give us some relief from the responsibility for the tragedy that we caused.
>
> When we attempt to assign responsibility in a case such as this, isn't it fair to inquire whether either of the drivers violated this law? Obviously the defendant did. Obviously the plaintiff did not, as you can see from the court's instructions as well as the evidence you have heard.
>
> When the defendant entered the intersection on the red light, this was a conscious decision that he made—whether the defendant proceeded into the intersection without stopping or, having stopped, went on—it was a decision that he made while knowing it was a legal violation. In that split second, the defendant suggests that the plaintiff should have acted differently, should have seen him sooner, should have done *something*. Although the plaintiff was not the one who "broke the law," the defendant now suggests that Mrs. Starr should have done something extraordinary to avoid the tragedy that he set in motion. We submit that it is patently unfair and unjust, after Mrs. Starr has been injured and her young child killed, for the defendant to suggest that "yes, after all, we did break the law; we are responsible in that regard, but somehow the plaintiff should bear part of that loss."

Proximate Cause

The concepts of cause in fact and foreseeability must also be simplified for the jurors. Many times, you may do so by direct evidence and demonstrative evidence, such as charts, blowups, photographs, and accident reports. As explained in chapter 16, you must logically paint a picture of your case in terms of time and sequence of events with the use of key points of evidence. Attempting to argue all the evidence will inevitably confuse the jurors. Argue and reiterate your strongest evidence. Because of the infinite variety of types of argument that might be appropriate in this respect, it is impossible to detail any patterns of argument. Your main goal should be to display your strongest points of causation in repetitive fashion. If creatively argued, almost any evidence of causation may be used. For example, envision a case where there is no direct evidence that the defendant's negligence caused the collision. Further, no circumstantial evidence of skid marks, point of impact, or vehicular damage tends to incriminate the defendant. Perhaps the sole evidence of proximate cause in this most undesirable situation, other than the plaintiff's testimony, is an accident report that appears to be partially incomplete. With that situation in mind, here we go.

> Ladies and gentlemen of the jury, we told you at the beginning of this trial, on the voir dire examination, that we would not be here more than a day or two and that you would have to decide who caused this collision without any eyewitnesses. At that time, however, we also told you that a preponderance of the evidence, a slight tipping of the scales of justice, would tell you that the defendant caused this needless collision that crushed John Parker's arm.
>
> We also mentioned that our proof would be with the type of evidence the law calls "circumstantial evidence." [*Discuss circumstantial evidence instruction.*] This simply means that for John to prove that the defendant ran the red light in this case, we are not required to produce any eyewitnesses to this fact. Indeed, even if we had, the defense would have been arguing that it was not sufficient. I believe you can see from their attitude and demeanor that if we had produced a witness sitting behind the defendant's car who had seen her go through the red light, the defense would have argued that such a witness could not see well, was not paying attention, or for some other reason was not being truthful or credible.
>
> The law recognizes that there are few accidents, if any, that are witnessed by a nun with perfect twenty-twenty eyesight, who was situated in just the right position and was doing nothing but observing the light and the defendant. This is the reason that we have the "circumstantial evidence" instruction. Because, you see, circumstantial evidence may be the strongest evidence of all.
>
> So it is with this accident report filed by the police officer who questioned the defendant after John had been rushed to the hospital. Why were there so many questions left unanswered on this form? Question: "Was the traffic light facing you red at the time you entered the intersection?" No answer. Why didn't the defendant

answer? Why not at least say something? Was it because the defendant didn't know, couldn't remember, or just didn't want to say?

Question: "What did your vehicle do before the collision?" No answer. Why was nothing said? I'll tell you a good reason. When you don't answer a question, it certainly cannot be said later in court that your answer was a lie. Wasn't this the strategy of the defense? Keep the facts broad. Keep everything wide open until trial, and then suddenly pick out the plaintiff and point the finger at him. Why select John? Well, he was the most seriously injured, his damages were extraordinary, and no one else could say anything to the contrary.

The preponderance of the evidence, both direct and circumstantial, establishes that the defendant caused this needless collision. [*At this point, discuss in detail your version of the wreck, referring to charts and graphs and so forth.*]

Arguments Peculiar to Automobile Injuries

A detailed discussion of damages is presented in chapters 22 through 27 of this work. Many arguments regarding injuries from an automobile collision, however, are closely connected with, or at least tangential to, the issues of liability—usually because the effect of a driver's negligence is part of a continuous episode of liability. Consequently, such arguments may be made to end a discussion of liability on a "high note," before any detailed argument of damages. A couple of the more popular arguments of this kind follow.

Burning Memories

In this case, it is not the hell of the flesh we must understand, it is the hell of the mind. It is not the burning and scarring of the body that is so vital to understand, it is the burning and scarring of the soul. As the blind poet John Milton once said, "The mind is its own place, and in itself / Can make a heaven of hell, a hell of heaven."[4]

We have no difficulty proving the injuries and pain that Ernie sustained. We have photographs. But we all have difficulty understanding the hell that his parents were cast into. We cannot take a photograph of the mind.

I did not really appreciate the effect a tragedy like this can have on a parent until I began to understand what is presented here. Every

---

4. PARADISE LOST bk. 1, ll. 254-55.

raging fire, every car that explodes, every tremendous car crash brings back to these parents the memory of their dead son and the senselessness and needlessness of his tragedy.

A few days before we began this trial, I went out to dinner with my family. We went to a nice restaurant. At the bar portion of the restaurant they had a television set on. They were showing a Rockets basketball game. No one was really watching the television except for a couple of ladies who were sitting at the bar. Everyone else was enjoying their supper. The next time I looked up, the television screen was filled with flame and fire. One scene after another of automobiles crashing into each other and fire spewing out was flashed on the television. I do not know whether they changed the channel or whether this was just a commercial. Yet I do know that, from the evidence we have heard, such an experience would have devastated these parents.

When you lose a son, as they have, there are many constant reminders. His room. His pictures. His things. But these parents have a peculiar reminder. Every time an eighteen-wheeler speeds by them on the freeway, they are reminded. Every time they see on television conflagration, fire, explosions, and cars crashing into each other, they are reminded. Every time they pass the Dolan Road overpass, they are reminded—reminded of burning memories that will haunt them forever.

Impact of Steel

When we made our opening statements to you, we told you of the severe impact that occurred when the defendant's truck smashed into Jane Hogan's little Datsun. Until the evidence was presented, however, I doubt that any of us could really appreciate the horror of that scene. You now know that when the defendant was not paying attention—when he flew over the overpass at more than sixty miles per hour—his truck demolished Jane's car, which was stopped at the end of a long line of traffic. You now know that the impact of that collision was so great that it tore the motor mounts from Jane's car. Her car was struck so suddenly and violently that it literally jumped more than one hundred feet beyond the far side of the intersection. Think of that distance—*one hundred feet*. Try to visualize being in a vehicle that is struck by such a tremendous force. When Jane's car was rear-ended, the defendant's truck actually crushed more than half of her car and catapulted it into the cars ahead of her. You now know that this tremendous blow paralyzed Jane from the waist down. The reckless impact of steel on steel—ending life, as she knew it, forever.

Defenses

Plaintiff's Responsibility

The general concepts of arguing comparative responsibility, discussed in detail in chapter 16, can be applied to virtually all personal injury cases. In an automobile case, however, some specific matters deserve attention.

In responding to the defendant's assertion that the plaintiff was negligent, you must compare and contrast the conduct of the defendant-driver with that of the plaintiff and emphasize that the defendant has the burden of proof on the plaintiff's negligence. It is equally important, however, to explain that the plaintiff had no legal obligation to anticipate or expect the negligent conduct of the defendant. Depending on the particular facts of the case, you may want to stress one or more of the following responses:

> The plaintiff has no legal obligation to anticipate the negligent conduct of another, since this occurrence is unexpected. Obviously, if we all had to drive in anticipation of the negligence of others, we would hardly be able to get anywhere. The law says we have the right to expect that others will obey the law, just as we do.

. . . . .

> Proper lookout is defined as that of an ordinarily prudent person. It is not the lookout that the extraordinary person might keep. We do not expect or demand that our drivers have bionic vision.

. . . . .

> Physical obstructions to the plaintiff's visibility [*discuss obstructions*] existed. Certain conditions [*specify*] limited his ability to keep a proper lookout.

. . . . .

> Even if you find that the plaintiff did not keep a proper lookout, he cannot be held partially responsible for his injuries unless this improper lookout was a proximate cause of the damages.

. . . . .

Given the speed of the respective vehicles and/or the plaintiff's ability to see the defendant's vehicle immediately before the collision [*discuss reaction time*],[5] could anyone believe that the plaintiff could have avoided this collision?

. . . . .

The question is not whether the plaintiff might have swerved the car so that the impact would have been different. The question is not whether the plaintiff might have applied the brakes a split-second earlier and lessened the impact. The defendant has not offered one shred of evidence that if either of these things had occurred, the damages sustained by the plaintiff would have been any less.

. . . . .

It is the defendant's burden to prove that the plaintiff was not keeping the lookout of an ordinary person and that, if he had been keeping it, the collision would have been avoided. If the defendant has not proved this by a preponderance of the evidence, then he has not proved his defense—he has not established a basis for you to hold the plaintiff responsible for a percentage of the damages the plaintiff sustained.

Unavoidable Accident

Generally, the defense argument of unavoidable accident is based on one of three factual sources: weather conditions (wet pavement, icy roads, fog, and so forth), roadway obstructions or conditions (animal crossings, oil spills, and so forth), and automobile conditions (tire blowouts, steering column malfunctions, and so forth). In all three situations, it is appropriate to make several common points. First, explain that there are very few truly "unavoidable accidents." A vignette or two may illustrate this fact to the jury. Second, emphasize the length of time that the defendant knew of the condition he contends was the genesis of the collision. Obviously, the longer he knew of the danger, the greater is the likelihood that he was negligent in failing to compensate for the condition. You may want to rally your argument around the precautionary measures taken by the defendant, especially when other drivers

---

5. As a matter of law, the time for a normal driver to react to danger under normal conditions is three-fourths of a second. Mobil Oil Co. v. Dodd, 528 S.W.2d 297 (Tex. Civ. App.—Corpus Christi 1975, writ ref'd n.r.e.).

encountered the condition but were not similarly affected. Given these precepts, you can then explain the instruction[6] on unavoidable accident stated in the court's charge and argue the rhetorical.

> The next excuse you heard from the defense was that of "unavoidable accident." They tell you that the collision that maimed Betty Meyers was not the defendant's fault, because he could not avoid it. In other words, what the defendant means is that "it was the rain's fault."
>
> That defense takes the cake, ladies and gentlemen. The tragic collision on the I-59 freeway could have been avoided by one simple act on the defendant's part—pulling over to the side of the freeway and waiting for the rain to slacken up. But what do we hear? "Blame it on the rain; it was the rain's fault." When you consider this defense in the jury deliberation room, you will see the court's definition of an unavoidable accident. It states, "An event *not proximately* caused by the negligence of any party to it."
>
> We know that the defendant's conduct caused this horrible wreck. The only question remaining is whether the defendant was negligent. We discussed negligence at the beginning of this trial, and you know that all negligence means is that a person did not do something that a reasonable person would have done. I submit to you that the defendant was negligent for several reasons. You remember on cross-examination that he said he had been driving in the rain for about twenty miles before the wreck. The defendant said he had to stop or apply his brakes at least thirty to forty times for that twenty miles because it was raining so hard. You now know that the defendant could not see Betty before he crashed into her. And we haven't faulted the defendant because he could not see. We have never expected the defendant to have extraordinary vision. What we have expected, however, is that the defendant would have enough common sense to pull over and wait for the rain to clear, as Betty had done, instead of barreling through it in a reckless and negligent manner.
>
> Perhaps the argument that this collision was unavoidable would not be so ridiculous if the facts were different. I would have to concur with the defendant, for instance, if the thunderstorm had poured down just moments before this collision. If the rain had started abruptly and he did not see Betty Meyers while slowing down and trying to pull over, this case *would* be different. But how can the defense say this accident was unavoidable under the present

6. *See* 1 STATE BAR OF TEXAS, *supra* note 2, PJC 3.04 (2d ed. 1987).

facts? Would a reasonably prudent driver continue to drive for twenty miles when it is raining so hard that he can only see five to ten feet of pavement in front of him? When other drivers are pulling over because they can't see either, is it reasonable to try to beat the odds? Of course not. We all know that we can't drive in dangerous weather conditions with impunity. When we know that it's raining too hard to see, when the roads are terribly slick, and when other cars are pulling off to the side of the road, we cannot blame the rain for the catastrophes that we cause. Such a defense makes about as much sense as the actions of the defendant in maiming Betty Meyers forever.

Sudden Emergency

There are essentially two ways to attack the sudden-emergency defense, depending on the facts of the case. In most cases the defense arises because of the sudden turn, lane change, or stopping of a third person that causes the defendant to collide with the plaintiff's vehicle. These situations can hardly be described as "true" sudden emergencies, simply because the defendant's negligence played a major role in producing the emergency situation. For example, in a typical "rear-ender" case, the defendant's car may have been approaching an overpass. After reaching the crest of the overpass and beginning his descent, the defendant immediately finds a line of vehicles backed up in a traffic jam. He has no time to avoid the collision, *mainly because he was following the cars in front of him too closely*. Under such circumstances, there is no doubt that the sudden emergency did exist; the question is whether the situation was a product of the defendant's own negligence. In such a scenario, you can effectively argue that the defendant's negligence caused the emergency.

A different approach is required, however, when the "true" sudden emergency occurred through no fault or negligence of the defendant. For instance, if a deer suddenly darts out in front of the defendant's vehicle, an emergency situation is suddenly present. The driver swerves to avoid hitting the animal and instead collides with the plaintiff's vehicle. In this factual context, your argument should have a different focus: you can no longer contest the validity of the emergency but must instead address the propriety of the defendant's actions upon being confronted with the emergency. In other words, you may concede that the situation was due to a sudden emergency but point out that the defendant should have applied his brakes and swerved onto the shoulder of the road instead of crossing into the plaintiff's lane. Moreover, when the true sudden-emergency defense is raised, a portion of the court's instruction[7] becomes particularly salient to your argument—the part of the

7. *Id.* PJC 3.03.

instruction that states that the defendant's conduct in an emergency is not negligence "if, after such emergency arises, he acts as a person of ordinary prudence would have acted under the same or similar circumstances."[8] Stress this fact to the jurors if evidence supports the defense argument of sudden emergency. Often, as in the hypothetical situation noted above, though the event may indeed present an emergency, the defendant's negligent conduct will still be the proximate cause of the plaintiff's injury. To illustrate this technique in the true sudden-emergency case, consider the following:

> Ladies and gentlemen, the defense has told you that Mr. Jackson was acting in an emergency situation when he swerved to avoid the large dog that unexpectedly darted in front of him on the I-10 freeway. The evidence indicates that there was indeed an emergency at this time. When you decide this case, you will notice His Honor's instruction about emergencies. I want you to look carefully at the last part of that instruction. It says that a person will not be negligent in an emergency situation *if* he acts as a person of *ordinary* prudence would have in that emergency. What this means, ladies and gentlemen, is that we always have certain duties, even when we are in an emergency situation. You now know from the evidence that Mr. Jackson did not own up to his duty—one that was easy to accomplish. Mr. Jackson was negligent by swerving into Bart Connors *because a reasonable person would simply have applied his brakes, pulled off onto the shoulder of the road, and not have harmed anyone*. Can it be reasonable to forget the cars approaching from the opposite direction and to veer head-on into their path?

Other Defense Arguments

If the defendant's argument raises other, less frequently encountered defensive issues, such as "sole proximate cause," the proper response should follow the general principles that have been demonstrated throughout this discussion.

Circumstantial Evidence and the "Disputed Red Light"

One of the most common types of automobile cases involves a disputed red light: the plaintiff will testify that the defendant ran the red light, while the defendant claims the plaintiff ran it. The trial of the case usually becomes a swearing match. Sometimes the plaintiff will be fortunate because an eyewitness will testify in his favor—that the defendant ran the red light. Of course, the defense may have two or three witnesses who state the contrary.

---

8. *Id.*

The problem in such cases is obvious: the jury may disregard the plaintiff's version of the collision because a greater number of witnesses have corroborated the defendant's story. You must certainly stress the credibility of the plaintiff's eyewitness, but don't overlook the fact that circumstantial evidence[9] in the form of physical facts may provide your strongest argument.

In this regard, the actual observations and findings of the investigating officers become particularly critical. That direct evidence will usually locate one or more of the following: the area of damage to the vehicles, the place in which the vehicles came to rest immediately following the collision, the points of skid marks, and the final resting place of any debris dislodged from the vehicles at the time of collision. To use this information, it is vital to understand the general principles of accident reconstruction and dynamics.[10]

Consider the following as a fairly typical scenario: a collision occurs between the plaintiff's vehicle and the defendant's delivery van at the intersection of streets *X* and *Y*. The defendant's story is that he was headed south when he pulled up to the intersection and stopped at the red light facing him on *X* Street. He also states that when the light turned green, he proceeded into the intersection. Thus, it is his contention that the plaintiff ran the red light and collided with his van. In contrast, the plaintiff testifies that the light facing him from an easterly direction on *Y* Street was green when he proceeded into the intersection. He further states that the defendant ran the red light and collided with his vehicle.

Assume further that, while the defendant has two eyewitnesses who state that the plaintiff ran the red light, the plaintiff has no such eyewitness testimony. The direct evidence of the investigating officers demonstrates that the defendant's van was damaged on the front right side and that it came to a resting place approximately thirty-five feet across the intersection on the right shoulder of the road. With this evidence, the plaintiff's expert witness in accident reconstruction is able to calculate the defendant's speed at the time of impact. His opinion is that the speed was approximately twenty-five miles per hour. From this testimony, it is apparent that the defendant could not have

---

9. Under the Texas Pattern Jury Charges, the term *circumstantial evidence* is defined as follows: "A fact may be established by direct evidence or by circumstantial evidence or both. A fact is established by direct evidence when provided by documentary evidence or by witnesses who saw the act done or heard the words spoken. A fact is established by circumstantial evidence when it may be fairly and reasonably inferred from other facts proved." *Id.* PJC 1.07.

10. The basic principles and formulas involved in the field of accident reconstruction can be found in 1 H. PHILO, LAWYERS DESK REFERENCE §§ 6:16-:19 (7th ed. 1987). Additionally, this work lists various books and articles in the field of accident reconstruction. As noted therein, one "good source" to consult in this field is the "Summary of Accident Investigations," distributed by the Bureau of Motor Carrier Safety, U.S. Dept. of Transportation, Federal Highway Administration. *Id.* § 6:19, at 701-02. Concerning the use of expert testimony regarding accident reconstruction, see generally 11 P. KELLY, BLASHFIELD AUTOMOBILE LAW AND PRACTICE § 431.3 (rev. 3d ed. 1977 & Supp. 1988).

stopped at the intersection before the collision, as he claims he did. The point of impact was approximately ten feet into the intersection, and it would have been impossible for the defendant's car to have accelerated from zero to twenty-five miles per hour within the space of ten feet. Hence, this is circumstantial evidence that the defendant never stopped at the red light. It is evidence that can be "fairly and reasonably inferred" from direct and expert testimony. As a practical matter, this evidence is more probative than that of the eyewitnesses for the defense; its credibility cannot be impeached. Within this framework of the evidence, emphasize the significance of circumstantial evidence and explain why it should be given more credence than the eyewitness testimony.

> How long did the eyewitnesses, Mr. Jones and Ms. Grayson, have to observe this wreck? A second or two? Does a split-second glimpse of a wreck outweigh cold hard facts? We all know from the evidence that Mr. Jones and Ms. Grayson are fine, reputable people. They have told you exactly what they *thought* they saw. But it would have been physically impossible for this wreck to have occurred as they have described it to you.
>
> The defendant could not have stopped at the red light, given these physical facts. The circumstantial evidence tells you that it was impossible for this to occur. While the plaintiff may be outnumbered by the defendant's witnesses, their testimony is not as strong as circumstantial evidence. And this is true in many cases. Because circumstantial evidence cannot be contradicted, it is stronger than direct evidence in cases like this. The reason is that, unlike the failings of human recollection, circumstantial evidence will never change.
>
> Witnesses' perceptions and memories, however, do change. We have all heard stories of innocent people being sent to jail—not because of circumstantial evidence—but because of eyewitness testimony. A witness was simply wrong or mistaken about what he saw. Which would you feel more comfortable with? Testimony by a person who says, "I saw Mr. Smith shoot Mr. Brown," or evidence that Mr. Smith owned a gun and stated that he would shoot Mr. Brown, Mr. Brown was found in his house dead from a bullet wound, Mr. Smith was stopped while leaving that house, and a spent pistol shell was found in his pocket?[11]
>
> We all know there is less room for error when such facts exist. And so it is with this case. You now know that the defendant was going twenty-five miles per hour at the point of impact. You know

11. Analogies can be very effective in arguing circumstantial evidence. See generally ch. 12.

that the impact occurred about ten feet into the intersection. So finally, you now know that the defendant could not have reached a speed of twenty-five miles per hour within that ten feet, if he had stopped at the red light like he says he did. From that evidence, the only explanation is that the defendant negligently ran the red light and carelessly caused this wreck.

Arguments for Specific Plaintiffs in Automobile Cases

Passengers

The type of argument desired in the passenger case will, as a practical matter, initially depend on whether the plaintiff-passenger's suit is against a third-party driver or his host-driver. Although there are no longer any statutory distinctions between such cases,[12] there are certain pragmatic differences. The primary difference is, of course, that the host had some previous relationship with the passenger, whereas a third-party driver did not. If the plaintiff was a passenger, there was some degree of acquaintance between him and the driver, whether it was based on hospitality or on a carrier-for-hire situation. By contrast, the third-party driver did not occupy the status of a good samaritan; he and the plaintiff were total strangers. For that reason, an argument against the host should be premised on the plaintiff's innocence, the plaintiff's reliance on his host-driver's care (to keep a proper lookout, to operate the vehicle prudently, and so forth), and the defendant's exclusive control over the operation of the vehicle. Obviously certain exceptions to this principle exist if the plaintiff knew that his host was an incompetent, reckless, or drunk driver.[13]

For cases involving a third-party driver, however, the previously discussed arguments in this chapter regarding the liability of a driver or employer can be used. Even more importantly, the conduct of the plaintiff, who *usually* played no part in causing the wreck, can be contrasted with that of the

---

12. In Whitworth v. Bynum, 699 S.W.2d 194, 197–98 (Tex. 1985), the Texas Supreme Court held that the Texas Automobile Guest Statute (now codified at TEX. CIV. PRAC. & REM. CODE ANN. § 72.001 (Vernon 1985)) was unconstitutional. Before that time, the statute precluded a negligence claim by a gratuitous guest who was a *relative* of his host-driver. *Id*.

13. *See, e.g.*, Sargent v. Williams, 258 S.W.2d 787 (Tex. 1953); Schiller v. Rice, 246 S.W.2d 607 (Tex. 1952), respectively, which state that the passenger may be contributorily negligent in such situations. In a suit by a guest against the driver, the negligence of the driver will not be imputed to the plaintiff-passenger even if both were engaged in a joint enterprise. *See, e.g.*, LeSage v. Pryor, 154 S.W.2d 446 (Tex. 1941). In the ordinary case the guest is under no duty to stay awake in order to guard his safety. McMillian v. Sims, 112 S.W.2d 793 (Tex. Civ. App.—Galveston 1937, writ dism'd by agr.).

defendant.[14] The following two arguments respectively depict these techniques in a suit against a host-driver and a third-party defendant-driver.

> When we began this case we told you that we expected these two defendants to point a finger of accusation at each other for this grave collision. And that's what they have done. You have seen Mr. Donaldson blame Mrs. Franks and, of course, Mrs. Franks has said that Mr. Donaldson was responsible for this wreck. What we did not expect at the beginning of this trial, though, was that Mr. Donaldson would say that even if he was negligent in causing this collision, it was partly the fault of the plaintiff, Pat Sims. This defendant would have you believe that an innocent passenger controlled the driving of his truck as if she had a remote control. He says that Mrs. Sims guided him, told him the manner in which to operate his vehicle, gave him directions, and guided him through the neighborhood.
>
> After hearing all the evidence in this case, I know you can appreciate the weakness of this defense. When Mrs. Sim's car broke down at the grocery store, she accepted a ride from Mr. Donaldson, a man who lived only a few blocks away. It was evening, and Pat wanted to get home, but she obviously was not in as big a hurry as was Mr. Donaldson. Wheeling around the corners, this way and that, Mr. Donaldson runs head-on into Mrs. Franks, only a block away from Pat's home. Pat is hurled against the glass windshield, which breaks and slices the nerves in her face and arms. Notwithstanding his actions, Mr. Donaldson wants you to believe that Pat Sims was responsible for her own scars, her own permanent nerve damage.
>
> Remember one of the questions that Mr. Donaldson's attorney posed to Pat? "You saw the other car approaching from around the corner before Mr. Donaldson did, didn't you?" What motive could the defendant's attorney possibly have had in asking that question? The only possible incentive was to somehow imply that Pat Sims contributed to this collision. Think about how silly that is. Here we have a lady sitting alongside a man who is just as familiar with the neighborhood as she. Should she be expected to direct him in the operation of his truck? Is the lady responsible for the direction and movement of a truck that she was not even qualified to drive? She had no commercial license. She didn't know how to operate a manual transmission.

---

14. In a third-party suit, the driver's negligence will be imputed to the plaintiff-passenger if they were engaged in a joint enterprise. *See, e.g.*, LeSage v. Pryor, 134 S.W.2d 446 (Tex. 1941).

If the facts of the hypothetical case above are slightly changed so that the third party is the primary target of liability, the attorney could argue the following:

> That defense is a new one on me, ladies and gentlemen. When someone does not slow down at a yield sign and causes a wreck, they come into court and tell you that it was the fault of a passenger in the other car. Why does Mrs. Franks say that Pat Sims is to blame? I'll tell you one reason. She does not want to accept her responsibility. A preponderance of the evidence has proved that Mrs. Franks's negligence caused these terrible injuries to Pat Sims. But Mrs. Sims is no more responsible in this courtroom than she was on the day of that horrible wreck. The defense aptly demonstrates this fact because their line of attack is to blame first the other person who was driving and, if that fails, then blame the other person who was not driving.

Pedestrians

The arguments that should be given in a pedestrian case depend greatly on whether the plaintiff is an adult or a child.

Adult pedestrian. In the case involving an adult pedestrian, compare the duties that the parties owed toward one another. Although both parties had the obligation of keeping a proper lookout, the jury should be made to understand that the effects of a driver's negligence are certainly more egregious than those of the pedestrian. Additionally, it is imperative to discuss reaction time, especially if the plaintiff is alleged to have been negligent: simply relate that the pedestrian did not have time to evade the defendant's vehicle. You can reinforce the principle in the juror's minds by emphasizing the distance that a car will travel in a few seconds at a given rate of speed.

> What did the defendant expect Mrs. Samuels to do when he came barreling around the corner of Smith and Pease streets? Did he believe a seventy-two-year-old woman like Mrs. Samuels could suddenly leap across the crosswalk as, perhaps, Carl Lewis could? Was it reasonable for this defendant to have been wheeling a four-thousand-pound vehicle around an intersection such as this? We have heard the defendant's excuse. "Mrs. Samuels contributed to her crippling injuries because she entered the crosswalk on a wait signal." But could the defendant have really seen the crosswalk signal in a split-second before he crippled Mrs. Samuels?
>
> It is true that the defendant was not exceeding the speed limit at the time he turned the corner and rammed into Rose Samuels. However, ladies and gentlemen, he was negligent because common sense tells us that a reasonable person does not hurl his automobile

> around a corner such as this without knowing what may be on the other side. A reasonable person slows his vehicle down when making such a turn. He keeps a proper lookout as he makes a turn like this.
>
> You now know from the evidence that this reckless defendant was doing thirty miles an hour when he rounded that corner. His car traveled at least thirty-two feet before he hit his brakes. His car then skidded along another forty feet or so.[15] You now know the horror that Mrs. Samuels experienced in less than two seconds. Because that's all it took, ladies and gentlemen—not even two seconds. She heard the screeching of tires and turned her head, only to realize her utter helplessness. Is this how we respect our elders, or do they not have any right to walk in our cities? Should we succumb to the arguments made by this callous defendant, or do the rights of human flesh and soul outweigh those of a machine of steel?

Child pedestrian. If the victim is a child pedestrian, the care he was exercising is obviously less important. For example, in the typical child dart-out case, it is the unreasonableness of the defendant's conduct that must be considered. Given the child's perception at his particular age, how could he have been responsible through negligence? Although pedestrians have the duty to keep a proper lookout,[16] the jurors are not likely to consider the conduct of the child in the same light as that of the adult defendant.

> Can we still remember what it was like to be seven years old, ladies and gentlemen? What understanding did we have of the world about us? When we were coming home from school in the afternoon, anxious to play with our friends, and we ran across the street, what were we thinking? The defendant has argued that a seven-year-old child should be more responsible—should watch for traffic before darting out into a street. Yet were we preoccupied with such thoughts when we were seven years old?
>
> This careless defendant speaks of the need for care by a child. But I did not hear him speak of the care that an adult driver should

---

15. These data are based on VEHICLE SPEED AND STOPPING DISTANCE COMPUTER (1983 & 1986) (available through Lawyers and Judges Publishing Co., Del Mar, Cal.).

16. The pedestrian and the driver have analogous duties in that each is required to keep a proper lookout for the other. In certain circumstances, each can be negligent as a matter of law; further, a pedestrian's negligence may bar recovery even though the pedestrian may generally have the right-of-way. Townsend v. Young, 114 S.W.2d 296 (Tex. Civ. App.—Fort Worth 1938, no writ); Norris Bros. v. Mattinson, 118 S.W.2d 460 (Tex. Civ. App.—Fort Worth 1938, writ dism'd w.o.j.). See generally 8 TEX. JUR. 3d *Automobiles* §§ 318–322, 398–403 (1980), for a further discussion regarding the rights and duties among pedestrians and drivers.

> exercise. Of whom would you expect the greater understanding of danger and the need for care—little Melissa sitting over there or the thirty-eight-year-old man who sits across from her—the negligent driver who caused this tragic wreck?
>
> When we speak of the responsibility and duties that adults have toward children, what do we mean? We know that children often cannot protect themselves. Adults therefore have the duty to protect children against themselves. Is it not the duty of an adult, when operating a deadly machine in a school zone, to move heaven and earth in an effort to protect our innocent children from the slightest danger and heedlessness? Someone needs to remind this defendant that children are to be "seen and not hurt." During our existence we serve in the capacity of guardians. We protect. We foster. We nourish. We certainly do not crash our automobiles into our children to forever haunt them with the torture and agony of pain and terror.

Cyclists

In a cyclist case an effective argument is often a hybrid of those used for the plaintiff-pedestrian and for the plaintiff-driver. In other words, your argument should contain certain principles that are appropriate to the pedestrian as well as to the driver. As with the pedestrian, stress that the cyclist has as much right to enjoy our roads and streets for leisurely travel as does the driver of a motor vehicle. Compare the physical makeup of a bicycle or motorcycle with the weight and size of an automobile or truck. Point out that while the cyclist has the same legal duties as a driver,[17] the cyclist will not be insulated from the effects of another driver's negligence as would one who is riding in or driving a vehicle: the cyclist is not enclosed within the metal framework of a vehicle. As in an argument for the driver, though, reaction time is an important consideration. In fact, unlike the driver of a motor vehicle, the cyclist will often experience difficulty in acceleration once he has stopped. Obviously, if a collision involves a stationary cyclist, a discussion of reaction time becomes that much more significant.

> We have all heard the expression that it's "like riding a bicycle; once you have learned, you never forget how." I believe that statement is a correct one, to a point, ladies and gentlemen. While our ability to ride a bicycle may never be forgotten, it seems that our muscular

17. *See generally* Dunn v. Sears, Roebuck & Co., 371 S.W.2d 731 (Tex. Civ. App.—Houston [1st Dist.] 1963, writ ref'd n.r.e.); Kelly v. Hamm-Tex Distrib. Co., 337 S.W.2d 608 (Tex. Civ. App.—Waco 1960, writ ref'd n.r.e.).

coordination in balancing and steering that bicycle is not so easily remembered after a long period of time. Perhaps I did not really appreciate this fact until I went bicycle riding with my family some weeks ago.

My sons, of course, took off in a flash on their bicycles, with my wife in hot pursuit. And I started out all right. I got the bike moving after a couple of seconds and began to take off, even though it had been some ten or fifteen years since I had ridden a bicycle. I was doing fine until after I reached the first stop sign. Once I had started off again, I could not stop the bicycle from wobbling and I had to extend a leg out to the ground to keep from falling over. You see, ladies and gentlemen, it had been so long since I had ridden a bicycle that I had forgotten that it takes several seconds to get a bicycle moving once you have stopped. After a block or so, I caught up with my wife and children and we pedaled about a mile. I really enjoyed that bicycle trip, and I noticed that everyone else seemed to enjoy it, as well. Although I don't do much bike riding, I appreciated the fact that our cyclists have just as much right to enjoy their leisurely travel as do the drivers of automobiles.

The defense you have heard in this case would have that right reduced to a privilege they could take away at any given whim. You have heard this defendant say that he couldn't stop in time and that Mr. Rosenberg should have gotten out of the way. Even though he only had two or three seconds at the most before the defendant's car slammed into him, they suggest that Mr. Rosenberg could have avoided this tragedy. Is it reasonable to believe that this forty-six-year-old gentleman could have darted across the street on his bicycle in those two or three seconds? Should we have to be champion cyclists when we ride down our streets in order to avoid the reckless and heedless automobile driver? You now know that this case is not so much a question of fault as it is one of right. We all know whose negligence caused these tragic injuries. The question before you is, Will you condone such conduct and, in essence, say that no one other than the careless driver has the right to travel on our streets and in our neighborhoods?

Arguments for Specific Defendants in Automobile Cases

While the principles and arguments described in this chapter apply to automobile cases in general, certain specific defendants deserve individual attention. The truck driver was discussed above; arguments regarding two other specific defendants, common carriers and intoxicated drivers, remain to be explored.

Common Carriers

The most consistently important aspect in arguing liability against a common carrier concerns the standard of care. It has long been the law in Texas that a carrier must exercise a "high degree" of care toward its passengers.[18] Thus, the focus of your argument will often be the duty the defendant owed the plaintiff. Another important issue in the carrier case is control. Point out that the bus, cab, or train was within the exclusive control of the defendant. The plaintiff, as a passenger, had no opportunity to avoid a collision or mitigate the effects of the carrier's negligence. Address the issue of safety, too. Often evidence in the form of the defendant's policies and procedures, or a violation of them, will provide ammunition for your argument. You may also effectively contrast the cost associated with the carrier's marketing and advertisements with the cost that carrier has expended to ensure the safety of its passengers.

> How could Mrs. Sloan have contributed to her injuries in this case? This bus was entirely under the control of the driver. Its routes were controlled by the Black Cat Bus Lines. This is why the law says that bus companies owe the "highest degree" of care toward their passengers. The passenger's duty is simply to act reasonably. Was it unreasonable for Mrs. Sloan to stand up and begin to exit the bus at the transit stop? The defense has suggested that she contributed to her injuries because she did not grasp the railing while exiting the bus. They tell you that if she had, she would not have fallen to the floor of the bus as the driver suddenly began to take off. Is this reasonable? Should Mrs. Sloan have had to carry her packages with her off the bus one by one—with one package under one arm and one hand on the railing for every step that she took? Would the bus driver have actually waited for her to make several trips on and off the bus to retrieve her packages and luggage? Of course not. This negligent driver did not even wait for Mrs. Sloan to exit *once* before he up and took off without any warning.
>
> But to a larger extent, ladies and gentlemen, it is not entirely the bus driver's fault. He is merely the right hand of the bus company. He travels their routes at the times they dictate and in the manner they order. All this is done to make a profit. We know from advertisements we see and hear on television and radio and in the newspapers that these bus companies want to attract the paying passenger. You now know that Black Cat Bus Lines spends hundreds of thousands of dollars on such campaigns. You've all seen

18. *See* Dallas Ry. & Terminal v. Travis, 78 S.W.2d 941, 942 (Tex. 1935); Delta Airlines v. Gibson, 550 S.W.2d 310, 312 (Tex. Civ. App.—El Paso 1977, writ ref'd n.r.e.); Skyline Cab Co. v. Bradley, 325 S.W.2d 176 (Tex. Civ. App.—Houston 1959, writ ref'd n.r.e.).

> their ads, "Why fly, when you can get there in comfort with Black Cat?" Does safety matter, or should we expect the sudden starts and stops when we attempt to exit these buses? Should passengers be hauled around like so many cattle, or should safety be their primary concern? Perhaps if Black Cat had placed some sign to warn Mrs. Sloan that you have to exit at your own risk, she might have grasped that railing. But this is not the question you must determine. You have to decide whether Black Cat was negligent because it did not use the *highest* degree of care when Mrs. Sloan attempted to get off its bus.

The status of the carrier's driver may also be vital to your argument. Although a bus driver is usually an employee of a particular company, the same may not be true for his automobile counterpart—the cabdriver. It is very common in the taxicab industry to label the driver an "independent contractor." This artificial distinction is most often employed for litigation purposes. Typically, the driver purchases or leases his vehicle from the company; the percentage of his fares that he provides the company is little or nothing.[19] Even then the company dispatches the driver to certain locations at various times.[20] Since the cab company remains liable under the doctrine of respondeat superior,[21] your argument should conform to the concepts of negligent entrustment and negligent hiring that were discussed earlier in this chapter.

It is very unlikely that the cab company could ever insulate itself totally from liability for its drivers' negligence.[22] If such a defense is viable, however,

---

19. *See, e.g.*, Rodriquez v. Zavala, 279 S.W.2d 604 (Tex. Civ. App.—San Antonio 1955, no writ).

20. *Id.* at 605–06.

21. *Id.* at 607; Martin v. Weaver, 161 S.W.2d 812 (Tex. Civ. App.—El Paso 1941, writ ref'd w.o.m.).

22. Article 883 of the Revised Civil Statutes provides in part: "[C]arriers of passengers, goods, wares, and merchandise for hire, within this state, on land, or in boats or vessels on the waters entirely within this state, *shall not limit or restrict their liability as it exists at common law*, by any general or special notice, or by inserting exceptions in the bill of lading or memorandum given upon the receipt of the goods for transportation or in any other manner whatsoever." TEX. REV. CIV. STAT. ANN. art. 883 (Vernon Supp. 1988) (emphasis added). The term *common carrier* includes taxicabs. *See* Skyline Cab Co. v. Bradley, 325 S.W.2d 176 (Tex. Civ. App.—Houston 1959, writ ref'd n.r.e.). Accordingly, courts have held that the taxicab driver is an employee rather than an independent contractor. *Rodriquez*, 279 S.W.2d at 606–07; *Martin*, 161 S.W.2d at 814–15. Even if the employer does not exercise any control or direction over the driver's work, it is also clear that some municipal ordinances may prescribe that the company is responsible for its driver's negligence. For instance, section 46-17 of the Houston Code states the following: "The permittee shall be responsible for anyone operating under his permit whether he be an employee or another person operating under such written agreement. Any person driving or operating a taxicab upon the streets or other public property

other vicarious liability arguments may still be employed against the cab company under certain circumstances. One possible theory of recovery is the doctrine of ostensible or apparent agency.[23] Although there presently appear to be no Texas cases to support the use of the ostensible agency doctrine in the typical cab case, it seems plausible that the employer can be held vicariously liable for his drivers' acts under this concept.[24] Briefly stated, this doctrine will impute liability to a party for the negligence of his independent contractor if the party has manifested to the plaintiff that the contractor is its employee and the plaintiff is injured in reliance thereon. These manifestations may be accomplished by word, conduct, act, or deed.[25] The argument necessary for a favorable plaintiff's verdict under this theory thus emphasizes the defendant's representation or "holding out" that the cabdriver was its employee, as well as the passenger's reliance on that representation.

> For the first time, ladies and gentlemen, you and John Wells have heard a new defense in this case. You have heard the Orange Cab Company say that they are not responsible for this tragic wreck, because the cabdriver was not their employee. They say that this cabdriver was an independent contractor—someone who just worked on his own and hired out to the Orange Cab Company. I'm not going to quarrel with that defense. I'm not going to try to convince you that this negligent cabdriver was an employee of Orange Cab. Frankly, John Wells is most willing to let you decide that question.
>
> But I do have a big problem with the defendants' attorneys telling you that Orange Cab cannot be responsible. They tell you that the driver was not their employee, but they do not tell you the most important question, the one that you will have to decide. That

---

of the city is presumed to be an employee of the permittee or to have entered into such written agreement." HOUSTON, TEX., CODE § 46-17 (1987).

23. The ostensible agency doctrine is based on RESTATEMENT (SECOND) OF AGENCY § 267 (1958), which provides: "One who represents that another is his servant or other agent and thereby causes a third person justifiably to rely upon the care or skill of such apparent agent is subject to liability to the third person for harm caused by the lack of care or skill of the one appearing to be a servant or other agent as if he were such." *Id.*

24. The theory of apparent agency has been used in medical malpractice cases in Texas against hospitals for the negligent acts of an independent contractor-physician. *See* Smith v. Baptist Memorial Hosp. Sys., 720 S.W.2d 618 (Tex. App.—San Antonio 1986, writ ref'd n.r.e.); Brownsville Medical Center v. Garcia, 704 S.W.2d 68 (Tex. App.—Corpus Christi 1985, writ ref'd n.r.e.). Thus, since the doctrine is invoked to remedy the tortious injuries of one who has been harmed by the ostensible agent of another, it appears that there is no justifiable reason to preclude an application of such doctrine to the automobile-cab case.

25. See Tottenham, *Current Hospital Liability*, 28 S. TEX. L. REV. 1, 8–9 (1987), for certain factors that will support a jury finding on representation.

> question, ladies and gentlemen, is not whether the driver was an employee; it is whether the Orange Cab Company *represented* to Mr. Wells, in any way, that the driver was an employee. When you decide the questions at the end of this trial, you will find that *this* is the question that His Honor wants you to decide. Not whether the driver was an employee, but whether Mr. Wells knew that the cabdriver didn't work for Orange Cab. Remember what the evidence told us? When John Wells phoned for a taxicab, he called the Orange Cab Company. A cab pulls up that has "Orange Cab" plastered all over it. Inside is a man who is wearing an Orange Cab cap. Was John Wells required to have some sixth sense that told him the driver did not work for Orange Cab? Of course not. By putting this negligent driver in their cab and on our roads, the Orange Cab Company *represented* that this was their cab, their driver. It was good for business. It helped make a profit. It made sure that people like John Wells would *rely* on their drivers for safety. The name Orange Cab Company was conspicuous when Mr. Wells saw the cab *and* when he stepped inside it. He didn't see any signs stating, "This is not our driver—enter at your own risk." You now know why there weren't any signs of this sort. It's because if there were any such signs, people might not rely on the Orange Cab Company, might not feel safe in an Orange Cab. In other words, it might not make a profit.

Intoxicated Drivers

Arguments in cases involving intoxicated drivers vary greatly depending on the personality and approach of the victim's advocate. One method, described toward the end of chapter 16, is to compare the conduct and the degree of care of the defendant with those of the plaintiff. When using this approach, be very careful with the content of your argument. Unless there are questions raising gross negligence and punitive damages, you cannot argue that the defendant should be "punished" for his conduct.[26] A carefully worded

---

26. For a list of cases that hold such argument to be reversible error, see Boone v. Henry, 151 S.W.2d 323, 325 (Tex. Civ. App.—Fort Worth 1941, no writ); Allis-Chalmers Mfg. Co. v. Board, 118 S.W.2d 996, 1000 (Tex. Civ. App.—Amarillo 1938, no writ); Nicholson v. Nicholson, 22 S.W.2d 514, 519–20 (Tex. Civ. App.—Eastland 1929, no writ). Note, however, that the standard of review in these cases required a reversal if there was any "reasonable doubt" of the effect of such argument on the jury. *See, e.g., Nicholson*, 22 S.W.2d at 517. Under current standards of appellate review, this rule of "presumed prejudice" is no longer applied to improper jury arguments. *See, e.g.*, Dillingham v. Lynch, 516 S.W.2d 694, 702 (Tex. Civ. App.—Austin 1974, writ ref'd n.r.e.). The present standard holds that such argument will be harmless error unless it was "reasonably calculated to cause and probably did cause the rendition of an improper judgment." *See, e.g.*, Aultman v. Dallas Ry. & Terminal, 260 S.W.2d 596, 599 (Tex. 1953).

argument may have the same effect without being improper.[27]

> The defendant was negligent in this case, ladies and gentlemen, as a result of his drunkenness. It caused him not to have the ability to properly operate his car. No one gets drunk by accident. When we start to drink, it is of our own desire, our own volition. And the same is true when we decide to drink too much.
>
> My friend Terry Jackson has only asked for his actual damages in this case. He has not asked that you award him any damages to punish the defendant. But on behalf of Terry, I would say that because of the defendant's drunkenness, there can be no room for compromise on the issue of damages. In this case, you need to be very careful when you are deliberating to make sure that Terry's damages equal the full amount. Terry is entitled to the full amount of his damages not only because they have been proved but also because if you do not award them, the system will be compromised.

If gross negligence and punitive damages have been pleaded and supported by the evidence, a different type of argument can be particularly effective. This argument is intended to impress on the jurors their power to stop the intoxicated driver. You may state that, while the legislature may pass laws against drunk driving and the criminal judiciary may penalize it, neither method has proved tremendously successful; in contrast, the jurors' power to assess punishment extends beyond the mere fine or overnight stay in jail. This is not to say that the argument should be based entirely on punishment. Although you want to anger and motivate the jurors to the point of punishing the drunk driver, your argument should also convey that the driver has the *obligation* to pay for the plaintiff's damages: payment is not a form of penalty but, rather, a form of just compensation. The following argument portrays this approach:

> The power with which you are vested in this case extends beyond any particular decision that you might reach. It is true that you have the power to make this callous defendant compensate my friend Todd Cook, but the power does not die once your verdict has been rendered. This power will live on in the form of a message, a warning, to other drivers who drink before they drive. The warning is that we will not tolerate the drunk and careless driver on our roads.

---

27. It seems that only blatant appeals for punishment are improper. *See, e.g., Nicholson*, 22 S.W.2d at 519.

When I was preparing my notes to speak with you, ladies and gentlemen, I really wasn't sure what to say about drunk driving. I truly could not think of anything that had not already been said on this very timely and serious subject. I thought to myself that we all know our legislature passes laws against drunk driving, but this won't stop it. Our criminal judges have the power to assess penalties against drunk driving, but this cannot end it. I thought about how our news media reports about people being crippled and killed by the drunk driver, yet this does not stop it. The reason, ladies and gentlemen, is that not much is ever said about the drunk driver's obligation. Sure, we know that these drivers may receive fines or be thrown in jail for the weekend, but we never hear of their obligation to compensate their victims.

So I realized when I was getting ready to talk with you that the *obligation*, the *duty*, of the drunk driver must be confronted. This is the only power I have—the only thing that I can do to stop drunk driving. Quite simply, that is to persuade you to use *your* power.

You now know that you *have* such power. By your verdict, you can now make people think twice about drinking before driving. This power will never die because the message is that they will have to "pay" for the suffering that they cause. It will be a constant reminder. No other person or entity but you possesses the power to hit them where it hurts—in their pocketbooks.

We have often heard attorneys say, "If you have tried five or ten automobile cases, you have tried them all." In a general sense, this proposition is valid: the concepts of duty and responsibility, negligence, and proximate cause will indeed be consistent in many automobile cases. The arguments used to explain these elements of liability, however, can always be improved and strengthened. Similarly, arguments concerning the defenses raised may be constantly revised to meet the facts of a given case. It is always important to identify and implement the arguments that will be beneficial for a particular plaintiff or detrimental to a specific defendant. In sum, an attorney's experience with earlier automobile cases may provide valuable insight for the preparation of his argument but should never dictate its content.

19

Premises Injuries

THE GENERIC TERM *premises injury* represents a number of different, yet similar, situations. In these cases, because of the variety of ways people receive injuries while on certain premises and the infinite number of different types of premises on which these injuries may occur, no simple classifications of argument are possible. The type of argument most effective for the victim depends greatly on the type of premises injury case in dispute, so some categorization of the different types of premises injury cases is helpful. Here are ten of the more common types of premises injury cases:

- Injuries in retail stores (e.g., slip and falls)
- Injuries in office buildings (e.g., escalators and elevators; carpeting)
- Injuries in commercial lodgings (e.g., falls; security precautions)
- Injuries on leased premises (e.g., unlighted stairways; defective stairs; apartment swimming pools)
- Injuries on unimproved realty (e.g., hidden holes; concealed stumps; pipeline explosions)
- Injuries in public stadiums and facilities (e.g., defective designs and railings; inadequate maintenance)
- Injuries from electrical sources (e.g., upon and inside buildings)
- Injuries in residential areas (e.g., electrical and structural defects in the home; landscaping maintenance)
- Injuries on recreational property (e.g., paths; slides and swings; amusement parks)
- Injuries on public streets and walkways (concealed signs; inadequate lighting and railings)

The multitude of different types of premises injury cases make it difficult, if not futile, to suggest any given rules of argument. For instance, a slip-and-fall case that occurs in a retail or grocery store will differ vastly from a case in which a child has broken a leg while playing on a vacant lot. In the former situation, the legal issues revolve around the duty owed to an invitee, such as the employees' and employer's maintenance of the premises. In the latter instance, however, the legal duty at issue will merely be the landowner's provision of a reasonably safe area for a licensee. While there are no general rules, however, there are general guidelines to follow.

Contrasting and Comparing Defendant with Plaintiff

In almost every premises injury case, you have the opportunity to compare and contrast several important factors between the parties—for example, the defendant's control, knowledge, responsibility, and marketing efforts and the plaintiff's innocence. These factors paint a picture for the jury and form a framework within which to build the plaintiff's case. Reduced to its essence, this evidence can give the jurors a new view: they may themselves see the defendant's premises as a trap for the unwary. Danger, of course, has a common meaning, but you can elevate the vice associated with dangerous *premises* into a powerful weapon for the victim.

You must also help the jurors empathize with the plaintiff's cause. All too often, people tend to believe that one who is hurt in a fall or collision should have been more careful and alert. We are all acutely conscious of the reactions people manifest when another person falls, trips, stumbles, or collides with an object. The initial reaction is surprise and concern, but, if the person is not seriously injured, that reaction may fade into a smile or chuckle. The advent of television's "slapstick humor" may have been the greatest impetus for such modern-day behavior. Whatever the cause may be, some people view these situations with an almost insensitive disregard for the victim, thinking that they would have been more cautious and attentive. After all, in its most definitive sense, intelligence may be regarded as nothing more than an awareness and appreciation of one's surroundings. The defense will naturally suggest that the plaintiff should have been watching what he was doing or where he was going, and you must dissuade the jurors from believing these suggestions at the earliest moment possible. Direct the jury toward the victim's plight and the *defendant's* callousness, insensitivity, and disregard for human welfare. These concepts are exemplified in the following arguments.

Stress the Plaintiff's Innocence

To portray fully the plaintiff's innocence, develop the theme that the plaintiff had a right to shop or travel safely on the defendant's premises—that the plaintiff was merely exercising and enjoying a right common to all. Modern shopping centers or business facilities are not undeveloped, unexplored, or unkempt. They are man-made environments wherein the greatest attention to detail is given to attracting a customer and realizing a profit. Society demands safety in these facilities and on these premises as a necessary consequence of civilization. We do not expect the slippery surface or the unfixed footing when we patronize our shopping establishments. We expect only to be customers, and the merchant expects that we will be *paying* customers. He expects to provide us with a safe facility in which to shop. Similarly, we do not envision the dangerous obstacles or impediments in our recreational paths. In our cities and communities, people do not anticipate the unmarked excavation or the stop sign hidden behind a growth of underbrush. The plaintiff's innocence is based largely on the fact that these conditions represent a danger to all of society.

> All the plaintiff was required to do was exercise the prudent care that the ordinary, careful individual would have exercised under the same or similar circumstances. The law recognizes that all of us may at times be inattentive—this is particularly so when there are distractions. When Walter Mays was cutting a roadway on the defendant's land, there were men and machines all about, moving and hauling brush, trees, and the like. Surveyors were set up, measuring and making recordings for the depth of the grading. We have all seen these types of operations at one time or another.
>
> And Walter was a big part of this job. From the evidence, you now know that he was a man who took great pride in his work. He was hired to drive a Caterpillar over the defendant's land, to plow earth, and to grade land for the pouring of concrete. Walter knew nothing about what lay hidden beneath that land. He knew only that the defendant wanted it cleared. Neither the defendant nor anyone else told him of the natural gas pipeline that lay a foot beneath the surface.
>
> You now know that Walter was churning that earth and rock when the Caterpillar struck the pipe buried in the defendant's land. You now know what the explosion must have been like—steel and flesh being ripped apart by an inconceivable force—fire and heat burning what was left of Walter and melting the steel of his Caterpillar. Who among us could say that he or she would have known of the concealed pipe, would have cautiously propelled that machine over the surface? The very purpose of this innocent man's job was to grade the defendant's land with speed and efficiency.

Stress the Defendant's Marketing Procedures

If the defendant is a private retail or grocery store, emphasize the impact that advertising and marketing have on a customer. The nature of signs and displays presented in alluring form, shape, and color are all calculated to result in a purchase. Point out that but for such advertising, the plaintiff might not have been injured. In other words, perhaps the plaintiff would have recognized the danger if his eyes had not been drawn to and transfixed on the goods the defendant had displayed in an enticing manner. The plaintiff's attention, however, was not focused on his own safety but, rather, on the defendant's imaginative display. Caution was neither a concern nor a reality.

> These defendants are in the business of selling merchandise. The more they sell, the greater the profit. They consult specialists to give them advice on the ways to attract a customer's attention. The signs

> that the store uses are in different shapes; some of them are moving; they are of different colors. Everything is calculated to focus the customer's attention and to provoke and inspire a purchase. But no thought is given to another subject—the safety of the person who makes all this possible—the purchaser. Mrs. Johnson was dazzled by a scene that sprang from the minds of ambitious and zealous advertisers. The kaleidoscope of color and sales inducement drew her forward. The sales promoters were right. They were successful in capturing Mrs. Johnson's attention. But in so doing, this store ignored the safety of their customers. They allowed the aisle to be cluttered with boxes.

To emphasize the defendant's marketing procedures, consider contrasting the position of the victim with that of the premises owner by using parallelism:

> The defense asks, "Why should we be responsible for Mrs. Jackson's injury?" They suggest that Mrs. Jackson is as much to blame for her fall on their freshly waxed marble floor as they are. To that argument we would suggest that there is a big difference between the position this hotel occupied in regard to these premises and that occupied by Mrs. Jackson.
>
> The Grand Hotel provided these premises. They promoted their use. They proclaimed that they were safe. They profited when this lady used them.
>
> What did Mrs. Jackson do? She paid.

Stress the Control the Defendant Exercised over the Premises

Another important distinction the jurors should understand is the defendant's exclusive control over his premises and the plaintiff's resulting lack of control. In virtually every premises injury case, the plaintiff, as an invitee or licensee, had no right to inspect the premises with a discerning eye or to repair the premises if that was necessary. The plaintiff cannot order the defendant's management to provide safe conditions for its patrons. The plaintiff cannot design and implement safe walkways within which to shop. The plaintiff cannot provide the maintenance for the defendant's office building or commercial lodging. The plaintiff can only expect that the defendant does these things because they are within the defendant's exclusive control. The defendant's control pervades every aspect of its premises, from the arrangement of its goods to the surface of its floors. Thus, the defendant controls whether or not someone will be injured on its premises.

> In this case Mrs. Johnson fell over a large decorator rug that was in the defendant's lobby. As you have heard, she was on her way from her room to the conference area where this meeting was to be held.

As she walked forward, her foot became entangled in the rug, which caused her to fall, injuring her hip. It was a severe fall, as you have seen from the injuries.

How did her foot become caught in this rug? It is a thick decorator rug with ruffled edges. Mrs. Johnson would not have been able to lift that rug with her foot. You have heard from Bill Elway, the plaintiff's expert, that these rugs should be affixed and attached to the floor. This was a responsibility of the defendant. It ordered the rug, it bought the rug, it installed the rug, and it was responsible for the rug's becoming a trap for the innocent guest such as Mrs. Johnson.

This hotel has a duty to protect its guests. It has a duty to correct or warn of hazardous conditions, especially if those conditions are not visible. It has a duty to anticipate that the attention of persons using its lobby may be focused on their activities rather than the floor. People using this hotel are human beings, not animals who walk around on all fours, keeping their heads to the ground.

On the other hand, the guests of the hotel owe no duty to the hotel. Simply look at the court's instructions, and you will see that the only duty owed by Mrs. Johnson was to herself.

Why does the law impose these duties on the operator of a hotel? Because a person in business for profit invites customers to use his establishment in order to make a profit. There is also the difference in the opportunity to observe the danger. Here the hotel had this rug in place for some three or four years. It placed the rug in the lobby. It had the rug cleaned and replaced. The opportunity the hotel had to discover this dangerous condition was long and significant. Mrs. Johnson, on the other hand, had no opportunity to discover the danger. She had but a few seconds. She had the right to assume that the hotel premises would be safely and carefully maintained. She had the right to assume that the hotel would not place any traps for her or the other guests.

The hotel had the only opportunity to correct this dangerous condition. You have heard from the testimony that the cost of securing this rug was minimal. Was the profit motive of this large chain, which operates hotels throughout the country, so great that a few dollars needed to be shaved from their budget at the cost of the safety of those who would be using their facilities?

The issue of control is also of paramount importance in cases where the plaintiff has been injured by an independent contractor on the premises of the owner. In the typical scenario, the owner has contracted with a third party for the performance of some work on the premises. During some construction, excavation, maintenance, or similar activity, an employee of the independent contractor receives an injury while working on the premises. Under current Texas law, the landowner will be liable for the plaintiff-employee's injuries if the landowner has *retained the right to control* the subcontractor's work but failed to exercise reasonable care in so doing.[1] Therefore, you must convince the jury that the right of control rested with the defendant-landowner.

> You have seen and heard evidence in this case that Beta Construction was hired to do a job for the Acme Corporation. You know from the evidence that the construction of this multimillion-dollar shopping center was to last two years, with Acme having final approval of the building specifications. You now know that Acme dictated what types of materials would be used for the installation of electrical wiring. Acme had the right to control the manner in which that wiring was installed. Acme had the right to change the building plans and, as a matter of fact, if Acme was displeased with Beta's work *at any time*, it could have ordered the work changed or could have fired Beta if the work was not to Acme's satisfaction.
>
> Acme enjoyed this right of control. It was an advantage to be able to order the manner and method in which its shopping center would be built. But now, when the time has come for Acme to bear the responsibility that comes along with the ability to control, Acme shrugs off that obligation. For the first time Acme now says it really was not able to control the installation of wiring. Acme has told you that it was Beta's job to determine whether any of the wires were "live" at the time Johnny Rogers was electrocuted. Even though Acme representatives were present to supervise this procedure and yet never inspected the wiring or objected to Johnny's rigging that wire, they want to shirk responsibility for it.
>
> It is only after twenty-four thousand volts surged through Johnny's body, destroying muscles and veins, that Acme does not want control. Only now, in the midst of this trial, does Acme Corporation say, "Well, it was out of our hands" and "What's done is done."

Another variation of the argument regarding control is to expose the childish nature of the defendant's position. The following analogy might be helpful:

> Ladies and gentlemen, as I was listening to the defense's argument, I was reminded of an experience that most of us shared as children. All of us remember a friend from our childhood who furnished the

---

1. Exxon Corp. v. Quinn, 726 S.W.2d 17, 20 (Tex. 1987); Redinger v. Living, Inc., 689 S.W.2d 415, 418 (Tex. 1985); Tovar v. Amarillo Oil Co., 692 S.W.2d 469, 470 (Tex. 1985); *see also* RESTATEMENT (SECOND) OF TORTS § 414 (1965).

> ball to play with; in my experience it was David Morrow. Because it was his ball, David dictated the way we would play. Whenever a close call arose, his ruling controlled. That was because it was his ball, and thus at any time he could exclude us if he didn't like the way we played. As is the way in life, David's ownership interest gave him the right of control.
>
> David often reminded us that he was in charge, and we all knew that if he was not satisfied with our conduct, he retained the right to take his ball and go home. Isn't it funny, though, that David was the first to disavow responsibility when the ball went through a neighbor's window.
>
> From the evidence in this case, Acme reminds me of David. They have the ownership. They have the right of control. But they possess the same level of maturity as David did, because they shrug off the responsibility that comes along with ownership and control. And today you are not here to consider the consequences of a broken window—but of a shattered life.

Contrast the Plaintiff's Knowledge with the Defendant's Knowledge

As an element of proximate cause, the defendant's knowledge of the condition of its premises is crucial to a jury finding in the plaintiff's favor. Contrast the plaintiff's lack of knowledge with the knowledge of each of the persons in the chain of the defendant's employ. For instance, in a case in which the defendant's stairs have been alleged defective, establish the chain of knowledge through each employee who was aware of such defect. The knowledge of the manager, the maintenance crew, the rental persons, and others who may have been aware of the defective stairs would be imputed to the defendant. Stress to the jurors that knowledge of each of those persons is knowledge of the corporation. In contrast, the plaintiff is not so charged with the knowledge of others. Therefore, how could the plaintiff have seen or known of the defect? The plaintiff, as a lessee or a guest, must accept that the stairs are safe and in good condition.

> How could Mrs. Johnson have known that this three-foot culvert was alongside the defendant's jogging path? When she was jogging at nighttime and the park was not adequately lighted, how could she have known that the culvert was a hidden trap for the unwary?
>
> The defendant's construction manager, Mr. Jake Brown, testified that he knew the culvert was there, he knew that a new string of lights needed to be installed, but he didn't think there was any hurry, because the culvert was only three feet deep.
>
> The groundskeeper testified that he knew of the culvert and had suggested that a railing be put up. He *knew* of the danger, you see, because he was in charge of maintaining the jogging path. You

> know now what he knew then—that someone could break a leg while running along the path at nighttime. The defendant also knew this, because its employees knew. The law says that when an employee knows something like this, his employer is charged with this knowledge.
>
> So the defendant knew, from its construction manager, of the culvert. It knew, because of its groundskeeper, that the jogging path was dangerous. In spite of all this knowledge, what did the defendant do? The defendant pretended the culvert wasn't there; it knew, but it ignored the obvious. The obvious danger. The obvious trap.

One reason for comparing the knowledge of the plaintiff with that of the defendant is that in most premises injury cases, except those involving very transient conditions, the condition of the premises can be demonstrated by either direct or circumstantial evidence.[2] As illustrated above, if the injury has resulted from some *fixed* part of the premises—stair designs or concrete faults, for example—direct evidence will usually establish the defective condition. If the defect on the premises was less permanent, however—faulty stairs or unsecured carpeting, for example—there may be no direct evidence to establish that the defendant was responsible for the defect or that he knew or should have known of it. Thus, circumstantial evidence will be required. And, finally, if the defective condition was merely temporary—objects on floors, for example—it may be very difficult to prove knowledge of the existence of the defect. At least some circumstantial evidence will be required to show that the defendant knew of the dangerous condition before the plaintiff's injury occurred.[3]

Do not be overly alarmed at the need to use and rely on circumstantial evidence. As discussed in chapter 18, in many instances circumstantial evidence is more credible than direct evidence. In fact, some premises injury cases can be more easily proved with circumstantial evidence than with eyewitness testimony.

> The Food Mart employees have told you that none of them knew there was hand lotion covering part of the floor in aisle nine. Two of these defense witnesses admit to seeing Shirley Carroll slip and fall in that aisle. But Food Mart says that no one knew of the slippery surface. Since no witness said that Food Mart knew of this, the defendant's attorneys have suggested that we have not proved our

---

2. *See, e.g.*, Carney v. Kroger Co., 455 S.W.2d 329 (Tex. Civ. App.—Houston [1st Dist.] 1970, writ ref'd n.r.e.).

3. *Id.* at 331; *see also* H.E. Butt Grocery Co. v. Johnson, 226 S.W.2d 501 (Tex. Civ. App.—San Antonio 1949, writ ref'd n.r.e.).

case by a preponderance of the evidence. Does that defense make sense to you?

If we had brought you a witness who said that he saw a Food Mart employee clean up the glass from that broken bottle of lotion, what would you think? You would think that someone was lying—either the witness or one of the Food Mart employees. Because the testimony was *contradictory*, you might not know whom to believe.

But no one that *we* know of saw that happen. What we *do* know, though, is that two small pieces of broken glass were found next to where Mrs. Carroll fell. This, ladies and gentlemen, is two pieces of circumstantial evidence that cannot be contradicted.

Why were there only two pieces of glass found? Where was the rest of the broken container? The label? The cap? The large pieces of glass? Did a thoughtful customer decide to clean up part of the mess, put it in his pocket, check out through the line at Food Mart, and carry it outside to later dispose of it? Is it reasonable to believe that this happened, ladies and gentlemen?

We have proved our case to you because a preponderance of the evidence tells you the only reasonable explanation: a jar of lotion falls from a shelf and breaks in aisle nine. A Food Mart employee sees this and picks up all the broken bottle except two small pieces. The Food Mart employee disposes of the vast majority of the broken bottle. But the employee doesn't clean up the spilled lotion. Along comes Shirley Carroll, searching for the items on her shopping list. Unfortunately, she steps on that lotion, her feet give way, and she lands square on her back in the middle of the aisle.

Arguing Comparative Responsibility

In addition to the basic factors or concepts discussed above, the single most important theory at issue in the premises injury case is invariably whether the plaintifif should bear some responsibility because of his own negligence. The quality of the defendant's conduct and of the plaintiff's conduct must therefore be contrasted for the jury.[4] In the premises injury case, a few specific arguments may be particularly helpful.

The Plaintiff's Reliance

The defense argument will often be dominated by the contention that the plaintiff did not have the right to rely on the safety of the premises. If this

4. See ch. 16 for a discussion of comparative responsibility.

assertion becomes apparent, place the circumstances surrounding the plaintiff's injury in a proper perspective for the jury. Point out that one does not ordinarily go about the streets or move around in a merchant's facility with his senses highly tuned to a state of exceptional alertness for danger. Using rhetorical questions is one effective way to demonstrate the fallacy of this defense contention.

> On what conduct by the defendants *did* Valerie Brown have the right to rely? How much time in the light of normal human activity did she have for reflection? The defendants have told you that she should have been more careful, that she should have been watching where she was walking.
>
> Valerie went to the grocery store for her family. She was looking for the bargains that the defendants advertised in their flyer sheets. We all do this. We all check for the listed price and search for the different types of articles on our lists. As shoppers, we have a right to believe that the people who own and operate a store will keep their floors reasonably safe.
>
> And the defendants know this. They know that when shopping carts are filled, people cannot see the floor of the aisle beneath them. The defendants know that the shoppers search for the best prices possible, not for the slippery surfaces. They know that we believe the floors will be safe. In fact, the defendants *expect* us to shop in a cost-efficient manner. Why else would they advertise and display their goods as they do?
>
> If Valerie Brown acted, as she obviously did, like any other mother grocery shopping for her family, then she wasn't negligent. She only had to be an ordinary shopper. The law doesn't require us to watch our steps or to search beneath our shopping carts every time we are in a store.

"See No Evil, Hear No Evil, Speak No Evil"

Sometimes the defense will maintain that there was no defect on the premises. The argument is usually predicated on the fact that none of the defendant's employees saw the condition that injured the plaintiff; therefore, the condition could not have existed. This contention may be effectively rebutted with the following argument:

> As I was listening to the defendant's argument, I could not help but remember the famous sculpture of the three monkeys—one who had his eyes covered, one who had his ears covered, and the last one, who had his mouth covered. I'm sure you have all seen this at one time or another. Do you remember the caption that appears

below, "See No Evil, Hear No Evil, Speak No Evil"? Well, that is what the defendants' argument reminds me of in this case.

The defendants haven't flat out called George Lathan a liar, but they have implied it. They say that they never saw a large pool of grease in the parking garage; they say that no one told them of the grease in the garage. But you know, I am not sure that any of the defendants, like the three monkeys, would admit to it even if they had seen the grease.

No One Else Was Hurt

Similarly, the defense may argue that someone other than the plaintiff needed to have been injured in order for the premises to have been dangerous. Essentially, they will contend that a number of people walked across the particular entrance, exit, or other part of the premises without being injured. They will argue that since other people—some of whom no doubt were old or infirm or had poor vision—were not injured, the plaintiff must have been negligent. If this argument is advanced, never forget its specious nature.

The defendants have told you that no one but Jackie Gordon was injured on these stairs. They point to the fact with pride and tell you that since no one else was injured, Jackie must have been at fault. That argument sounds real good, but you know there is a big difference between a good sound excuse and an excuse that sounds good.

From the evidence we have brought you, there is no doubt that the wooden railing on the defendants' stairs was splintered and rotted through. You know now what Jackie did not know—that this railing would collapse if it was pressed on in a certain manner.

The other people at the defendants' apartment complex are fortunate that they were not injured on these stairs. They can thank their lucky stars that they didn't grab that railing on the rotted part while they were climbing. But the defense says Jackie Gordon was negligent. She didn't see that the railing was rotten. They suggest that others must have because no one else had been hurt. Think about that argument. They say, "We are not responsible, because others had managed to avoid this obviously dangerous railing, this trap." Where would this reasoning lead us? If one person climbs these stairs safely, is it fair for the defense to say, "Well, the railing is dangerous, but we don't need to fix it, for one person has passed safely." If ten—or a hundred—pass safely, then even less the reason.

What if, instead of this being a case of negligence in maintaining an apartment project, it involved negligence in operating an automobile. The defendant ran a stop sign, but, because the other

> driver either saw in time or was not near the intersection, no collision occurred. So the defendant runs the next stop signal and the next. Finally, on the one hundredth try, he crashes into Jackie's car. If the defense were to make the same argument there that they have made here, you would not consider it for one minute. Some of you might even laugh at it. But isn't that exactly what they are using here—as a defense—as an excuse?

Arguments in Response to Defense Experts

Existence of Dangerous Condition

As earlier noted, the defense may contend that the alleged defect or condition never existed. To bolster its case, the defense will often call an expert to testify that the defect didn't exist or that it was not dangerous. If there is testimony that the defect never existed, compare the cost of correcting the condition with the cost of the expert's testimony.

> The defense then called Mr. Stone, their so-called expert on these types of swing set defects. You all remember his testimony. "The swing at Hillview Park was not defective. The reason that the chain broke loose at the crossbeam was that Rhonda Stevens was swinging too high."
>
> This defense really astonished me. I was amazed not only because little Rhonda weighed about sixty-five pounds when this swing snapped loose and paralyzed her for life, but I just couldn't believe the manner in which this defense was made.
>
> I heard all these scientific formulas and weight-and-speed ratios. I heard all these physics calculations about force and stress loads on the swing set.
>
> And you heard, on cross-examination, that the cost of putting a bigger, stronger bolt on the swing set was about sixty cents. You heard, on cross-examination, that Mr. Stone is being paid three hundred dollars an hour by the defendant for his testimony.[5] Isn't it a shame that the defendant did not pay sixty cents to correct the defect on this swing set, instead of three hundred dollars an hour for its hired expert?

---

5. On the cross-examination of an expert in Texas, the attorney may inquire about compensation for the expert's testimony. *See, e.g.*, Russell v. Young, 452 S.W.2d 434 (Tex. 1970); Texas Emp. Ins. Ass'n v. Garza, 557 S.W.2d 843 (Tex. Civ. App.—Corpus Christi 1977, writ ref'd n.r.e.). Thus, jury argument regarding that evidence is likewise permissible.

If the expert testifies that the condition may have existed but was not dangerous, this argument can be effectively modified. With a slight change in the argument, you can contrast the total cost of the defense with the cost of correcting the condition. The following paragraph could replace the last paragraph in the argument above.

> And the defense doesn't stop there. You have seen the exhibits and depositions and the attorneys used to defend its position. You now know that Mr. Stone was hired at three hundred dollars an hour for his testimony. By my calculations, the defendant has spent over a thousand dollars for his testimony alone. You now know that no expense was spared by the defendant. Thousands and thousands of dollars were spent to convince you that the swing set that crippled Rhonda was not dangerous. Though the defendant would not spend sixty cents to make that swing safe, they will spend thousands of dollars *to prove to you* that it *is* safe.

Defendant's Relationship with Defense Expert

Another common argument in response to the defendant's expert focuses on his relationship with the defendant. Pointing out that the expert is not an in-house member of the defendant's staff, but merely an independent hired voice, can greatly reduce the expert's credibility. Obviously, this approach is suitable only if the defendant's enterprise is such that the expert's full-time consultation would be economically feasible.

> As you have heard, the Payne Corporation spent thousands of dollars for their expert's opinion. In fact, they went all the way to Michigan to hire Mr. Watson—the construction expert who regularly testifies in boiler-related explosions. Although neither the Payne Corporation nor Mr. Watson had ever heard of the other before Harry Edwards was killed in a boiler explosion at the AMEX plant, they have come to know each other very well. Fly him in. Tell him about the construction job. See if he will testify that the boiler explosion was not our fault.
>
> This expert's opinion, ladies and gentlemen, might have some validity if the Payne Corporation was truly *confident* about his abilities and skill. But Payne values his opinion only *in this case*.
>
> Mr. Watson never worked for the Payne Corporation before this trial. If he truly is the construction wizard that Payne would have you believe him to be, why didn't Payne hire him to work for their corporation? Why not put him on the payroll? Let him assist in the prevention of boiler explosions and construction injuries. For the amount they have spent on this defense, Payne Corporation could have hired two or three Mr. Watsons.

> Is the Payne Corporation truly concerned about safety, as they say they are, or do they care only about money? Does the destruction of human life get their attention, or can you only do that by your verdict?

Inevitability of Accident Even If Repairs Are Made

In some cases the defense will argue that even if the dangerous condition had been repaired or corrected, the plaintiff might nevertheless have been injured. If this occurs, use expert testimony to point out that there was a *good chance*[6] the plaintiff would not have been injured had such repairs been made. Additionally, indicate that the defendant is the last person who should speculate about the prevention of the plaintiff's injury.

> The last defense of the city is one of insolence. Their attorneys tell you that even if the guard railing alongside the overpass on Market Street had been repaired, Mr. Carpenter's truck might still have crashed through the railing. Their experts say that when Joel's truck went out of control, it would have broken through the railing anyway.
>
> Since when does the city have the right to predict what Joel Carpenter's chances of survival were? After hearing the testimony of Mr. Jacobs, a man eminently qualified in engineering design work, you know that there is a real good chance that Joel would be here today if that railing had not been so flimsy. You remember Mr. Jacobs saying that it is "more likely than not" that Joel would not have dropped from the overpass had a sturdy railing been there to stop his car.
>
> But the defendant doesn't want you to give a dead man the benefit of any doubt. They tell you that even if the railing on the Market Street overpass had been repaired, it probably would not

---

6. In Texas, expert testimony regarding causation need not necessarily be couched in terms of reasonable scientific probabilities. *See* Jordan, *Expert Testimony—Cause of Present Physical Condition*, 29 TEX. B.J. 805 (1966). *See generally* Robinson v. Argonaut Ins. Co., 534 S.W.2d 953, 957 (Tex. Civ. App.—Fort Worth 1976, writ ref'd n.r.e.). Although the substance of the expert's opinion must relate more than a "possibility" of causation, Valdez v. Lyman-Roberts Hosp., 638 S.W.2d 111, 114 (Tex. App.—Corpus Christi 1982, writ ref'd n.r.e.), no particular word or phrase is required. This is because the jury's determination on causation is made from the substance of the expert's testimony. *See* Western Cas. & Sur. Co. v. Gonzales, 518 S.W.2d 524 (Tex. 1975); Otis Elevator Co. v. Wood, 436 S.W.2d 324 (Tex. 1968); Insurance Co. of N. Am. v. Myers, 411 S.W.2d 710 (Tex. 1966); Gibson v. Avery, 463 S.W.2d 277 (Tex. Civ. App.—Fort Worth 1970, writ ref'd n.r.e.); Insurance Co. of N. Am. v. Parker, 434 S.W.2d 159 (Tex. Civ. App.—Tyler 1968, writ dism'd by agr.). For further elaboration regarding the use of expert testimony, see ch. 21.

> save any lives. Think about that defense. "We won't fix a dangerous overpass for those who drive on our freeway, because we don't think a good railing would matter." Are we prepared to allow the city to play the prophet when our lives are at stake?

The content of argument in the premises injury case inevitably depends on the type of case being tried. Perhaps the only common factors are the plaintiff's innocence and the defendant's control, knowledge, responsibility, and use of marketing. Even for these factors, an effective argument must be molded to fit the facts of the case. Specific arguments on comparative responsibility or about the defendant's experts, however, can be constructed and modified by any plaintiff's attorney who expends some time and effort in preparing the victim's case. The specific arguments set forth in this chapter merely provide a guideline of common techniques. The overall effectiveness of a final argument in the premises injury case is limited only by the lawyer's creativity and imagination.

20

Product Liability

THE PRODUCT LIABILITY CASE is perhaps second only to the medical malpractice case in complexity. Preparing and delivering an argument in the product case involve unique challenges for the victim's advocate. Not only is the evidence likely to be more complex than in a workers' compensation, premises, or automobile case, but the legal concepts will be foreign to the jury as well. To appreciate this fact, one need only consider the differences in the concept of "unreasonably dangerous" that exist between manufacturing defects and design defects.[1] Further, the product case may involve multiple theories, and the court's charge may embody any combination of those theories—manufacturing defect, design defect, marketing defect, breach of warranty, and negligence.

Also, a greater range of facts may be encountered in a product case than in an automobile or premises case. Here are ten general classifications of product-related cases:

- Injuries from drug products (e.g., side effects from DES, intrauterine devices (IUDs), vaccines, and other medicines).
- Injuries from automobiles (e.g., defects associated with steering or braking mechanisms, crashworthiness, and seatbelts).
- Injuries from recreational vehicles (e.g., utility vehicle rollovers; defects in snowmobiles and motorcycles).
- Injuries from consumer and household products (e.g., defects in appliances, children's toys, television sets, and stereos; inflammable fabrics; impure cosmetics).
- Injuries from industrial equipment and machinery (e.g., defective valves, pipes, gauges, ladders, scaffolding, and welding tools; inadequate warnings for combustible liquids and gases).
- Injuries from agricultural products (e.g., defective tractors and other farm machinery; inadequate warnings for pesticides).
- Injuries from private residences (e.g., faulty architectural design; structural defects; inadequate roofing and swimming pool specifications).
- Injuries from commercial structures (e.g., faulty architectural design;

---

1. *See* 3 STATE BAR OF TEXAS, TEXAS PATTERN JURY CHARGES PJC 71.01, .02 (1982).

structural defects; insufficient stair-railing and elevator specifications; faulty parking lot and garage designs).

- Injuries from public utilities and facilities (e.g., products sold by third parties, including gas pipelines, electrical power lines, and unprotected sources; defective equipment in public parks and facilities and structural engineering defects thereon).
- Injuries from common carriers (e.g., manufacturing defects, such as mechanical failures in aircraft; faulty subway designs; defective rail transport structures; train derailings).

Because of the diversity in facts and legal theories, each product liability case calls for a fresh approach to argument. What works well in one product case may not serve the plaintiff's interest in another. This chapter explores arguments that may be effective in the product case. In no instance will all these arguments be proper in a particular case; that is why, in some instances, the following arguments may appear to be contradictory.

Paint a Picture of Your Case

To reflect accurately the issues in a product case, it may first be appropriate to give a short historical perspective. For example, there was a time in our legal history, during the nadir of consumerism, when the fundamental principle was caveat emptor, or "let the buyer beware." Few would seriously challenge the thinking that underlies our modern concepts of product liability. By making manufacturers and sellers legally accountable, we make them more responsible. Safety cannot be sacrificed in the name of profit. The manufacturers and sellers of products occupy a unique position. They alone have the ability to control the quality of their product. They conceive it. They design it. They make it. They market it. They service it. And, they place it in our hands.[2] A case theme commonly used to paint a picture in a product case involves an appeal to the concept of consumerism.

> This is a case involving public safety. The defendants manufactured and sold an automobile tire. The evidence will show that this tire was unreasonably dangerous, as that term is understood in law, by virtue of the way the tire was designed as well as the way it was made. As a result, every person, every family, every adult, adolescent, and child who rode in an automobile on which those tires were placed was under a constant threat of danger.

---

2. Any argument along these lines is obviously susceptible to the use of parallelism. See ch. 1 for an example of parallel language.

Emphasize Consumer Safety—Not Product Liability

Consistent with the "consumerism" concept, be conscious of the propaganda of insurance companies and manufacturers that has embedded in many people's minds the belief that there is something wrong with a product liability claim. Most people in Texas have a more conservative political philosophy than that which might be found in other parts of the country. In fact, some conservatives view the consumer movement as "harming business." Remember that the term *product safety* is less likely to alienate jurors of this political persuasion. Even the conservative-thinking individual will respond favorably to a theme based on product safety, which stresses that safety is everyone's business and that the jury, as the conscience of the community, is responsible for setting safety standards.

Explain the Product

Muster the evidence in an argument that describes the product and demonstrates its functions and foreseeable uses. The most common defense employed in product liability cases is, in essence, that the use of the product that caused the injury was not its intended use. It is important to emphasize that a manufacturer is responsible for foreseeable, not just intended, uses: the manufacturer may be responsible for the injured victim's actions as long as they were *foreseeable*. Analogies may be freely used in this regard. For example, someone who sticks his hand into a household fan is obviously not engaged in an act for which the fan is intended. Yet, such an event is entirely foreseeable. It is for this reason that such appliances are designed with safety screens.

Describe the Tragedy

Explain exactly how the victim's injuries occurred. Describe the events as if you were an eyewitness to the plaintiff's tragedy. A colorful narrative that outlines the events in chronological sequence will paint a graphic picture for the jurors. Then explain how the injuries could have been prevented. Even though the case may be submitted on a strict liability theory, which avoids the necessity of establishing negligence, the jurors will still want to know what the defendant did that was wrong and whether it was within the defendant's power to have prevented the tragedy.

Explain the Charge

It is particularly important in a product liability case to discuss the legal concepts and explain them to the jury.

If the cause of action is based on a manufacturing defect or impure product, the concept of *unreasonably dangerous* entails a danger beyond that which would be contemplated by the ordinary user of the product—one whose knowledge of the product's characteristics is common to the community.[3] In some instances the user of the product may not be the plaintiff; rather, the plaintiff may have been injured while the product was actually being used by a physician, a third-party industrial entity, or a third-party operator of a vehicle.[4] In such a case, point out to the jury that the court in its question is addressing the contemplation of the user—the third party; the plaintiff's expectations may not be particularly relevant.

In a design defect case, the concept of *unreasonably dangerous* involves the balancing test originally enunciated in *Turner v. General Motors Corporation*.[5] The question submitted to the jury on defective design requires a consideration of the utility of the product balanced against the risk involved in its use.[6] Early in the trial of such a case, it should be made clear that a determination whether the product was "defectively designed" is made by resort to this balancing test. For instance, the focus of the plaintiff's experts should be on this principle. Final summation is the opportunity to bring all this effort together.

> Question 1 asks whether the Tonto automobile involved was defectively designed at the time it was manufactured by Board Motor Company. You will note the court now submits to you the concept that we first discussed with you on the voir dire examination. A product is defectively designed if it is unreasonably dangerous, taking into consideration the utility of the product and the risk involved in its use. We are all aware of the general definition of utility. It means, in simple terms, usefulness. In considering this question you are asked to balance the usefulness of the Tonto against the risks involved in its use.
>
> When I asked you on the voir dire examination whether or not you could follow and apply this legal concept of defective design, each of you replied in the affirmative. There was a reason I asked that question. I knew then what you know now—that the evidence would show the risk involved in driving a Tonto was substantial and grave. You heard the testimony of an expert who recognized that the location of the gas tank was such that a rear-end collision could cause the gas tank to explode.

---

3. *See* 3 STATE BAR OF TEXAS, *supra* note 1, PJC 71.01.
4. *See, e.g.*, Ethicon, Inc. v. Parten, 520 S.W.2d 527 (Tex. Civ. App.—Houston [14th Dist.] 1975, no writ).
5. 584 S.W.2d 844 (Tex. 1979).
6. *See* 3 STATE BAR OF TEXAS, *supra* note 1, PJC 71.02.

You know now what I knew then—that this danger was recognized not only in the industry but by the defendant itself. The heads of Board Motor Company knew when they began running these cars off the assembly line that a rear-end collision, such as that involved here, could produce catastrophic consequences. They knew that what they had designed was a moving time bomb. A rear-end collision that would pose no particular threat to the users of other makes and models of cars would cause the Tonto to become an inferno.

You know now what I knew then—that Board Motor Company ignored the information available to them and chose to place the gas tank where they did in the face of this overwhelming proof of danger. They had an alternative location, a different way to place the gas tank. That location would not have interfered with the utility or usefulness of the product. It would not have made the Tonto any less fun to drive; it would not have made it any less reliable.

You know now what I knew then—that the decision to place the gas tank where it was placed was a decision made for economic reasons. In simple terms, it was cheaper.

Question 1 recognizes that there are some instances where the adoption of a design will result in lessening a product's utility. It will make it less effective or less useful. In other words, the adoption of a safer design, while it may make a product safer, may make it more difficult to use or make the product less effective for the purpose for which it is intended.

That is not the case here.

You now know the risk involved in driving a Tonto: if you were involved in a rear-end collision, the car would explode. Board's only justification or excuse is that this allowed them to manufacture the car for a few dollars less.

Would Mrs. Beatrice Williams and her husband, John, have been willing to pay those few extra dollars? Would anybody within the sound of my voice be willing to pay a few extra dollars in order to have a car that does not explode in a rear-end collision?

We submit that the answer to Question 1 is "yes." This has been established by a preponderance of the evidence. When you, as the court instructs, balance the utility of this automobile against the risk involved in its use, the answer is apparent.

A product liability case based solely on a marketing defect involves a situation in which the product was properly designed and manufactured, but the defendant failed to give adequate warnings or instructions for its safe use. Again, it is essential to discuss and explain the court's charge and definitions. In Texas the concept of adequate warnings and instructions means such warnings and instructions as could reasonably be expected to catch the attention of the reasonably prudent person in the circumstances of its use.[7] The content of the warnings and instructions must be of such a nature as to be comprehensible to the average user, to convey a fair indication of the nature and extent of the danger, and to explain how a reasonably prudent person could avoid the danger.[8]

If the product was not accompanied with any warnings, a different case theme may be required. For example, consider the case in which a worker was exposed to a toxic chemical manufactured by a third party. The chemical had no visible warnings with regard to its transportation. Assume further that the manufacturer is a large statewide corporation that employs thousands of people. In this type of case, your argument may be corporate responsibility, with environmental overtones.

> When the defendant, the Delta Chemical Company, manufactured this substance that they sold under their brand name "Chem-O-Lay," they knew that exposure to it could produce neurological impairment. They did not warn the workers, such as my friend Juan Gómez, that they should use gloves and wear masks and hoods while working with this chemical, which was supplied in its bulk form. Juan, as you have heard from the evidence, was required to get down into the railroad cars where this bulk chemical had been stored and stand in it. Shovel it. Breathe it. The exposure to this chemical produced in Juan the very type of neurological impairment that we have heard so much about. As a result of that exposure, Juan is not able to work, earn a living, or provide for his family.
>
> The defense says that they shouldn't be responsible for these injuries. The people that they sold the chemical to and the people who worked with it, such as Juan, were supposed to know better than to work in these tank cars without protection. That argument might be appealing to some. Someone might ask, "Well, after all, why should we hold this manufacturer of this chemical compound responsible? Even though their business affects the lives of millions of people across this state, all they did was make it and dump it into the tank cars for transportation."
>
> I wonder if our view of this case would be the same if, instead of simply selling this product without adequate warnings, the Delta Chemical Company had caused this product to be released into one of our Texas rivers or bayous. What if Juan, instead of being a poor, ordinary, common laborer, had been a big rancher who owned thousands of acres on the Brazos River bottom. Because the chemical had been dumped in the river, his cattle who drank from it died.

7. *See id.* PJC 71.04 Comment, at 238.
8. *Id.*

> When our winter Texas rains came and the Brazos rose, the chemical was spread over much of his acreage, polluting the grazing grounds. The claim would be that the defense, by their conduct, had effectively put the rancher out of business. He lost his herd. His grazing land was no longer safe. The damages in that case would probably equal or exceed what we are asking for on behalf of Juan.
>
> The defense would say that they didn't intend to cause that type of harm. All they did was make the chemical. "Don't blame us simply because we accidentally discharged some of our product into the Brazos River."
>
> I doubt that many of us would be very receptive to that type of argument in that type of case. So it should be here. A manufacturer should be required to warn the people who will be exposed to its dangerous substances. This requirement should be no less vigorously imposed than we would impose the requirement on the company to exercise care in seeing that its dangerous chemicals are not released into our waters, our air, our environment.

One expanding area of product liability law is the breach of implied warranty. In Texas the breach of implied warranty now applies not only to the implied warranty of fitness but also to some service transactions.[9] The recommended submission for implied warranty of fitness involves a series of considerations. Essentially, the jury is asked to determine whether the defendant knew the particular purpose for which the product was being acquired, that the plaintiff was relying on the defendant's skill in furnishing a suitable product, that the product was unfit for the purpose, and, finally, that the unfit condition was a proximate cause of the occurrence. If one or more of the causes of action being submitted involve warranties of fitness, explain the concepts embodied in the questions being submitted. In most cases the critical issue will be the third question in the series of inquiries—whether the product was unfit for the particular purpose for which it was purchased.

> When you consider whether or not this product was unfit, ladies and gentlemen, you will see that the court requires you to remember the purpose for which it was purchased. My good friend Andy Todencus bought this defendant's concoction for one reason only—to help generate hair growth in an effort to cure his baldness. That was its only purpose. That was what the "Ferasco Formula" was designed, produced, marketed, and sold for—to cure baldness.

---

9. *See* Melody Home Mfg. Co. v. Barnes, 741 S.W.2d 349 (Tex. 1987), in which the court held that the implied warranty of "good and workmanlike performance" extends to certain service transactions.

The hair salon that sold this dangerous product to Andy knew that its only use was to treat baldness. They knew this was the reason that Andy bought the "Formula." Andy didn't just go down to the drugstore and buy this product; he went to a business that was supposed to be knowledgeable about hair products. He purchased the Ferasco Formula from the defendants because he relied on their advice, their skill, and, he thought, their knowledge of the products that they sell.

How could this product have been fit for the purpose of treating baldness? You know now from expert testimony that none of the ingredients in this product were scientifically recognized as even *retarding* the balding process. Yet how was Andy to know? He followed the defendants' advice. He heeded the instructions. He applied the recommended portion of this disastrous recipe to his scalp every day for five weeks. From the scientific analysis, you heard that this product was full of certain steroid and cortisone agents. You now know that these ingredients were absorbed through the skin and into the bloodstream, where they accumulated in the reproductive organs and ultimately produced the medical problems about which there has been so much testimony in this case.

This was not a product that was "fit" for curing baldness. This was a concoction like those we have all seen in the old Western movies. Remember the scenes of a medicine man in the back of an old hardtop wagon? He would mix up some elixir that could cure baldness and all sorts of illnesses, including arthritis. Although the product was really a conglomeration of ingredients such as roots and herbs, snake venom, swamp water, whiskey, and the like, it would be marketed as a panacea—a wonder cure. The problem, however, was that the elixir in the medicine man's show was never fit for any of the purposes for which it was sold.

And so it is in this case. You know now that the Ferasco Formula was nothing more than a recipe for medical disaster. The difference, folks, is that the modern-day medicine man has been disguised as a hair salon business that promotes not only an unfit product but one that is life-altering as well.[10]

---

10. While most of the arguments in this book are realistic and, in fact, have been used by many advocates at one time or another, this story is obviously fictional. In any event, the argument should illustrate that the "medicine man show" analogy may be particularly effective in drug-related product cases to demonstrate that the product was "unfit." *See* L. SMITH, ART OF ADVOCACY: SUMMATION § 19.40 (1987).

Stress the Manufacturer's Knowledge

In many cases the evidence will demonstrate that the manufacturer or seller was well aware of the dangerous uses of its product but never warned anyone about them for fear of repercussions to its business. In such situations, stress the distinction between the legal culpability of an individual and that of a corporation—for example, "The evidence showed that the defendant's employees observed this use and did nothing about it."

Rebut Industry Standards

Written standards and specifications are frequently received into evidence during the trial of the product case. If the proof demonstrates that the defendant's product did not meet industry standards or specifications, this fact should obviously be stressed to the jury.

Oftentimes, however, the defendant's product met the published industry standards but was still responsible for the plaintiff's injuries. If appropriate, explain that these standards are minimal ones, long outdated and even regarded as inadequate by many manufacturers. Compliance with such standards, therefore, certainly cannot demonstrate that the product was safe for all its intended and foreseeable uses. If the defense argues that the industry standards are acceptable, however, a different approach may be necessary.

> The Acme Aluminum Ladder Company says that their thirty-foot extension ladder was not defective. It met the standards published by the industry. Even though the ladder bent under the weight of my friend Johnny Brown when he was carrying this bundle of shingles up onto the roof, they say their ladder was fine. Nothing was wrong with it. It met our standards.
>
> Isn't it appropriate that we ask: Who was responsible for promulgating these standards? Did Johnny have anything to do with it? Did other roofers who would be using the ladders in their work in Harris and Brazoria counties have anything to do with it? No, the authors of these standards are the manufacturers of these ladders. They are the manufacturers who know how these ladders will be used. They are the manufacturers who know that a common use of these ladders is by roofers—big men, like Johnny, who need their size and strength in order to do a hard job—big men who are strong enough to carry heavy loads of shingles up onto the roof. They say, "Our ladders shouldn't be expected to withstand such a load." They say that the industry has no way of expecting that ladders will be used in this way. That is why the standards didn't embody protection against such an event.

> These captains of industry don't make their living like Johnny did, in our hot Texas sun carrying bundles of shingles up onto roofs. Who are these people who set these standards? They are companies like the Acme Aluminum Ladder Company, which is seeking to avoid its responsibility in this case.

Use Expert Testimony

In the trial of a product case, the war often becomes a battle of experts. The plaintiff introduces expert testimony to the effect that the product was improperly designed, manufactured, or marketed. The defense has experts to the contrary. In some cases the defense chooses to support its product with its in-house staff; in others, an independent expert may be employed. The following arguments may be effective, depending on the scenario presented.

The In-House Expert

Most large corporate manufacturers have on their staff what is affectionately referred to as a "point man"—a person who is usually particularly adept at testifying and speaking on behalf of the company. Often this individual has had little actual "hands-on" participation in the design, manufacturing, or marketing of the product but will testify from corporate records, blueprints, and drawings prepared by others. If the defense calls this type of individual, you should stress certain points to the jury.

> When the defense paraded Mr. Flint before you to tell you that this pipe valve could not have been defective, he gave an opinion that was based on many factors. You heard only two of those factors from Mr. Flint—his review of the pipe valve and his knowledge of such equipment. According to Mr. Flint, the other factors don't matter much. It does not matter that he had never operated this deadly gas valve. He said that it was not important that he did not assist in the design of this valve. His opinion, he said, would have been the same even if he had.
>
> The certainty with which Mr. Flint delivers his opinions, ladies and gentlemen, is not surprising. I would not have expected that a man who owes his livelihood to the defendants would admit that their product was defective. After all, his opinion carries with it his continued employment.
>
> What does surprise me, however, is that evidently the Top Valve Supply Company only uses Mr. Flint's knowledge about valve explosions in the courthouse. You now know from the evidence that Mr. Flint does not design, inspect, or pressure-check these valves. Other people, supposedly, do that. What does Mr. Flint do?

> Well, he oversees and coordinates the work of the technical department, or so we're told. This means that he does the testifying, as you have heard, for his bosses.
>
> If the Top Valve Supply Company actually believes that Mr. Flint is such an expert on gas valve explosions, why don't they use him to inspect and test what they sell? He is already on salary. If he is so knowledgeable, why not get him to make sure these valves are not defective, rather than just using him to testify when the valve kills someone? I think you know the answer to that question—Mr. Flint's primary proficiency and skill is not in gas valves but in testifying at the courthouse. In other words, he is an expert only at being an expert witness.

The Independent Expert

The outside expert who testifies regularly for the defense is discussed in chapter 19. In summary, the credibility of the independent expert can be significantly diminished by arguments that stress the cost or fee for his testimony and the fact that the defense has employed him for this litigation rather than to assist in the designing, manufacturing, or marketing of their product.

The Overqualified (or Underqualified) Expert

Just as the quality of a book cannot be judged by its cover, the significance of an expert's testimony cannot be measured by his qualifications alone. Many times the eminently qualified defense witness's expertise is derived from a purely theoretical design or manufacturing standpoint. The plaintiff's expert, in contrast, may have no sophisticated degree or lengthy curriculum vitae in the area of his testimony. What he may possess, however, is firsthand knowledge of the product from a pragmatic standpoint. For example, the physician who has used a defective medical appliance may have given opinions about the appliance. The mechanic who regularly services defective tie rods may have testified about the condition of those rods. The industrial worker whose job requires him to attempt to operate a defective gauge may have testified about it. All these people would be considered experts, even though they may not possess degrees or certificates in those precise scientific fields.[11] In fact, having this type of expert is a decisive advantage for the plaintiff, which should not be overlooked. You can argue that only among the plaintiff's witnesses was there an individual who actually had "hands-on" experience with the product. He actually used it, serviced it, or worked on it. Contrast the experience and opinions of this expert with the qualifications and

---

11. *See* TEX. R. EVID. 702.

opinions of the defense experts. Point out that the defendant's experts never actually used the product. They never performed an operation using the medical appliance involved. They never attempted to repair or service one of their company's tie rods. They did not work with the gauge in the field. Often a plaintiff's advocate has discovered, following the rendition of a jury's verdict, that the most credible witness of all was the so-called lay expert.

Avoid Technical Terms

The lawyer who explains technical terminology in language that the average person can understand not only enhances his credibility but also increases the victim's chances of success. At least two different approaches to simplifying technical terms can be effective. The first method is self-deprecation. This style of handling scientific terms brings to mind Peter Falk portraying the fictional television character Columbo.

Another way to simplify difficult terminology is to subtly convey the fact that you have become familiar with this language by virtue of the time you have spent preparing the case. "The engineers who testified called this part the pressure valve. Its purpose was . . ." or "The experts refer to this scientific principle as . . ." The jurors must understand that you are not trying to deceive them by using terms or words they may not understand. By the same token, however, they must be made to appreciate that you have diligently expended the necessary time to educate yourself about complicated terminology. Placing technical terms on a chart or chalkboard with other demonstrative evidence is particularly effective in this regard.

If you use the second approach, you can also enhance your image with the jury by explaining exactly how you learned the terminology. Stress that you have read the technical journals, you have become familiar with the scientific standards, and you have obtained information and knowledge by discussing the matter with your experts and from deposing the defendant's experts.

Account for Absent Parties

Accounting for absent parties is discussed in chapter 2; it is particularly important in the product liability argument. Often, at the conclusion of the evidence, you may feel that the jury will consider the culpability of some entity that is not a party, particularly in the industrial situation where the jurors may believe that the plaintiff's employer contributed to the use of the product that produced the plaintiff's harm. In this situation, it is important to account somehow for the employer's absence. Generally, the most effective method is to point out to the jurors that they are to consider only the culpability of the parties who are before the court in this case. The issue is not whether the jury can conceive of other individuals or entities that may likewise be responsible. The only issue before the jurors is the culpability of the parties before the court.[12]

Account for Missing Evidence

Similarly, in some situations you may conclude before final argument that the jury will be concerned about some evidence that was not introduced. Usually, you will have been prohibited from introducing such evidence. Other product failures, for example, may be excluded because the trial court found that they did not occur under sufficiently identical circumstances. Some evidence about the history of the product may be missing. If there is any missing evidence that the jury might conclude is available to the plaintiff, you must account for its unavailability. Simply put, it is better to address such issues than to leave unanswered questions in the jurors' minds.

Clarify the Role of Circumstantial Evidence

In many product liability cases, circumstantial evidence plays a critical role. When it does, emphasize the court's instruction in this regard. A detailed discussion of how to handle the concept of circumstantial evidence in argument is contained in chapters 18 and 19.

Turn the "No Defect" Argument Against the Defense

If the defense persists in arguing that their product was not defective, you can turn that argument against them. Cast the defense in a disingenuous light by stressing the evidence from a commonsense standpoint. Emphasize the defendants' callousness in failing to correct the defect. Highlight the recalcitrance of the defendants by referring to their lack of concern for those who will be harmed by their product in the future.

> The thing that appalls me about this case is that the ABC Tool and Supply Company has persisted in arguing that its pressure gauge was not defective. We have all heard the evidence. This gauge was not equipped with safety glass. When it failed, the glass would shatter into thousands of jagged pieces. It was not equipped with a safety valve. If the gauge was exposed to certain pressures, it was certain to fail. That's what happened in this case. A gauge exploded, the glass shattered, and Bobby Ray Brown lost an eye.

---

12. The jury is to attribute a percentage of responsibility "to each claimant, each defendant, or *each settling person*." TEX. CIV. PRAC. & REM. CODE ANN. § 33.011(4) (Vernon Supp. 1988) (emphasis added).

But the defense insists that there is nothing wrong with their gauge. They made it that way on purpose. They like it. As far as we know from the evidence that has been presented, they continue to make the gauge the same way today. They intend to do it in the future.

The only hope that my friend Bobby Ray and the men like him who work in the oil fields have is your verdict. Only by your verdict can we hope that the ABC Company will reevaluate its position—that it will reconsider. Only by your verdict can we ever hope that those gauges will be equipped with a safety valve and shatterproof glass.

Stress the Time Element

In most product liability cases, the critical decisions made by the defendant occurred over an extended time. The defendant's decisions regarding design, manufacturing, or marketing were usually subject to some degree of scrutiny. This scrutiny is the responsibility of several individuals. It typically occurs over months or even years. Thus it is important to point out that, unlike many other situations in which an injury occurs, the decisions that led to the plaintiff's injury did not occur within a short span of time. They were decisions made over a long period—decisions that could have and should have been changed.

When the Jones-Manstown Corporation sold this deadly asbestos insulation, they made a business decision—a business decision after years and years of time to consider the consequences. For twenty years they knew that the fibers of this insulation would invade the lungs of anyone who breathed it. They knew that it would kill many people within a few years, while others would die a much slower and more agonizing death. At any time in those twenty years, Jones-Manstown knew that they could have changed their product or warned their customers.

You know that this despicable conduct was not the result of momentary oversight or inadvertence, ladies and gentlemen. It was a conscious decision—a decision made without any regard for the rights of those who would be exposed to the asbestos.

When a car wreck occurs because a driver was speeding or not watching where he was going, we might say that it was his fault but that it was an accident—an accident because his negligence occurred for only a few seconds.

When a surgeon makes a mistake and his scalpel strikes a major artery in the patient's body, he is negligent. One wrong incision and the patient is paralyzed. The conduct was his fault, but you have to remember that his conduct occurred within a few seconds.

Almost any type of injury that a person sustains from the negligence of another, ladies and gentlemen, is one that occurs in a moment's time. The defendant's conduct happens in a minute or two, a second or more, or even a fraction of that time.

Unlike the conduct of anyone else conceivable, however, the grossly negligent conduct of the Jones-Manstown Corporation occurred over twenty years. Seven thousand three hundred and five days of this conduct, causing so many lives to end—some of them extinguished in a year or two, others fading out after years and years of torment. No excuse, no reason, nothing on this earth can justify that type of conduct over so long a period of time.

Negate the Bad-Impact-on-Business Argument

There are some product liability cases in which the jury may think that a favorable plaintiff's verdict will have negative ramifications. Even if the defense does not choose to make this argument—and often they may not—you must address the problem. Some jurors may simply feel that the plaintiff's verdict might stifle business. To defuse this type of thinking, emphasize the public's concern for safer products.

As we have pointed out, this case involves significant issues. The Glasco Drug Company manufactured the medication that proved to be very useful in the treatment of arthritis.

Unfortunately, as a side effect it produced this medical condition, with the long name that some of us have had difficulty pronouncing—toxic epidermal necrolysis. Welts appear on your body. Your skin starts to slough and fall off. It is difficult to treat or cure. And sometimes, as in Mrs. Rosan's case, once it occurs it cannot be brought under control. You die the most agonizing death imaginable.

There is no question that the drug is dangerous. The answer to this question should be "yes." But there are those who would suggest that a verdict such as we have requested would stifle medical research. It will cause us to have fewer drugs available. But isn't it fair to ask who should pay the price for medical advancement? The manufacturers say we have to take chances if we are to have new drugs. I was brought up to understand that with every opportunity there is a risk. But I was also taught that the person who took the risk realized the reward. Mrs. Rosan will not realize the millions of dollars in profits from the sale of this drug. All she did was take the risk. When this company is graded on the research and investigation it did into this drug, it must be given an "F." But the company doesn't get the bad grade—Mrs. Rosan does.

So to those who would suggest that a verdict such as we have requested, a plaintiff's verdict, would stifle medical advancement, we would ask simply, Who is to pay for this advancement? Those who will profit or those who will perish?

Negate the Plaintiff's Responsibility

The plaintiff's comparative responsibility may be a factor in determining not only the amount of the plaintiff's recovery but also issues of joint and several liability. In this regard, you should be thoroughly familiar with chapter 33 of the Civil Practice and Remedies Code.[13] The concepts of approaching these problems involving the plaintiff's comparative responsibility, which are discussed in chapter 16, apply equally to the product liability case.

The effective advocate must temper his argument depending on the facts, the parties, and the evidence in the product liability case, with flexibility as his primary goal. If you develop the ability to look past the insignificant issues and contentions raised by the defense, simplify your evidence, and respond with your best arguments, you will find that the product liability case is but another enjoyable challenge.

13. *Id.* §§ 33.001-.016

21

Medical Malpractice

THE MEDICAL MALPRACTICE CASE is the most complex type of personal injury litigation discussed in this work. Automobile and workers' compensation cases may sometimes involve complex and difficult medical issues of causation or physical condition, and the trial of a product liability case may involve complex scientific matters in the area of liability. Medical malpractice cases invariably involve both these elements. The immediate problem for the plaintiff's advocate is to simplify the issues. The challenge is to take complex and arcane medical procedures, anatomical concepts, and scientific data and translate them into information the jury can understand, accept, and use in its deliberations.

The rules of organization, preparation, and flexibility discussed earlier are particularly critical in these complex cases. Likewise, it is imperative to inform the jury of the legal concepts that underlie the malpractice action.

The basic rule of flexibility is the most essential matter to bear in mind when you deliver a closing argument in the malpractice case. Most of the time, because of the complexity of the issues and evidence involved, it is unwise to try to summarize all that has transpired during the trial. Instead, reemphasize the strong points of the plaintiff's case that were not answered by the defense. Often, some of the defense arguments are not that significant to the case, and it may be appropriate to point this fact out to the jury. In malpractice cases, the jury can often be motivated by the fact that the plaintiff was helpless to prevent his or her own injury. Similarly, the jurors may be inspired by a desire to ensure that competent medical and health care will be rendered to people in their community. Finally, remember to consider those issues that may not affect the outcome in the legal sense but may affect the jurors' decision. Adopt the "jury view" and anticipate the positions that certain jurors may take during deliberations; confront these nonissues to obtain a favorable plaintiff's verdict.

Paint a Picture of the Case

Claims brought against health care providers are based almost exclusively on the theory of negligence. Negligence, however, is often a misunderstood concept, particularly in the medical setting. The nonprofessional's concept of this term may range from the belief that the doctor is responsible only if he intended to harm the patient to the belief that he is responsible for any medical complication. Try to dispel these misconceptions as early as the voir dire examination. In closing summation, address them again; discuss and analyze them. Whether negligence incorporates the concept of "ordinary prudence"[1] or whether, as some authorities suggest, it includes the concept of "reasonable and prudent,"[2] the standard must be confronted and explored. Physicians and nurses are accountable when they do not adhere to the standards of their practice, as are other professionals, such as lawyers, accountants, and bankers. When we seek the services of a physician or check into a hospital, we presume that those who are charged with our care will act carefully, prudently, and responsibly. Obviously, if we did not feel this way we would simply choose another physician or hospital. The patient relies on the physicians and nurses during all stages of his care. The patient assumes that the physician will make the proper diagnosis, or at least a diagnosis based on a good, reasonable, and careful analysis of the patient's complaints. In no area of human endeavor are we more dependent on, and at the mercy of, another individual than in the field of medicine. Most of us know little of medicine. We look to the doctor and his assistants, such as the nurses and therapists who work under his supervision, for our care and treatment. We believe what they say. We follow their recommendations. During surgical or other invasive procedures, we are completely at their mercy. We are either totally unconscious or at least partially immobilized by anesthetics. We cannot comment or suggest during the procedure that the physician should be careful. Instead, we must rely on his ethical and legal obligations to do so.

A medical or "malpractice"[3] case is simply the remedy that the law gives when a health care provider's failure to adhere to the standards of his profession results in harm to a patient. From the days of Babylonia with the Code of Hammurabi, civilized people have insisted on some protection from the careless physician. In those days the penalty was much harsher than it is today. Some four thousand years ago, the rule was, "If the surgeon has made a deep incision in the body of a free man and has caused the man's death, or has opened a caruncle in the eye and so destroys the man's eye they shall cut off his forehand."[4]

Our democratic peoples long ago discarded vengeance as the basis for remedy. For vengeance we have substituted the concept of full compensation. The injured patient will be compensated and made whole. If the patient's

---

1. This submission is recommended in 3 STATE BAR OF TEXAS, TEXAS PATTERN JURY CHARGES PJC 40.02 (1982).

2. *See* Hood v. Phillips, 554 S.W.2d 160, 165 (Tex. 1977).

3. Most trial advocates move to limine this term from the case and try to avoid it during argument because of the potential for misunderstanding by jurors. *See, e.g.* Perdue, *The Law of Texas Medical Malpractice*, 22 HOUS. L. REV. 1, 280, 555 (2d ed. 1985).

4. 2 THE BABYLON LAW § 218, at 81 (1955), *quoted in* C. KRAMER, MEDICAL MALPRACTICE 2 (rev. ed. 1965). There was a lesser penalty for injury to slaves. *See* C. KRAMER, *supra*, at 2 n.4.

health cannot be restored, the negligent physician must respond in damages. The injured patient may recover damages to compensate for the physical pain, the anguish and worry, and the loss of the ability to earn a livelihood.

Explain the Duty Concept

Like all tort cases, the malpractice case has four essential elements: duty, a breach of that duty (negligence), proximate cause, and damages. Among these elements, only the concept of duty is not a jury question.[5] Whether the defendant–health care provider owed the patient a duty of reasonable care is a question of law to be determined by the court. One or more jurors may question the duty concept during deliberations, however, even though it is not a part of the court's charge. A juror may say, "I don't believe that the physician should be required to act in such and such a way." Because of this potential problem, it is appropriate to stress to the jurors that the question of duty is not an issue to be determined by them. Explain that the court has already determined that the defendant owed this professional responsibility to the patient and that the only question before the jury is whether he carried out that responsibility in a safe, careful, and reasonable manner. After laying this predicate, you may then discuss and analyze the concept of negligence.

Address the Standard of Care

Once the jury understands the concept of duty, address the concept of the standard of care. The issue in the malpractice case is whether the health care provider acted with reasonable or ordinary prudence. This standard is determined by what a health care provider of ordinary prudence would have done "under the same or similar circumstances."[6]

> When Dr. Santania did this gallbladder surgery on Mrs. State, he cut the common bile duct. We have now heard what catastrophic results this surgical error brings. You have heard from the plaintiff's experts the steps that can be taken by a physician to see that this does not occur. Yet, in the face of this evidence, the defense still contends that Dr. Santania was not negligent. In essence, he says that he was as careful as he needed to be.
>
> If you examine the court's charge closely, and I know that you will, you will see that a physician, such as Dr. Santania, is required to use the prudence or care that would have been appropriate under

---

5. *See, e.g.*, Bryan v. Jenkins, 247 S.W.2d 925, 928 (Tex. Civ. App.—Waco 1952, writ ref'd n.r.e.).

6. *See* 3 State Bar of Texas, *supra* note 1, PJC 40.02.

the circumstances. What were the circumstances? He was attempting a surgical procedure handling, cutting, and sewing on the vital organs of this lady. How careful is ordinary care—ordinary prudence?

Like many of you, I have an old pickup truck that I use to run errands in. When I'm driving down our freeways in Houston with no load, just going about my business, I exercise a certain type of care. But if I load the truck up with a mattress and box springs, I don't drive the same way. Before I take off, I'll tie the mattress down. And, while I'm driving, I'm constantly checking in my rearview mirror to make sure that it hasn't come loose. The reason is that I know that if the mattress comes loose it could drop out on the freeway and cause somebody to have a wreck.

By the same token, if I were to be carrying a load of explosives in the pickup, I would want to be more careful. I would probably even arrange for a police escort.

How careful do we expect our doctors to be when they are performing surgery on us? This doctor either did not identify the common bile duct or identified something else as the common bile duct that was not. He cut it, severed it, and brought about this harm. Can we say in the face of all the evidence we have heard that the way he performed this surgery was in keeping with ordinary care—ordinary prudence—good and reasonable regard for his patient?

Discuss the Professional Charges

In some cases it is effective to blend in with the discussion of the concepts of negligence and standard of care a discussion of the professional charges made by the health care provider. In many instances the physician's charge for his services is quite substantial. In the hospital setting, invariably there are specific charges made for specific services. A common area of malpractice litigation involves nursing care. If the patient was kept in a special unit, such as in intensive care, special charges will have been made. The evidence will show that those charges include a fee made necessary because of the need for a skilled nursing staff. Consider the case where a young girl was brain-damaged because her endotracheal tube was allowed to become occluded while she was in the surgical intensive care unit:

> I am sure that some of you, having now heard the evidence, have been somewhat dismayed, bewildered, and confused at the defense attitude toward this case. From the beginning, they told you it was their position that they had rendered good and appropriate care to little Susie New. But we know from the evidence that Nurse Parker, who was caring for Susie, was not qualified to serve in that intensive

care unit. She was an LVN, not a registered nurse. Her experience in intensive care was limited to a brief period of orientation given her by the hospital before they turned her loose in the unit. Put on top of that is the fact that instead of caring for one or two patients, which is their recommended staffing pattern, she was caring for four patients on the day that this tragic event occurred. This nurse doesn't suction the tube, and, as a result, it becomes stopped up with mucus. When the tube stops up, Susie cannot breathe; she suffocates and suffers brain damage.

The defense says they are not responsible. They gave Susie the care that the law, you and I, and Susie's parents could expect. But if you will look at Exhibit 12, which is the hospital bill, you will find something significant. They charged Susie's parents four hundred dollars a day for her to stay in that unit. That charge is for the unit, the room, the bed. You will note on Exhibit 12 that there are other charges. Charges for the medication, catheters, and tubes that were used. They even charged for the facial tissues. What did that four hundred dollars represent? Obviously, not just the right to occupy that bed. As you've heard from the evidence, that four hundred dollars went primarily to provide nursing care. Both Susie's parents and their attending physician believed that that four hundred dollars was buying good, adequate, and prudent nursing care. A nurse who was qualified to serve in the surgical intensive care unit. A nurse who would have time to do the things for Susie that needed to be done. These parents paid for that service. They didn't get it. We suggest that this is simply another factor that you can look at when you address the defense argument that they were not negligent.

Negate the Loss-of-License Argument

The potential effect of a plaintiff's verdict on the defendant's professional standing must be addressed—not so much in response to an argument made by the defense but rather to anticipate jurors' concerns that will be expressed during deliberations. The jurors must understand that they are deciding a purely civil matter and that neither the lawyer nor the plaintiff is seeking to interfere with or revoke the medical license of the defendant. Stress the fact that the general skill or qualification of the doctor is not being questioned; at issue is only the manner in which this particular medical case was managed. Remind the jurors that they owe no allegiance to the medical profession and that they professed this on the voir dire examination.

Some jurors may be concerned that a finding of negligence will be a professional embarrassment to the defendant. It is important to contrast any such "embarrassment" with the permanent, substantial, and significant damages the plaintiff has sustained.

Emphasize Medical Literature and Standards

Before pursuing the malpractice case, the experienced advocate will have carefully reviewed and analyzed the relevant medical literature. The plaintiff's case will not be inconsistent with medical principles announced in the literature, and the literature will support the plaintiff's contentions. In these instances the plaintiff can demonstrate that the treatment rendered by the defendant was inconsistent with, or contradictory to, the principles stated in medical texts, journals, and articles. This demonstration can be a significant weapon in the plaintiff's arsenal. Remind the jury of the medical principles and how the defendant's conduct conflicted with those principles. The question then becomes simply whether those medical principles, as stated in the literature, are the correct principles of medicine. Emphasize the fact that the statements were written by noted scholars and medical practitioners. Highlight that these statements are presented in the objective environment of medical communication and are not written for the purpose of defending or prosecuting a lawsuit. Show that physicians in this state and throughout the nation study these basic principles.

> In this case the defense says that the fourteen-month delay in diagnosing my friend Rose Brown's breast cancer did not make any difference. Essentially, they have admitted that Dr. Sabawu should have been more alert to her problems. Certainly he should have appreciated the ominous potential represented by that lump that Mrs. Brown pointed out to him as early as November 1982. But, says the defense, even if Dr. Sabawu had diagnosed and treated the breast cancer at that time, the outcome would have been the same. This cancer would, as you have heard from their evidence, still have metastasized to other portions of her body.
>
> This case has become a battleground for scientific debate. You've heard testimony from experts called by both Mrs. Brown and the defense. Our experts have reminded us of simple facts of which most of us were already aware. "Early diagnosis can make the difference in treating cancer." Dr. Franks and Dr. Jankowski have indicated that in their opinion, if this cancer had been diagnosed in its early stages and Mrs. Brown had been operated on at that time, the spread—the metastasis—of this cancer would not have occurred. The two defense experts testified essentially that no one can tell and that they do not believe this to be an established scientific fact.
>
> But you have heard more than just the testimony of these warring factions of physicians. We brought you statistics from the nationwide study conducted by the National Cancer Institute in Washington, D.C. This statistical evidence is compiled from the results at all the major medical institutions that treat cancer across

> this country. We brought you articles from medical journals, such as the one that appeared in the *American Journal of Oncology*. The statistics show that the earlier diagnosis would have made a difference in Mrs. Brown's case. The medical writers indicate that earlier diagnosis would have made a difference in Mrs. Brown's case. The principles announced by these eminent authorities in the field of medicine all indicate that earlier diagnosis would have made a difference.
>
> When you address this issue of legal causation or, as the lawyers and judges call it, "proximate cause," we would ask that you look at all the evidence. Consider not only the testimony of the witnesses but also the basis for their opinions. We ask that you ask yourselves and your fellow jurors this question, What makes the most sense and represents what you would consider sound medicine—the defendant's position now as it has been announced by him and his experts—opinions that are presented now that his conduct has made an appointment with death for this lady—or that which has been clearly established by the scientific research and literature? The results of the National Cancer Institute study were not devised, arrived at, or published either to defend or prosecute this or any other case. Those eminent medical articles that announced the principles you have heard so much about were not written with a lawsuit in mind. Rather, they were objective, considered, and educated pronouncements. They represent the body of scientific thought from which all doctors draw in their day-to-day practice.

If the defendant tries to reject the victim's claim because of the inability of medical science to prove it clearly, place special emphasis on the superior nature of the testimony of the plaintiff's attending physician. Stress the fact that the testimony of this witness was based on observations made over a long period, in the course of trying to heal the plaintiff. Then compare the testimony of that witness with the testimony of the defendant's medical witnesses, who examined the plaintiff briefly, for the sole purpose of testifying at the trial.

In summing up the medical issues in a case, it is often highly profitable to read to the jury excerpts from both the opening statements of the defense and the testimony of the medical witnesses. In the voir dire or opening statement, the defendant's lawyer may have stated a medical contention that either has not been proved at trial or has been fully disproved. As discussed earlier, referring to medical books and treatises that support the plaintiff's right to recover will be most helpful to his cause; in many cases trying to sum up the medical issues involved without mentioning such books would be like trying to find some unfamiliar street in Houston without the benefit of a city map. Stress the great significance of the literature in question with respect to the issues involved. Make it clear to the jury that before the defense medical witnesses were confronted, the authenticity and relevance of the work were established by expert witnesses. The following argument differs only slightly from the previous one:

> These medical studies were made to enlighten the medical profession in its never-ending quest to cure the sick, to heal the afflicted. Their authors received no fee to come here as witnesses. They advocate the cause of no one who is here before you. When you take one of your family to a doctor for a medical consultation, are you not most vitally concerned with what medical science has found out about the sickness or condition for which you are seeking help? What would you think of your doctor, with regard to his diagnosis and treatment of anyone dear to you, if his opinions were opposed by nationally known specialists, not recognized by physicians who practiced in that medical specialty?
>
> The plaintiff has no monopoly on the literature of medicine. Yet when his doctor testified to the fact that, although the medical test performed on Jack Thomas was negative, that result did not mean that he did not have this condition, the defense did not challenge the truth of that statement. Why didn't they challenge it? They would have if there were writings in the medical libraries to prove that the witness was wrong.

Argue the Rhetorical

Rhetorical questions[7] can be particularly effective in the malpractice case: many prominent trial lawyers use this technique.[8] The argument depends on the facts of the case, of course, but here are some of the more commonly argued rhetoricals:

- Who was caring for this patient during this time?
- What kind of medical care do you want the doctors of this community to render?
- Couldn't the defendant have at least picked up the telephone and talked with a consultant?

---

7. *See* ch. 13 on the use of rhetorical questions.

8. The New York trial lawyer Moe Levine is perhaps most notable for his use of this type of argument. *See generally* M. LEVINE, SUMMATIONS: THE BEST OF MOE (1967); M. LEVINE, SURGICAL MALPRACTICE: SURGICAL ERRORS AND ACCIDENTS AND PROFESSIONAL LIABILITY TO THE INJURED (1970).

- If the emergency room physician had any question about this EKG, shouldn't she have at least consulted her superior?
- When Nurse Jones realized that her unit was understaffed that evening, shouldn't she have at least inquired of her supervisor whether any additional help was available?

These questions may drive home the desired point even more effectively than an affirmative statement.

Make the Issue Bigger Than the Case

It is often particularly appropriate in malpractice cases to remind the jury that the issues of the case are larger than the narrow questions submitted to them by the court. The beau ideal of trial advocates, Clarence Darrow, was noted for this approach.[9] Explain that the issue involved is not simply whether this particular plaintiff should recover damages. Although that issue is certainly important, it is too small in the abstract. The real issue is the type of medical care that people have a right to expect and demand. Stress that the community, speaking through this jury, has the right and the duty to establish what is and what is not accepted as proper medical practice. All of us, at some time in our lives, will come under the care of these doctors. Comment that you would personally feel disgusted to learn some years from now that this kind of thing happened again to some other citizen of this community. Tell the jurors that if they approve these medical practices and find that the defendant was not negligent, then all that we would be able to say to future victims is, "Well, we tried a case like that some years ago and that jury, speaking for this community, approved those medical practices."

Defend the Unpopular Position

In conjunction with making the issues appear larger than the case, you may also have the opportunity to defend an unpopular expert opinion. If the defense has more than one expert in a malpractice case and the plaintiff has only one physician, remind the jurors that the opinions of a majority should never be considered correct merely because they are the most popular.

---

9. Although Clarence Darrow tried primarily criminal and labor cases, a study of his summations is certainly helpful to any trial lawyer. A specific example of this type of argument was used when he defended Thomas Kid on criminal conspiracy charges. *See generally* I. STONE, CLARENCE DARROW FOR THE DEFENSE (1941 & reprint 1971): "I do not appeal for him; that cause is too narrow for me, much as I love him and long as I have worked by his side. I appeal to you not for Thomas Kid, but I appeal to you for the long line—the long, long line reaching back through the ages and forward to the years to come—the long line of despoiled and downtrodden people of the earth." *Id.* at 134.

Emphasize for the jurors that their decision should be based on the *credible* evidence, not merely the greater amount of testimony or larger number of experts: argue that, even though the defense has brought forth more doctors to justify the defendant's conduct, their opinions cannot be given greater credence than those of the plaintiff's expert on the basis of numbers alone.

You may wish to strengthen your "credibility" by defending the unpopular position of your expert witness. You can use anecdotes liberally in this situation, depending on the arguments advanced by the defense.

> In the government's investigation of the shuttle explosion, it came to light that Allen McDonald, one of the engineers at the launch site, disapproved of the scheduled launch because he felt that the temperature was too low. It was his position that the cold temperature affected the safety of the launch and particularly the integrity of the O-rings. Mr. McDonald was overruled by a number of other engineers and representatives. Indeed, there is no question that his view was by far that of the minority. Yet, we know now in retrospect that it was not safe to make the launch that morning.
>
> Unfortunately, on the occasion in question, Mr. McDonald became the target of verbal criticism and castigation because of his position. History, however, tells us that he was right.
>
> There are other historical examples to which we could refer to illustrate this point. The right, proper, and just view is not always the "popular" view. Before his election as President, Jack Kennedy wrote a book called *Profiles in Courage*. That book was devoted to a discussion of many men in American history, such as Daniel Webster and Thomas Jefferson, who had sacrificed their positions and power because they held views that were unpopular at the time but that history tells us were correct. Perhaps the best example in President Kennedy's book that we would be familiar with is that of Sam Houston: when the Civil War broke out, he opposed secession.
>
> But all these historical figures, whether they are as recent as Allen McDonald or as remote as Sam Houston, teach us that we cannot always measure right, safety, or what is just by the opinions of the majority.
>
> In a malpractice case, for example, there will always be more physicians to step forward and defend the questioned conduct than there will be to withstand the pressures against unpopular opinion. As you have seen in this case, Dr. Eacham's opinions were belittled and berated by a team of doctors for the defendant. Their insolence was a product of their teamwork. After all, Dr. Eacham's opinions only represented the views of one man, said the defense. In short, they scorned his opinions, not so much on their merit but because they were unpopular in this case.

> Ladies and gentlemen, the defense seems to be that you should condone by your verdict the medical practices of the defendant because his friends say that those practices are acceptable. As throughout history, however, the real question that confronts you is whether you search for what is right or, instead, for what is popular.

Anticipate the "Nontreating Doctor" Argument

The plaintiff may, for various reasons, choose not to call the treating physician as a witness. The defense may argue that he should have done so. Respond that plaintiff's counsel is not the only lawyer with subpoena powers. The plaintiff does not need the subsequent treating physician to make a case, because other highly competent expert testimony was presented. Suggest that perhaps the defense needed the treating physician and is trying to put the matter off on the plaintiff. Point out that it is difficult to obtain a local expert who will testify, because of professional or social contacts between the expert and the defendant-physician. Tell the jury that the witness must be paid for his time spent preparing and testifying because of his many commitments—some of which include teaching medical students to avoid such poor practices as have been documented in this case.

Justify the Foreign Physician

It is very difficult to secure expert testimony from a physician who practices in the same geographical area as that of the defendant: a testifying expert will usually be criticized, ostracized, and treated as something of a pariah. Because of this attitude within the medical profession, the victim's lawyer is often required to look beyond the immediate community for expert assistance. The physician testifying in a malpractice case in Jasper may actually be teaching or practicing in Dallas. The plaintiff's expert in Houston may be a physician who practices or teaches in Phoenix, Los Angeles, or Boston. In such instances the defense will often persist in arguing that the plaintiff should explain why he had to go so far to get an expert to support his cause. Many trial judges prohibit the plaintiff from going into the so-called conspiracy of silence that exists in the medical profession during the trial of the case.

A defense argument that the plaintiff should explain the need to get an expert from outside the community, however, may open the door for a vigorous reply:[10]

---

10. Texas courts have long recognized that an argument, although ordinarily improper, may become justified if the opponent's argument invites the reply. *See, e.g.*, Hartford Accident & Indem. Co. v. Thurmond, 527 S.W.2d 180, 193-94 (Tex. Civ. App.—Corpus Christi 1975, writ ref'd n.r.e.); Dyer v. Hardin, 323 S.W.2d 119, 127 (Tex. Civ. App.—Amarillo 1959, writ ref'd n.r.e.). The limitation, however, is that the response must be reasonable considering the provocation. Seeley v. Eaton, 506 S.W.2d 719, 721-22 (Tex. Civ. App.—Houston [14th Dist.] 1974, writ ref'd n.r.e.).

In his closing summation, Dr. Jackson's lawyer has asked why we had to go to Boston for our expert testimony if our case against Dr. Jackson was so strong. Most of you are smart enough to know the answer to that question without my having to address it. We have all heard of the reluctance of one physician to testify against another. We even have a term for it in law and medicine. It is called the "conspiracy of silence." It isn't that all the doctors will come forward to support what this doctor did. Instead, they simply conspire to remain silent while realizing that this will prevent the truth from being known and, in turn, protect this doctor. While we may be offended by this approach, we cannot be overly harsh. I, for one, can understand the reluctance a physician would have to testify against another doctor who practices in the same community, the same state, when he knows that he will see that defendant at some time, on some occasion, after the trial. At a professional meeting. At a social event. At a medical convention.

But I do have difficulty with the lawyer who will stand and make this an issue when he knows what the circumstances are. This defense lawyer knows the difficult position in which any injured victim is placed when the issue is that of medical care. He knows of the conspiracy of silence. He knows of the reluctance to testify. Notice the defense didn't suggest that Dr. Boyd was not qualified. He had performed as many neurosurgical procedures as had Dr. Jackson. From the evidence, he had performed more procedures, more complex procedures than the defendant. The only thing about Dr. Boyd's testimony that was challenged by the defense was his opinions. Of course, the defense didn't like what he had to say. But did what he had to say make sense to you? Doesn't it make sense that when you're doing this type of neurosurgery, these precautionary steps are taken to ensure that the subarachnoid space is not entered? When he said that, when he outlined for you the way that these crippling, maiming, catastrophic injuries could have been avoided, he looked you in the eye. I think all of you formed the impression that Dr. Boyd was intelligent, honest, and sincere. I have heard no argument from the defense that he was anything other than that. They don't question his qualifications. They don't question his integrity. They just don't like what he has to say and where he comes from.

So, in response to the defense question of why we had to go to Boston to get an expert, I would follow with what is perhaps a more significant, a more meaningful question to you: Is it right for the defense to make an issue of this when doctors refuse to talk in the aftermath of these types of tragedies?

Address Your Expert Witness's Fee and Time

A typical defense tactic in cross-examining the plaintiff's expert is to dwell at length on the expert witness's fees and charges. Probably in no other form of personal injury litigation will the expert's fee be as substantial—usually because the plaintiff's expert, to become familiar with the case, must spend substantial time reviewing extensive records, reports, diagnostic tests, and in-house hospital policies and procedures. This situation always casts the plaintiff in a dilemma. If he calls an expert to testify who has not spent a great deal of time in preparation, the expert becomes vulnerable because of his lack of familiarity with the facts of the case. If, on the other hand, the plaintiff's expert makes an in-depth review, he is criticized because of the amount of his charges. Explain this dilemma to the jury, and consider asking, "Which would you rather have us bring you, an expert who simply glanced at the matter and formulated opinions or an expert who was committed to a thorough, comprehensive, in-depth review of the matter?"

It may be appropriate to contrast the time spent by the plaintiff's expert with that spent by the defense: if the defense expert has spent less time than your witness in reviewing the matter, let the jury know. Sometimes the defense is blessed with a generous expert who is serving free of charge. If the defense can get its expert to donate time and appear, you may want to ask why the defendant did not readily consult that expert before diagnosing and treating the plaintiff.

Mention the Defendant's Failure To Recognize Authorities

Before our new rules of evidence became effective in 1983, it was common practice for the defendant and his experts to refuse to recognize any published materials as authoritative. The earlier rule had been that if the witness refused to recognize the source as authoritative, it could not be used for impeachment.[11] The present rule allows any published work that has been recognized by any expert to be used for substantive evidence as well as impeachment;[12] in other words, for the published work to be used for impeachment, it is not necessary that the witness be familiar with it or otherwise accept or recognize it. Despite this change in the rules, many defendants still refuse to recognize medical texts, journal articles, and other published works as authoritative even though the document is obviously one with which the doctor is presently

---

11. *See, e.g.*, Bowles v. Bourdon, 219 S.W.2d 779, 783 (Tex. 1949); Seeley v. Eaton, 506 S.W.2d 719, 723 (Tex. Civ. App.—Houston [14th Dist.] 1974, writ ref'd n.r.e.).

12. Tex. R. Civ. Evid. 803(18); Wellborn, *Article VIII: Hearsay*, 20 Hous. L. Rev. 477, 526 (1983) (Texas Rules of Evidence Handbook).

familiar or to which he has had some exposure in the past. Intransigence of this sort provides excellent material for argument to the jury:

> You have heard Dr. Davidson testify throughout this trial that he did not recognize any text, study, or journal article as authoritative. We referred him to Nelson on pediatrics. "I don't accept it." We referred him to Harrison's text on internal medicine. "It's not an authoritative work." We referred him to five separate journal articles dealing with this problem—dehydration of the young infant. Articles in the *Journal of Pediatrics*, the *New England Journal of Medicine*, and others. He hasn't read them, or, if he has, he doesn't accept them. To Dr. Davidson, Dr. Davidson is the only authority. No one else knows anything about the diagnosis and treatment of an infant who is experiencing severe fluid loss from vomiting and diarrhea. No one but Dr. Davidson knows the impact of dehydration on the infant. If he is so knowledgeable, so brilliant, so smart, maybe he should write a book. We could slip him in very neatly in our medical libraries between "A" for arrogance and "B" for baloney.

Counter the Twenty-Twenty Hindsight Contention

In a malpractice case the defense will often argue that all the plaintiff's expert testimony is based on twenty-twenty hindsight. According to this line of reasoning, because they had the benefit of looking back on the medical events, the plaintiff's experts are not to be believed. They knew that the plaintiff's course of treatment was going to lead to death, disability, or some type of injury; they are judging the case after the fact.

Stress that your expert's testimony was necessarily based on the medical records.

> What was the basis for Dr. Randolph's opinions? All his opinions resulted from his analysis, review, and consideration of the medical records prepared by the defendants—Dr. Brown and the nurses at General Hospital. None of these records were made by Mr. and Mrs. Boudreaux. Certainly none of them were made by little Cheryl; she could not even sign her own consent form for the surgery since she was not of legal age. Can anyone point to a single entry in any of these records that was made by these parents or this little girl? For heaven's sake, until after this tragic event occurred and we obtained the medical records for them, they had no idea what was there. Our expert's opinion was based totally on medical records. Records prepared by the defendants. Records in their keeping, their custody. Records of which they are the sole author.

Then stress that the records show that the plaintiff's treatment should have been handled differently. Explain to the jury that if it followed the defense counsel's reasoning, any analysis of an event is with twenty-twenty hindsight. The fact that the defendant's actions can be evaluated in light of their consequences does not change the fact that the actions constituted a deviation from the accepted standards presented to the jury. A different approach to analyzing events would stifle any type of scientific research, learning, or improvement.

Clarify the Role of Circumstantial Evidence

Specific examples and the concept of arguing circumstantial evidence are discussed in chapters 12, 18, and 19. In all but the few malpractice cases in which the plaintiff's proof on liability is based on direct evidence, it is particularly important to stress the significance of circumstantial evidence. Invariably, the defense will assert that observations were made that were not documented in the records: some aspect of the surgical procedure that was not mentioned in the records was performed; some medical or nursing contacts were made with the patient although they were not recorded. Invariably, the medical records will conflict with the testimony of the plaintiff, his relatives, and his friends. For this reason, it is important to clarify the role of circumstantial evidence in the jurors' minds. Point out that the court's charge clearly indicates that a verdict may be based on circumstantial evidence. Circumstantial evidence is to be given no less weight than direct evidence. If the jury could not follow the court's instructions on this matter, there would be no instances of medical negligence in which the plaintiff would ever have a remedy: in all instances of medical injury, the plaintiff must make his case by expert review of the defendant's records. In virtually no instance will an independent advocate who understands the medical principles involved have been present during the occurrences in issue. You may also argue that, in some instances, circumstantial evidence is more reliable than direct evidence.[13]

Neutralize the Presence of Physicians and Nurses

In some situations, particularly in rural areas, the defense will have various physicians and nurses present for the closing summation. Some defense counsel believe the presence of these spectators has a chilling effect on the jurors in their deliberations. Neutralize their presence by pointing out that the only possible reason they have chosen to attend the argument is to affect the jury in its verdict. Rhetorical questions may be particularly effective:

---

13. See ch. 18.

- Where were these nurses when Mrs. Holmes was crying out for help?
- Where were these doctors when it was obvious that Mr. Johnson's peritonitis needed to be medically treated?

Interject the "No Apology" Argument

Experienced malpractice litigators know that the most common impetus that leads the injured patient or members of his family to go to an attorney is the desire for a meaningful explanation of the injury. Often the malpractice victim or his family has become frustrated by the inability to obtain any information or explanation of how or why the medical injury occurred. During argument, remind the jury that if the doctor is so sincere in his belief that he did nothing wrong, why didn't he ever approach the patient or his survivors to explain what happened? You may demand rhetorically: "Who are these people who hold the destiny of their fellow man in the palms of their hands and yet do not have the compassion to come and explain to him what happened after it occurred?"

Stress the Time Element

Medical malpractice cases differ from other classical forms of personal injury in one significant respect: the incident complained of usually occurred over a significant period of time. Whereas in an automobile case, industrial accident, or other personal injury case, the defendant's negligence may have occurred within a few seconds, in most malpractice situations the defendant's negligence occurred over a protracted period. In surgical cases the plaintiff can usually demonstrate that the procedure lasted many minutes or even hours. Seldom is the defendant under any pressure of time to conclude the procedure. Thus, if the defendant negligently performed the procedure, this negligence occurred at a time when he had the opportunity to reflect, consider, and deliberate. If the malpractice occurred in a hospital or office, these time considerations may become even more significant.

Thus, in many cases you must stress the fact that the defendant's negligence occurred over extended time and was not the result of an alternative chosen under exigent circumstances. Sometimes you can blend this argument with other considerations to drive home the fact that the medical injury is a result of more than a momentary oversight.

> When we talk of Dr. Camp's negligence in his treatment of Calvin Dunston, of what are we speaking? One time—one incident—a few seconds of carelessness? The evidence in this case has brought home to me something that I have believed for a long time. The human body is amazingly resilient. Not only can it withstand disease and

injury, it has the amazing capacity to absorb and recover from improper medical care—but not from a battering of medical negligence like that shown in this case.

After the abdominal surgery was performed on Mr. Dunston, the evidence tells us that he began to develop an infection. That infection first manifested itself on the second postoperative day, when he began to have a fever. Dr. Camp saw the patient that day and did nothing.

That night Calvin became delirious. He was sweating profusely. The nurses were concerned enough that they decided to call the doctor. He gave a few orders over the phone but wouldn't come.

The next day, the patient—our friend and neighbor, Calvin—was experiencing pain, the likes of which fortunately none of us will probably ever know. Agonizing, intense pain. He was sweating, the wound was draining, and he was hallucinating. Again, a call to the doctor with no result.

Then, when they finally took Calvin to the operating room, it was too late. For almost one hundred hours this man went without any significant medical attention.

We are not dealing here with a case of a person who is careless for a few seconds or even a few minutes. This carelessness, this neglect, this indifference went on for hours. The hours passed into days. It is clear from the evidence that if at any time during this inexcusable ordeal Dr. Camp had taken any reasonable steps to deal with Calvin's problems, we would not be here today.

After he saw his patient each time or talked to the nurses, do you think Dr. Camp was thinking of him? Was Dr. Camp further considering the problems? Was he concerned about the treatment and outcome? Or, having seen the patient or talked to the nurses on the phone about him, did Dr. Camp simply dismiss the matter? The evidence shows that Calvin and his wife were thinking of the doctor. There wasn't an hour during this critical period of time when they weren't thinking of him. Wondering when he would come and see Calvin next. Wondering what he might do for Calvin. Thinking that surely this doctor, with all his knowledge, would address Calvin's needs and do something—anything to help him overcome the vice of infection that threatened his life.

Simplify the Issues

The basic premise underlying all successful plaintiffs' arguments in malpractice cases is simplification. The complex nature of these cases mandates that the issues be simplified. Almost all the techniques discussed earlier are useful for this purpose. For example, analogy can be particularly useful in helping the jury understand medical principles. In a malpractice case involving the failure of nurses to report symptoms of increased intercranial pressure and its predictable effects, the following argument might be effective:

> The human brain sits in a sealed compartment. A significant part of that sealed vault or compartment is composed of cerebral spinal fluid. It has much the consistency of water. The brain floats upon and is surrounded by this fluid. When, because of an injury, such as was sustained by young Parker Raymond, the brain begins to swell—this fluid is displaced. To help you appreciate this concept, let's refer to a common example. Most of us have squeezed the juice out of an orange. Increased intercranial pressure, brought on by brain swelling, is much the same type of thing. The tissues of the brain, because of the swelling, are traumatized and displaced. Because of the displacement of the tissues, they cannot receive their natural nutrition, which is supplied by the vascular system of the brain. So, as with the orange, the longer this condition is permitted to exist, the more the trauma occurs to the brain. If you've ever looked at an orange after the juice has been squeezed out, you have some idea of the effect that increased and unrelieved intercranial pressure has on the brain.

Similar analogies can be used in cases involving misdiagnosis of myocardial infarctions; the human heart can be likened to an electrical, four-chambered pump. Cancer can be likened to a hostile army constantly mobilizing and building for war; if we can attack and destroy the army before it establishes a beachhead, the chances are great that the army will be defeated.

You must simplify not only the medical concepts but the legal concept of negligence as well. Ominous symptoms and medical signs represent red flags or warnings to the physician. The physician who overlooks a series of ominous symptoms and positive diagnostic and lab reports is much like the driver who proceeds past several road signs warning that the road ahead is closed and dangerous. In each case, presenting a simplified view demonstrates that the plaintiff's injuries are the inexorable result of the defendant's acts.

Although medical malpractice cases are highly complex, the skilled advocate who uses all his arsenal of weapons for communication and persuasion has a good chance for success.

PART 7

Specific Arguments on Damages

Man's inhumanity to man
Makes countless thousands mourn!

—Robert Burns, "Man Was Made To Mourn"

22

Arguing Damages—Generally

TO ARGUE EFFECTIVELY FOR DAMAGES, the advocate must bring to his arsenal all the techniques of persuasion, inspiration, and motivation. The damages award may be significantly affected by the jury argument—either positively or negatively. It is often said that "two lawyers could try the same case and one would get a one-hundred-thousand-dollar verdict while the other would get a two-million-dollar verdict." This aphorism highlights the importance of oral advocacy on the question of damages.

The skilled advocate is able to coalesce and blend the medical and scientific evidence with proof regarding how the injuries have affected and will continue to affect the plaintiff. An inadequate award may be returned by a jury because the plaintiff's lawyer—

- failed to understand the physiology and anatomical principles involved;
- failed to understand the significance and meaning of the various medical findings;
- failed to understand the mechanism of injury;
- failed to understand and communicate how the injury has affected the plaintiff's ability to live and enjoy life; or
- failed to understand the economic consequences of the injury.

To argue effectively for damages, you must understand and appreciate the miracle of the human body: the fantastic structure of the bone and the marrow within, which produces several hundred million cells every second; the beating heart, which pumps in and out one-sixth of a quart of blood every second for seventy years; the liver, within which a thimbleful of substance carries on as many chemical processes as a six-story factory; the brain, which has millions of connections and mysterious functions of consciousness. The human skin, for example, is a profusion of organic structures in a thin layer. It contains networks, cables, antennas, switches, glands, blood-vessel loops, alarm mechanisms, and many chemical and physical mysteries that our medical instruments have yet to fully explore and understand. The skin is one of the largest organs in the human body. The entire skin weighs twice as much as the liver or the brain. It receives one-third of the circulating blood, and its surface extends over twenty thousand square centimeters. One square centimeter of human skin contains two sensory apparatuses for cold, twelve sensory apparatuses for heat, three million cells, an average of ten hairs, fifteen sebaceous glands, one yard of blood vessels, one hundred sweat glands, three thousand sensory cells at the ends of nerve fibers, four yards of nerves, twenty-five pressure apparatuses for the perception of tactile stimuli, and two hundred nerve endings to record pain.

Armed with a rudimentary appreciation of the human body, interlace your argument with the basic concepts and principles explored in this book. Once you have mastered these techniques, you may select and incorporate certain specific damages arguments.

Reconsidering Basic Techniques and Tactics

Using a Case Theme

A brief review of the basic techniques and tactics discussed in earlier chapters will be valuable in assessing how to proceed with the damages argument.

If damages are a significant issue in the case—for example, if the evidence will support a conclusion of catastrophic, permanent, or significant injuries—incorporate some reference to the plaintiff's injuries within the case theme.[1] Avoid adopting a case theme that concentrates solely on the questions of liability. A case theme employing the principle of multiple references was recently developed in a medical malpractice action against a hospital and neurosurgeon. The evidence showed that the plaintiff, who had experienced hydrocephalus since birth, received a shunt revision in one of the major Houston hospitals. Following the revision, the shunt became occluded or obstructed, resulting in increased intercranial pressure. The nurses in attendance failed to observe and report to the attending physician the complications that were occurring. During critical periods after the surgery, the parents expressed concern to the nurses. As a result of the unrelieved obstruction, the teenage plaintiff sustained significant brain damage. The following case theme was employed to incorporate reference both to the liability aspect of the case and to damages.

> This case was brought because the hospital would not listen.
>
> On three separate occasions, this hospital would not listen to simple truths and facts that were being put before it. First, on the night of July 13 and the early morning hours of July 14, when Pippa Victor was experiencing symptoms, signs, and indications of increased intercranial pressure, the nurses would not listen. They ignored her complaints of photophobia, vomiting, headache, lethargy, and disorientation. They didn't notify her doctor. The hospital and its nurses would not listen.

---

1. See ch. 1 for a complete discussion of the case-theme concept.

After this inexcusable incident occurred, the hospital would not listen a second time. As the evidence began to mount that this needless, inexcusable failure to respond to her needs had caused significant, irreversible, and crippling brain injury—they refused to listen again. Instead of accepting the medical evidence that was mounting, they began to look around for some explanation other than that which was obvious. The hospital and its doctors would not listen.

Finally, for the third time, they will not listen again. After the evidence has been developed about Pippa through her lawyers—they will not listen. We have accumulated evidence from medical witnesses, laypersons, teachers, and rehabilitation experts from across this state. Not only does that evidence demonstrate in an overwhelming fashion that the care Pippa received at the hospital was inadequate, negligent, and unjustifiable, it also proves what that inexcusable conduct has wrought. You have heard witness after witness testify about the nature of Pippa's injuries. They have told you that she cannot find her way to the women's restroom and back to the family's table in a restaurant—that she cannot remember the names of even her closest friends and relatives. You have also heard that she will never be capable of marrying, having children, or raising a family. Yet, for the third and final time, the hospital and its lawyers will not listen.

Perhaps they will listen to you when you return your verdict.

The Concepts of Communication in Arguing Damages

You must effectively employ all the levels of communication when arguing damages. Verbal content must be appropriate for the facts of the case. Proper vocal and physical aspects of communication must be used to the utmost. Finally, you must be capable of transferring feelings to the jury that are appropriate for the facts of the case and that are calculated to bring about a full understanding of the impact that the injuries have had on the plaintiff.[2]

Subliminal Persuasion

It is essential to employ the concepts of subliminal persuasion, such as the jurors' feelings of obligations to a plaintiff they believe is worthy, their desire to be consistent with their notions of right and wrong, and the importance of scarce and valuable information. It is equally important to identify "non-issues" that may have arisen during the trial of the case and might be used to

2. See ch. 3 for a discussion of these concepts.

motivate the jury toward a favorable verdict—particularly on the damages questions.[3]

Selecting and Using Words

When arguing damages, be extremely careful in selecting the words to describe the plaintiff's injuries. Avoid impotent, limp, and weak language (as urged in chapter 10); use power words at every opportunity. Compare the following arguments:

> As a result of the defendant's negligence, Mrs. Ruby McIntyre has been rendered disabled. Her paralysis certainly, we think, would make it difficult if not impossible for her to get a job. It appears to us from the evidence that she has a good amount of mental anguish as a result of these injuries. The defendant has pointed out that she's not in any physical pain. That would appear to be the case. However, we still feel that these injuries are significant because they have rendered this lady disabled. She can get back and forth only by the use of a wheelchair. She has been damaged significantly, and it is for that reason that we have asked for the damages that are prayed for in this case.

By contrast, the following argument incorporates power words:

> What is the price of carelessness, recklessness, and indifference? It is a crippled and maimed body. Ruby McIntyre cannot stand, walk, or go up a flight of stairs. It is an Olympic challenge for her to get in and out of a taxicab or automobile. You saw the taxing of physical resources that was required when she simply moved from her wheelchair to the witness stand. Ruby is a bright, intelligent, and loving mind imprisoned in a wretched half-corpse. For four years she has been paying the price for the defendant's carelessness. Her entire future was mortgaged on that eventful day back in 1984. Every minute, every hour, every day for the rest of her life will be spent in retiring that debt.

Using Metaphors

Using metaphors is an effective and easy way to energize the argument on damages.[4]

---

3. See ch. 4 for a discussion of subliminal persuasion.
4. See ch. 11 for a discussion of using metaphors.

What did these people lose when Toby Kennedy died on February 14, 1986? The cold, scientific evidence tells us that they lost a nineteen-month-old male, twenty-eight and one-half inches tall, weighing thirty-four pounds. But in him was that which cannot be described or measured scientifically—all of the hopes and dreams of his parents. He was the masterwork of an artist. A painting that was destroyed entirely after only the first few brush strokes of color had been applied. When the artist began that painting, he knew that it would be magnificent. He had a view in his mind's eye of the picture he would create. A painting as perfect as that hanging in the great galleries to be seen by thousands of people. A sculpture as spectacular as one outside a public building where it stands to be admired by throngs. A symphony so sweet that it would be played over and over before the admiring multitudes.

The artist would get a warm feeling in his heart every time he saw someone admiring his painting. The composer would have tears in his eyes every time he heard his symphony played.

But that work was destroyed before it was even really started. A child is much like a great work of art. The rearing, training, education, and direction of a child are the fashioning of a personality—a human being—no less than that of the sculptor who puts his hands to clay.

But there is one difference.

When the painting is destroyed, the artist may buy a new canvas and begin again. The composer whose mind is still filled with the music that only he has heard can renew his efforts to write his great symphony. But these parents can never again have this child. He is lost forever.

Using Poetry and Biblical Passages

If you have considered using poetry in your argument (discussed in chapter 11), you may also wish to consider using biblical sayings and passages. These types of references are used almost exclusively in arguing damages. Years ago, when the population of this state was typically rural, high-school educated, and Christian by religious preference, the great trial lawyers liberally sprinkled their arguments with biblical references. The nature of the Texas population has changed dramatically in the last three decades. Particularly in our larger metropolitan areas, juries may be composed of people who have several college degrees, who are agnostic or atheist, or who follow various faiths, such as Judaism, Hinduism, and the forms of the Islamic religion. By the same token, in some areas of the state the people still largely resemble in educational background and religious preference the juries made up of their mothers and fathers some thirty years ago. The lesson should be clear: in using biblical references, consider the forum in which your case is tried. Using biblical references in the traditional sense may be offensive to certain jurors in some communities.

One reference often used in arguing damages is contained in *Galatians*, chapter 6, verse 2 (King James): "Bear ye one another's burdens, and so fulfil the law of Christ." Consider the two following methods of injecting this passage into argument. The first method might be appropriate in some areas of the state but offensive to some jurors in others; the second approach would invariably be used in the metropolitan areas.

> When it comes to considering this victim's damages in this case, it is appropriate that we heed the teachings of the Bible and of our Savior. In *Galatians* it is said, "Bear ye one another's burdens, and so fulfil the law of Christ."

Contrast that approach with the following:

> In seeking guidance on this most important issue of damages, it is important that we turn to the philosophers and inspired men of history. There is a good book that many of us have read. Actually, it is a book made up of many books. One of the books in that great and inspired work is called *Galatians*. In that book, chapter 6, verse 2, we are reminded that we must be willing to "bear one another's burdens." In so doing, we fulfill the law of the Creator.

Using Embedded Commands

Using embedded commands is a particularly forceful and effective technique in arguing damages. Invariably, the skilled advocate will have touched on damages in some detail during the voir dire examination and will have obtained, at a minimum, the commitment from the jury that it will approach the question of damages with an open mind. Embedded commands may be used to appeal to that commitment.[5]

These techniques and tactics can vastly increase the effectiveness of your argument on the damages issues. The remainder of this chapter examines specific types of arguments that may be advanced on these issues.

Jurors' Misconceptions of Damages

The natural indifference and apathy many jurors will bring to their deliberations pose a compelling challenge for the victim's advocate. In many cases,

---

5. See ch. 13 for a discussion of embedded commands, with specific reference to damages.

especially those involving fairly serious injuries, jurors have at least two misconceptions about a damages award:

- There is no amount of money that would pay for the kind of pain and suffering the plaintiff experienced. The money won't make him any better (or in the case of death, bring back the loved one, and so forth).
- If we give the plaintiff $30,000, he will have enough to go to college. If we give him $40,000, he will just buy a fancy car with it or waste it, and so forth.

A number of responses can dispel misconceptions of this type. Several such arguments are found throughout this chapter. Here is one:

> In order to do your job and render a verdict in this case, you must know and understand what Peter Bard has experienced. The reason we have people decide these cases—the reason we have a jury system—is that the law places a high premium on human life. Agony and pain, when sold, must go at a high price. Only people can evaluate pain and suffering. Our system works—our country works—because our citizens have come to realize that all our lives are inextricably interwoven.
>
> There are those who would dispute this type of thinking. They say that people are selfish, that they will not help one another. Yet this is not true, particularly of this jury. Juries are made up of superior people.
>
> Of all the many people who were brought to the courthouse this week, you were chosen to determine this most serious and substantial matter. Of all the people originally brought into the courtroom, you were selected to determine this case. I am reminded of the definition given by a famous lawyer, Robert Ingersoll, of a superior man: "The superior man is the providence of the inferior. He is eyes for the blind, strength for the weak, and a shield for the defenseless. He stands erect by bending above the fallen. He rises by lifting others."[6]
>
> There are those who cannot understand and will not understand another's suffering. In this instance it is not only your privilege to do so but also your responsibility. As you come to discuss, understand, and know what our friend Peter Bard has been through, one of you may say, "There is no sum of money that could compensate him for the pain. There is nothing we can do that would make

---

6. *Liberty*, in PROSE—POEMS AND SELECTIONS FROM THE WRITINGS AND SAYINGS OF ROBERT G. INGERSOLL 202 (3d ed. 1888).

the pain go away or change the pain he will have in the future." Of course, this thinking is flawed and inadequate. You must fully compensate for the pain. To say that there is no sum of money that would compensate Peter Bard is only to recognize that his pain and suffering have been substantial. To believe and follow that statement is to abandon your commitment in this case.

Other people may say or consider what Peter Bard will do with the damages awarded by you. Obviously, this has nothing to do with your determination. Those people would not know that there are expenses and obligations that the plaintiff will have to satisfy out of any judgment. He will not receive all the money found by you. But even if he did, what he could do with the money, or what he will do with it, is of no consequence. It is the same as though a valuable piece of property had been destroyed. If, for example, this case were brought by a company that had had a million-dollar piece of property destroyed by the acts of another, would the jury for a moment diminish the damages because of the fact that the owner of the company could buy a house with it or invest it? Of course not; but there have been juries that have decided cases on that basis. I have had jurors tell me that they found a certain amount of damages because they felt that with that sum of money the plaintiff was going to be able to do a certain thing. This is improper, and the judge does not want you to approach this case in this manner, because there are things that we cannot tell you—things that affect and determine the amount that the plaintiff may actually realize from the damages found by you. And in any event it would not be proper to consider the case in this way. If this were the way to do it, the judge would have simply asked you what sum of money would be necessary for the plaintiff to buy a house and provide for his medical expenses.

The "Golden Rule" Argument

In an effort to overcome the jurors' misconceptions, many trial lawyers have gone over the line and made arguments that courts have declared improper as violating the "Golden Rule" argument.[7] In Texas it is well settled that it is improper to suggest that the jurors should return the same type of verdict that they would expect if they were in the plaintiff's shoes.[8] A suggestion that the

7. See generally 6 TEX. JUR. 3d, *Appellate Review* §§ 767-769 (1980), for a discussion of the "Golden Rule" argument.

8. *See, e.g.*, Fambrough v. Wagley, 169 S.W.2d 478, 481-82 (Tex. 1943); Plains Transport, Inc. v. Isaacs, 361 S.W.2d 919, 923-24 (Tex. Civ. App.—Amarillo 1962), *writ ref'd n.r.e. per curiam*, 367 S.W.2d 152 (Tex. 1963); Red Top Cab Co. v. Capps, 270 S.W.2d 273, 275 (Tex. Civ. App.—Austin 1954, writ ref'd n.r.e.).

jury should "do unto others as you would have them do unto you," however, may not constitute reversible error.[9]

Hence, the rule is sometimes misunderstood. For example, it may not be improper to request that the jurors place themselves in the plaintiff's posture in order to understand the effect of the injuries.[10] Proverbs or sayings like these are often used to illustrate the point:

- A Mexican proverb says, "Only the person who carries the sack knows the weight of the burden."
- As Romeo observed below Juliet's balcony, "He jests at scars that never felt a wound."[11]
- The Navajo Indians had a saying that you must stand in the moccasins of a man before you can understand the difficulty of his journey.[12]

Whether you resort to adage, saying, anecdote, or analogy, your goal is to impress on the jurors the fact that they must fully appreciate and understand the plaintiff's suffering and limitations before they can be expected to translate those factors into just compensation. Your fear is that some jurors may unduly dwell on what they perceive as an effect on themselves—that they will consider some real or imagined pecuniary interest of theirs or otherwise accept some improperly selfish motive and return an inadequate award. Such considerations should and can be rejected without violating the Golden Rule principle. Consider the following argument, which incorporates anecdotal references to historical examples:

> When you consider the damages to which Paul Brownley is entitled, I know that there are those who will suggest that the sums we have asked for are too great. Some may suggest that since these are the figures suggested by Paul and me, surely something less would do.

---

9. *See* World Wide Tire Co. v. Brown, 644 S.W.2d 144 (Tex. App.—Houston [14th Dist.] 1982, writ ref'd n.r.e.), where the court stated that the "Golden Rule" jury argument was not per se improper, because it required the jurors to look "with equal solicitude to the rights of both plaintiff and defendant." *Id.* at 145-46; *accord Fambrough,* 169 S.W.2d at 480-82.

10. *See Fambrough,* 169 S.W.2d at 480-82. Note that the line of demarcation for the Golden Rule argument is crossed and that such argument becomes reversible error when its effect is to ask the jurors "to give the plaintiff what they would want if they were injured, rather than what the evidence showed plaintiff was entitled to receive as compensation." *World Wide Tire Co.,* 644 S.W.2d at 146. Thus, an instruction to the jury to disregard such an argument may not suffice; and even under the "harmless error" test, this type of argument may be reversible. *Id.* at 146-47.

11. Shakespeare, *Romeo and Juliet,* act 2, sc. 2, l. 1.

12. Although this proverb, absent more, should be proper, similar language was held to be reversible error when it was combined with an appeal for the jurors to "[g]ive [the plaintiff] the same hearing that you would want to have if you stood in their place and they sat in yours." *Plains Transport, Inc.,* 361 S.W.2d at 923-24.

The defense has argued that under our law one cannot take a person's money and give it to another without proof. We would reply that under our law if a person proves a certain amount of damages, the finding of less than that sum by the jury is just as wrong.

To consider these damages properly, you must understand what these injuries have meant to my friend Paul Brownley. The Mexicans who originally settled this great state had a saying: "Only the person who carries the sack knows the weight of the burden." In order to measure the amount of money that should be found as damages for Paul, you have to, as the Mexican proverb goes, "carry the sack."

I have no doubt that you understand the inherent fairness of what we are asking you to do. How could anyone reasonably translate pain and agony into money damages unless they fully understood the pain and agony? But every time I address jurors on this issue, I am concerned that something bitter, unfriendly, and selfish may enter into their verdict. There is the fear that someone may think or say that, after all, these injuries that were produced by this irresponsible conduct are someone else's problem. Why should we really concern ourselves?

I could remind you that under your oath you are obligated to render a fair verdict. To many people, though, this would be no answer to the concern. Some of us are old enough to remember what occurred at the outbreak of World War Two. Others have certainly read about it. Hitler had remilitarized the Rhineland and had taken over Czechoslovakia and Austria without a shot being fired. He proposed to annex Poland. The Poles were prepared to fight. England and France had a treaty with Poland that provided that if Poland was attacked, they would come to Poland's aid. History tells us that some of the English opposed this. They didn't feel that English blood should be spent in support of Poland. In France the cry was, "Why should French blood be spilled in support of the Polish people?"

It was the farsighted statesmen of the day, men such as Churchill and de Gaulle, who realized that the war with Germany was inevitable. If the Western democracies had not joined forces, Hitler would have been allowed to pick them off one by one.

One hundred and fifty years ago, in this state, men and women from Tennessee, Ohio, Louisiana, and other states came to Texas to join in the fight for independence. Santa Anna had denied basic rights to the American settlers here. Davy Crockett explained his commitment to the cause this way: "If you have a he-bull goring a neighbor's stock, it whets his appetite. Before long the bull is goring yours."[13]

It's easy for one to say that Paul's problems are his own. But we know, from the evidence, that what happened to Paul could happen to any of us. Our only protection against this type of irresponsibility is the knowledge that we can find shelter—we can find justice—within the law. The one thing that we should all have learned from history as well as from our daily living is that our security, our liberty, our health, our pursuit of happiness are only as secure as our neighbors will make them. As the British poet John Donne reminds us: "No man is an island, entire of itself; every man is a piece of the continent, a part of the main."[14] We all remember that pleasant piece of British writing. It expressed the simple truth that we are all in the business of living together. My neighbor's problems must be my own. The individual or company who irresponsibly brings about injury is as much a concern to me as he or it is to the person who was injured. For, as the British poet said at the conclusion of his essay, "And therefore never send to know for whom the bell tolls; it tolls for thee."[15]

The "Per Diem" Argument

The essence of the per diem concept is that damages for elements such as physical pain and mental anguish should be evaluated on an hourly or daily basis or on the basis of some other increment of time. These arguments have long been accepted by our appellate courts, so their use is not error in Texas.[16]

The per diem argument can take many shapes and forms; it can be used in arguing both past damages and future damages.[17] While the underlying premise may be constant, this argument affords great variation depending on the characteristics and inclinations of the particular advocate.

The argument usually takes one of two basic forms. First, you can suggest a total figure for damages on each particular element, represented on a blowup or other visual aid, and then support that figure with the per diem approach. A second method is the converse approach. You can suggest the per diem analysis, with the rationale of the argument leading the jury to the

---

13. *The Alamo* (United Artists 1960).

14. *Devotion XVII*, in DEVOTIONS UPON EMERGENT OCCASIONS (1623).

15. *Id.*

16. *See, e.g.*, Sunset Brick & Tile, Inc. v. Miles, 430 S.W.2d 388, 390 (Tex. Civ. App.—Corpus Christi 1968, writ ref'd n.r.e.); Louisiana Ark. Ry. v. Mullins, 326 S.W.2d 263, 268 (Tex. Civ. App.—Texarkana, writ ref'd n.r.e.), *cert. denied*, 361 U.S. 966 (1959).

17. *See, e.g.*, Hernandez v. Baucum, 344 S.W.2d 498, 500 (Tex. Civ. App.—San Antonio 1961, writ ref'd n.r.e.).

desired figure. At the end of the explanation, use a visual aid to illustrate the monetary amount.

Here is an example of the first approach:

> Part *d* of Question 9 asks you to find the damages that would reasonably and fairly compensate Blanche Davis for her mental anguish in the future. You have now heard the testimony, from both physicians and others, about Blanche's injuries. In this tragic and senseless automobile collision of October 2, 1983, Mrs. Davis sustained these very severe injuries to her left arm. Glass and steel were propelled into her arm with the same velocity as if she had been shot. Muscles and nerves were severed. Skin and flesh were torn. She has been left with a part of her body that is now not only of limited use to her but also ugly and disfigured. Because of the extensive scarring, she can wear only a long-sleeved dress. Because of the injuries, she cannot use her left arm to comb her hair or to get something off a shelf.
>
> We have sought the sum of one million dollars for this element of damages [*point to the visual aid*]. I know that when that sum was mentioned on the voir dire examination, some of you seemed a bit skeptical.
>
> But you now know the basis for that figure. You realize that our friend and neighbor Blanche Davis is now thirty-three years of age. According to the statistics published by our government in the life tables that were admitted in evidence before you, Blanche has a life expectancy remaining of just over forty-six years. Forty-six years of the type of frustration, torment, and agony that you have heard about in this courtroom. 16,801 days. 403,224 hours. It is appropriate for you to look at Blanche's damages in this manner. This is the way that this lady will experience the mental torment, agony, and anguish of which there has been so much evidence—day by day, and hour by hour. Viewed in this context, the damages we are asking you to find become almost trivial. About two-fifty an hour. A few pennies under sixty dollars a day.
>
> Who among us is willing to be so harsh as to say that these damages are unreasonable? Two-fifty an hour, less than sixty dollars a day for the mutilation, disfigurement, and crippling of this lady's body.

The second type of argument—first suggesting the per diem approach and then disclosing the amount—is as follows:

> Part *d* of Question 9 asks about the damages that should be awarded for my friend Blanche Davis's mental anguish in the future. In order to address this significant and critical issue, you must concern

yourself with what should be properly considered. How should you, as jurors, approach this question? Obviously, you will want to consider the nature and extent of the injuries that Blanche has sustained, as well as the type of anguish, agony, and frustration these types of injuries produce. You have heard the evidence about the tearing of muscles and nerves that this defendant's negligence caused. You have heard from the doctors and seen photographs showing how this lady's skin was torn from her body, leaving the grotesque and hideous scarring that requires her to wear only long-sleeved dresses. Wear clothes that will cover the scars. Wear something so that the only ones who have to look at it will be Blanche and her husband. You have heard of the frustration and bitterness that flow from this type of injury. Frustration when you cannot use your arm to comb your hair or to take a small box down from a shelf in the kitchen.

Yet, in addition to the injuries, there is another consideration that is equally important in your formula. That is the time over which this anguish and agony will be experienced. The evidence before you includes the United States Life Tables, Exhibit 2. According to those life tables, Blanche, who is now thirty-three years of age, has a reasonable life expectancy remaining of just over forty-six years. If you multiply forty-six by the number of days in a year and hours in a day, you will see that it translates into 16,801 days—403,224 hours. What approach could be more fair than for you to consider the nature and extent of her injuries, her agony, her worry, and the time over which this will occur? You have heard from her doctors that they have done, medically, all they can do for Blanche Davis. She is forever left with the crippling effects of these injuries and the grotesque scarring. Most of you are aware of what the minimum wage as prescribed by Congress is today. If you were to find that this fine lady, by her proof, should be awarded a little under two-fifty an hour for this element of damages, you would arrive at the sum of one million dollars, which is reflected on this chart [*point to the visual aid*]. That hourly rate would be well below the minimum wage. But we do not suggest a figure to you. We only suggest that in evaluating this element of damages, it is appropriate that you view it the way that she must experience it—on an hourly basis. You have heard from the evidence that there is hardly an hour when she does not experience some limitation as a result of the use of her arm. There isn't an hour when she doesn't worry about the scarring. Her injuries have caused her difficulty sleeping. We simply suggest what we feel is a reasonable and fair approach. Arrive at whatever figure you feel would be appropriate to compensate Mrs. Davis on an hourly basis, and then multiply it by the number of hours that she has left in this life. The number of hours that she must deal with the crippling effects of these injuries, her agony, her anguish, and her worry.

Future Damages

Virtually all the substantial jury verdicts that are returned in Texas involve some element of future damages. Perhaps the greatest failing of the inexperienced advocate is the inability to inspire and motivate the jury in this area. This process must begin on the voir dire examination and be continued in final summation. Point out that, under our procedure, the jury is to decide damages in this case for all time. The plaintiff cannot return in five or ten years and suggest that the award was inadequate. Instead, the jury must hear all the evidence, including the medical testimony, and make its determination not only of damages that have already occurred but of those that will occur in the future as well—over the lifetime of this plaintiff.

The impact of future damages may vary greatly depending on the facts of the case. In some instances the proof will be that, while the plaintiff will have damages in the future, the really grave consequences will be in the immediate future, that is, the years immediately following the jury's verdict. In other cases more remote events will visit the most significant harm. Some injuries may produce a type of traumatic arthritis, the most disabling and troubling effects of which may not be experienced for decades. Some damages or injuries to vital organs may also fall in this category.

If there is evidence of permanent, irreversible harm or damage, you should devote a significant amount of your argument to those damages in the future. Here are a few matters to consider:

- Under our system, all damages, including future damages, must be determined in this lawsuit.
- The plaintiff does not have the right to return if, as predicted by his physicians, he develops additional problems or additional limitations.
- The life expectancy of the plaintiff is a significant span of time. (The per diem arguments discussed above may be helpful on this point.)

Illustrate the Length of Time Involved

Unless you explain and elaborate, the jury may not be able to conceptualize the extensive period of time that is involved with injuries of a permanent nature. Consider the case of a woman who is forty-eight years old at the time of trial. According to the United States Life Expectancy Tables,[18] she is

18. 2 NATIONAL CENTER FOR HEALTH STATISTICS, VITAL STATISTICS OF THE UNITED STATES, 1980, § 6, *Life Tables*, DHHS Pub. No. (PHS) 84-1104 (1984).

expected to live thirty-one more years. To help the jury understand the magnitude of that period of time, you could point out that over the time of her future damages and injuries, two separate generations will have started the first grade and one will have graduated from college. A child born today will have gone to school, graduated, gone to college or trade school, entered a profession, married, and had children, and his or her children would be in school at the time the plaintiff dies and is finally freed from the effects of the injury.[19]

Consider the "Whole-Man" Argument

The premise of the "whole-man" argument is that, because the body is an entity, it is impossible to separate or segregate one portion from the whole. The noted New York trial lawyer Moe Levine is credited as the author of this persuasive approach. This well-known advocate, who secured many plaintiffs' verdicts before juries in the eastern states, firmly believed that the whole-man concept was inconsistent with a per diem type of argument.[20]

When Moe Levine talked of the total man, or the whole man, he was referring not only to the injured person but also to the person's entire family. When a man is injured, his whole family becomes injured. The victim's injuries affect his or her ability to live and enjoy life.[21] But the essence of the whole-man concept is that you cannot selectively injure just a part of a person's body.

> Ladies and gentlemen, when a woman is injured, such as you have before you, it is the whole woman. We have heard the testimony from the physicians that because of Diane Wilson's fall in the Q-Mart store, she suffered two ruptured intervertebral discs. The surgeons, with all their skill, knowledge, and training, have not been able to take from her the pain and agony that were brought about by this defendant's carelessness. She was operated on in 1983. A laminectomy was performed, but still she had pain. She was operated on again that year—still the pain. In 1984 the doctors performed what they called a fusion. They took bone from her hip and placed it in her spine. Still no relief from the pain.
>
> Someone might suggest, "Well, just her back hurts." But we all know that when we hurt, we hurt all over. When we were created in the image of our maker, a single body and mind came into being. When you have constant back pain, you are deprived of all the

---

19. The concept of future damages is discussed in ch. 23.

20. *See* M. LEVINE, SUMMATIONS: THE BEST OF MOE 82 (1967); M. LEVINE, STRUCTURE AND FUNCTION IN ADVOCACY 56 (1968).

21. *See* M. LEVINE, SUMMATIONS, *supra* note 20, at 83.

simple pleasures and enjoyments that most of us take for granted. You cannot enjoy a movie or television show, because if you sit too long in one position you become uncomfortable and ache. After a while, the pain becomes unbearable to the point you have to take medication and lie down. You can't enjoy a night of dancing, because your back hurts. Doing simple housework sends you to the chair, couch, or bed. You become irritable and difficult to live with. It places strains on your marriage. You're not the type of parent you want to be.

Have any of you ever experienced a severe toothache? Someone might suggest that, after all, it's just your tooth that is infected or abscessed. But you know that with a severe toothache you cannot think or concentrate on your work—you cannot function. You pray for the hour to arrive when you will see the dentist who will be able to put that misery aside.

Q-Mart's mindless blundering in failing to clean up this quart of oil that was spilled on their floor caused injury to this whole lady. Try as they may, they cannot isolate this injury and its effects to the back or, even as you have heard, the discs, ligaments, and nerves that were damaged in this fall.

Specific Damages Arguments

Denounce the Remorseful Defendant

While it is settled law in Texas that the plaintiff cannot, in a negligence action, introduce evidence of subsequent safety precautions,[22] this rule will not prevent the defense from doing so.[23] Particularly in cases involving egregious conduct, gross negligence, or claims for punitive damages, the defendants will introduce evidence and proof that they have changed their policies and procedures. Their goal is to be placed in a position to argue that they are remorseful, sorry, and repentant about the facts and circumstances that led to the plaintiff's injuries. In essence, the defense argument will be, "We're sorry; we've changed; don't be too hard on us in your consideration of damages." If this argument is injected by the defense, you should address it.

Consider the case in which a number of individuals have been injured in a spectacular automobile-truck collision. The evidence has established that the driver of the defendant's truck had received seven speeding tickets in the year immediately preceding the accident. He was driving a truck with bad brakes.

---

22. TEX. R. CIV. EVID. 407.

23. This is because under the terms of the rule, those facts would not be introduced "to prove negligence or culpable conduct." *See id.*; *see also* Blakely, *Article IV: Relevancy and Its Limits*, 20 HOUS. L. REV. 151, 212-19 (1983) (Texas Rules of Evidence Handbook).

The company, by its own records and admissions, has budgeted absolutely zero dollars under the line item "safety" for the twenty years that the company has been in existence. Both actual and punitive damages are sought. At trial, the defense offers evidence that the company has changed its policies, that it now routinely checks the driving records of its employees, that it is more vigorous in discharging unsafe drivers, and that it now spends significant sums in the area of safety, educating and orienting its drivers and maintaining its equipment. In this type of situation, consider this argument:

> The defense has suggested that we should not be too harsh in evaluating their conduct in this case—that the damages that we have sought, both actual and punitive damages, should not be found by this jury—that something substantially less than that should represent your verdict. The cry of the defense is, "We've changed; we're better now; it can't and won't happen again."
>
> As most of you are aware, we are trying this case in the Harris County Civil Courthouse. Right across the street is the criminal courthouse. They have a saying over there that we do not hear too much on this side of the street. The saying is that the defendant "wants the ride but not the rap." This is merely an aphorism that recognizes that those who break our laws are always willing to enjoy the profits of their misadventures but will go to great lengths to avoid the responsibilities. Let's think about this for just a moment. How often have we ever heard of a burglar who has successfully stolen from our neighbors' homes on hundreds of occasions, walking into the police station and saying, "I'm sorry for what I've done; I want to make it right"? How many of those who rob our convenience stores and cleaners turn themselves in following their sprees? How many rapists who have terrorized our neighborhoods confess and say that they will never rape again? No, we all know from experience that what happens is that the burglar finally gets caught. The armed robber is somehow tracked down. The rapist is finally identified. It is only after they are caught that we see any type of remorse. All indications are, and it seems very clear, that these types of people will persist and continue in their unlawful activities until they are caught. Why? Because they profit from these activities or receive some other type of gratification. That is why most of us are somewhat skeptical of the person who engages in a continued and lengthy course of law-breaking who, on being captured and brought to the bar, claims, "I've changed. It won't happen again."
>
> There is no question that the Octagon Trucking Company profited from its irresponsible, reckless, and unjustifiable practices. You make more money when you hire marginal drivers. You can hire marginal drivers for less than what you have to pay the good, conscientious, responsible driver. You make more money when you

> don't maintain your trucks. Maintenance of truck tires, brakes, and safety devices costs dollars. You make more money when you do not have to spend that money to check driving records. You profit more when you do not have to budget funds for driver education, safety programs, and safety enforcement.
>
> What caused this so-called change in company policy at Octagon? Was it the occurrence of this accident, or was it the realization that they would have to face a jury who would be charged with assessing this company's responsibility in terms of money damages? We leave that determination to you, but it appears to us that it is an important question that must be asked.

Urge the Right Verdict for the Right Reason

Many fine advocates have used the approach of urging the right verdict for the right reason.[24] In a sense, this concept is a corollary to, or outgrowth of, the "sympathy" response explored earlier in this book.[25] The crux of this persuasive technique is to challenge the jury's thought processes. The essence of the argument is that the jury's verdict, whether it be for the plaintiff or defense, must not only be the "right" verdict but must also be based on a proper consideration of the proof.

> Esteemed counsel for the defense has just concluded his summation by suggesting to you that to find the damages we asked for in our opening remarks for our neighbor Gilda Lawrence would be wrong. At the risk of prejudicing the rights of my friend—this good woman—I must tell you that we do not ask for a verdict that is necessarily right or wrong. It is a peculiar imbecility of our times that we insist on measuring human endeavor with a preconceived and well-defined longitude of right and latitude of wrong. Who knows, in the last analysis, what is absolutely right or wrong? We're not dealing here with computers or adding machines. No machine can decide a case for a jury. Machines will never be used to decide conflicts between people or to appraise damages. Machines can't feel. Machines can't suffer. Machines do not dream and do not hope. Only people do, and so only people can decide. But we are, of course, concerned with your verdict. We are so concerned about your verdict that our concern does not end with whether it is right or wrong. It does not end with whether or not we recover the damages we have asked for or whether you find some smaller, inadequate figure, such as suggested by the defense.

---

24. *See* M. LEVINE, SUMMATIONS, *supra* note 20, at 26.
25. See the discussion under "Closing Argument" in ch. 2.

If you find these damages, as suggested by the defense, you might be finding the right verdict. But if your reason for making that finding is that such an award might be less of an economic burden on the defendant than would a larger award—this would be the wrong reason. If you refuse to find the damages asked by us because you believe that it might be financially onerous to the defendant or have some other economic effect, it would be a verdict for the wrong reason. It would not be a verdict you could be proud of, because while your verdict might have been right, your reason was wrong.

If you find the damages we have sought because you feel sorry for Mrs. Lawrence—because you pity her—again, that might be the right verdict, but it would be for the wrong reason. We ask that you find the damages we have prayed for—damages that have been proved by a preponderance of the evidence—because the irrefutable evidence is that this lady has been so horribly injured. The measurement of those injuries by the legal standards and instructions that have now been given to you by the court requires a finding of those damages.

And so, in response to the defense suggestion that they are entitled to your verdict on this crucial issue of damages, we would say to you that we ask for even more. We also ask that you return a verdict that is based on the right reason—a consideration of these damages, injuries, and losses. A strong, determined, considered analysis of the evidence in this case. A consideration of what the plaintiff has lost. A consideration of how long this fine lady must agonize because of the effects of these injuries. A consideration of the shrinking value of the dollar. A consideration of how needless and senseless this event was. If you do that—and we know you will—then not only will you return the right verdict, but it will also be a right verdict for the right reason.

Consider Not What Was Taken But What Was Left

Some advocates make the mistake of focusing their damages argument on what was taken from the plaintiff by the injury, rather than on what was left. In some cases it may be appropriate to remind the jury that the most important element of damages is not what you take from a person but what you leave him. Take the example of a man with 20/20 vision. He has an accident and is left with 20/40 vision. The defendant, by his conduct, has taken a substantial amount of the man's vision. But what remains still permits him to see. However, if you take a person with 10/200 eyesight—a person who may barely see the light—and blind him, you have left him with nothing. Consider the following argument in a death case in which a widowed woman has lost her only son:

> It is our human nature that when we look at a case such as this—one involving the death of a son—we concentrate on that which was lost. That which was taken. We overlook and ignore that which was left. This is but an illustration of the old axiom that you can have two people looking at a glass that has water in it. One person will observe that the glass is half full, and the other will observe that it is half empty.
>
> This lady lost a son. That is what was taken. We have discussed with you the meaning and magnitude of that loss. Let us now turn to a brief consideration of what was left. The candle whose light the defendant extinguished was seventeen years old. But more importantly, it was this lady's only son. It was her only light. If a man or woman is in a room with three candles burning and you extinguish one of them, the room gets a little darker. But if there is only one candle in the room and you extinguish it, you plunge that person into total darkness. So it is here. What this defendant has left is a woman all alone. She now has no one to brighten her day. No one to ask after a hard day's work, "How did things go at the office today?" No one to comment to during a football game, "What did you think of that play?" No one who is interested in how she feels. No one who cares about what she thinks. No one with whom to share things.
>
> This fine lady lost a son. But more importantly, we must consider what this defendant has left her with.

Differentiate Between Price and Value

Sometimes, you may feel it necessary to explain to the jurors that it is the *value* of the plaintiff's damages that they must ascertain. This explanation is particularly important in discussing nonpecuniary elements such as pain and suffering. Many jurors will approach these questions skeptically because they have no figures (unless a "per diem" approach is used) for a guideline. Try to guide the jurors in the direction of *evaluating* the plaintiff's damages, not just determining them. Indeed, the very concept of value implies that the worth of something must be considered, rather than its price.

> The definition of a cynic is one who knows the price of everything and the value of nothing. There is a difference between price and value. Price applies to something we can purchase or sell; it represents the amount of money that is obtained or paid in the transaction. Value is the worth of something to the individual.
>
> That distinction is particularly significant in personal injury cases such as this. There is no price for pain and suffering or mental anguish. You cannot purchase them off the shelves at the grocery store or by the gallon at the service station.
>
> When we talk of the loss of a loved one, such as the death of a son or wife, the initial question is always, Whose son? Whose wife?

Yours or mine? We might feel that that amount of money could not possibly replace our own son. The same concept would apply to physical pain or mental anguish.

Let me give you an example of what we are talking about. Many of us know of shut-ins—the elderly people who, because of their physical limitations, are not as active as they once were and spend virtually all of their days in their homes, apartments, or rooms in nursing homes. Each of you may have a mother or a grandmother who would fit this picture. If you've been around these people very much, you know that their television sets are the center of their daily activities. They use those sets to keep in touch with the world, to stay familiar with what is going on, to be entertained, to remind them of happier times in the past, to bring them laughter and enjoyment. It is their touch with reality and the outside world. It is as though they have someone with them around the clock. They are not alone. Phil Donahue, Merv Griffin, Johnny Carson, and a countless line of people visit with them every day. The price of their television sets may be four to five hundred dollars. But if you were to go to these elderly people and say to them, "I will give you what you paid for that set. Even though it is a used set, even though you have enjoyed it for a couple of years, I will take it off your hands. I will give you the four to five hundred dollars you paid for it. The only thing that I demand is that you not buy another set. You can never own a television again." Those poor shut-ins, in every case, would not accept your offer. They would not sell. That is because the *value* to them of that television is greater than the money that you are offering them.

There is a difference, folks, between price and value. When we face the question such as presented by this case, we are controlled by the principles of value and not price. This is because my good friend Pat Cain did not voluntarily subject himself to this injury and the resultant pain, disability, and impairment. He didn't voluntarily trade his physical and mental torture for the defendant's money. Indeed, no one could seriously argue that Mr. Cain or anyone else would voluntarily do so. These things were cast on him by the defendant's negligent conduct.

Emphasize That Damages Have Been Earned

One of the more common errors made by advocates when arguing damages is to incorporate such phrases as "we ask that you give these damages" or "the plaintiff should be given damages in this amount"—phrases that merely reinforce in the jurors' minds the concept that their damages award is in some measure gratuitous. Instead, stress the fact that the damages you seek were earned by the victim and that they represent just compensation. Consider the following argument in a case involving the amputation of the plaintiff's leg at the knee:

> Palmer Richardson has earned the damages that we have asked for by blood, sweat, and tears. He has earned those damages in the four years following that tragic collision on Interstate 10 that left him crippled, maimed, and disfigured for life. He earned them with a broken heart when he was told in the hospital that they would have to saw off his leg at the knee in order to save his life. He earned them in the days that followed with the agonizing pain that could not be controlled with even the strongest medications that the doctors dared to give him. The months of physical therapy that followed were agonizing and cruel. The damages that we seek for that pain and anguish were earned in those months in the hospital. He earned the damages in the months that followed, as he learned to use the prosthesis that enables him to walk.
>
> In years to come he will earn the rest of these damages. The future holds for him only more agony, more frustration, and more sorrow. The doctors have told us how the use of this prosthesis will cause him to experience irritation, inflammation, discomfort, and pain. Every time he is turned down for employment because he has an artificial leg, he will be earning these damages. Every promotion he loses—every advancement denied him—every future moment of frustration and agony must be represented in your award.

Distinguish the Impairment from the Injury

You must also distinguish between the need to prove injury or disability and the need to prove its exact medical source. Consider a case in which the plaintiff is complaining of a neck injury. The plaintiff's physician testifies that the plaintiff had a compression fracture of the cervical vertebrae at C-5 and C-6. The defendant's doctor says that the condition, which has resulted in some narrowing of the vertebral bodies, is a congenital anomaly. To the victim's advocate, it makes no difference whether or not the plaintiff has a fracture of the cervical spine; the question is the impairment of living. As far as the victim is concerned, the fact that his neck has now become a medical battleground on which fine doctors may wage their scientific wars does not make any difference. He only cares that he once had a symptom-free spine but is now suffering pain and disability.

> John Jones would ask, "Can you cure it?" His treating physician, Dr. Elton, has said, "We can't cure it, because you have a fractured spine and this is irreversible and you have damage to the surrounding tissues and, therefore, we can't cure it." But the defense's doctor has said, "We can't cure it, but you didn't have a fractured spine. You

just had soft tissue injury, and we would suppose you had some scar formation and some involvement of nerves in that area and of muscle fibers, but you can't cure this. But you didn't have a fractured spine."

Does it really make a difference, ladies and gentlemen, whether or not John Jones had a fractured spine? Haven't we made it clear that we don't care whether the bones were broken? We care whether the life has been impaired, whether pain has been inflicted, whether suffering has distracted this fine man from his pursuit of whatever pleasures there are in living. Isn't this what we're concerned with?

Address the Attacks on the Plaintiff's Character

Subtle and sometimes ill-conceived disparagements of the plaintiff's character and standing in the community are a part of many defense attorneys' strategies. Of course, an in-depth investigation and examination of the plaintiff's personal habits and tendencies are sometimes appropriate: for example, if the plaintiff contended that the injured victim enjoyed a substantial earning capacity before the incident in question, proof to the contrary would be relevant and appropriate. The victim's advocate must recognize these situations. But even if the plaintiff's counsel has admitted to the jury at the outset the shortcomings of the plaintiff, the defense may insist on overemphasizing this element of proof. In other cases defense counsel will try to interject into the case evidence and considerations whose only value is in prejudicing the jurors' minds against the plaintiff.

These attacks are aimed at the issue of damages. The defense often hopes that if the jurors see the plaintiff as less than an honorable and upright citizen, this view will affect their determination of money damages. Such an attack, whether by direct or cross-examination of witnesses, introduction of records, or argument, requires a vigorous reply.

Consider the case of a laborer who received two fractures of the os calcis, a fractured femur, and vertebral fractures in a fall from the side of a building. The plaintiff was an itinerant window washer. The plaintiff's case is a product liability action brought because of the defective eyebolts that failed, causing his scaffold to fall so that the man plunged three stories to the street below.

> The Atlas Bolt Company's case is one punctuated by innuendo, interspersed with insinuation, and supported by suggestion. They say John Allen is not entitled to the damages that have been proved and prayed for in this case. They refer to the medical records indicating that this poor laborer drank four to six beers each evening. He has been married twice and has children living in another state. He ran away from home when he was twelve. He worked for ten different employers in the last three years.

These facts about John were brought out by the defense. We didn't hide them or attempt to conceal them. But is it not legitimate to ask, For what reason did the defense dwell on these matters?

A courtroom is not the place where we should discuss who can throw stones at whom. We don't ask that you search your own hearts and say to yourselves that if you were in this position, if you had to bring a lawsuit to recover damages for an obvious wrong, is there ever a part of your life that you would not want to be disclosed. You have seen what happened here in this courthouse. Every facet of John's life, every time he stumbled, every time he fell along the way have been brought out for you to scoff at if you wished. And for what purpose? To prejudice your consideration of the damages that should be found in this case.

What other purpose could the defense have had? Why would they dwell on these matters except in an effort to get you to dislike this man—to get you to say, "If we don't like John, we're not going to consider his rights—and never mind the law."

John may have done some things of which he's not proud. He may have done some things that are worthy of your criticism. But the thing that has brought us to the courthouse was John's attempting to do an honest day's work for an honest day's wages. He attached his scaffold to the eyebolts manufactured by this defendant—bolts that were by every scientific measure defective and destined to break and shatter—destined to cause the men who were supported by them to fall and be either injured or killed. There is no suggestion that John was anything other than innocent on the occasion in question. Can we stand in some ivory tower, some mountaintop retreat, and look down upon this modest workman and say that he is so far beneath us that we will not consider his rights? Or instead of that, will you do what you have dedicated yourselves to do by agreeing to serve as jurors, to say to yourselves that there is no class, there is no creed, there is no color, there is only the principle of abstract justice to which you are dedicated?

We have heard the philosophers and poets remark that not even the smallest sparrow falls without his passing being noted. John was a very small sparrow indeed. Some might consider him as plain and simple a man as they could ever meet. In that respect, some people would agree with the defense. But he was not a bad man. You have heard nothing bad about him. If he had perpetrated crimes, you would have heard about them. You heard of weakness. You did not hear of any evil.[26]

---

26. For another example of the type of case in which this argument may be used, see M. LEVINE, SUMMATIONS, *supra* note 20, at 31-47.

Create Some Bonding Between the Jury and the Victim

Even if the defense has not vigorously attacked the plaintiff's character, it is still appropriate to try to create some bond between the jury and the plaintiff. Most victims are people of modest means, average incomes, who live in typical neighborhoods with simple and ordinary family relationships. So it is with most members of the jury. Take a few minutes of your argument on the damages issues to reinforce this natural bonding.

> What sort of people are Karver and Naomi Burns? This is an important question for you. It is significant to your deliberations on this question of damages. We must face facts. These are simple people. Ordinary people. They may seem important to no one except themselves and God. They live the kind of life you heard about. He is a mechanic for Al Davis Chevrolet. She works as a nurse at Ben Taub Hospital. They have two sons.
>
> Can you understand and appreciate what it meant to these people to come into this court and lay open before you—their neighbors, but still strangers to them—the most sacred and private parts of their lives? Do you think they welcomed or looked forward to the experience? Certainly not, but they were compelled to do so by our legal procedures.
>
> So what kind of folks are these? They are people just like you and me and many others we know. Like your neighbors. Like your brothers and sisters, or your mom and dad. They had the same dreams. The same ambitions. The same hopes and wishes for themselves and their children. They sought nothing more out of life than that which they could earn by an honest day's work.
>
> But those hopes and dreams were shattered on the night of July 3, 1984, in this tragic collision. It is the value of those hopes and dreams, the value of those lives that you must now translate into money damages.
>
> Bear in mind we are not suggesting that you should say to yourselves, "What would I say if this were to happen to me or my wife or my husband?" That type of thinking destroys impartiality. I know most of you would say to yourselves that you wouldn't want it to happen to you and you don't even want to think about it. So instead of that, our appeal is for objectivity. Twelve neighbors looking at their neighbors. What has this accident done to these lives? What will life be like from now on?[27]

---

27. The last paragraph of this argument represents a close, but probably proper, circumvention of the Golden Rule problem. *See supra* notes 7-12 and accompanying text.

Challenge the Jury

In recent years we have seen a heightened effort and commitment of financial resources by insurance carriers and corporations to affect public opinion. Time and again the public has been reminded of a need to place limits on jury verdicts or otherwise control them—particularly on the issue of damages. A vigorous voir dire may help dispel some of these misconceptions or form the basis for a challenge for cause. Despite all these efforts, you will still meet with attitudes of varying hostility toward the concept of large or adequate damages. A direct challenge to this type of thinking may be appropriate:

> When you retire to the jury room to consider your verdict in this case, our thoughts, best wishes, and prayers will go with you. It is our fervent hope that you will somehow find within yourselves the courage to do what frequently is an unpopular thing. It is much easier, much simpler, much quicker to find for the defendant on these issues of damages. We realize the natural reluctance on some people's part to award adequate damages—the damages we have prayed for—in a case such as this. And so it is our fervent hope and prayer that you will find the courage to properly appraise the case and that there will be among you jurors who, through experience and the appreciation of life, know the effects of crippling, maiming, and disabling injuries. There are those of you who have been in our hospitals, which to many are places of death. Places where the creaking of the wheels at night are the sounds of death—where moans, groans, and tears are the signature of torment.
>
> It's a sad commentary, but a true one. Many of us have come to accept the proposition that a human being can tolerate any amount of pain. An individual can overcome any disability. Provided—provided it is the pain of another. It is another's disability. It is another's loss of wage-earning capacity and ability to provide for himself and his family. In this trial we have challenged that way of thinking. We ask only that you have the strength, courage, and fortitude to challenge it in your deliberations.

The "Can'ts" of Arguing Damages

Just as certain damages arguments are effective in raising the jurors' consciousness, there are some negative considerations in preparing such an argument. There are three principle "can'ts" of arguing damages: you can't—

- make undue and inappropriate emotional appeals.
- seem greedy.
- make a "Mack truck" out of a "Tonka toy."

You Can't Make Undue and Inappropriate Appeals to Emotions

One of the principal arguments the defense may stress is the "sympathy" argument. A similar problem that may arise when this argument is given (and even when it is not) is the emotional appeal. If you contemplate making this type of argument, be extremely careful. First, there are many cases in which an emotional appeal may simply not be appropriate. Depending on the facts, the jury, and the opposing counsel, this type of argument may not be warranted. Second, an obvious appeal to emotion will be seen for what it is.

An argument appealing to emotion will be effective only when all the following circumstances are present:

- You truly feel the emotion and need not feign, fake, or stage it.
- The facts of the case fully support the emotion.
- The jury is composed of individuals who are capable of sharing the emotion.
- The emotional content is an intrinsic part of the evidence and the facts in the case.

A variety of emotions may be the subject of legitimate appeals. An argument may contain an appeal to anger based on the defense's callousness and, at some other point, an appeal for empathy or understanding of the plaintiff's plight.

Many advocates make the critical mistake of trying an emotional appeal in cases where it simply will not be accepted by the jury. They attempt to inject an inappropriate emotion into a case, or they extend their emotional appeal beyond the bounds that the evidence and the jury can support. An appeal for anger at the defense is appropriate only if the evidence has clearly demonstrated some callousness of the defense or some obvious disingenuity on the part of the defense counsel. Likewise, a tearful plea for adequate damages can be shared by the jury only in cases involving a substantial loss that is sincerely felt by the trial advocate.

You Can't Give the Impression of Being Greedy

The advocate who inadvertently, through inexperience or a lack of analysis, leaves the jury with the unmistakable impression that his claims and demands for damages are unrealistic and excessive has made another critical mistake: he has lost any meaningful chance for an adequate jury verdict because his credibility was destroyed when he argued for totally unrealistic damages.

Plaintiffs' counsel often ask, "How much can I safely argue for?" In every case there is a figure beyond which the jurors become incensed, believing that the plaintiff's counsel is looking for more than just compensation. One approach to this problem is to ask yourself what damages might be found acceptable and reasonable by your strongest juror.

The exact damages figure is not the only factor that may produce an impression of greediness. The advocate's demeanor and the vocal and verbal qualities he projects may also cause him to be cast in this unfavorable light. In short, you must always be mindful of the physical and nonverbal cues that are explored in detail in part 2 of this work. To have any hope of recovering full damages, your argument must have conveyed the following characteristics:

- Honesty—you have not misstated any evidence or appeared less than candid in the presentation of your proof.
- Sincerity—you genuinely believe in your case.
- Preparation—you have obviously worked hard and diligently on the case and have presented the evidence in an organized, expeditious fashion.
- Integrity—all your actions in the case have been consistent with ethical and professional principles.
- Candor—you have faced up to the unfavorable proof and have not ignored it.

If the jurors have formed these types of impressions and you have not otherwise left the impression that your demands on damages are excessive, there is every reason to believe that the jury's consideration of damages will lead to the desired conclusion—that full and complete compensation is justified in the case.

You Can't Make a "Mack Truck" out of a "Tonka Toy" (or how to argue the small damages suit)

A corollary to the preceding two principles concerns the small damages suit. Most novice advocates begin their trial practice on personal injury cases involving modest or minimal injuries. All too often these cases are lost completely or inadequate damages are awarded, because the plaintiff's counsel didn't heed the admonition that "you can't make a silk purse out of a sow's ear." Candor plays a critical role in these types of cases. Recognize that there is some natural skepticism toward reasonable compensation in the small case: some jurors are inclined to feel that the plaintiff should have ignored his remedy and borne the loss himself. Consequently, you must confront the nature of the plaintiff's injuries. At the same time, you must remind the jury that even modest cases require full consideration and just compensation:

> At the beginning of this trial we told you that this was not the biggest case that would be tried in Harris County this year. The injuries produced by the defendant's carelessness were, thank goodness, capable of being treated and cured. You have heard from the evidence how Mrs. Wetzel, with the help of her physician, Dr. Lawrence Seaver, was able to recover from the effects of her injury

within three months. Although she was still in pain and had discomfort at that time, Dr. Seaver felt that Mrs. Wetzel had essentially reached maximum recovery. For that reason, you will see from the court's charge that we have only asked for the past damages of medical expenses and physical pain and mental anguish. Mrs. Wetzel feels pretty good today. She still has some vague aches and pains but nothing like that which she experienced for several months after this accident. Nothing like the pain that drove her to take muscle relaxants even though they upset her stomach. Pain that caused her to drive fifteen miles round-trip three times a week for two months to physical therapy. The defense suggests she didn't need that treatment. But her doctor thought she did. And does anyone really think that someone would spend that time and money and yet not seek any compensation for future pain, in the hopes of building a lawsuit?

We were candid with you. We were honest with you. We told you that this was a small case. We have only asked for twenty thousand dollars in damages, which includes the thirty-five hundred dollars in medical expenses, with the remainder going for pain and suffering and mental anguish.

I know that there are some who would suggest that Mrs. Wetzel is not entitled to that sum or even a fraction of it. Whether they say it or not, they believe that those types of matters should not be decided at the courthouse. They are the same type of people who would turn our courthouses into playpens for the rich. They would say that justice can live and thrive only in the neighborhood of corporate lawsuits and catastrophic injuries.

Who is being unreasonable in a case such as this? Mrs. Wetzel, who from the beginning asked only to be compensated fairly for the injuries caused by the defendant, or the defense, who has insisted from the beginning of this trial that they did not owe her a penny? When the defense refused to accept and honor their legal obligation, this lady did all that she could properly do. She hired an attorney and filed a lawsuit.

To those who might suggest that she shouldn't be here, that you shouldn't award these damages that she seeks, we would pose a couple of questions. First, do you honestly want us to return to the days when people were expected to extract their own justice? There was a day not too long ago in this state when, if a man suspected his neighbor of stealing a cow, he went out and hanged him. I don't believe that any of us would accept a return to those concepts, those days. The second question is but an extension of the first. If we say that this courthouse exists, that our judges serve, in order to ensure that we all have a place to go with our complaints, then at what point do we say the cause is too small? Obviously we would not deny the courthouse to the corporation that has lost millions of dollars because of business fraud. I doubt seriously that anyone would suggest denying it to someone who has been paralyzed for life because of the negligent conduct of another. But where do you propose to draw the line? At what point do you propose to say to Mrs. Wetzel and all of us, "If you're injured as badly as *X* I will consider your cause and award full damages, but if you're injured less than *X* was you should simply forget about it"?

The law does not draw that type of line. As the champions of justice and the ultimate arbiters of this dispute, you must not draw it either.

Punitive Damages

If the evidence warrants a recovery of punitive damages, the victim's attorney will usually have ample ammunition for his argument. The difference between having this evidence and using it in the most effective manner, however, separates the skilled advocate from the unskilled advocate. No matter how persuasive the evidence may be, the advocate who merely rants and raves about the defendant's conduct has not made the most of his argument. The skilled advocate, by contrast, may display anger, disgust, and indignation; yet in so doing, he or she will transfer feelings and emotions that motivate and inspire the jury. In short, there is a big difference between motivating the jurors and lecturing them to find punitive damages.

The experienced plaintiff's attorney may have a variety of arguments with which he can inspire a large punitive damages award.[28] The content of his argument, obviously, will depend on the facts in the case at bar. From a liability standpoint, punitive damages arguments were illustrated in earlier chapters.[29] The amount of punitive damages argued or sought in a particular case, however, presents another problem. As with other elements of damages such as pain and suffering, no monetary amounts may be easily ascertainable. Emphasize to the jury that for the defendant's conduct to *change*—not just to get the attention of the defendant—the damages must be substantial and significant.

You may decide not to argue for a specific quantum of punitive damages, leaving it to the jurors to choose a precise amount. The facts of the case often dictate which method will be more effective.

If you assert a specific amount, though, it is often helpful to justify it in some fashion. One common argument, similar to the "per diem" argument,[30]

28. Remember that for lawsuits filed after September 2, 1987, an award of exemplary damages "may not exceed four times the amount of actual damages or $200,000, whichever is greater." TEX. CIV. PRAC. & REM. CODE ANN. § 41.007 (Vernon Supp. 1988).

29. See chs. 18 and 20.

30. See discussion beginning at *supra* note 16.

is to base a punitive damages award on a certain portion of the defendant's business income. The amount is usually predicated on some evidence of the defendant's annual income,[31] which is multiplied by an arbitrary length of time; the product of this simple calculation yields an amount of punitive damages to be suggested to the jury. If the defendant's business is extremely profitable, another method is to multiply its annual income with some small arbitrary percentage. Again, the product can be suggested as punitive damages.

Sometimes the multiplier, whether a percentage or a length of time, has some particular relevance to the punitive damages computation. Although the defendant's income will remain a constant, you may choose a multiplier with some special significance to arrive at a figure you want to suggest to the jury.

> What sum of money will make this callous corporation more responsible? You now know from the evidence that their truck driver had no license for almost five months before he crippled our friend and neighbor Joe Watkins. And the XYZ Corporation knew it—they knew for one hundred and forty-four days that every time Joe turned on the ignition of their massive forty-thousand-pound machine of steel, some member of our community was in danger.
>
> The court's charge tells you that punitive damages are to punish, to make the defendant more responsible. We know now that the XYZ Corporation makes about eighteen million dollars each year, ladies and gentlemen. Every day, whether or not they are responsible, they rake in about fifty thousand dollars. That is the amount of money they made yesterday, the amount they are making today, and the amount they will make tomorrow. In fact, that was the amount they made during each of the one hundred and forty-four days of their conscious irresponsibility and indifference.
>
> You can make the XYZ Corporation responsible, folks, but only if you equate punishment with money. The XYZ Corporation could not understand your verdict any other way. One hundred and forty-four days of grossly negligent conduct at fifty thousand dollars a day equals nine million two hundred thousand dollars of punishment. That is the price of safer trucking companies, safer truck drivers, and safer freeways for our families. That is the amount of punitive damages that will keep this type of conduct from ever occurring again.

---

31. Evidence of the defendant's financial condition is both discoverable and admissible as it relates to a claim for punitive damages. Lunsford v. Morris, 746 S.W.2d 471 (Tex. 1988); Birchfield v. Texarkana Memorial Hosp., 747 S.W.2d 361 (Tex. 1987).

Arguments Concerning Specific Types of Damages

In chapters 16 through 21, the more common types of personal injury actions are discussed. Those chapters present not only the general approach to arguing liability in a particular type of case but also specific identifiable arguments that might be considered. Chapters 23 through 27 concern different and specific types of damages and are therefore presented in a different format. Each of these chapters essentially represents an essay—a practical and philosophical "stream of consciousness" relating to the particular type of damages element. This format has been followed for a number of reasons.

First, unlike the argument on the question of liability, the damages argument rarely involves a "checklist" approach.

Second, to argue the elements of damages successfully, some time must be devoted to what is essentially a philosophical and somewhat esoteric exercise. The trial lawyer must contemplate pain, anguish, and the inability to work and provide.

Third, the argument of damages represents but an extension of the unique personality and character of the victim's advocate. In no other area of forensic persuasion is this more true.

Finally, it was apparent that any effort to approach these subjects in any other manner would be futile. For instance, few burn cases have much in common. The effects of a brain injury are peculiar to the portion of the brain that was damaged. A hip fracture that has resulted in some disruption of the acetabulum is completely different from a hip fracture in which this has not occurred. The list could go on and on.

For all these reasons, the following chapters, 23 through 27, are offered primarily for provocation and contemplation rather than for any other purpose.

A Note About Chapters 23 Through 27

Chapters 23 through 27, which concern argument about particular types of damages, are presented in a slightly different format from the rest of this book. The preceding chapters primarily consist of instructional essays, with examples of specific jury arguments that might be made in particular hypothetical cases. Chapters 28 through 31 contain sample jury arguments that the author has given in actual trials. Chapters 23 through 27 follow neither format but, it is hoped, combine the virtues of both.

Because of the nature of jury arguments on damages, an expository essay or list of subjects to cover would hardly capture the flavor of this delicate and critical area of argument. Because of the importance of adapting each jury argument on damages to the unique facts of each case and to the personal character of the victim and each advocate, sample jury arguments, whether from hypothetical situations or actual cases, are of limited value. Instead, these chapters offer, in a jury argument style, demonstrative examples of the types of things you should consider when talking with a jury about damages. Some of these suggestions may be lifted verbatim and transposed into jury arguments; others will require modifications to adapt them to the facts of an individual case. These are thoughts and suggestions of the types of ideas that should be offered to a jury to assist it in evaluating damages, and it seemed that the most effective way to convey those thoughts was through the voice of a trial lawyer.

Some language in these chapters stressing the seriousness of the injuries received by the plaintiff may raise questions in the reader's mind. First, none of the arguments that follow are meant to be in any way demeaning or degrading to handicapped individuals. The champion of the handicapped is the victim's advocate who secures full compensation for those who have been left impaired as a result of irresponsibility. To meet this challenge, the advocate must convey to the jury the total impact of physical and mental incapacities. Also, in some portions of these chapters there appear to be inconsistencies: at one point physical pain is described as the worst of afflictions, while in a later chapter the same description is used for mental anguish. The reader will recognize that this seemingly inconsistent language is suggested in both instances so that the jury may fully appreciate the magnitude of the victim's injuries.

23

Physical Pain

PHYSICAL PAIN is our ageless enemy. Its allies are fear, despair, and agony. From the dawn of time, we have fought to avoid it, paid great sums to elude it, resorted to both science and religion to control it, and died to escape from its tyranny. It is a cruel master, choosing as its victims the helpless and the sick, who are least able to bear its oppression. It is in attendance at every human birth, loves to prey on children, and plagues us in our last minutes of life. It has destroyed marriages, authored family ruin, and pillaged lifelong friendships. It writes the scripts for suicide and euthanasia. In severe cases, it breeds compassion; in lesser ones, indifference.

The words used to describe pain are countless. Words such as tormenting, burning, excruciating, agonizing, severe, cruel, harsh, throbbing, horrendous, gnawing, and grinding all have been used to characterize it; but to one afflicted by it, no words are adequate. Though beyond verbal description, its boundaries are easily defined. It is encapsulated within flesh, bone, muscle, nerves, tissues, and vital organs.

Physical pain can be the greatest form of agony and torment. It is the scourge of life and death's extreme disgrace. It is a perfect form of misery and the worst of all evils. It forces even the innocent to lie, and it overturns all patience.

How do we describe pain? The great modern minds have had no more success defining and communicating the concept of pain than did the ancient philosophers. Some might say that it is the only friend of care and want and that its constant companion is an insatiable hunger: hunger for peace, comfort, relief, and happiness. When one is visited with pain as a result of the conduct of another, the law says that the victim must be compensated. If there is no compensation, or if the compensation is inadequate, the victim becomes nothing but a coolie on whose shoulders are placed the burdens created by another. Think of how often we express in our daily wishes the hope that others may be free from pain. Phrases such as "have a nice day," "have a safe trip," or "drive carefully" all express our wishes for continued health and freedom from pain. On anniversaries and birthdays we say, "Many happy returns." At weddings the common wish is for "a long and happy life together." Very seldom do we wish for anyone to have great wealth or fortune. This is because we all silently recognize that health, well-being, and freedom from pain and disability are much more important and valuable than any monetary or financial reward. Who among us has ever met a person who, in the long run, would accept a lifetime of agonizing pain in return for great financial wealth or success? "The poorest man would not part with health for money, but the richest would gladly part with all his money for health."[1]

Consider the legal and philosophical attitudes regarding pain. Although our Constitution forbids "cruel and unusual punishment," many states allow very controlled forms of capital punishment. It is ironic that even when overriding societal concerns require the taking of a human life, the most extreme form of punishment, we go to great lengths to ensure that this ultimate punishment is administered as painlessly as possible. Four thousand years ago, in the days of Hammurabi, a person who injured another was required to suffer in a like manner, including death in appropriate cases.[2] This was the famous "eye for an eye, tooth for a tooth" code of justice. In ancient Rome the value of pain was never slighted. As Julius Caesar once remarked, "Those who will of their own accord give themselves to death are more easily found than those who can bear pain with patience."[3]

Under the present laws of our state, we have the right to resist when someone tries to rob us of our possessions. We even have the right to kill, if necessary, to defend our personal property. But what remedy do we have if someone invades the house of our soul? What if they steal from us a part of our most valuable possession—our good health? All of us live for the enjoyment of life—we work, strive, plan, dream, create, so that we can have the time, and a place, and loved ones with whom we can enjoy life's richness. What person lives solely for the sake of mere biological existence? If this was what God intended us to be, our species never would have survived the prehistoric age.

Thus, any discussion of pain must involve the following three categories:

- The experience
- The effects
- The evaluation

The Experience

To experience physical pain is to be imprisoned in a world of loneliness and isolation. The initial reaction upon being thrust into this darkened dimension is one of anger, shock, horror, and humiliation. As the physical torment continues, the mind must compensate for the anguish of the body. The brain attempts to block out that which is unbearable. A superhuman effort is

---

1. C.C. Colton, *quoted in* THE DICTIONARY OF PERSUASIVE PHRASES FOR LAWYERS 112 (H. Kornblitt ed. 1962).

2. Urch, *The Law Code of Hammurabi,* in THE LAWYER'S TREASURY 64, 70 (E. Gerhart ed. 1956).

3. *Quoted in* W.G. BENHAM, PUTNAM'S COMPLETE BOOK OF QUOTATIONS, PROVERBS, AND HOUSEHOLD WORDS 634a (1926).

required to concentrate and remain rational. Inevitably, the ugly portrait of pain is painted on the faces and bodies it has inhabited. The victim cowers, cringes, flinches, and grimaces. Yet even these outward appearances cannot adequately communicate what is happening within the soul. The pain sump is collecting the spirit of dreams, ambition, hope, confidence, and faith. The human soul is drained and distilled, leaving only a sediment of desolation, despair, depression, desperation, gloom, and bitterness. Anxiety and panic control one's mind during the isolation of the night as the agony of pain wrenches the body. Hours of darkness endlessly drag on toward dawn, the only remnant of hope being that somehow the change from night to day will bring some degree of relief. Anyone who has been ravaged by pain knows that it is not merely one part of the body that is affected; it is the entire body and the mind that suffer. There is no dividing line between the mind and the body.

It is easy to quantify the pain of another in terms of time. For a person afflicted with pain, however, a simple measurement of time cannot begin to express the extent of his anguish. It is not a matter of months or years of pain but of hundreds or thousands of days and nights, with scarcely a noticeable beginning or end. The person in pain lives these days and nights an hour or a minute at a time, often counting time by the clock instead of by the calendar. Time is often considered an absolute, but it is not. A minute, sixty seconds, can be the blinking of an eye or an eternity. There are countless examples in each of our daily lives that can be used to illustrate this point. When you are reading a good book, watching something interesting on television, playing golf or tennis, you have probably noticed how fast the time seems to fly. If you are visiting over a cup of coffee with a friend, you may have found yourself glancing at your watch, realizing that you had something else to do, and remarked, "Look at the time. I didn't realize I had been here that long." An exciting movie or sporting event that captures our attention never seems to last two or three hours. After a couple of days off over the weekend, we return to our offices or jobs on Monday and remark to our coworkers, "Gee, the weekend just flew. It seems like I just left work a short time ago."

Yet when we face pain, agony, and tragedy, time stands still. Even the mildest form of pain, such as a toothache, can make it impossible to enjoy certain simple pleasures. When the dentist asks us to come into his office for an hour of dental work, we think to ourselves that one hour is a long time to be in that chair. That hour of dental work may seem interminable, even though the work is performed with the benefit of modern anesthetics and is, in most instances, relatively painless. A minute of excruciating pain, however, does not pass like a minute on the golf course, a minute visiting with good friends, a minute at a football game, or a minute watching a good movie. Minutes of pain become hours, hours of pain become days, and days of pain become eternities.

Who are the heroes of the persons who suffer persistent pain? For most, they are the physicians who cast the splint, the nurses who administer pain medication, or the family members who furnish the ice pack or the heating pad. These people are the only hope for those locked in a tortured body. They are the saviors who alleviate the hurt and ease the pain. They are the givers of mercy.

There are moments of pleasure for even those in intense pain. The pleasure comes from the medication, the injection, and the pill that provide fleeting relief. As John Keats observed in 1818, however, just as pleasure is often a visitor, the pain clings cruelly to us.[4] Because of the ache, the discomfort, and the misery, we suffer in solitude and either callously ignore those whom we love or lash out at them in frustration. To that end, "life is not life; it is only a state of languor and suffering—the image of death"[5]—that feeds the perpetuating cycle of pain. While awaiting this end, though, we painstakingly strive to maintain a certain degree of mobility, of independence, and, if possible, our dignity. At times like this, our pleasures are merely fantasies; our pains are the only real things that exist.[6] Pain is all we know. Pain is all we feel. Pain is all we can remember.

The Effects

Show me a man in severe pain, and I will show you a person who has lost all track of time—a man who cannot remember when the pain began. He knows only that his pain is now, that it is harsh, and that his life is a blur.

Show me a man in severe pain, and I will show you a wife who lives in fear and sorrow. She is afraid for her husband—frightened that the pain will not end, tearful that he will not be able to work and provide for their family, and fearful that she will never again have a whole partner. Sorrow eats at her soul like a cancer because a part of her is in pain. She knows only that his pain is her pain.

Show me a man in severe pain, and I will show you crying children who cannot understand why their father has to suffer. The four-year-old daughter begins to feel deserted because her mother spends all waking hours with her father, while her father seems unaware of her existence. The seven-year-old son lives with depression because he cannot play ball, wrestle, or even laugh with his dad. He realizes, for the first time in his life, that his father is not immortal.

Show me a man in severe pain, and I will show you relatives and neighbors who silently begin to provide countless services for the family—the aunt who keeps the children every evening so that the wife may be with her husband; the man next door who mows their yard along with his own; the

---

4. ENDYMION bk. 1, l. 906 (1817).

5. Rabelais, *quoted in* THE NEW DICTIONARY OF THOUGHTS: A CYCLOPEDIA OF QUOTATIONS 262 (T. Edwards comp. 1957).

6. SAMUEL BUTLER (1612-1680), *Satire upon the Weakness and Misery of Man*, ll. 81-82, in 2 THE POETICAL WORKS OF SAMUEL BUTLER (G. Gilfillan ed. 1854).

church members who donate food and who begin raising money to support the family.

Show me a man in severe pain, and I will show you a tragedy that saddens all of those who know and love him. People he has not seen for years send presents and cards when they learn of his suffering. Fellow employees pitch in to buy the family a gift, and they assure the husband that he will get well and be able to return to his old job.

Show me a man in severe pain, and I will show you a tapestry of tragedy. The person who was once so healthy and content is now a monument to agony and despair. Who can say that it matters only to that man himself, his family, his relatives and friends? The suffering and sadness diminish us all.

Show me a man in severe pain, and I will show you someone who has looked into hell. To the person in pain, hell is the compass point on his chart of life. Although theologians, philosophers, and scholars may debate whether there is a hell after death, the ideological squabble is meaningless to the person in pain. His injury and its effects have become his "window into hell," through which he sees the torment of the ages. Even for those who are not religious, it cannot be denied from their accumulated imagination that nothing worse than physical pain exists on earth. Pain is the tool of torturers, the scourge of humankind, and the means by which we can create a hell on earth. A man in severe pain has, to his own satisfaction, long ago settled the theological debate concerning the existence of hell.

Show me a man in severe pain, and I will show you a historian—someone who knows that history is replete with the anecdotes of men and women who chose death rather than to suffer unendurable pain. From the remote times of ancient Rome to the more recent days of nineteenth-century Texas, death has been a solution for the problem of intolerable pain. In those earlier days of Texas, the familiar expression was "save a bullet for yourself," because torture at the hands of Comanche Indians was a real possibility. The Comanches were known to be so ruthless and cruel in their torture that they would brutally mutilate and mangle their captives and then suspend them over the smoldering fires of their own homes.[7] Despite the value and sanctity of life, no man, woman, or child would endure such agony if that person had an extra bullet. Men killed their own children, their wives, and themselves out of necessity, because the alternative was unthinkable. In more recent times, in settings ranging from the desolate battlegrounds of world wars to hospital wards for victims of diseases such as cancer and AIDS, we continue to hear pleas for death—the ultimate inhumanity—as a humane alternative to enduring continued physical pain.

---

7. See, e.g., accounts of Comanche tortures in J. MICHENER, TEXAS 461,672 (1986).

The Evaluation

Physical pain is so agonizing, so tormenting, so disturbing that most of us refuse to think about it. At the sight of someone inflicting pain upon the innocent, we become angry and uncomfortable; we cannot force ourselves to watch. When we hear of another's pains, we prefer not to listen. It is human nature to turn our minds from the knowledge of other people's troubles just as we must turn our minds from the thoughts of our own eventual deaths. If we did not have that mental block, the ability to remove ourselves from the shocking reality of pain and its effect on a man or woman, we would all be the victims of unbearable anxiety and frustration.

When was the last time you seriously considered the tragedy of starving children in Ethiopia, the state of political prisoners held by terrorists in the Middle East, or even the problem of drug trafficking in our own country, which results in the addictions and deaths of so many young people? In these troubled times, we feel the need to classify agony and despair in terms of sterile political "issues." We try to rationalize the pain of others through our own eyes. Because we cannot control the pain, the hurt, the anguish, we tune it out entirely.

Sure, we can deal with pain as an abstract concept, in the language of political rhetoric, in the cold calculation of numbers. If we talk about the Holocaust victims of Hitler's Germany in terms of the number of victims, we can avoid coming to grips with each individual's pain. If we talk about war atrocities in which thousands of men and women were tortured or mutilated, we can deal with those numbers. Yet, if we make pain personal, if we push it up close where we can see it, hear it, feel it, or smell it, we are forced to close our minds and hearts to it.

Remember the last time you visited someone in a hospital? A feeling of obligation and concern undoubtedly prompted your visit. You arrived at the hospital with a strong, healthy, and able body. After a short visit with your friend or relative, you probably left as quickly as you could. What excuse did you give? Was it the familiar apology that you were leaving so soon because you did not want to disturb the patient, your friend or family member? Despite the reason, you most likely left because your healthy body and mind could not tolerate the atmosphere of a hospital. Although the hospital is a place of healing, it is still a place of pain, torment, and dying. And as time goes by, rarely will you forget the suffering that confronted you.

When we are forced to evaluate the pain of someone else, we find our task incredibly formidable. Unlike the priest, rabbi, doctor, psychiatrist, nurse, or social worker, most of us have rarely tried to truly understand the pain of another human being. We have to draw on our past experiences to empathize with the suffering of another. What better way could there be to assess pain than through the collective wisdom of twelve strangers? It is somehow easier to receive and absorb information about pain in a community of twelve, which provides both a buffer and a support group. The unity of twelve minds provides a wisdom that can evaluate anything.

The victim of physical pain does not ask the strangers for sympathy; he or she asks to be compensated. The woman who wakes up in the middle of the night, with cold tears of reality rolling down her face, is not crying for sympathy; she is crying because of pain. Sympathy for a victim of pain comes through family and friends; it should not be awarded in the courtroom. Sympathy does nothing to compensate for the pain and suffering. If a child has a horribly painful disease and the pain can only be alleviated by expensive medication, what is the price of his pain? The child suffers not from a lack of sympathy but from a lack of compensation. The compensation he needs is whatever is required to relieve his pain. What parent could ever deny his or her child this simple relief because the medication was too costly? Can you imagine the little boy's parents sitting with him one morning, almost feeling the pain themselves, and saying to their son, "Your medicine is so expensive that we think a better use of that money would be made in a practical investment, such as common stock or savings bonds."

It is true that no amount of money will ever cure a person's tormented body. The compensation for pain is pleasure—the exact opposite of the harm that has been done. When one injures the body of another, who is that person to say that the victim is not deserving of compensation, of pleasure? What right is it of the wrongdoer to set the price of another's pain? The person at fault can easily preach tolerance when he has never been made to feel the pain. It is easy to criticize and belittle another's injuries. But that type of evaluation only adds to our own tortures, it only feathers the arrows of our enemies, and its resolution only provides us with little sleep.

Isn't it strange that the only place where pain becomes cheap is in the courthouse? We spend billions of dollars a year in this country in quest of cures for diseases, in quest of means to alleviate pain. In our scientific advances, the worth of the individual is considered paramount. Every drug that we have permitted to be marketed and sold to the public has been one that was designed, tested, and produced under the strictest of regulations. Medical research companies in the United States have almost unlimited resources through federal funds, grants, and even private and charitable donations. All the money is of secondary importance; the primary motivating factor is the safety of those who will ultimately benefit from the drug or the medication.

When corporations fight among themselves, there is never any quarrel about the fact that the loss of profits, loss of business, or loss of property is worth millions of dollars. Yet when we talk about the individual and the pain and agony that irresponsible conduct can bring, it is only then—in the courtroom—that pain becomes cheap.

What price tag does good health and freedom from pain carry in our country? Those who suggest that there is no price tag have not truly considered the world in which we live. In a day and age where anesthetics may run several hundred dollars for a surgery, who would undergo the operation without gladly paying that money? What person in pain thinks that the twenty-dollar shot of novocaine is too expensive?

Who are those in our society who are recognized for their superior health and physical abilities? Athletes. Their health and well-being carries an incredible price tag. Show me a professional baseball pitcher who is worth two million dollars a year when he cannot play because of his pain; tell me of the football or basketball star who can still earn his multimillion-dollar salary when his career has ended because of permanent pain and injury. To say that the ordinary person, however, is not entitled to reasonable compensation for his or her pain is to discriminate against and demean the value of human life. What man or woman does not cherish good health as much as any professional athlete does?

Pain is something that a person lives with because he cannot hire a substitute to take his place. If someone could suffer for those in pain, what would be the hourly rate? In cases of severe pain, do you think that a substitute could be found, regardless of the salary that was offered? Even if someone could be found, how long would he or she be willing to work? The person who hires on for a single day at two hundred dollars knows that his suffering is not infinite. He can see the light at the end of the tunnel. What would happen if that person were left in such pain for the rest of his life? Would that two hundred dollars suddenly become an unfair trade? Would it provide fair and reasonable compensation for a lifetime of agony?

Vince Lombardi once said that "fatigue makes cowards of us all." Fatigue is a very mild form of discomfort compared to pain. If fatigue makes us cowards, consider what pain does to us: it robs us of our pleasure, our mobility, our concentration, our dignity, our self-respect, our enjoyment of life, and, in extreme cases, our will to live.

Ultimately, physical pain is the most unbearable and intolerable affliction known to us. Financial ruin can be inconvenient and embarrassing, but with a good bankruptcy lawyer it can be tolerated without significant changes in life-style. Personal disgrace can be humiliating, but it can be endured with a change of scenery and a fresh start. Mental anguish can be debilitating if you are intent on being preoccupied with it, but there are ways to "put it out of your mind" and go on with your life. But there is no escape from physical pain and no satisfactory way to tolerate it. There are various medications that we euphemistically call "painkillers," but they do not kill pain. They merely postpone pain until the effects of the medication fade away, and in the meantime they dull the senses, so that the patient may not feel as much pain but does not feel anything else as acutely, either. Life with pain medication may be preferable to life without medication, but it becomes its own private hell—a life of perpetually dulled senses, where you are absolutely dependent on a little bottle of pills to make it through each day. Life with pain, with or without pain medication, is a constant, unrelenting, intolerable nightmare.

Many of the world's great religions teach that there is an afterlife consisting of something like what we call heaven and hell. Different religions, and different individuals practicing those religions, have different concepts and images of heaven and hell. Yet these versions of heaven and hell have one common thread: heaven, the ultimate reward for the virtuous, is characterized by the absence of pain; hell, the ultimate punishment for the evil and the wicked, is permeated by the most severe form of retribution imaginable by us—physical pain. At least those banished to hell get to wait until this life is over before they are forced to endure this punishment. For those injured by the carelessness of another, it does not matter that they are virtuous and deserving of heaven; it makes no difference that they are not evil and not deserving of hell. Innocent though they may be, they are forced to endure that unthinkable and unendurable feature that most of us place in our worst version of hell—physical pain. What greater injustice can there be?

24

Mental Anguish

THINK FOR A MOMENT about the human mind . . . From it flows all of that which has distinguished us from the other creatures of this planet. The human mind gives us the ability to think, plan, invent, create, and advance. What other quality do we possess that distinguishes us from God's other creatures? The horse is swifter. The ox is stronger. The lowly sponge is more durable and resistant to disease. The butterfly is more beautiful. The ant and fly are more prolific. The dog and cat have more acute senses, greater agility, and superior reflexes. But none of these creatures can think as we can.

Politicians refer to the human mind as America's greatest resource. Physicians and scientists declare it to be the least understood and most complex of the human organs. Theologians tell us that within the mind the soul resides.

Only the human mind can contemplate abstract concepts, such as justice, truth, fairness, and charity. Only the human being can understand that his existence is mortal, that death is inevitable, that tomorrow will be different from today. Why is the family dog so happy to see us when we return from a day's work? Scientists tell us that it is because the dog is unable to contemplate or understand the future. To the family pet, our absence is a terminal event. Our return at some future time is beyond its contemplation. Only the unlimited resources of the human mind have enabled us to survive, prosper, and control this planet to the exclusion of all other species. Because we could plan and contemplate the future, we were able to plant and harvest crops. Our mastery of mathematics, engineering, and metallurgy enabled us to build great cities, in which we can control our environment, provide for our comfort, and protect against the ravages of nature. Only human understanding of physics and aerodynamics has made it possible to leave this planet and return safely.

But with every blessing bestowed upon the human mind, there is a corollary disadvantage. Because we can contemplate justice, we also recognize injustice. The ability to anticipate a satisfying and rewarding future also enables us to despair in the face of tragedy. Because we can experience pride and satisfaction in our physical appearance and our personal and professional successes and accomplishments, we can also be tormented by disfigurement, failure, and physical limitations.

All the great religions of the world, Christianity, Judaism, Islam, and Hinduism, share the belief that our minds and bodies are one. Afflict the one, and the other inevitably will be impaired. The greatest author in the history of the English language, William Shakespeare, observed that it was the contents of the mind that made the body rich.[1]

Another gifted philosopher put it this way: "I find, by experience, that the mind and the body are more than married, for they are most intimately united; and when the one suffers, the other sympathizes."[2]

The blind English poet John Milton observed that "[t]he mind is its own place, and in itself / Can make a heaven of hell, a hell of heaven."[3]

The human spirit is nothing less than the sum total of our mental and physical health. Physical injury will inevitably produce mental anguish or despair. Yet agony of the mind does not require that the body be broken or the flesh be torn. Worry, fear, hopelessness, and despair can, of themselves, produce physical consequences. Science has long recognized that diseases such as high blood pressure, peptic ulcers, and chronic migraines can be produced by states of mind. On the other hand, a person who has the mental qualities of hope and the desire to live can often overcome the physical effects of injury or diseases that take the lives of others who feel that the window of hope and promise has been closed to them.

The story is told of the prisoner who volunteered for an experiment during World War II. Doctors were attempting to determine the amount of emotional stress that a soldier might experience on the battlefield. They told the prisoner that they were going to withdraw blood from him until he lost consciousness in order to see how much blood loss he could sustain. Actually, the doctors were not going to withdraw any blood from the prisoner. A large vial was placed in front of him while he was lying on an operating table, and the tubing was connected so that the vial would fill with what appeared to be his blood. As the vial began to fill, the prisoner's blood pressure rose, his heart rate increased, and, finally, he suffered a heart attack. Not an ounce of his own blood had been taken. These physiological effects resulted from the man's own perception, rather than what was actually happening to him. This story simply illustrates the axiom "Anguish of mind has driven thousands to suicide; anguish of body, none."[4] It also proves that the health of the mind is far more important to our happiness than the health of the body.

To contemplate fully the nature of "mental anguish" in its legal sense, four identifiable aspects of human emotion must be considered:

- grief and sorrow,
- worry and fear,

---

1. *The Taming of the Shrew*, act 4, sc. 3, l. 169.
2. Chesterfield, Earl of, *quoted in* THE NEW DICTIONARY OF THOUGHTS: A CYCLOPEDIA OF QUOTATIONS 408 (T. Edwards comp. 1957).
3. PARADISE LOST bk. 1, ll. 254-55.
4. C.C. Colton, *quoted in* THE NEW DICTIONARY OF THOUGHTS, *supra* note 2, at 410.

- the loss of enjoyment, and
- the inability to obtain recognition and self-satisfaction.

Grief and Sorrow

The first aspect of mental anguish, grief and sorrow, is based on the premise that human agony is not dependent on direct physical injury to the victim. The woman who has lost her lover, her companion, her confidant, and her best friend of twenty years—her husband—may suffer and agonize more as a result of that loss than she would from the most catastrophic injury.[5] So it is with the parent who has lost a child. Broken hearts are much more difficult to heal than broken bones. "On the sands of life sorrow treads heavily, and leaves a print time cannot wash away."[6] Grief is not peculiar to the human being. A cow that loses her calf will despair for a period of time. A cat that loses a kitten will search for it for a few days. But a man or woman who loses a loved one will never forget. For humans, "[t]he wrinkles of the heart are more indelible than those of the brow."[7] As people, we recognize that the anguish experienced as a result of death can only be fairly measured by reference to the loss suffered by the individual. "Grief is a matter of relativity; the sorrow should be estimated by its proportion to the sorrower; a gash is as painful to one as an amputation to another."[8]

For most of us, the unexpected, inexcusable, and avoidable loss of a loved one represents a tragedy of immense proportion. The inheritance of death is grief, sorrow, mental pain, and agony.[9] Where there is sorrow, there is holy ground.[10] Sorrow makes a silence in the heart.[11] Joy has its friends, but grief, its loneliness.[12] It is sorrow that humanizes our race.[13] It is grief that makes the heart sick and worry that consumes it.[14]

---

5. Before the supreme court's decision in Sanchez v. Shindler, 651 S.W.2d 249 (Tex. 1983), it was appropriate to instruct the jury in wrongful death cases not to consider any amounts by way of consolation for the decedent's death or for any sorrow, anguish, or grief suffered as a result of his death. *See* 3 STATE BAR OF TEXAS, TEXAS PATTERN JURY CHARGES PJC 81.04 (1982). This exclusionary instruction and comment are now obsolete. *See id.* (Supp. 1984).

6. Henry Neele, *quoted in* THE NEW DICTIONARY OF THOUGHTS, *supra* note 2, at 631.

7. Madam Deluzy, *quoted in id.* at 265.

8. Francis Thompson, *Shelley*, in THE DUBLIN REVIEW (July 1908), *quoted in* J. BARTLETT, FAMILIAR QUOTATIONS: A COLLECTION OF PASSAGES, PHRASES, AND PROVERBS TRACED TO THEIR SOURCES IN ANCIENT AND MODERN LITERATURE 990b-91a (13th ed. 1955).

9. Damages for mental anguish, including grief, sorrow, and mental upset are recoverable in an action for wrongful death. *See* Moore v. Lillebo, 722 S.W.2d 683 (Tex. 1986); Sanchez v. Shindler, 651 S.W.2d 249 (Tex. 1983).

10. Oscar Wilde, *quoted in* THE NEW DICTIONARY OF THOUGHTS, *supra* note 2, at 632.

11. ROBERT NATHAN, *Sonnet VII*, in A CEDAR BOX (1929).

12. *Id.*

13. Owen Meredith, *quoted in* THE NEW DICTIONARY OF THOUGHTS, *supra* note 2, at 633.

14. Talmud, *quoted in* THE DICTIONARY OF PERSUASIVE PHRASES FOR LAWYERS 180 (H. Kornblitt ed. 1962).

When we were created, we were imbued with magnificent capacities; we can love, sacrifice, feel guilt or pride, or worship the Creator. But with those gifts came a burden. God bestowed upon us not only the ability to feel grief, sorrow, and anguish but also the inability to ignore those feelings. As the American writer Washington Irving noted: "The sorrow for the dead is the only sorrow from which we refuse to be divorced. Every other wound we seek to heal, every other affliction to forget; but this wound we consider it a duty to keep open; this affliction we cherish and brood over in solitude."[15]

It has been our nature to use every gift, talent, and faculty to assist ourselves in demonstrating and documenting our grief and sorrow. Indeed, we have no artistic, creative, or innovative inclination that has not been enlisted in the memory of a loved one.

It is our nature to commemorate, memorialize, reminisce, carry in our thoughts, keep a memory alive, enshrine in memory, keep in mind, impress on our minds, treasure, hold dear, brood over, and keep forever.

It is our nature to keep memoirs, mementos, remembrances, and tokens to remind ourselves of a loved one.

It is our nature to build monuments or museums or to erect tombstones. But it is also our nature to recognize that it is the memories of a lost loved one that we carry in our minds that are the true monument. It is not the great marble monuments that cause us to grieve over the untimely deaths of such great men as Lincoln and Kennedy; it is the memory of their accomplishments and the emptiness that we all feel over their loss.

It is our nature to place upon the final resting place of a loved one a flower that is appropriately called the "forget-me-not."

The remembrance of lost lives has inspired people to courage. The British poet Rudyard Kipling, following the loss of English soldiers in battle, wrote, "Lord God of Hosts, be with us yet, / Lest we forget—lest we forget!"[16] In Lincoln's Gettysburg Address in 1863, America's greatest humanitarian remarked, "The world will little note nor long remember what we say here, but it can never forget what they did here." "Remember the Alamo" was the rallying cry of our distant cousins at the Battle of San Jacinto. "Remember the Maine" was the inspirational motto of Americans during the Spanish-American War. "Remember Pearl Harbor" was posted across this nation in bold letters during World War II.

It is our nature to commit our wounded hearts—our grief and sorrow—to poetry. Edgar Allen Poe's poem "The Raven" deals with the emotion that he felt for his lost love, Lenore. Although she had been dead for many years, he still had vivid memories of her that were aroused by embers of a fire.

---

15. *Rural Funerals, quoted in* J. BARTLETT, *supra* note 8, at 446b.
16. *Recessional*, st. 1 (1899).

It is our nature to write songs that remind us to remember and cherish lost loved ones. The popular "Abraham, Martin, and John" deals with the memories that we all still cherish of great men of this country who have fallen to the assassin's bullet.

Grief, sorrow, and anguish over the loss of a loved one are not only a part of human nature; they are also qualities that we all respect and admire. Yet the law clearly says that it is wrong for someone, through his or her carelessness, to visit this melancholy on another.

Those who are responsible for the loss of a loved one always assure us that "time heals all wounds." But those who give lip service to this hollow platitude ignore the great and grand virtue that the human possesses. It is our nobility that enables us to grieve and anguish.

Likewise, the authors writing of death always suggest that the loss of a loved one is lessened by the store of pleasant memories—recollections and remembrances of good and happy times. But in making such an argument, they forget that it is the recall of joy and happiness that forms the crucible out of which pain and hurt flow. The visions of the past only serve as poignant reminders of the pleasures and comforts that we can never know again. Only those who have taken a life suggest that grief and sorrow should be purchased cheaply. When these types of defenses and arguments are offered, we must remember that it should not be the prerogative of those who have visited another with grief, sorrow, and sadness to set the price.

Worry and Fear

The second aspect of mental anguish, worry and fear, may arise in the personal injury case in several forms. The man who is injured in a fall from the side of a building because of defective scaffolding will experience incalculable fear during the seconds that he is plummeting to the earth. The woman who is told that the only relief for her back and leg pain is surgical invasion will experience hours of torment, both before and after the back surgery. The young man who, because of a maiming and crippling injury, is unable to work faces decades of worry and fear over his inability to provide for himself and his family. Of the various shades of mental anguish, worry and fear are probably the most difficult to convey to others. Most of us approach these terms from an objective standpoint. But no one can truly understand the worries and fears of another. It is this subjectivity that confounds the assessment of damages.

Worry is not capable of quantification. Fear is not scientifically measurable. Thus, these human emotions have amazed the anatomists, confused the chemists, and remained shrouded in mystery to the mathematicians and physicists. Those who study human emotions, such as psychiatrists, classify them in terms that are general, at best. The reason should be obvious. Even though we are all capable of experiencing most human emotions, each of us has a unique emotional capacity. Some people love with a dedication and fervor that defies description. The emotional attachments of others are loose and fragile. So it is with worry and fear. The high-wire artist who walks across Niagara Falls on a cable, because of his training and emotional background, has little fear. On the other hand, the elderly woman attempting to cross an empty street may be in mortal fear. Some veterans were able to survive Vietnam with little emotional scarring. Others found themselves rendered permanently dysfunctional and are institutionalized for life. Yet, objectively, they were subjected to the same combat experience. These and other examples should make it clear that to understand another's mental anguish is a challenging task at best. Most of us recognize the human emotion of worry, but we cannot fully understand the extent to which it is experienced by another.

It is, therefore, appropriate to ask rhetorically: Are worry and fear proper elements of damages in the personal injury case? Some would suggest that, because of the difficulty of proof, they are not. But we all recognize that the effects of the shattering of bone or tearing of flesh are not simply those of physical pain. When the body is violated physically or the heart is broken emotionally, the mind is scorched and the soul weeps. Doctors of the human body often succeed quickly; but a doctor of the mind, a psychiatrist or psychologist, has a much longer, more difficult, and more uncertain road to travel. The scars of the soul are the slowest to heal.

It is sometimes suggested that the worry and fear of a particular individual are unusual, that the person's reaction to an event was not that which would be anticipated or predicted by statistics. But in considering the mental anguish sustained by one individual, we can obtain little solace from facts, figures, and statistics. Leave that approach to the scientists and statisticians. Those who find their answers in the computer will be confounded by the concept of mental suffering; they will not be able to understand it. Fear and worry are unique and intense human emotions. That is why in the personal injury lawsuit we have people decide these issues.

Think about it for a moment. What professionals do we recognize as being knowledgeable in the area of human emotions? Psychiatrists, psychologists, ministers, social workers, and teachers. All these fine professionals have been trained in different disciplines. They have been taught not merely to see what is on the outside but to look within as well. All of us know inherently that the most meaningful measure of worry and fear is that which a person finds within.

Worry and fear are inseparable. When fear appears, you can rest assured that its blood brother, worry, will not be far behind. What we fear most is the unknown. Evel Knievel could jump twenty cars with his motorcycle and be fearless. But if you and I attempted such a feat without having tried it before, we would be wrapped in total and immeasurable fear. With the gravely injured, the single word that hurts the most is *permanent*. All of us have been ill from time to time. Some of us have suffered serious injury. Most of us have labored through those illnesses, diseases, or injuries with the knowledge that one day we would recover. The word *permanent* breaks the soul.

A wise teacher once asked his students what was the saddest thing they had ever seen. One of his pupils answered that the saddest thing was a bird that could not fly. Another suggested a young deer that could not walk or run. Finally, after hearing all responses from his students, the teacher answered that the saddest thing in the world was a person without hope.

Remove a person's hope and you cast him into a whirlpool of fear and worry—troubled waters that the law calls mental anguish.

Worry and fear are the most brazen of thieves. They steal from us hope; they rob us of our faith; they destroy our expectation and plunder our confidence.

Worry and fear are harsh and insensitive employers. They come and demand our attention during all hours. They make us toil for them even as we sleep. They offer no holidays, no benefits, and no compensation. They make their most difficult demands at the very time when others are reaping the most enjoyment and comfort. They treat those over whom they preside more brutally than any master ever abused a slave.

Worry and fear are the most vicious of our enemies. They surround, while leaving no path for retreat. As noted by an English novelist, their natural allies are the dark, physical pain, public ridicule, poverty, and loneliness.[17] Their goal is to immobilize, disarm, weaken, and subdue. The only compromise acceptable to them is absolute surrender.

Forty-five years ago, America and its allies were locked in a great global war against an axis of tyrants. The Commander in Chief of this country who successfully guided us through that conflict was a courageous man, whose disease had confined him to a wheelchair. In 1941 in a message to Congress before we entered the war, Franklin Roosevelt declared that for the future to be secure, "we look forward to a world founded upon four essential human freedoms: freedom of speech and expression, freedom of worship, freedom from want, and, perhaps most important, freedom from fear." Our people, our elected officials, indeed every segment of American society have remained true to that principle announced that day. We have spent billions on defense so that our people may be free from the fear of foreign aggression. We have spent billions on law enforcement and erected prisons so that we may be free from the fear of criminal acts. We have spent billions on medical research so that we may be free from the fear of disease. Isn't it ironic that only in the courthouse are fear and worry said to enjoy only a modest value? Only when those responsible for planting the seeds of fear and worry in another's mind are called before twelve citizens to account for their actions do we hear that fear and worry should come cheap.

---

17. HUGH WALPOLE, THE OLD LADIES, *quoted in* J. BARTLETT, *supra* note 8, at 930a.

Loss of Enjoyment

The march of civilization has been fueled by our pursuit of happiness. Few of us labor and toil for the sake of work alone. Instead, we labor so that we can sow the seeds for happiness and pleasure. Even the most tireless worker will tell you that his toil is but a bridge to better times. Men and women work, strive, sacrifice, and endure in the name of what we call the enjoyment of life. Most citizens recognize that a neighbor who has been injured or crippled through the carelessness of another is entitled to just compensation. The concept of an injury that diminishes one's earning capacity is readily understood. But when the painful and crippling effects of that injury bring about a loss of the enjoyment of life, the concept of just compensation becomes clouded and obscured.

Our Founding Fathers pronounced in our Declaration of Independence that all men are created equal and that they are "endowed by their Creator with certain unalienable rights; that among these are life, liberty, and the pursuit of happiness." These are not empty and hollow phrases. The pursuit of happiness—the enjoyment of life—is a fundamental guarantee of our government. Laws are passed, statutes are enforced in courts, law enforcement organizations are created, and armies are maintained in an effort to ensure this inalienable right. Thomas Jefferson, the principal author of our Declaration of Independence, declared that it was the care of human life and happiness that was the first and only legitimate object of good government.[18] William Somerset Maughan, the English novelist, wrote that it is happiness that ennobles the character sometimes, but "suffering, for the most part, is what makes men petty and vindictive."[19] Many other writers have described happiness. One calls it "wine of the rarest vintage,"[20] and another describes it as something that makes up in height for what it lacks in length.[21] Jean-Jacques Rousseau said, "The thirst after happiness is never extinguished in the heart of man."[22]

Happiness and the enjoyment of life are more infectious than the most contagious diseases. The person whose cup is filled with joy, comfort, and satisfaction will find that these qualities spill over into the cups of all those around him. Some say that there is not only a right to happiness but a duty of happiness as well. According to another writer, being "happy ourselves is the most effectual contribution to the happiness of others."[23] And the Russian

---

18. *To the Republican Citizens of Washington County, Maryland, quoted in id.* at 375a.
19. THE MOON AND SIXPENCE ch. 17 (1919).
20. LOGAN PEARSALL SMITH, AFTERTHOUGHTS, *quoted in* J. BARTLETT, *supra* note 8, at 822b.
21. [*Title of poem*] (1942).
22. LES CONFESSIONS bk. 9, *quoted in* J. BARTLETT, *supra* note 8, at 345a.
23. SIR JOHN LUBBOCK, THE PLEASURES OF LIFE, *quoted in id.* at 664a.

novelist Tolstoy wrote, "Happy families are all alike; every unhappy family is unhappy in its own way."[24]

Good health can never ensure happiness, but pain, disability, and physical limitation, like a dreaded virus, will always attach to that part of the human heart where happiness and enjoyment reside. The German philosopher Schopenhauer observed that "the two foes of human happiness are pain and boredom."[25] It is the person who is happy and enjoys life who is the optimist, the dreamer, the enthusiast, the idealist, the romanticist, and the visionary. As one poet put it:

> You have to believe in happiness,
> Or happiness never comes. . . .
> Ah, that's the reason a bird can sing—
> On his darkest day he believes in Spring.[26]

Most of us, each day, express the wish that those we meet will find comfort and enjoyment. "Have a nice day." "Enjoy yourself." "Have a good time." "Have fun." In these sayings we express to each other the value that we all place on the ability to enjoy life. There are men and women who paint "just for fun." While their pictures and paintings might not meet with artistic approval, we recognize that it is the doing of that which gives pleasure. We play golf for amusement; we fish for sport. We take pleasure trips—travels that carry us to no particular place to do no particular thing. Your neighbor "delights" in his yard work. You and your spouse had "the time of your lives" on your last vacation trip. Your child's camping trip was "a blast." The trip to the museum was a "big time." The softball game you played in was a "picnic." The sailboat cruise around Galveston Bay was a "riot."

It is our nature to be happiest when we are playing, gaming, sporting, jesting, relaxing, frolicking, being entertained, joking, laughing, romping, celebrating, rejoicing, or "just passing time."

What is life without pleasure? It is biological existence—nothing more and nothing less. It is as sad as a flower that will never bloom or a bird that will never fly. It is a simple recipe for torturing a soul. A Hemingway who could not write, a Remington who could not paint the West, a Ginger Rogers who could not dance, a Jesse Jackson who could not preach or speak, a Van Cliburn who could not play piano, a Mark Spitz who could not swim, an Amelia Earhart who could not fly. They would all exist, but would they truly live?

---

24. ANNA KARENINA pt. 1, ch. 1 (1875-76).
25. ESSAYS. PERSONALITY; OR, WHAT A MAN IS, *quoted in* J. BARTLETT, *supra* note 8, at 461b.
26. Douglas Malloch, *You Have To Believe, quoted in id*. at 889b.

How should we view the assessment of damages for an injury that deprives a neighbor or friend of the enjoyment of life? Life without the ability to enjoy and participate in the things that give us pleasure and satisfaction is like marriage without love; like a child without spunk, energy, and imagination; like a family without a loving home; like a ship without a port.

How do we measure in damages the loss of the enjoyment of life? The person who has been robbed of pleasure will be left with constant reminders of that which was stolen. The woman who used to pride herself in making her own clothes becomes envious of her friends and neighbors who make their own clothes. The man who loved to play golf on weekends finds agony when his friends discuss their last round of golf. The woman who prided herself in her yard work becomes jealous of her neighbor who gardens. As Shakespeare observed, "But, O, how bitter a thing it is to look into happiness through another man's eyes!"[27]

The Inability To Obtain Recognition and Self-Satisfaction

The aspect of mental anguish that involves an inability to obtain recognition or self-satisfaction might best be termed the "ignobling of man." The concept has been aphoristically stated as, "He who steals my purse steals trash, but he who steals my good name makes me poor indeed."[28] Various types of tragedies yield this type of mental suffering in their wake: the woman who once took great pride in her appearance but finds herself scarred and disfigured for life; the robust and athletic man who suffered amputation of a limb or was otherwise crippled and cannot participate in sports; the bright and promising student who suffered brain damage and can function only at the lower levels of intelligence; the husband and father who prided himself on his financial ability to provide for his family but is now physically unable to do so; the career woman who suffered an injury causing physical limitation and now finds the windows of opportunity closed to her.

The ennobling of the human being by the Creator was done without prejudice. Self-esteem is as important to the man as it is to the woman. Pride in one's appearance and accomplishments is as vital to the young as it is to the old. Self-respect is no less important to the Christian, Jew, or Moslem. The need for respect knows no racial barriers.

Good health is the foundation on which the essence of the human spirit depends. The Old Testament Apocrypha tells us that health and good estate of

---

27. *As You Like It*, act 5, sc. 2, ll. 41-42.

28. This aphorism is paraphrased from Shakespeare, *Othello*, act 3, sc. 3, ll. 158-62, where Iago says to Othello: "Who steals my purse steals trash; 'tis something, nothing; / 'Twas mine, 'tis his, and has been slave to thousands; / But he that filches from me my good name / Robs me of that which not enriches him / And makes me poor indeed."

body are above all gold.[29] Even before these teachings, the ancient Greeks recognized that "to lose one's health renders science null, art inglorious, strength unavailing, wealth useless, and eloquence powerless."[30]

The flower of good health yields many blooms: confidence, positivity, self-reliance, fearlessness, faith, and assurance. The ability to work and provide for one's self and one's family yields the sweet fruit of dignity, worthiness, and respect. The desire for personal recognition is the fuel for the fire of human existence. Would any of us strive and work as hard at our jobs and professions as we do if our accomplishments were not recognized by others? Would the artist paint if there was no one to see the picture? Would the musician play if he knew no one would hear his music? Samuel Johnson, British author in the seventeenth century, observed that it generally happens that assurance keeps an even pace with ability.[31] And Joseph Conrad wrote more than a century later that a man's real life is that accorded to him in the thoughts of other men by reason of respect.[32]

There are few sports that people play by themselves, unobserved and in isolation. Even the average-to-poor tennis player obtains satisfaction from that occasional good shot. The golfer who is only a duffer and who shoots in the hundreds plays with his friends and colleagues in search of the satisfaction and admiration he may receive for that one shot, or that one par on one hole out of eighteen.

Of all the human values, virtues, and emotions, pride is the most difficult to understand. Personal pride in our endeavors is the genesis of our greatest accomplishments. It is pride that causes us to work hard and gain that promotion; it is pride that drives us as parents to devote our energies and efforts to our children in the quest for their success; it is pride that keeps our houses clean, our yards neat, and the corner laundry in business. From the bosom of pride is born the brilliant surgeon, the concerned teacher, the successful homemaker, and the great athlete. As Mark Twain said of the steamboat captains who sailed the Mississippi, "Your true pilot cares nothing about anything on earth but the river, and his pride in his occupation surpasses the pride of kings."[33]

Both men and women take pride in their personal appearance. The American novelist Gertrude Franklin Atherton wrote that people "love the lie that saves their pride, but never an unflattering truth."[34] And America's

---

29. *Ecclesiasticus* 30:15, THE APOCRYPHA OF THE OLD TESTAMENT (Revised Standard).

30. Herophilus, *quoted in* THE DICTIONARY OF PERSUASIVE PHRASES FOR LAWYERS, *supra* note 14, at 150.

31. 2 THE RAMBLER No. 159, *quoted in* DICTIONARY OF QUOTATIONS 34 (B. Evans comp. 1968 & reprint 1978).

32. UNDER WESTERN EYES pt. 1 (1911).

33. LIFE ON THE MISSISSIPPI ch. 7 (1883).

34. THE CONQUEROR bk. 3, ch. 6 (1902).

famed poet Robert Frost suggested that mental agony occurred when there was "nothing to look backward to with pride and nothing to look forward to with hope."[35] Shakespeare noted that it was always pride that fell with fortune.[36]

It has been said that while pride is not a virtue, it is the parent of many virtues.[37] It is this parent and its progeny of virtues that may be wounded and killed when the body is crippled or disfigured. If pride dies, humiliation begins looting the grave of what little self-respect may be left. Being a victim of carelessness that produces an incapacitating injury is like being visited by a disagreeable relative. It comes without invitation, stays when it is not wanted, and demands to be placed in charge of the whole household. But the most disagreeable thing about disability is that when it pays its unwelcome visit, it insists on bringing its obnoxious cousins, shame and disgrace. Is the gruesome accounting that is required to find fair damages for incapacity or disfigurement to be limited simply to the balance sheet? Are we confined to the imbecilic arithmetic of lost wages or medical expenses? A good man represents more to himself and his family than simply a paycheck. A good woman represents more than simply a contribution to the family income or a good housekeeper. A good person's injuries represent much more than the expense of having a doctor and hospital patch him up.

The price that humankind has for centuries placed on pride is indelibly etched in the annals of history. Pride has written the scripts for war, divorce, business resignation, family quarrels, the breakup and dismantling of corporations, and an inexhaustible list of actions by men and women that we sometimes characterize as irrational, illogical, or senseless. The Bible speaks of men who would rather lose their lives than lose their pride. The history books tell us of men and women who chose to die rather than live with indignity.

Our famous Texas novelist Larry McMurtry recently wrote a classic work about life in Texas in the middle nineteenth century. The book is called *Lonesome Dove*, and it is about two middle-aged men who were once feared and respected Texas Rangers. The two Rangers, Gus and Call, make a cattle drive from Texas to Montana. Toward the end of the story and just short of their destination, Gus is ambushed by a band of renegade Indians and wounded with two arrows in his left leg. In his wounded condition he is barely able to make it to the nearest town. By that time infection has set in in the wounded leg and is beginning to spread to the other leg. Call learns of Gus's plight and leaves the cattle drive to check on his lifelong friend. The doctor explains to Call that the wounded leg was amputated and now, because the

---

35. *The Death of the Hired Man*, ll. 103-04 (1914).

36. *As You Like It*, act 1, sc. 2, l. 233.

37. John C. Collins, *Aphorisms*, *quoted in* DICTIONARY OF QUOTATIONS, *supra* note 31, at 555.

gangrene has spread, the other leg must come off or Gus will die. But Gus refuses, telling the doctor, "I might could get by without the one, but I can't without both" and later explaining to Call: "I've walked the earth in my pride all these years. If that's lost, then let the rest be lost with it. There's certain things my vanity won't abide." The only request that Gus makes of Call is a promise to take Gus's body back to Texas to be buried in a special place on the south Guadalupe River, where he had found his best happiness. Gus eventually dies of the gangrene, and the last two chapters of the story focus on the long journey that Call makes in a buggy, carrying Gus's body in a coffin packed with charcoal and salt to preserve it.

McMurtry's book is about pride: Gus's pride in not wanting to live without any legs; Call's pride in fulfilling a promise.

When we come before a jury of twelve friends and neighbors with our pride ravaged, our self-esteem maimed, and our self-respect crippled, we must look for another source of pride—that which resides in each member of the jury. It is the same type of pride that drove Call to bring Gus's body back to Texas. Perhaps Abraham Lincoln expressed it best in his first inaugural address in 1861. In that address he asked, "Why should there not be a patient confidence in the ultimate justice of the people? Is there any better or equal hope in the world?"

25

Future Damages

A WISE MAN once said, "We are always looking to the future; the present does not satisfy us—our ideal, whatever it may be, lies further on."[1] We always live prospectively, never retrospectively.[2] The ordinary human has the faith that gives him courage to face the present with confidence and the future with expectancy. But imagine our destiny if we could not dream, if we had no thought of a better tomorrow, no hope of promising times ahead, no possibility of a rewarding future. Imagine life if it were only a continual succession of tragic pasts. Imagine a future that is only the past repeated, entered through another gate. If a person's only fate was based solely on scarred memories, he would perceive life through never-ending anguish, agony, and torment. A crippled body may serve only as a constant reminder that any satisfying future must be in another world, in the life that we believe follows the death of the body.

In arriving at your verdict in this case, you must answer a number of questions about future damages. This is the law's requirement, not our desire. We wish these matters could be handled another way. We would prefer that this jury would address only the damages that have occurred in the past. We know you would be more comfortable with that type of responsibility. We wish that, in ten or fifteen years, we could bring back this group, or another body of fair-minded people dedicated to justice, to decide the damages that have occurred in the intervening time—and then, over the lifetime of this victim, continue the same process. But that is not the law. Rather, the court charges you with the responsibility of determining all damages for all time. The decision you reach in this case will be binding on this victim for the rest of his life.

That is why we brought you evidence like the life expectancy tables, the medical proof, and the statistics. These are facts. But getting the facts is only one half of the job. The other half is to use them intelligently. Sometimes the hardest thing about facts is to face them.

Someone may want to talk about this victim's hopes for the future. During the trial of this case you have heard the defense examine several

---

1. Ezra Hall Gillett, *quoted in* THE NEW DICTIONARY OF THOUGHTS: A CYCLOPEDIA OF QUOTATIONS 226 (T. Edwards comp. 1957).
2. Friedrich H. Jacobi, *quoted in id.* at 226.

witnesses who told you what "could happen" that would make this victim's situation better. We did not object to this evidence, but I think we all recognize that what "will be" is a long way from what "may be."

We have all been ill, sick, or had a problem we thought would consume us. In every instance, when we went to bed at night, our one thought was that tomorrow would be a better day. In everyone's life, both faith and fear sail into the harbor of the mind. With most of us, only faith is allowed to anchor. But few of us have ever had to face the word *permanent* as it applies to a crippling or maiming injury. And even when all the doctors and the knowledge of medical science tell us that the injury is permanent, we still hold on to the "may be" rather than living with the "will be."

As this evidence about what "may be" was introduced by the defense, we did not object. We recognize that hope is what keeps us all living and going on with life. In this victim's case, it is this hope, however dim, that will keep him alive. We did not object to the evidence, because we did not feel it appropriate to destroy what little hope this victim may be holding on to that is shedding some light into a rather dismal existence. While it is appropriate that this victim keep his hope, his ray of light, it is not appropriate for that hope to form the basis of your verdict. Instead, your verdict must be based on the evidence—on facts. Facts do not cease to exist just because they are ignored. While evidence, reality, and reasonable medical probability all form the basis for your verdict, they will not give this victim something to live for.

It has been suggested that the victim is a courageous individual. You have courage when you are the only one who knows you are afraid. We did not object to the evidence offered by the defense on those things that are remote, speculative, and good, because we did not want to take from this victim what little hope he has. By the same token, while we would not take that hope from him, I think it reasonable to ask of you that you base your verdict not on that ray of hope but rather on that darkness this defendant's conduct has cast upon the victim for the rest of his life. This man's future has been taken hostage by the defendant's conduct. In our troubled world, we have learned all too well the folly of making concessions to those who would seize hostages.

When you answer these questions about future damages, that will be the end of it—for all time. The victim cannot come back to this judge a year from now, or five years from now, and say, "Your Honor, I need a new trial. The jury made a mistake. All those hopes and suggestions that things would get better did not materialize—they did not happen."

All of us have faith in the future. Faith in the future is what makes the farmer plant his seeds in the spring, the parent save for his children's college education, and the family take out a thirty-year mortgage. Without faith in each other, we could not board an airplane, take the elevator up to this courtroom, or even get on the freeway to go home this evening. Our faith in each of you was demonstrated when you were selected to serve on this jury. We all know that our faith in each other will be reflected in your verdict.

Injury to a Child

It is said that a person has grown old when he has forgotten what it is like to be a child. The assessment of fair damages to a child who has been maimed and crippled must be made through the child's eyes. Only if we view injury in this manner can we hope to do justice. Likewise, to fairly assess future damages we must understand the relationship between these parents and this victim. The old expression that there is only one perfect child in the world and every parent has it is a simple recognition of the unique and very special relationship that exists between all good parents and their children.

Childhood is that wonderful time when all you have to do to lose weight is take a bath. The only thing that children wear out faster than shoes are parents and teachers. It seems that the thing most children save for a rainy day is lots of energy. And while healthy children may tear up a house, they will never break up a home.[3] A child's ear is a delicate instrument that cannot hear a parent's shout from the next room but picks up the faintest tingle of the ice cream vendor's bell. There is nothing thirstier than a child who has just gone to bed or hungrier than a child between mealtimes. Children disprove the basic law of physics that matter cannot be created: simply love a child, and the love will be returned a hundredfold. Children are the best home furnishings. The best Christmas gift of all is the presence of a happy family all wrapped up with one another.

The terms *innocence* and *childhood* are synonymous and interchangeable. It is said that children and fools cannot lie. In the Beatitudes, Jesus called the peacemakers the children of God. Children are like wet cement—whatever falls on them makes an impression. Children need strength to lean on, a shoulder to cry on, and an example to learn from. A child is a magical creature; you can lock him out of your workshop, but you cannot lock him out of your heart.[4]

A philosopher once observed that if you confront a child, a puppy, and a kitten with sudden danger, the child will turn instinctively for assistance, the puppy will grovel in abject submission, and the kitten will brace its tiny body for a frantic resistance.[5] The famed poet Elizabeth Barrett Browning said that a child's sobbing in the silence curses deeper than the strong man in his wrath.[6]

The hallmark of Western civilization is a humane regard for the lives and health of children. It was not always so. In early Rome there was an island in

---

3. These descriptions of children are found in E. McKenzie, 14,000 Quips & Quotes for Writers & Speakers 70a (1980 & reprint 1984).

4. *Quoted in id.* at 53a.

5. Saki [Hector Hugh Munro], *The Achievement of the Cat, quoted in* J. Bartlett, Familiar Quotations: A Collection of Passages, Phrases, and Proverbs Traced To Their Sources in Ancient and Modern Literature 851b (13th ed. 1955).

6. *The Cry of the Children*, st. 13, *quoted in id.* at 518b.

the Tiber River where unwanted infants were left to die. The first orphanages were bowls in front of churches where abandoned babies could be left in the hope that they might live instead of perishing from exposure. The history of the enlightenment of humankind is a pattern of increased consideration for the young, especially in our nation. Our law has created special courts in which to try juvenile delinquents and special institutions where those found guilty may be kept away from hardened criminals. Why does our own state not allow teenagers to drink? Isn't it out of the belief that they may not have the needed maturity—the ability to appreciate the dangers and consequences of their actions? Why are laws concerning child abuse and child support so vigorously enforced? Isn't it because we know the children cannot defend themselves and so we must do it for them? When a child brings legal action for damages, in addition to the attorney who has been hired by the parents, a special lawyer is appointed for him. This lawyer serves as an officer of the court to ensure that justice is done for the child. This appointment is made in every case, for every injury to a child.

The fair evaluation of damages for pain, suffering, and impairment of a child requires that we bring with us a different perspective and a special understanding. An injured child possesses unique problems with respect to pain. The very young cannot describe their symptoms, so it is harder to diagnose and treat them. How does a child learn to cope with pain and crippling injuries? A child's world is one of fairy tales, cartoons, and comic books, where there is no such thing as tragedy. The woodsman slays the wolf before the wolf can harm Little Red Riding Hood. The Three Little Pigs find they are safe in the brick house even though they were threatened in houses built of straw and wood. Daffy Duck and Bugs Bunny are squashed, trampled, run over, or blown up, but they always recover. Fred Flintstone may be hit over the head with a club, but the lump goes away. Movies containing too much violence and tragedy are rated unsuitable for viewing by young children.

We all know that fear magnifies pain and mental anguish in a person of any age. But a child cannot build the same bridge over troubled waters as can an adult. Children lack the armor of maturity—an acquired stoic attitude that what cannot be endured must somehow be tolerated. They have been taught that pain means punishment or discipline: in a child, needless and accidental pain may plague the conscience as well as the soul. And we all know that medical science does not have the same freedom in treating a child with narcotics as it does an adult, because the child's body is less tolerant and may be more easily addicted. So the painful injury exacts a harsher toll from the child than from the adult.

Pain and anguish do not come to children in reduced doses like baby aspirin. The torture of broken bones and ravaged flesh may be the same for a child as for an adult, but it is magnified many times by the child's fear, which lies beyond the reach of any remedy—any pill, treatment, or therapy.

But it is not only pain and fear that are different for the child. Disfigurement embarrasses the adult, but it humiliates the child who must exist in a world of his peers. The innocence and frankness most of us so admire in children may, to an impaired child, be vehicles for scorn and ridicule. The adult who is physically different may feel uncomfortable, but the impaired child feels himself a pariah. The impaired child may come to view himself as a cultural outcast, a physical freak, a social exile. In short, "being different" may shanghai more of the child's personality.

And what of the family? Holidays like Thanksgiving and Christmas may be special times for you and me. Yet holidays may represent to this family only one more special occasion to reflect on the tragedy that has left their loved one disfigured or impaired. No one can doubt the devotion of this mother and father. But certainly no one would suggest that, because this victim has devoted parents, the damages awarded should be any less.

The damages you find for this victim will be placed in the registry of this court to be administered under the judge's supervision. This process is simply another way that the law says to all of us, "Use special consideration, use special care when you determine the damages in this case." The determination of damages for a child with permanent injuries is always a particularly challenging and troubling task for a jury. Simply consider the amount of time that is involved. During the time this victim must contend with the ravages of the injury produced by the defendant's negligence, three more generations will be born. We will have sixteen presidential elections. More than five separate groups of children will start the first grade and graduate from high school. This defendant, by his carelessness, has mortgaged a child's future. When you consider the value of that mortgage, you might want to consider the following admonition:

> Bitter are the tears of a child:
> Sweeten them.
> Deep are the thoughts of a child:
> Quiet them.
> Sharp is the grief of a child:
> Take it from him.
> Soft is the heart of a child:
> Do not harden it.[7]

Injury to the Elderly

A comfortable old age is the reward of a well-spent life. Life becomes brighter and brighter, and its meaning clearer, the longer we live. What has puzzled us in the past seems less mysterious, and crooked paths look straighter as we

---

7. Lady Pamela Wyndham Glenconner, *A Child, quoted in id.* at 853b.

approach the end. In this nation we venerate and respect the elderly. It is the elderly person who is the statesman, the professor emeritus, the retired gentleman whom the shop calls when a problem arises that no one can seem to solve, and the Sunday-school teacher molding young minds with a unique depth of wisdom. Henry Ford suggested that if you take all the experience and judgment of men over fifty out of the world, there would not be enough left to run it.[8]

This enlightened and respectful attitude did not always prevail. History tells us that certain tribes of Indians were known to shun many members of their clan when they reached old age; they would literally be cast from the community to die an isolated and lonely death. Primitive nomadic tribes were known to leave the elderly men and women at the side of the road rather than try to help them in their journey.

But we have come to realize that many people achieve their greatest accomplishments in their golden years. Daniel Webster, Thomas Jefferson, John Adams, and Benjamin Franklin performed some of their best work after the age of sixty. Louis Pasteur discovered a cure for hydrophobia after the age of sixty. John Stuart Mill, John Ruskin, and Ralph Waldo Emerson were beginning some of their best writings when they were sixty. At age seventy-three, Galileo discovered laws of astronomy that have never been supplanted. William Gladstone was prime minister of England at the age of eighty-five. Michelangelo completed his work at St. Peter's Church in Rome at the age of seventy-five—after having worked on this masterpiece for more than seventeen years. Today, Republicans point with pride to the accomplishments of Ronald Reagan. Democrats would hold up Claude Pepper and Lloyd Bentsen. Yet we would consider all these fine individuals senior citizens.

Our respect for the elderly arises not only from recognition of a potential for contributions to come but also from a sense of responsibility for contributions past. Ordinary senior citizens, people like this victim, were the builders of our roads, the drillers of our oil wells, our teachers, the men and women who nurtured us, the people who cared and protected us as children. They obeyed our laws, they paid their taxes, and it was their contributions in both money and time that gave us the great highways that we use today, our communication system, our schools, and our medical centers. If we compare the problems we have today concerning deficits and taxes with the problems their generation faced, we would all have to admit that they did not do a bad job.

As we grow older, we come to understand that age is determined more by state of mind than by number of winters passed. We do not stop laughing because we grow old; we grow old because we stop laughing. To be seventy years young is sometimes more cheerful and hopeful than to be forty years old.

---

8. *Quoted in* THE NEW DICTIONARY OF THOUGHTS, *supra* note 1, at 13.

But some people feel that an injury to an elderly person is somehow not as significant as an injury to a child or to a young or middle-aged adult. It has been suggested that things would be a lot nicer if antique people were valued as highly as antique furniture; unfortunately, many people do not hold that view. The argument is made that, because this victim is approaching the twilight of his life, the damages you find for his future impairment, disability, pain, and anguish should not be that great.

It is certainly true that nature endowed the young with many gifts. The young heal faster, they recover better, and they tolerate adversity and conquer it because of their vigor and spirit. Bones heal quickly, torn tissue repairs itself, and aches and pains pass with time in the young. When we realize these medical facts and their corollaries—that as we reach the golden years, our bones may not heal, torn tissue remains tough and inflexible, and the pain of an injury sometimes only compounds and worsens the discomfort of our many years of living—we realize the truth of the old adage that youth is wasted on the young.[9]

The older we get, the more precious our days become, the more valuable are the hours that permit us to do the things that bring us pleasure and satisfaction. The ability to be free from illness, pain, and disability is treasured by those who live in the twilight years. Most of us spend our lives working for the treasures we feel are hidden in those years. We sometimes neglect our families, ourselves, and our friends in the quest for the ultimate goal: to be in a position to do those things we denied ourselves for so long. How many times have we heard one of our parents, or some elderly neighbor or friend, say, "When I retire, I will be able to do all those things . . ." And we know it's possible. During the weekends, we see elderly folks at golf courses. We see them in social gatherings at churches and synagogues enjoying their games. We see them gathered in groups headed on a trip. On our highways, we see vans and buses of older people who are now seeing the country in a way that time and commitment have always denied them. And as we get older, we begin to realize that the time on this earth the Lord gave us is beginning to run out. We realize that there is more sand at the bottom of the hourglass—the years we have spent—than there is remaining at the top of the glass—the time we have left.

Picture two men trying to cross the desert on horseback. One has a keg of water, the other a small canteen that is only half full. If each man gives a cup of water to someone else, who has made the greater sacrifice? If two people are robbed on a bus, and the thief steals one hundred dollars from each passenger—one a millionaire and the other a widow who is traveling with her small life's savings—who has experienced the greater loss?

---

9. George Bernard Shaw, *quoted in* DICTIONARY OF QUOTATIONS 787 (B. Evans comp. 1968 & reprint 1978).

During the trial of this case, we have all joined hands and walked through the past. We have come to know this victim. We know his contributions, his work, the sacrifice he made to his family and his community. He had won his race, and it had become his turn to sit comfortably in the bleachers, enjoying the shade, while others competed for the gold, the silver, and the bronze. In determining future damages, we face a more difficult task. We must now all join hands and walk through the future. We must peer beyond the veil of tomorrow to understand the full impact of the defendant's negligence. We will each bring to this task the values, ideals, and virtues that were instilled in each of us by our parents and grandparents. Your verdict will be fair and just if it reflects those ideals.

Medical Expenses

Of all the questions involving future damages, one would assume that the cost of future medical and hospital care would be the least troubling. Certainly we all know the high cost of medical care that is associated with significant injury. It has been said, not necessarily in jest, that it is becoming more difficult each day to find a disease or injury we can afford. Many people view today's hospital emergency rooms as places where you can receive medical attention just as fast as you can prove your ability to pay for it.

Think about the question on future medical care this way: if one had to take so many thousands or millions of dollars and put them in a box—so that this victim could draw out what he needed to care for himself during the rest of his life—what should that box contain? The evidence demonstrates that this victim will require future medical care in the form of medicines, hospitalizations, and physicians' fees. The message is clear: for the rest of his life, as soon as he pays one fiddler, another will begin to tune up. The calculation of future medical and hospital expenses is no easy task capable of solution by simple arithmetic. The old axiom "close enough for government work" will not do justice in this case. In determining future expenses of this sort, using the concept that a budget is what you can stay within if you go without produces not only injustice but further harm, as well. The tragedy all of us have already recognized is magnified.

In considering future damages, we must consider the rising cost of medicine, newer drugs, which always seem to be more expensive, spiraling private nursing care expenses, and increasing hospital room rates, not to mention inflation and the like. Most of us remember the time when two hundred dollars was the down payment on a car; now it is a fraction of the sales tax. Today it costs more to amuse a child than it did to educate his father.

During this trial the defense has suggested there may be cheaper ways to go. This approach has reminded me of Oscar Wilde's definition of a cynic—

one who knows the price of everything and the value of nothing.[10] To this victim, the much-needed brace is never overpriced. Special orthopedic mattresses and pillows are not luxuries; they are necessities. The medicine he purchases to limit his pain or give him some relief is not a leisure item. What right does the one who causes such anguish and trauma have to discount the worth of these expenditures? What privilege does that person enjoy to dismiss the cost of even simple things, like bed sheets and towels, as being too great?

Isn't it strange that ours is a country where millions of dollars are spent each year in the quest for cosmetic surgery and cures, but the anticipated cost for surgeries that are necessary to repair bones, tissues, and ligaments is discounted by some in the courtroom. We enjoy life in a land where all aspire to investments, earnings, and income. Whether we invest in bonds, stocks, gems, or precious metals, we hope to prosper so that we may enjoy. Our thoughts of a better, safer, and more secure tomorrow are the basis for those decisions. Who among us would decide that an investment for one's future health does not deserve equal, if not greater, recognition? It is medicine and treatment—relief from suffering—for which the crippled go searching, not scenery or fame or fortune.

Some of you may be aware of the recent work of many art historians and artists in repairing Michelangelo's famous Sistine Chapel. The goal of this team of artists and scientists was to restore that renowned work of art so that it could be preserved and viewed as it was meant to be seen. Before the restoration, much of Michelangelo's masterpiece had been lost to the ravages of time. During many stages of the restoration work, there were revelations of color, luster, beauty, and form that had not been seen since the seventeenth century. Millions of dollars were spent so that paintings unique in the world could be enjoyed. A work of art unlike any other was repaired and restored with the greatest of care. Cost was not a concern.

The human body must be equally appreciated and admired. There are no two alike in this world, nor will there ever be. When this work of art, of creation, is ravaged and torn, does it not equally deserve repair? Should we view with cynicism money provided to repair—to try to restore—work not of mortals but of our Creator?

The medical expenses awarded for this victim cannot be changed in the future if they should become inadequate. It is not possible to go back and award any additional funds to cover these expenses. This tragically injured person has no power to barter for medical care in the future. There are no special sales for hospital services and doctors' treatments. Medical attention is never sold at a discounted rate. Coupons cannot be clipped out and used to cut hospital costs.

---

10. *Lady Windermere's Fan*, act 3, *quoted in* J. BARTLETT (14th ed. 1968), *supra* note 5, at 839b.

This victim's future will be a constant financial war—fought to balance resources against needs. And we all know what happens if this victim loses that financial war. If he is lucky, someone else will assume the burden of this loss. Perhaps a relative, a friend, or even a neighborhood fund drive will ease the financial strain. They will do so for the sake of friendship and love—that which comes in the guise of charity. But if your verdict is just—if the sum of money you find for future damages is adequate—this victim will never need to turn to charity. A just verdict not only ensures that the victim's future medical needs will be met; it also ensures that the victim will retain that dignity of which he was not robbed by the defendant's conduct.

Physical Disfigurement

Scars

Rightly or wrongly, we have always placed a high value on physical appearance. From childhood we learn that beauty is good, that a pretty face is synonymous with virtue, and that we are all to take pride in our physical appearance. As children we were taught from fairy tales that the handsome prince gets the fair maiden. We learned that even a common girl could become a beautiful princess with the help of a little magic and a glass slipper. The meaning of beauty's opposite was also instilled in us at an early age. We learned to fear the wicked, ugly witches of *Hansel and Gretel* and *The Wizard of Oz*. We were taught to despise the ugly stepmothers in *Cinderella* and *Snow White*. We read about the mean, ugly old woman in the shoe who whipped her children. We were told of an ugly little man named Rumpelstiltskin, who had a particularly nasty habit of extortion when it came to young children.

Most of us know, however, that real beauty is only skin deep. We try to teach our children that a beautiful heart more than offsets the handicap of a homely face.

But we would be blind if we did not recognize society's attitude toward beauty and good looks. We all grow up watching beautiful and handsome movie stars, many of whom go to great lengths to retain their physical appearance. One of the largest and most profitable industries in this country is the cosmetics industry. Our friends and neighbors buy creams, lotions, hair conditioners and tints, wigs, and nail polish to improve their physical appearance. Orthodontists earn fortunes straightening teeth. Plastic surgeons become rich and famous by altering people's physical appearance. We spend billions of dollars each year in maintaining and improving our appearance. It is the desire of every man and woman to look attractive, good, beautiful, honest, virtuous, and acceptable.

But what happens if our physical distinction is from some deformity of flesh? When the flesh is scarred and the scars are visible to any naked eye, what is the effect on our self-image, our self-confidence? Some would say that it is only a temporary emotional loss that will heal with time, but those people have never themselves been the subject of ridicule.

Scars of the flesh have always been a symbol of hate, pain, and anguish. Some of you will recall the movies and television series, such as *Hang 'Em High* and *Branded*, in which the heroes were punished and left with permanent physical scars by which they could be identified. More recently, movies like *Mask* let us know the suffering and despair that a teenager with a grotesque physical appearance must face. In most of the stories that are written or told, a scar is a mark of pain or a symbol of vandalism.

Many of you have been to museums where beautiful paintings are displayed. What would happen if, in our presence, someone were to take out a knife and slash the canvas of such a piece of art? We all know that the person would be arrested and a trial would be held. The defense would have to explain the defendant's actions—to justify the destruction of the artist's skillful work. Imagine the defendant arguing that he had cut only a small part of the painting, that only a portion of the masterpiece was disfigured. Would not that kind of defense be laughed out of the courtroom? So it is with even a small scar to any human being. The permanence of the jagged and cruel cut is one thing that time will not erase. It pierces the texture of skin and transforms it into a brand of ugliness. It is a merciless mark on a creation of God.

Who among us has never felt different or out of place at one time or another? In most instances the cause may have been our form of dress at some social event, our ideas or thoughts expressed in public, or perhaps merely some act or conduct to which others took exception. It has happened to all of us at some time in our lives. When it does, most of us experience humiliation, embarrassment, and torment, if only for a brief time. We are all affected by the way others perceive us, even if we do not want to admit it to ourselves. But most of us shrug it off, and we become stronger individuals—less affected by the views of others. But this is not to say that we ever become insensitive or indifferent to the beliefs or attitudes of others; most human beings do not enjoy that quality.

Suppose that the awkwardness, the shame, or the loss of self-worth were an experience that would never end. Take a moment to examine your true feelings about being stared at by strangers, being unable to make eye contact with acquaintances, or even being ashamed to be seen with your families. These are just some of the experiences that the scarred person does not want to face. These are the sorts of graphic injuries that breed pity and rejection for life.

Dismemberment

Fear strikes deep in the heart of any person who faces amputation. For some, the limb may be lost quickly. Flesh, tissue, bone, and nerves are severed even faster than the mind can fathom. The nerve endings send a message of terror. Horror gathers in the mind, races through the body. The face displays confusion as shock sets in. Pain begins to surface. All this happens within a matter of seconds. It is only then that the brain will acknowledge the dismemberment. Only thereafter does the mind try to evaluate, to compensate.

Others are tortured by pain before the fear can accumulate. They may have an arm or leg ripped more slowly from the body. They experience the pain along with the horror as they feel the amputation. Fear gives way to the pain.

You cannot amputate a part without lessening the whole. A tragic loss of a limb devastates the body's coordination and strength. Even simple tasks like buttoning a shirt become a herculean task for a person with one hand. The entire body tries to adjust, to compensate for the missing part. A man with one leg wears a prosthesis—a piece of plastic that does not cushion his hip as he moves. After a time, the hip becomes painful and sore; the nearby muscles are inflamed and swollen, and so they cause him backaches and pains he has never before experienced.

You cannot remove a portion of the body without affecting the soul. As time goes by, the brain does not forget the missing limb. We have all heard this phenomenon described as the "phantom limb." This term means simply that the mind denies the loss of the limb that the nerve endings still feel. He is constantly reminded that he is less than a whole being—that his spirit is not intact. He feels as did some ancient Indians that, by dismemberment, the soul is severed as well.

You cannot sever a part of the body without fear, worry, and anguish taking their toll. This fact is evident from the challenges facing any amputee. Forget the looks of repulsion he sees cross the faces of others when their attention is inevitably drawn to the stub of what used to be his arm. Forget the sleepless nights with dreams of horror and torture. Forget the loss of confidence and self-image he had before his children became embarrassed that he is unlike other fathers. All of those pains are inconsequential to him when they are compared to the pain he sees his family going through. His former pride in having a productive job is now replaced with worry that his wife and children will have no financial security. His cane and his crutches are symbols of misery and despair. The missing leg haunts him with frustration and pain.

Most of us are familiar with the old television series *The Six Million Dollar Man*. Lee Majors portrayed an astronaut who lost most of his limbs in a plane crash. The scientists rebuilt him—they gave him new limbs that were stronger, faster, and better than ever before. The story was of course a fantasy, describing feats that medical science cannot do. But most people would probably agree that, if our doctors had these capabilities, a person who is dismembered because of another's fault should be entitled to the restoration of the lost limb. The amputee should recover the costs necessary to repair his arm or leg—not to make him whole, because that is something that could never be done—but to award him the best prosthesis known to science.

Until that fortunate medical and scientific knowledge has arrived, no amount of money can do this for him. We simply do not have the knowledge, the tools, the training, the ability. The damages that should be found for an amputee will always represent something less than full justice, since complete justice cannot be accomplished. By awarding damages, a jury can only try to provide the medical care that the victim will need; to award him the money that he would have earned in the future had he been healthy; and, to the extent possible, to see that he will be made comfortable in the years he has left. Even if a jury were to do all this and more, it still would not have done what the law envisions—"to make the plaintiff whole."

Burns

There is no greater pain imaginable than the pain that radiates from burning flesh. Even a slight burn caused from a lighted oven, a hot engine, or an open flame can be excruciatingly painful. When the heat is removed, the skin wrinkles and blisters. Pus forms. The blister peels. The underlying skin is raw and extremely sensitive. But gradually it toughens, and a small scar may be left in its place. It is usually a configuration of mottled skin, a blemish on the tone of skin color.

Others notice the burn and ask us what happened. In fact, if we are around many acquaintances, the conversation may often turn to the subject of our burn. How many times have we had this happen to us? So many people may comment on our burn or ask about it that after a few days we become tired of having to recite the story. But in a couple of weeks the burn heals well enough that we can use the arm or hand again. The burn has almost disappeared.

The future of a person who is horribly burned, in contrast, is an inferno of misery and suffering. The burns are so very painful for so long. The skin appears more melted than mottled. The pigment of the skin suffers such a mutation that it never regains its composition. Keloid scarring forms. The skin takes on a reddish hue as the scars thicken. The results are predictably catastrophic: the person becomes a living mummy—hidden behind layers of seared flesh and scars.

Psychologists say that, as time goes by, the victim loses his self-respect, which is replaced by anger and frustration. Other people do not ask this person the story behind his burns. The results speak tragically for themselves; they tell a story that even a brash person is embarrassed to ask about.

Fire has always been the tool of torturers. In that dark portion of man's soul where corruption, hatred, and bigotry live, the concept of torture by fire was born. If we were to ask people their vision of hell, most of them would describe a place of eternal torment and agony. It would be a place of fire. Before the enlightenment of man, both witches and saints were burned. Remember the ordeal of Joan of Arc? Torture or death by fire has always been the tool of bigots and oppressors, because it is within them that a part of the human spirit that is profane, vulgar, and ugly resides.

A person who survives serious burns finds himself facing future life with a body so terribly disfigured that he cannot accept it as his own. Other people try not to stare for fear of seeming insensitive. Children are frightened by the victim's appearance. His own family suffers with him because they know of the pain. The family dog becomes the only member of the family that sees the victim without change. The burn victim who used to be outgoing, lively, and secure is now introverted and withdrawn. Mirrors in the bathroom become daily reminders of the defendant's carelessness and neglect.

But it is not only the flesh that is destroyed by fire, it is also the spirit and the soul. Personalities become scarred and leathered just as do arms and legs. Today's television and movies are filled with scenes of fire and conflagration. Cars crashing into each other and bursting into flame, houses exploding, and rooms on fire are entertainment to most of us—simply a part of the plot and action. But to the burn victim this is not entertainment but, rather, torture. Even the cozy fireplace may seem threatening.

As we contemplate what might be fair compensation for this victim, who was tragically burned and who must suffer the effects of the defendant's negligence for the remainder of his life, it might be appropriate to consider for a moment a story that is told about ancient Greece. In ancient Athens, the great Greek scholars, statesmen, and philosophers struggled with the concept of justice. For some time they debated about the statement of a simple principle from which, if it were followed, justice would always result. Finally they agreed on the statement of a principle so simple and yet so meaningful that it has been repeated down through the ages. You will find reference to it in the writings of John Locke, Thomas Jefferson, and Oliver Wendell Holmes: "Justice is insured when those who have not been injured are as indignant as those who have been."[11]

Physical Impairment

Brain Damage

Injury that produces brain damage may leave in its wake various physical impairments. The words we use to describe those impairments paint dark and ugly portraits of the brain-damaged victim. The victim who has motor impairment is referred to as spastic, uncoordinated, an invalid, crippled, or a handicapped person. Brain damage that impairs the victim's mental processes produces people who are called slow, stunted, stupid, mentally retarded, dullards, or unteachable. If you think about it, these are some of the kinder phrases that are used.

We all recognize that the brain becomes a mind when it is fortified with knowledge. When we are up to our ears in trouble, we can use the brain—that part of us that is not submerged—to get us out of trouble.

The normal person who has no motor, neurological, or mental impairment can set and drive life's agenda. But the mentally impaired have no such

11. This anecdote is from a fictionalized television movie and is most likely apocryphal.

freedom. For most of us, one of the most important aspects of our lives is what we consider "independence." Many whole, complete, and healthy men and women have died throughout the history of this country because they did not feel their independence was secure. Our revolutionary war was the War of Independence. Our ancestors believed that citizens could not be considered independent when their lives, fortunes, and future were determined by a foreign government. Today independence is not only necessary for pride, it is also synonymous with it. All of us believe it is important that we paddle our own canoe, stand on our own two feet, can look any man in the eye and tell him where to get off, are self-sufficient, come and go as we please, and are free as a bird. Perhaps the famous American poet Longfellow put it best in describing the village blacksmith:

> His brow is wet with honest sweat
> He earns whate'er he can,
> And looks the whole world in the face,
> For he owes not any man.[12]

This brain-damaged victim cannot paddle his own canoe; rather, he must depend on relatives and friends for steerage. And when we look into his future, we must face even harsher facts. As time passes, the crippled mind suffers even more erosion. No new experiences can be perceived, no sensations felt. One of the greatest minds of all time, Leonardo da Vinci, put it well when he said, "Iron rusts from disuse, stagnant water loses its purity and in cold weather becomes frozen; even so does inaction sap the vigors of the mind."[13]

But this victim has memories of his past. Sometimes he cannot understand that he is injured, that the world goes on without his conscious awareness of it, that he will not improve. The frustration sets in—frustration at not being able to learn, at not recognizing familiar faces. He cannot adequately communicate all his wants and needs. His presence may seem childlike, but he is not like a normal child. His mind does not continue to grow. It will atrophy and decay.

Some of us have elderly friends or relatives who may have a disease like Alzheimer's. We know they have an extremely short memory. They will lapse during a conversation and not be able to remember what we were saying. They have incredible difficulty in collecting their thoughts. They depend on others, family and friends, for their survival. Senility can produce much the same confusion and many of the same frustrations. Whenever we see such a friend or family member, our hearts go out to them. We all believe that a mind-altering disease in the elderly is one of the most tragic realities of life. We

---

12. *The Village Blacksmith, quoted in* DICTIONARY OF QUOTATIONS, *supra* note 9, at 344.
13. *Notebooks, quoted in* J. BARTLETT (14th ed. 1968), *supra* note 5, at 174a.

find some comfort, however, in knowing that our grandparent or friend experienced a good life, a full and complete life.

But this victim was brain-damaged early in life's journey. He will never know the pleasures of retirement or grandchildren. He will never be able to take pride in his work and family. He has been deprived of his worth, his enjoyment, his quality of life. Consciousness, as we know it, has been stolen. Biological existence is his reward.

The touching book *Flowers for Algernon*, by Daniel Keyes, is a story that documents the pain of a mentally retarded person. Some people will recognize the movie *Charly*, which was based on this book. In the movie, Cliff Robertson plays a man mentally retarded since birth. He worked in a factory as a janitor. But Charly was chosen for a medical experiment to cure his mental handicap. The surgery was a success. Charly was not only cured, he developed a brilliant mind. There was only one complication: the cure was only temporary. After a period of months, Charly would return to a state of retardation. At the end of the movie, right before the change, Cliff Robertson was the epitome of a man without hope—a man whose anguish was all the greater because he knew what his life could have been. The story was about dreams, ambition, and hope—qualities we all possess but qualities we take for granted. *Charly* teaches us that the destruction of the human mind is a much more severe trauma to any person who has experienced what we call independence. It is only because he has known what he could become that he is devastated by what he has left.

Some might look down on this victim because of what he has become. However, it was a very wise man who once observed that there is only one time in our lives when we have the right to look down on another—that time is when we are willing to stop, extend a hand, and help that man up.[14]

Paralysis

Most of us know of the famous prison Alcatraz. Located in San Francisco Bay, it is now a museum. But for years it served as a place to house our most dangerous and violent criminals. The cells were five feet by nine feet in size. In each cell there was a bunk, a toilet, and a sink. In many of the castles in Europe, there are dungeons with even smaller cells. Their ceilings were intentionally built low enough that a prisoner could not stand; their dimensions did not permit a prisoner even to lie down. But the cells of Alcatraz and of those castles were larger than the one to which this victim has been condemned by the defendant's negligence.

When I was a child and went to the beach with my friends, we always played a certain game. We would dig a hole in the sand, and one of us would

14. This observation is attributed to Jesse Jackson, who used it in a speech during his 1988 presidential campaign.

get into it. Then the others would fill up the hole with sand and pack it down tight. After a while we would take turns, and another boy would get in the sandpit; he would also be covered up to his head with sand. Invariably, one of us would be trapped in the sand for a lot longer than the others. The rest of the gang would get interested in something else and would run off laughing. The person who was left in the sand would start pleading to be let out, but no one would be there to dig him out. Minutes would seem like eternities. The seven- or eight-year-old who was buried in the sand would become terrified. He would eventually start crying and screaming for someone to let him out. Usually an adult would walk over and help the unlucky one get out of the sand.[15]

The paralyzed victim faces life trapped in a sandlike tomb. But unlike the boys on the beach, he has no one to let him out. This victim is serving a life sentence as an invalid. He is a prisoner condemned to the smallest cell that could be envisioned by the harshest jailer. There is no possibility of parole and no chance of pardon.

For the rest of us, our world knows no limit. Think about it. Even our times of greatest frustration and despair would be times of elation for this victim. We go to the doctor's office and discover that we will have a two-hour wait. During that time we may pace the office. We may get up and find some magazines to read. We may go down the hall to the restroom or downstairs to get a cup of coffee. Perhaps we will walk outside and buy a newspaper and return to the doctor's office. We are frustrated and agitated by the wait and our waste of time. But if this victim could even do those simple tasks under those circumstances, I am sure he would gladly trade for any damages and compensation that you will find as part of your verdict.

This victim cannot eat with dignity; someone must feed him. He cannot brush his teeth or comb his hair; someone must do these things for him. He cannot even use the bathroom by himself; someone must attend to those needs for him.

He has to live vicariously, through the actions of others. He may have recreational privileges, but he cannot participate. He is a spectator in the game of life. We give him television privileges, but television only reminds him of everything he cannot do. We give him reading privileges, provided there is someone handy to turn the pages of the book for him. We give him mobility in one of science's modern marvels—the motor-driven wheelchair. But his dreams are filled with visions of a man running, jumping, and playing. When his wife or children lift him out of bed every morning, no adventure awaits him. His life is only another day of physical existence.

To properly accomplish the gruesome accounting of fair and just damages for this type of catastrophic injury, we must look to many ledgers,

---

15. This colorful analogy is found in J. SMITH, THE ART OF ADVOCACY: SUMMATION CA-69, 3-S.06 (1987).

including the value of the burden that this defendant's conduct has placed on the victim. The agony, the torment, the fear and mental anguish are parts of that burden.[16] The medical expenses that will be required to care for this crippled and maimed body for the rest of its life is but a part of this burden.[17]

But what about the other ledger sheet? That which has been taken. That which is lost. This defendant's conduct robbed this victim of what we call freedom. The ancient Greek philosophers observed that freedom is nothing more than the right to live as we wish.[18] The freedom of a man is judged by the volume of his laughter and the peacefulness of his sleep. But, conversely, it is said that the freedom of slaves is measured by the lengths of their chains. If you but view this victim's loss of freedom in that way, we are sure your verdict will be just.

---

16. See ch. 24.
17. See the discussion on medical expenses in this chapter.
18. *See, e.g.*, Epictetus, *Discourses* bk. 2, ch. 1, § 23, *quoted in* B. STEVENSON, THE HOME BOOK OF QUOTATIONS 722 (10th ed. 1984).

26

Loss of Earning Capacity

MOST OF US have a pretty good understanding of today's economic realities. If you live within your income, you will live without worry—and without a lot of other things. The outcome of the income depends on the outgo for the upkeep. Today people not only cannot live within their incomes, they cannot even live within their credit cards. Growing families have a way of outgrowing everything—especially their incomes. Today a fellow can go broke by just staying even. Things that cost two hundred dollars to buy a few years ago now cost three hundred dollars to repair. Some folks might suggest we are just getting stronger. Twenty years ago it took two people to carry fifteen dollars' worth of groceries; today a child can do it.

A crippling and permanent injury that produces disability will require a jury to determine loss of earning capacity. Determining an amount of money to award for loss of earning capacity is one of the most misunderstood and perilous tasks of a jury. Some folks see the word *loss* and the word *earning* and assume that this element of damages involves a cold calculation of actual income, discounted by a disability factor and multiplied by working life expectancy. A jury that restricted itself to this kind of number-crunching, however, would not only be callous and insensitive but would also apply the law of Texas incorrectly. We have juries to decide these cases because they pose tough questions. If the simple arithmetic of earnings times the percentage of disability times the life expectancy would do, we could turn to the computer, but we have people decide these issues. We choose people to decide these issues because it is only working men and women who can grasp the concept that a healthy body and a good job translate into more than the numbers that show up on our W-2s at the end of the year. People understand that work is not simply the challenge of today but the opportunity of tomorrow—opportunity for advancement, better pay, and better benefits. People understand that if you cripple a man, you do not simply injure him today, you maim his future.

The questions submitted to you by the judge ask what is the victim's loss of earning *capacity*. When judges and lawyers and lawmakers use words, we must presume that they choose those words and use them for a reason. Words are the tools of the law trade, and we must interpret those words in such a way that each of them has meaning. Think for a moment about why His Honor deliberately chose to ask you about this victim's loss of earning *capacity* and not just loss of earnings projected into the future. He chose those words because there is a big difference between a mechanical calculation of loss of earnings and the broader concept of loss of earning capacity, and the loss of earning *capacity* is what you will be called on to determine in this case.

The well-settled law of this state provides that it is possible to recover damages for a loss of earning capacity even if the injured person goes back to work, in the same job, for the same amount of money, or even for a greater amount of money. Now this concept bothers some people at first, because it seems as though the victim is recovering damages for lost earnings when there are no lost earnings. There are several reasons, however, why it is fair and just to award damages for loss of earning capacity in this situation, even though the loss does not show up immediately in the bottom line on the first few paychecks.

First, when an employee is injured, his employer, as a gesture of goodwill, may allow the employee to keep his job at the same rate of pay despite the fact that the employee is no longer physically capable of performing all the tasks he could do before the injury. This arrangement may last for weeks, for months, or even for several years, and as long as it persists there may be no appearance of loss of earnings. However, does anybody really expect the employer to carry the disabled employee for the rest of his working life? As the years pass, the initial sorrow and pity begin to fade, the unfortunate injury becomes a distant memory, and the need for an able-bodied employee who can do all the tasks required by the job increases. Management personnel may change, and new people in decision-making positions may lack the personal contact and bond of loyalty necessary to continue paying a full salary to one who is not fully capable of doing the job. Even if management personnel stay the same, the injured worker must remain with the same company to reap the benefits of this kind of arrangement; he cannot expect a new employer to compensate him on a full-time basis for a job he is not fully capable of performing. Before his injury, the worker was free to ply his trade anywhere in the marketplace. The elimination of that option is truly a loss of earning capacity for the injured worker.

Another reason that actual earnings immediately after an injury may not accurately reflect loss of earning capacity in the future is that it may be many years before the full extent of an injury is known. The injured victim may initially experience some healing, but that appearance of healing may be offset by long-range degenerative changes in the body and the development of complications, such as posttraumatic arthritis. He may be able to return to the same job initially, but he may not be able to perform that job several years later.

Finally, calculating future loss of earning capacity based on whether the injured employee returns to the same job at the same rate of pay sets up a value system that rewards malingerers and punishes the industrious, the determined, and the proud. The fact that an injured worker may return to the job under these circumstances does not guarantee that he will continue to be able to do the job, or that his employer will give him the opportunity to do so, for the rest of his working life. Moreover, as a matter of public policy, do we want to tell injured workers who crawl back to the workplace under these circumstances that they will be punished because their first few paychecks after their injury are comparable to their preinjury take-home pay and they therefore have no loss of earning capacity? Can we afford to tell these proud souls that they are not entitled to compensation but that the injured victims who resign themselves to injury and make no attempt to reenter the workplace will be rewarded? If this victim considered this lawsuit simply a road to riches—as some have suggested—then why didn't he sit down by the side of the road and wait for your verdict to usher him out in style? This victim worked because he had to, not because he wanted to. He did not want his family to do without. He would rather endure pain and agony than the disgrace and humiliation that comes from experiencing poverty and accepting charity.

But we face yet another problem when we analyze the concept of loss of earning capacity in the future. Victims of injuries do not get to choose at which point in their careers as wage earners they are injured. Most careers involve periods of training and apprenticeship, when actual earnings are relatively low compared to the potential for considerably higher earnings in the future. If a person is injured during this period, his future earning capacity should not be measured by the relatively low income he was earning at the time of his injury. Once again, your function as a juror is not to determine the actual earnings realized before the injury and multiply them, but to determine the victim's loss of earning *capacity*.

The concept of earning capacity also allows you to consider the wage earner's freedom of choice. An uninjured worker is free to choose a career and an employer. Although the worker may have the capacity to earn a large sum of money, he may choose to work in a job where he is realizing less than his full earning capacity because of various noneconomic considerations. Nevertheless, that uninjured worker has the freedom to choose at any moment to change jobs to make more money. If that worker becomes disabled, however, his freedom of choice is gone. When determining that worker's earning capacity, you are not limited to the precise amount the worker was earning in the job at which he chose to work before his injury. That injury has deprived the worker of his freedom of choice and eliminated his capacity to choose to enter a more lucrative career for which he is qualified. Therefore, his earning capacity has been reduced by considerably more than the actual amount he was earning in the job in which he chose to work immediately before his injury.

When evaluating earning capacity in the future, you are also entitled to consider the economic reality of inflation. You may draw on your own experience in understanding that inflation occurs, that the value of the dollar decreases, and that salaries throughout society as a whole tend to increase. You may consider that trend when you determine loss of earning capacity; you are not required to freeze the victim's earnings in time at the date of his injury.

You should also be careful not to equate a percentage of physical disability with a percentage of reduction in earning capacity. For example, a laborer may injure his back to the point that a doctor says he has a twenty-five percent disability. This statement means that his back is twenty-five percent less strong than it was before the injury, when it was a healthy back; it does not, however, mean that the worker has only a twenty-five percent reduction in earning capacity. If he had spent his life doing hard physical labor that requires a one hundred percent healthy back, the fact that his back is disabled, even partially, means that he is completely incapable of doing the kind of work for which he is trained. In that circumstance, a twenty-five percent physical disability could cause a one hundred percent reduction in earning capacity. If my pickup truck has a flat tire, I might say it is only twenty-five percent disabled, since three out of four tires are still in good condition. But even if it is only twenty-five percent disabled, I can tell you that I would not want to haul a load in it.

Some people are bothered by the fact that loss of future earning capacity is a speculative element of damages. That means there is a certain amount of guesswork involved in determining a loss of earning capacity in the future. Unless the injured victim had a lifetime employment contract that would guarantee a definite income for the rest of his life, it is impossible to determine his loss of earning capacity in the future with precision. Nevertheless, the fact that this element of damages involves some speculation does not make that loss any less real to the victim. Most of us do not work simply because we love our jobs. Even if we enjoy the work we do, most of us would admit that our primary reason for doing that job is to earn enough income to make house or rent payments, to put food on the table and clothes on our backs, to put us behind the wheel of a drivable car, and, we hope, to have a little bit left over to do the things we want to do. Juries understand that somehow our outgo always exceeds our income. Everything we need either keeps going up or breaking down. This victim, like most of us, made his living a few dollars at a time. Like the child trying to stay on the seesaw, he had to struggle every month to keep things in balance. When a disabling injury occurs, however, the expenses remain the same, if they do not increase, but the income required to meet those expenses is reduced or eliminated altogether. This defendant's conduct threw this victim off the seesaw. Just how far are we willing to let him fall?

I cannot help but find it somewhat strange when it is suggested in a case like this that a worker's earning capacity has no real or significant value, that it is an element of damages that is somehow speculative or should be diminished or discounted. We all know that corporations and business entities consider it a very real element of present value.

In other areas of our society and our economy, future earning capacity is treated as a very real element of present value. For example, when a business is sold, accountants and consultants can put together a financial statement that speculates about the future earning capacity of the business. That future earning capacity becomes one of the assets on which the value of the business is based. Even if the business is not sold, its owners can go to a bank with that same financial statement and borrow money, using the business as collateral. The future earning capacity of the business is accepted as a legitimate part of the equation for determining the value of the business.

With a worker, however, the rules are quite different. Although the worker also has a future earning capacity, he cannot go to the bank and borrow an amount of money equal to his future earning capacity. The only asset the worker has other than his future earning capacity is his healthy body. Unfortunately, if you take away the latter, you diminish, if not destroy, the former. Banks are willing to bet that a business will remain productive, regardless of what happens to individuals in the business, because individuals can be replaced and the business can continue to function. When a worker is injured, however, there are no replacements available, and his productivity and earning capacity will be affected, if not completely destroyed.

The jury in this injury case, however, is not a bank, and it is not in the business of lending money based on sufficient collateral. Rather, its function is to determine how much a working person has been injured when his sole assets—his healthy body and his future earning capacity—have been diminished or destroyed.

Jurors are sometimes startled by the figures produced when loss of earning capacity is calculated. If a fairly young person is seriously injured and his earning capacity is seriously reduced for the rest of his working life, the projection of his future earnings over many years can generate some high-dollar figures. It may shock some of us to learn that a blue-collar laborer in his twenties may have a future earning capacity of over a million dollars. But the reason that figure is shocking is not that it is more than the worker would have earned in his lifetime, but because we are accustomed to thinking of income in terms of weeks, months, or, at most, years. We are used to our life's earnings dribbling in a little at a time over many years, not all at once in a lump sum. And believe me, if this victim had his choice, he would have preferred to have it that way, too. As a result of the actions of the defendant, he will not have that option. Instead, this victim has only one opportunity to recover the money he would have earned with a healthy body, the money he will never again have the opportunity to earn.

Some of us think that large figures for the loss of earning capacity should not be given to common laborers but should be reserved for the big-wage earners in our society, the doctors, the stock market investors, and the presidents of large corporations. Those people are not the only ones whose lives and future earning capacities are worth money. Whether that money is earned at an hourly rate, a week at a time, year after year, or made in big deals and big annual salaries, any person whose right to earn income is diminished deserves to be compensated. There is no disgrace, and no legal disadvantage, in being a working person. It is not what a person does, but rather how he does it; it is not what he is, but who he is, that counts. After all, the greatest man of all time was a carpenter by trade. The loss suffered by a carpenter or any other worker should be accorded the same significance and the same fair measurement as that of the doctor, the stock market investor, or the corporate officer.

27

Death

DEATH is an enigma.

Of all our human experiences, more has been written about death than any other. Simply examine a topical index for the Bible, philosophical works, or books on poetry, and you will see that we have been absorbed with the contemplation of death since the birth of time. The enigma is that, for most of us, the contemplation of death—whether our own or that of a loved one—is so distasteful and repulsive that we refuse to let it enter our minds.

Death has been glorified when life is sacrificed for country, cause, or principle. Shakespeare immortalized this glorification of death in his play *Julius Caesar*: "Cowards die many times before their deaths; / The valiant never taste of death but once."[1] The certainty of death that we all acknowledge has been expressed in many ways. Benjamin Franklin said, "In this world nothing is certain but death and taxes."[2] Longfellow put it, "The young may die, but the old must!"[3]

At death we leave behind us all that we have and take with us all that we are. Death is said to pay all debts,[4] square all accounts,[5] and quit all scores.[6]

A German proverb describes death as the poor man's doctor.[7] Shakespeare described death as "passing through nature to eternity."[8] The Good Book tells us that the death of the wise man is the same as the death of the fool.[9]

---

1. Act 2, sc. 2, ll. 32-33.
2. *Letter to M. Leroy* [1789], *quoted in* DICTIONARY OF QUOTATIONS 152 (B. Evans comp. 1968 & reprint 1978).
3. *The Cloisters, quoted in id.* at 152.
4. MICHAEL DE MONTAIGNE, *Essays* bk. 1, ch. 7, in THE COMPLETE WORKS OF MICHAEL DE MONTAIGNE 38 (W. Hazlitt ed. 1888).
5. Charles Reade, *quoted in* H. KORNBLITT, THE DICTIONARY OF PERSUASIVE PHRASES FOR LAWYERS 219 (1962).
6. James Shirley, *Cupid and Death, quoted in* B. STEVENSON, THE HOME BOOK OF QUOTATIONS 377b (10th ed. 1984).
7. German proverb, *quoted in* H. KORNBLITT, *supra* note 5, at 219.
8. *Hamlet*, act 1, sc. 2, l. 73.
9. *Ecclesiastes* 2:16.

But even though we all may accept death as the final chapter to any life, it always carries a note of tragedy. Mark Twain said that "[e]ach person is born to one possession which outvalues all the others—his last breath."[10] The Bible described death as the king of terrors.[11] Theodore Roosevelt once mused that "[d]eath is always and under all circumstances a tragedy, for if it is not, then it means that life itself has become one."[12] It is the tragedy of death that has caused scholars and philosophers to note that the good die first[13] and that death strikes down the innocent and young.[14]

But recognizing the inevitability of death in no way diminishes *our* cause. The fact that some of our loved ones may have given their lives to protect freedom and justice can serve as no safe refuge to garrison the defense in this case. Death is not the issue. Rather, the issue is cast in the terms of our Texas statute—"wrongful death." Our Texas wrongful death statute is founded on a simple premise: that one who by his conduct steals from us a member of our family must respond fully at the bar of justice. This principle—this law—can be traced back centuries through American and English jurisprudence. Our enlightened English cousins felt that vengeance should hold no office in the law. In earlier times, justice was simple and swift: if one caused the loss of another's life through carelessness or irresponsibility, he forfeited his own. The Enlightenment brought a different perspective. Life itself was too valuable to confiscate as a punishment for negligent conduct, and restitution was substituted for vengeance. The responsible party would be called to account for the value of the life that had been taken. Likewise, the defendant would be responsible for the harm done to the family members that followed in the wake of the death.[15]

Placing a value on a human life has always been a difficult and troubling task. The challenge is complicated when we consider the amounts paid for certain material goods. Racehorses in this country often sell for millions of dollars. Paintings, sculptures, and pieces of jewelry may go for tens of millions. When we read accounts of these sales in our newspapers, we often ask ourselves how a painting or an old book could be worth that kind of money. Such an item does not earn anything, no one is dependent on it, and

---

10. *Pudd'nhead Wilson's New Calendar* ch. 6, in 2 FOLLOWING THE EQUATOR, *quoted in* J. BARTLETT, FAMILIAR QUOTATIONS: A COLLECTION OF PASSAGES, PHRASES, AND PROVERBS TRACED TO THEIR SOURCES IN ANCIENT AND MODERN LITERATURE 763a (14th ed. 1968).

11. *Job* 18:14.

12. *Letter to Cecil Spring-Rice* [March 12, 1900], *quoted in* J. BARTLETT, *supra* note 10, at 847a.

13. William Wordsworth, *The Excursion* bk. 1, *quoted in id.* at 516a.

14. CHARLES DICKENS, THE OLD CURIOSITY SHOP ch. 72 (A. Easson ed. 1977).

15. The arguments in this chapter are directed solely to a discussion of damages recoverable in wrongful death actions other than for mental anguish. These damages—pecuniary loss and loss of companionship and society—are set out in 1 STATE BAR OF TEXAS, TEXAS PATTERN JURY CHARGES ch. 8 (2d ed. 1987 & Supp. 1989). Consideration of arguments that may be appropriate on the issue of mental anguish in a wrongful death action are discussed in chapter 24.

certainly there can be no human emotion associated with it. The reason for these sales prices should be obvious: those paintings, racehorses, and pieces of jewelry are worth those millions of dollars because they are unique. Each is one of a kind, and never can another like it be created. But isn't that quality even more relevant in valuing human life? Isn't that the reason the philosophers have said that any man's death diminishes us[16] and that we understand death for the first time when he puts his hand on one we love?[17]

Do we as a people—as a nation—place a higher value on animals and inanimate objects than we do on human life? Of course not. We might spend billions of dollars to make sure an astronaut returns from space. We do it because human life has such great value in our society. If persons are lost at sea, we spare no expense in trying to find and save them. Hundreds of millions of dollars a year are spent on medical research. At our fine medical institutions in Houston, Dallas, San Antonio, and Lubbock, men and women are engaged in all types of medical research. A search for answers. Answers leading to the effective treatment of injury and disease. Answers that will save lives.

Remember Jessica McClure, the little girl who fell into a well in Midland? Her plight and rescue became an American epic. Untold amounts of resources—equipment, scientific expertise, and time—were sacrificed in the effort to save that infant. As we all followed this saga, none of us—no one—questioned the wisdom of sacrificing those resources and assets to save that little girl. No one questioned the cost.

And so it must be that this is our approach and understanding of a wrongful death action. The victim's loved ones do not ask for vengeance. They ask only for that which the law has, over centuries, determined as a just remedy—the value of the life that was taken. A jury's task in this kind of case is a gruesome type of accounting. If the measure of compensation were merely the pecuniary contributions the victim would have made to the loved ones, we would not need twelve citizens like you. A computer would do. Rather, we must also consider and place value on the individual traits and qualities of the one who has been snatched from the family by the defendant's conduct. Qualities such as advice, counsel, love, comfort, companionship, and society. Values that are uniquely human. Qualities that this person shared with many of us, our friends, relatives, and neighbors. But, nonetheless, virtues and ideals that lead us to conclude that this life was special. It was one of a kind.

Death of a Son

It is said that God laughs every time he makes a boy. The Greek philosopher Plato noted that "[o]f all the animals, the boy is the most unmanageable."[18]

---

16. John Donne, *Devotions XVII*, in Devotions Upon Emergent Occasions (1623).
17. Madame De Staël, *quoted in* The New Dictionary of Thoughts: A Cyclopedia of Quotations 128 (T. Edwards comp. 1957).
18. Laws 808, *quoted in* J. Bartlett, *supra* note 10, at 96a.

Boys are found everywhere but seldom standing still. They may be climbing a tree, digging a hole, crawling under a bush, or building something that they haven't quite figured out yet what it will be when it is finished. A boy is truth with freckles on his face, beauty with a frog in his pocket, the wonders of a mind that can master the multiplication tables, and the hope of the future with a poster in his room that says, "He who dies with the most toys wins!" Boys have insatiable appetites for hamburgers, french fries, ice cream, comic books, action movies, and summer vacation. They can pretty well do without girls, Sunday school, "mushy" movies, and dressing up for church or Sunday school. To a father, being with a son is like being subjected to an inquisition. "Why does it work?" "Why is the sky blue?" "Why does a compass always point north?" are but typical examples of the meanderings of the inquisitive mind of a young son. To mothers, boys can sometimes be an aggravation. They can clutter up a room faster than three adults can clean it. But simply ask any mother about her son and watch the pride appear on her face as she reaches into her purse for those photographs that she loves so much to share with other people.

It is against this backdrop of the nature of boys that the defense in a wrongful death case must be considered. The flaws or imperfections in the character of the victim of the defendant's negligence should give the defense little comfort. The argument that the victim was less than perfect and that, therefore, damages ought to be less is specious on its face. There are no perfect boys.

When I was growing up in the forties, there was a radio show called *Jack Armstrong, All American Boy*. We were all taught that Jack Armstrong was our hero. But Jack Armstrong was not perfect. He failed high school algebra. He lost his job. Jack's adventures and the things that we listened to were one series of catastrophes after another. In between fighting saboteurs and spies, he had trouble with school and his friends. He never had any adventures with his mother or father because, after all, there is nothing more dampening to an adventure than to have a parent along. So, I guess, it could be argued that Jack was not close to his folks. But the radio show taught us that he loved and respected his parents and he represented principles and ideals that we should all aspire to. He was not perfect, but he was our ideal, our hero.

For a number of generations before that, young boys were thrilled by the adventures of Tom Sawyer and Huckleberry Finn. Tom was far from an ideal boy. He was constantly in trouble and not above taking advantage of his friends. Remember how he tricked Huck Finn into painting the fence for him? Tom Sawyer was not perfect, but he was our hero.

Today and in years past, we have had many kinds of heroes to look up to. People in government, sports, religion. The recent heroes that come to my mind are people such as Jack Kennedy, the Reverend Martin Luther King, Earl Campbell, and Glenn Davis. We know that each of these men has had problems and imperfections in his personal life. Nonetheless, we still consider them our heroes because of what they accomplished, what they represented, and their values to us. The truth of the matter is that there is no such thing as perfection in human life. It is often said that the only perfect man who ever lived walked on foreign lands two thousand years ago. The defense approach would have us look for the flaw and ignore all that was good.

The death of a son is one of the most tragic and significant losses we can experience. While we are all aware of the love that is shared between husband and wife and between brothers and sisters, it is still the loss of a child that for thousands of years has been recognized as the most significant. This is because the bond between parent and child is greater than any bonds that can exist between other human beings. The Greek philosopher Sophocles described sons as "the anchors of a mother's life."[19] One of Shakespeare's characters in *The Merchant of Venice* says, "The boy was the very staff of my age, my very prop."[20]

We may love and be devoted to our wives and husbands. We may love and support our parents. We may be close to our brothers and sisters. But the love a father and mother feel for a son is different. The mother carried that child and brought it into this world. The father nurtured that boy from the time of his birth. In every son resides a part of the mother and father. A son is God's way of giving us some sense of immortality on this earth. We know that even after we are gone a part of us continues to live and contribute to humankind.

That is why the "good books" speak so often and so favorably of the relationship between mother, father, and son. The Bible tells the story of the prodigal son. The boy wasted his fortune but was still taken back with open arms by his father.

The Old Testament tells us that when God chose to challenge Abraham's faith, he called on Abraham to sacrifice his son. God did not permit the sacrifice but, rather, chose it as the supreme test of Abraham's faith.

And, when it became time for the good Lord to make the ultimate sacrifice, the Good Book tells us that he gave his only son. These examples merely illustrate the kind of sacrifice that for thousands of years we have felt goes with the loss of a son.

Many years ago a boy was skating on some ice. The ice gave way, and he fell through. He was rescued by a gentleman who happened to be fairly wealthy. They became good friends, and the man sent the boy to college. The boy studied diligently, became interested in science, and ultimately discovered a drug from a mold. Shortly after his discovery, the man who had sent him to college, who was now quite elderly, developed pneumonia. The new drug was administered to the man, with the result that he recovered. The boy was Alexander Fleming, the discoverer of penicillin. We do not suggest

19. *Phaedra*, frag. 612, *quoted in id.* at 83a.
20. Act 2, sc. 2, ll. 60-61.

that the son these parents have lost would necessarily have become an Albert Einstein, a Picasso, or a Michael DeBakey if he had lived. However, he might have been the teacher who inspired children to become good citizens and to go to college. He could have been the policeman who was there at some critical time to prevent an accident or a crime. Perhaps he could have been simply the good neighbor who, by example, helped this community to be a better place to live.

Someone may suggest that, with time, these parents will forget the loss of this son. It is a legitimate proposal, but one that would never be suggested by anyone who has experienced this tragic and catastrophic loss. How often are we asked in daily conversation, "How many children do you have?" I am always proud to say, "Three." But the father or mother who has lost a son must answer, "Well, I had three, two daughters and a son, but my son was killed."

Every time those parents are asked that simple question—"How many children do you have?"—they are reminded of that loss. They are reminded not only that their son died but also that their son's death could have been prevented. It was caused by the carelessness, the recklessness, the negligence of someone else. Remember when we started this case? The first thing you did was a simple task: you filled out your jury-information cards, on which there is a blank for "Children." Most of you had no problem with that. But these people sitting before you, if they had filled out that card, what would they have put? They would have probably put "Three" and then explained, if any lawyer had asked, "Well, we had three children, but our son was killed."

When someone suggests that the passage of time will somehow quiet these parents' hurt, I cannot help but be reminded of a poem about the loss of a son. It goes like this:

> I shall see his toys and his empty chair.
> And the horse he used to ride,
> And they will speak with a silent speech
> Of the little boy that died.[21]

Death of a Daughter

Little girls are the nicest things that happen to people. Somewhere between the blossoms of spring and the laughter of summer resides the spirit of a daughter. Little girls are freedom in pigtails, innocence sitting next to a puddle while making mud pies, and independence with a pout on her face. Little girls like playing in mommy's makeup, having tea parties in their playhouse, and

---

21. Joshua Davenport Robinson, *The Little Boy That Died*, st. 3, *quoted in* J. BARTLETT (13th ed. 1955), *supra* note 10, at 643b-44a.

dressing up with bows and ribbons. They always seem to smell of lilacs and springtime. To men, one of life's unsolved mysteries is what young girls giggle about. But to everyone, they are, without doubt, the sweetest of God's creatures.

It is often said that when a son marries, we do not lose a son but, rather, we gain a daughter. This saying simply recognizes the nurturing and support that a girl bestows on her parents, as well as those of the man she marries.

These parents were always there when this little girl needed them. When she tried to take her first step, her mother and father were there to catch her if she fell. When she went to school the first day, they were there to see that she got there all right and did well. They were there when she needed help with her homework. They were there when she learned to swim. They applauded her accomplishments in school, and they shared her failures. They helped in the difficult adjustments from childhood to womanhood. They shared the joy of her first high school prom. When she was sick they not only supported her, but they treated her, as well. They would have been there as long as she lived.

And she would have been there, had she lived. She, like all good daughters, would have helped and supported her parents as the years began to take their toll. She would have been there to do the jobs around the house that they could no longer do—jobs that are difficult to hire someone to do, even if you have the money. If her parents had become sick, she would have been there to comfort them, to treat them, and to give them hope and encouragement.

These parents were there when this victim needed them. But their daughter will not be there when these folks need her—not because she would not have wanted to, but because the conduct of the defendant has taken her from them.

In days past we used to hear of daughters being taken for ransom. Such adversity still occurs in our unsettled world today, unfortunately. What do you think these parents would give to have their daughter back? All they have? All they could borrow? All they could accumulate for the rest of their lives from themselves and their friends? When I contemplate this type of tragedy, I cannot help but recall the words of one of America's most beloved poets, Edgar A. Guest:

> Little girl, just half-past three,
> This is what you mean to me,
> More than all that money buys,
> More than any selfish prize,
> More than fortune, more than fame,
> And I learned this when you came.
> Other fathers know it, too.
> Nothing matters more than you.[22]

---

22. *To a Little Girl*, in COLLECTED VERSE OF EDGAR A. GUEST 708-09 (1934).

What is the fair measure of these parents' tragedy? Old people die with their achievements, reputations, and memories. But the graves of children are filled with opportunities that were never realized and dreams that will remain unfulfilled. This young lady had not reached the point of selecting a vocation. We do not know what she might have become in our society. She might have become a secretary or a schoolteacher—both honorable professions for earning a livelihood. She might have become the owner of her own company, a doctor, or a nurse. She might even have become an attorney who would have earned fees commensurate with those of these great lawyers who represent this defendant.

The awesome task facing you would make many cringe and tremble—the task of translating the value of this little girl's life into mere dollars and cents. It seems profane and vulgar that we must do it, that we must assess the quality of life in dollars. But that is the only measure these parents have.

All the members of this jury have reached an age where you have determined what your mission in life will be. All of us remember when we were young: we thought we might become president, a famous missionary, or a head of a corporation or that we would reach a similar lofty position. As we age, we mature. Many of us conclude before we reach middle age that maybe our mission in life is to be the best mother or father we can be. That is a noble mission, one that befits many of us. But when a daughter is taken from us, our life's mission becomes a failure. We no longer have our dreams for the future. We have only our despair for what might have been. The court's charge speaks in terms of loss of aid, comfort, society, love, and companionship. But to me, this is just the law's way of saying that you are to consider in determining compensation for these parents the value of their unfulfilled dreams. The happiness they would have shared with their daughter when they learned she had found "the right fellow." The joy of seeing the first grandchild. The warmth that only a daughter can bring when she spends Thanksgiving or Christmas with her parents. The nurturing and care that only a daughter can bestow on us when we become old and infirm. The warmth that she brings to our hearts when she says, "Mom—Dad, I love you most of all."

Death of a Husband

Husband. You can tell so much about a woman by the way she says the word. Show me a woman who is happily married, and the word rings with contentment, pride, security, and satisfaction. Show me a woman who has lost her husband to death—a widow—and when you hear the word flow from her lips, there will be loneliness, worry, and grief.

Husbands come in all sizes, shapes, heights, and colors. But regardless, they have one thing in common. Each was chosen by "the little woman" to spend the rest of her life with. Most husbands are neither very successful nor very poor. Usually they are running somewhere in the middle of the pack.

Husbands aren't just handy—they are essential. How else would a wife get the mechanic who didn't fix her car bawled out, her zipper unstuck, the buttons on the back of her blouse buttoned, her appearance praised, or a hug and a kiss just when she thinks her world is falling apart.

This victim in his lifetime was a symbol of his family's security and its aspirations for the future. He was the source for satisfying all its needs—housing, clothing, health, education, and savings—and he had the means of nourishing and expanding life. No one need tell you what a calamity it is to lose a family's pillar of strength, reliability, and security.

What happens to this woman now and hereafter becomes the subject matter of the damages portion of your verdict. This is the bitter bookkeeping, the grisly audit of death, which cannot be avoided. Someone may suggest that this life that was lost should be measured simply by what this victim would have contributed to his wife over his lifetime through his salary and earnings. Such an approach is false and counterfeit on its face. Any of us would reject the notion that we should be viewed as simply a paycheck to our families. Merely looking at the court's charge will convince you that this is not the law's approach. His Honor tells you that you must place a value on such imponderables as the loss of care, advice, counsel, love, comfort, companionship, and society. This widow's life today is much different from her life before the tragedy that took her husband. Before that, she spent a portion of each day with him. They got up together and visited in the morning before they both left for work. At night they had more time together. When she woke up in the middle of the night, she had him with her. On the weekends, they went grocery shopping together, watched the ballgames, enjoyed the children, and did many things we would consider simple pleasures. They went to church regularly together. They spent the holidays together with their children and other members of the family.

Today this lady is alone. Now she has to make the decisions that her husband used to make or that they made together. She cannot hand that stubborn bottle to her husband and say, "Darling, can you get this off for me?" That tall man is no longer around to reach the things on the high shelf that are beyond her reach. Her world is now empty.

In a few years, when their youngest daughter leaves, she will be completely alone. Years from now she will think about your verdict as she struggles to make it alone. This lady has not even considered remarriage, and, to be brutally frank about it, the prospects for her would be very slim in any event.

For twenty-five years, this couple had worked for the future. They were happy and satisfied with their lives, their jobs, and their families. The phrase "building a life together" may be hackneyed and worn, but it applies so well to these people. Where is this lady to find her happiness? She will be alone. Yes, she will take pride and satisfaction in her children, their families, and their accomplishments. But, in contemplating what the future holds for this lady, I could not help but feel it appropriate to share with you a short portion of a poem by Edgar A. Guest:

> They're all away
> And the house is still,
> And the dust lies thick
> On the window sill,
> And the stairway creaks
> In a solemn tone
> This taunting phrase:
> "You are all alone."[23]

Death of a Wife

It is said that a family consists of a husband who gets an idea, children who say it cannot be done, and a wife who does it.[24] When God created the world, he must have surely realized that without wives there would be total chaos. A wife is what makes a family work. She can get a man to the office on time, children up, fed, and dressed for school, and still, in many instances, appear on time at her own job looking attractive, relaxed, and ready for a day's work. She can handle the family's finances, shop for groceries, school supplies, and clothes for the children, and still find time to listen to her husband's tall tales and laugh at his jokes.

The wife comes to view her family with a fatalistic resignation. No matter how she slaves at cleaning, cooking, washing, polishing, sewing, mending, or ironing, her husband seldom notices. To him, home is a place for loafing.

Then there are the children. She cleans their clothes, sees that they get their baths at night, helps with their homework, encourages them to attend Sunday school and church, chauffeurs them to football practice and dancing lessons, and keeps nutritious and healthy meals on the table. But all through the years, Dad and the children never notice that she does not enjoy a complete meal that is uninterrupted; nor can they understand why she never seems to have anything to wear.

Studies done by our government and several independent agencies have demonstrated what has been suspected for so long. If one attempted to hire someone to do the tasks of a wife—a homemaker—the cost would be substantial.[25] But we cannot consider or follow that approach. Our law does not view

---

23. *Lonely*, in *id.* at 381.

24. This section, as well as the later section on the death of a mother, deals primarily with the traditional roles of women. Economic conditions and social changes are causing women to assume even greater family responsibility as wage earners and providers. Where appropriate, incorporate this important aspect of the victim's contributions into your argument.

25. The Houston Chronicle, July 24, 1979, reporting an AP wire release in the August issue of *Parents Magazine*, confirmed the annual cost of replacing a homemaker at $35,000 per year.

a wife as simply a maid, dishwasher, cook, handyman, gardener, chauffeur, and bookkeeper. If the law did, our task would be simple. But if this were the law's approach, we would not find in the court's instructions reference to the loss of aid, comfort, society, companionship, love, and affection.

America's noted jurist Oliver Wendell Holmes observed that "husband and wife come to look alike at last."[26] A sixteenth-century English author wrote that a good wife makes a good husband.[27] She laughs at her husband's jokes, not because they are clever but because she is. It is said that the road to success is filled with women pushing their husbands along. A Greek philosopher noted that "[m]an's best possession is a sympathetic wife."[28] In more recent times it has been said that wives are young men's mistresses, companions for middle age, and old men's nurses. A good wife and good health are man's best wealth. Of all the home remedies, a good wife is the best.

We should think about these things as we ponder the value of the life that has been lost. Do you think this man misses his wife most when he finds himself making supper for the family or when he finds himself lying silently in bed—alone—at night. Do you think he misses her most when he finds himself having to do the laundry or when things are not going well—when the world seems to have turned against him—and that soft voice is not there to encourage him on. Do you think he misses her most when he is doing the family shopping or when in the evening he turns to share an idea he got from a book or a movie and finds that there is no one to share it with. Do you think he misses her most when he finds that the checkbook will not balance that month or when he awakes on a Saturday morning realizing that there is no one to spend the weekend with. Or maybe—just maybe—he misses her most when he comes in from work every day and stands for a moment in the living room of their little house waiting to hear those familiar words, "Welcome home, darling, how did your day go?"

Death of a Father

Male parents are known by many names. Pop. Dad. Father. The Old Man. Regardless of the name he goes by, a good father is a bigger-than-life combination of John Wayne, Billy Graham, Bob Hope, and Phil Donahue. It has been suggested that there are only two animals that sleep on their feet—horses and fathers with one-month-old babies. Fathers are men who buy toys at Christmas that *they* would enjoy playing with. The average father wears out a pair of shoes when the rest of the family wears out a set of tires. It has been said that one father is worth more than a hundred schoolmasters. The naturalist would

---

26. *Quoted in* H. KORNBLITT, *supra* note 5, at 153.
27. John Heywood, *Proverbs, quoted in* DICTIONARY OF QUOTATIONS, *supra* note 2, at 333.
28. Euripides, *Antigone*, frag. 164, *quoted in* B. STEVENSON, *supra* note 6, at 2140a.

tell us that the human is the only animal that even attempts to have anything to do with its half-grown young.

Fathers are always bigger, stronger, funnier, smarter, and more tolerant than other people. Their tweed jackets and khaki shirts smell of pipes and cigars. Their workshops are mystical places of tools and gadgets, and there is always the smell of sawdust in the air. Their libraries contain imponderable volumes of knowledge of things that seem so far beyond our ken when we are youngsters. A father's voice is a resonance of reassurance, security, and affection. Fathers have answers to problems, jokes we have never heard, and stories far more interesting than anything you would see on television or at the movies.

You can always pick the fathers out at the football or baseball games, plays, or recitals. For when *his* "little one" makes the play or comes on stage, his face lights up and you can see his chest stick out a little bit. "Dad" has the worst voice when he sings in church, the loudest laugh in the movie theater, the firmest handshake, and the most generous wallet.

The bond between father and child has been commemorated in song and script, from Eddie Fisher's recording of "Oh! My Pa-pa" to more recent country and Western ballads. In Jerry Jeff Walker's recording of "Desperados Waiting for the Train," a song about a son's relationship with his father, there is this simple refrain: "We were friends, me and this old man."

On the stage we had *Life with Father* and on television *Father Knows Best*. We all know of the biographies written about famous men by their children. But even ordinary dads have been the subject of books and stories. Many of us laughed and cried at *A Christmas Story*,[29] a recent movie adapted from the book about a boy who grew up in the forties and his relationship with his father.

One of the Reverend Billy Graham's favorite stories used in his sermons concerns a young girl. He saw her one winter day taking very long and difficult steps in the snow. When he asked her what she was doing, the little girl replied simply, "Trying to walk in my father's footsteps."

If you have ever had the opportunity to watch young children at play in your neighborhood, you probably have witnessed this scene. All at once one of the little boys or girls will jump up from play, saying, "I've got to leave now, my daddy's come home." Then watch that little one as he runs down the street to the man getting out of the car, shouting, "Daddy, Daddy, you're home!"

How much does the loss of a father mean to a young child, adolescent, or young person? Simply ask someone of middle age who enjoyed the full lifetime of a father's fraternity, companionship, and love. Such a man wrote the following poem:

---

29. Based on JEAN SHEPHERD, IN GOD WE TRUST, ALL OTHERS PAY CASH (1966).

Used to wonder just why father
Never had much time for play,
Used to wonder why he'd rather
Work each minute of the day.
Used to wonder why he never
Loafed along the road an' shirked;
Can't recall a time whenever
Father played while others worked.

Father didn't dress in fashion,
Sort of hated clothing new;
Style with him was not a passion;
He had other things in view.
Boys are blind to much that's going
On about 'em day by day,
And I had no way of knowing
What became of father's pay.

All I knew was when I needed
Shoes I got 'em on the spot;
Everything for which I pleaded,
Somehow, father always got.
Wondered, season after season,
Why he never took a rest,
And that I might be the reason
Then I never even guessed.[30]

This victim—this father—was a fixer. He repaired the washing machine, the family car, stuck drawers, and broken hearts. He was a builder—of shelves in the closet, bookcases in the children's room, the deck on the back of the house, and bridges of opportunity for these youngsters. He was the guide who would have helped them through the wilderness of life. He was the groundskeeper who tried to see that life's playing field remained level.

What do these children need now? Someone who would try to understand their needs and problems? Someone who would do everything within his power to ensure that the fair thing would be done by them? Someone who would not compromise any aspect of these children's lives and future? Someone committed to justice? You might think that I am describing a father. But in reality, I was describing the twelve people who must now determine the value of this father.

Death of a Mother

A Jewish proverb says that when God made man, he realized that he "could not be everywhere and therefore he made mothers."[31] It has been suggested

30. E.A. Guest, *Father, supra* note 22, sts. 1-3, at 28.
31. *Quoted in* B. Stevenson, *supra* note 6, at 1350b.

that next to God himself, a good mother most resembles the qualities of the Creator. An English author wrote, "Mother is the name for God in the lips and hearts of little children."[32] Maybe this is because "a mother's face and voice are the first conscious objects as the infant's soul unfolds."[33] Napoléon Bonaparte said, "The future destiny of the child is always the work of the mother,"[34] and Ralph Waldo Emerson wrote that "men are what their mothers made of them."[35]

A mother's heart is the child's schoolroom, her lap a lifeboat in life's stormy seas, her touch the greatest of all medicines. We know that there are many females of the animal species that will die to protect their young. But mothers in the animal kingdom care only for a body; mothers in the spiritual kingdom must also care for a soul, a mind, and a heart. That is why in the animal kingdom a mother will abandon her young as soon as they can fend for themselves. There are a lot of orphans in the animal kingdom. It does not take long in the animal order to generate and develop the brain of a monkey, because the monkey's brain does not have very much to do. But it takes a long time to develop the mind of a child, to inculcate ideals, virtues of honesty, truth, patriotism, and justice. Animals can leave their parents quickly, because they have no eternal destiny. But humans are under a different standard—a compulsory need to educate their offspring—and to fulfill this need, there must be a loving mother. The home is the schoolhouse of affection wherein a mother completes the work that was begun when the child was born. A poet questioned "What is home without a mother?"[36] Motherhood then turns into mothercraft, as biology hands the work over to ethics. The canoe can be quickly launched on the waters when it is made, but the big ship has to wait for engines because it has a better port. A tiny ball of incognizance needs much motherly care to become all that God destined it to be. Maybe that is why mothers oppose war: they realize better than anyone else how long it takes to make a man.

Motherly love requires greater attention to individuals of the species. A mother will love each offspring as if it were the only child in all the world, recognizing that human beings are not just individuals but persons. In the animal order, they are individuals; in the human order, they are persons. The difference between an individual and a person is this: individuals are replaceable, and persons are not. This is probably why every mother gives to a child a name that implies dignity, uniqueness, and individuality. There is no greater repudiation of communism in the world than a mother. Because communism

---

32. WILLIAM MAKEPEACE THACKERAY, 2 VANITY FAIR ch. 12, *quoted in id.*

33. Grandville Stanley Hall, article in *Pedagogical Seminary*, June 1891, *quoted in* J. BARTLETT (13th ed. 1955), *supra* note 10, at 565a.

34. SAYINGS OF NAPOLEON, *quoted in* B. STEVENSON, *supra* note 6, at 1350a.

35. *Fate*, in THE ESSAYS OF RALPH WALDO EMERSON 444 (1944).

36. Alice Hawthorne, [*title of poem*], *quoted in* B. STEVENSON, *supra* note 6.

denies the value of persons, it affirms that we are all like grapes and that we have no other destiny than to have our life ground out of us for the sake of the collective wine of the state. Every mother arises to protest and proclaim, "This child of mine is a person and may not be submerged in any totality of a class or a state or a race; he is unique; he has a name; he is my son (or my daughter)!"

A typical mother, seeing that there are only four pieces of pie for five people, promptly announces that she never did care for pie. The quickest way for a mother to get her children's attention is to sit down and look comfortable. It is said that mothers can have a few minutes to themselves at the end of each day by doing the dishes.

Mothers are easy to spot at any age. A young mother always has a streak of peanut butter and jelly on the sleeve of her best dress or a blotch of oatmeal on the top of her high heels, which she forgot to wipe off. An older mother has a purse full of photographs of her children and a litany of their accomplishments.

What did the loss of their mother mean to these children? You have heard that a man never sees all that his mother has been to him until it is too late to let her know that he saw it. But we know this, that every successful and famous person who ever lived would admit that he owed it to his mother. Abraham Lincoln once commented that all he was or hoped to be he owed to his angel mother.[37] Two thousand years ago, a teacher was scourged, tortured, and placed on a cross to die. The last person he asked for on earth was his mother.

While many poems have been written about the loss one feels on the death of a mother, perhaps the one most appropriate to these fine children, who must now await your verdict, is this by Edgar A. Guest:

Never a sigh for the cares that she bore for me,
Never a thought of the joys that flew by;
Her one regret that she couldn't do more for me,
Thoughtless and selfish, her Master was I.

Oh, the long nights that she came at my call to me!
Oh, the soft touch of her hands on my brow!
Oh, the long years that she gave up her all to me!
Oh, how I yearn for her gentleness now!

Slave to her baby! Yes, that was the way of her,
Counting her greatest of services small;
Words cannot tell what this old heart would say of her,
Mother—the sweetest and fairest of all.[38]

37. *Quoted in id.*
38. *Mother, supra* note 22, at 6.

PART 8

Illustrative Arguments

Do but set the example yourself, and I will follow you. Example is the best precept.

—Aesop, "The Two Crabs"

A Note About Chapters 28 Through 31

Chapters 28 through 31 contain forensic arguments adapted from actual cases tried by the author. The names of the parties, attorneys, witnesses, judges, and medical authorities have been changed to protect their anonymity.

These cases involve various types of issues and injuries. It is important that the trial lawyer not become too "structured" or fall into the habit of giving essentially the same argument in all cases. Argument must be adapted to the facts of the case, the makeup of the jury, the court in which the case is tried, the geographical area in which the case is being determined, the personalities of the defense attorneys involved, and the position taken by the defense. In each of the following arguments, conscious decisions were made based on those factors.

28

The Case of the Redundant Oxygen

A Product Liability Argument

THE MINOR PLAINTIFF was born prematurely, weighing two pounds and three ounces at birth. He was administered between 32 to 40 percent oxygen on a continuous basis for ten days, resulting in a condition known as retrolental fibroplasia (RLF) that rendered him totally and permanently blind. The malpractice case against the treating doctors was settled for $100,000 by attorneys who had originally handled the case before the author became involved. Suit was filed against the hospital and the manufacturer of the incubator. The evidence showed that giving supplemental oxygen in those quantities for the length of time involved could cause RLF and that the manufacturer-defendant knew this fact but failed to establish policies and procedures to prevent the practice. The corporate defendants offered only $25,000, believing they could convince the jury that the sole cause of the RLF was the negligence of the settling doctors who had ordered the oxygen. The jury found both the hospital and the manufacturer negligent and awarded damages totaling almost $2 million.

The argument in this case illustrates several of the principles discussed earlier in this work, concerning both general concepts of forensic argument and the strategy of arguing a product liability case. Perhaps the greatest challenge presented was to persuade the jurors against attributing the greater part of the responsibility for the plaintiff's injuries to the physicians who had prescribed the supplemental oxygen.

Opening Argument

May it please this honorable court. Ladies and gentlemen, needless to say it is my privilege and, indeed, my honor to be able to address you on behalf of Rusty Smith. Lawsuits have a way of getting pretty mean, particularly when there are significant issues and substantial money involved. And for that reason I've asked Rusty to stay outside the courtroom—because the comments I make are going to be about Rusty and they're going to affect Rusty, and what you are going to do will be something that Rusty will have to live with. Your verdict will live with him for the rest of his life, but it is not appropriate that he hear what the lawyers say. It's appropriate only that he hear your verdict, because that's the important thing.

But I would be ungrateful if I did not, at the very beginning, take this opportunity on behalf of Rusty and his mother to thank you for your patience and attention during a very long and difficult trial. I know we have imposed on you at a very personal time of the year for all of us around Christmas. And I know that your service has been difficult. It's taken you from your families and from your work. But the one thing I've noticed the few times I have looked over at you is that each and every one of you, to the man, to the lady, has been paying the strictest attention to the evidence, in order for you to do what you have sworn to do. And that is to decide this case based on the evidence, that the right thing would be done by Rusty. I want to thank you for that patience, and I want to apologize to the extent that we have had to bring you into this tragedy.

Fortunately, though, ours is a system where we have the opportunity to try to remedy a tragedy when it occurs. And our system is one in which I believe. I know that statement comes as no surprise—my being a lawyer—but I also know that you believe in it very strongly, because it's the one chance you really have to make your voice heard. It seems to me that you can vote for representatives, and they may be elected to office, but if they speak for us at all, it is only indirectly. A jury is a very direct form of decision-making—a direct way of deciding the way that you want certain things to be run, of deciding how you want certain people to behave. In a case like this, you decide with your verdict what is proper and who is responsible as well as who is not.

Our system works because everyone does his job. My job, as Rusty's lawyer, has been to bring evidence for your consideration. This has been a difficult case. It has taken us some time to gather the evidence and bring it to you. I've tried the best I know how to be professional and ethical in the presentation of the case on behalf of Rusty, and I hope I have done that. If I've offended anyone by anything I've done, I apologize. But I think we've been straightforward with you, and I think we've presented our case in an honest and up-front manner. I believe we have proved those things that we said we would in the very beginning of this case, on the voir dire.

You have also noticed the difficult job His Honor has had in this case. From time to time, it has been a very busy one that required tough legal rulings on objections. The judge has also written the charge you will take with you to the jury room. That has been his job—to handle the legal matters.

By virtue of that charge you will receive shortly, you will now have the most important job of all. The judge's job, my job, is nothing at all compared to your job. And that's because your job is to decide the case. Your decision is final; there is no appeal from your decision. We have all heard of civil cases being appealed. And we have a fine court of appeals down the hall on this floor; we have a supreme court in Austin, and they take civil appeals. But civil appeals are not had on the wisdom of a jury. They're on legal matters. Did the judge correctly exclude evidence? Did he correctly include evidence? Appeals are decided on things of that nature, legal matters. But no one can set aside your verdict. This judge cannot rewrite your verdict for you. If you make a mistake, Rusty can't go down the hall to the court of appeals and say, "Hey, those folks made a mistake! I need you to rewrite my verdict." Because they can't do it. They don't have that power. The only people who have the power to decide the facts are you; you are the supreme court of the facts of this case.

I know that some of you are already wondering what facts will be decided. You will see that there are a lot of questions the judge asks of us. What are we deciding? You will recall on the voir dire examination when we told you what we would prove. The defendants told you that we would not. But we backed up our contentions with proof for you and the court. The judge is the one who renders judgment. He renders a judgment based on your decision, your verdict. And we said that after the jury's verdict, your verdict, Rusty would be entitled to the damages found by you for what he has suffered. The defendants, on the other hand, have contended from the very start of this trial that Rusty is not entitled, that he is not deserving of your verdict, for he lacks the proof to receive it. And so they say that they don't owe Rusty anything—that they are entitled to the judgment, regardless of what you find by way of damages. So there are only two judgments that are sought—two judgments that are as different as night and day. Only one of these two judgments can be rendered by the judge. The one that is rendered depends entirely on your verdict—your decision on the facts. But don't think for a minute that he can change your answers to make it come out the way you would like or render the judgment the way you want. He can't—unless you give him the right answers. It is because you can change your answer to any single one of these issues, and thereby change the verdict completely, that His Honor's judgment may change from night to day. That's how important your verdict is. That's how important your answers to these issues are. That's how automatic it is.

In fact, when you come in and your answers are read out loud, every lawyer in the courtroom, every reporter who will be here, will hear each answer and know what judgment the court must render. IT IS THAT AUTOMATIC. And so I hope that none of you will say when you get back to the jury room, "Well, we're just giving an advisory verdict. We're just advising the judge of what we think ought to occur." Nothing could be farther from the truth. You're not advising anyone of anything—you are deciding this case.

You will notice that the issues in this important charge are broken down, and the first ten issues that are submitted to you deal with responsibility. Who is responsible for Rusty's blindness? The last three issues deal with the damages he has sustained and will continue to suffer. They're broken down in that order for a reason. And your answers to those first ten issues are crucial, because you answer them before you even get to the damages issues. Your answers must be based on evidence, and they have to be answered properly. Because if you make a mistake, an error, you change the entire result of this case. That's why in the court's charge, Instruction 3, the court tells us right off the bat, "since every answer that is required by the charge is important, no juror should state or consider that any required answer is not important."

Every single answer has got to be answered right. You have got to score a hundred on Rusty's test for him. A seventy-five won't do it. It won't pass this test. I wish it could, but seventy-five or even eighty won't do for Rusty. He has to have a hundred—a perfect score.

There are also a couple of other instructions that are particularly appropriate for you to remember when you confront these issues. They are all important, but on the first page you'll find that the judge tells you foremost and in particular that "you are the sole judges of the credibility of the witnesses and the weight to be given their testimony." Now what does that mean? Well, you've heard a lot of witnesses, and your job as the jury is to remember the motives of the witnesses. What interest do they have in the verdict? Were they consistent? Did they change their story? Does it make sense? What did they have to say? YOU judge the credibility of the witnesses. YOU decide how much of a witness's testimony you want to believe. YOU can believe all of it or none of it or only a part of it. That job is left to your wisdom as the jury—to decide the credibility of the witnesses.

Only after those instructions, which are so very important, come the questions you must answer. And even then they are based on one final instruction. They are to be decided on a "preponderance of the evidence." Preponderance of the evidence is defined for you as "the greater weight and degree of credible evidence." You take only the evidence that you decide is credible. Who said something that made sense to us? Who said something important without a special motive? Who said something, not because of an interest in your verdict, but because it was true? You take only that evidence and place it on the imaginary scales of justice, and, if it tilts ever so slightly, it has become a preponderance of the evidence. There is no question of doubt. Nothing depends on being proved beyond a shadow of a doubt like a criminal case. Preponderance of the evidence is the measure for Rusty in his case.

You will see that the questions on responsibility inquire essentially about three entities. The charge asks about the responsibility of the manufacturer, it asks about the responsibility of the hospital, and it asks about the responsibility of these two doctors. As you will see, contrary to what the defense told you on voir dire over a month ago, these folks are not considered alike in the eyes of the law. The charge lets you know that they are not alike—that they are judged differently, that their responsibility is measured differently. And that again, for example, is one reason that every issue, every word, is there for a reason. That is why it is so important—why it takes days for a judge to put a charge together. Because the words are so significant, and they have to be just right. Nothing can cause an error any quicker in a case than a wrong word being in that charge. Every word in this charge has been gone over and over, and that's how important the words are.

There is in this charge, for instance, a concept or word that is used throughout: negligence. Even though it's the same concept each time it is typed in the charge, even though it is spelled the same way, it's measured very differently among individuals, such as doctors, and a hospital or corporation, such as Aerobator. When we talk about the specific issues you will see why that is so and why it has to be so. A corporation in law is responsible for everything it knows. A corporation in law can't say, "Well, we knew that over in the medical department, but marketing was sending out that information and they didn't know it." The corporation cannot deny that knowledge. It cannot do that. The corporation that operates a hospital cannot say, "Well, the medical staff didn't know it, but we had these statistics." No corporation can do that. The knowledge of the corporation is judged by the knowledge of all its departments, all its members. And that is why negligence as to a corporation is measured on a different scale than the negligence of an individual—because they are charged with the knowledge of all their departments and all their individuals. One department cannot escape the corporate responsibility, the corporate duty, because something was done by another department. One department cannot say, "Well, we knew that, but we didn't tell the other departments; so it's not our fault." That doesn't work. That is not the law. That is something you now know to help answer these difficult questions.

Issue 1 asks whether or not this incubator, as it was designed by the manufacturer—by Aerobator—and sold to the hospital in 1968 was defectively designed. You will notice that the court tells us what defective design means. A defective design is a design that poses an unreasonable risk of harm. An unreasonable risk of harm—Judge Carter has written there for you to use—means that some feature of the machine threatened harm to the infants who needed the incubator to the extent that the incubator, as designed, should not have been placed in the channels of commerce by prudent manufacturers aware of the risks involved.

You should know that there are some products that are as safe as you can make them. And even though there is some risk in them, they can be released into commerce, into our hands, because they are the safest that can be made. But if there is knowledge of the risk involved so that a prudent manufacturer would have changed the design or put some information on the product, done something differently—then they should not release that incubator, being aware of the risks involved. And looking at it today, if a manufacturer aware of the risk would not have released that incubator, then it was defectively designed.

We know from the evidence that this machine was designed in the early sixties. It was designed at a time when it was believed that 40 percent oxygen concentration was safe. This machine incorporated the 40 percent feature all over it. This machine had a red flag that went up or down when it exceeded or fell below 40 percent oxygen. Red flag went down if you were under 40 percent. It went up if you're over 40 percent. It had 40 percent references in the literature. Forty percent is "high oxygen"; low oxygen is less than 40 percent. The idea of a 40 percent cutoff was intertwined completely in the design of this incubator, and yet, when the information came to the manufacturer that 40 percent was not safe, they did nothing to change the design. When they found out that 40 percent was not safe, what practical use was there—what necessity—to have the flag on the machine? How does it help the doctor? How does it help the nurse? Why not have it at 30 percent, at 35 percent? How does it help in the treatment of children? What does it do except mislead the doctors and nurses who are going to be using the machine? They were made to believe that as long as the red flag is down, we're safe. A child can't get retrolental fibroplasia in low oxygen. But the manufacturer knew that was not so, that it was not true. And they continued to manufacture the same machine, with the same type of design and the same 40 percent misconception, even though they knew.

It seems to me that a risk of harm involves danger and the chances of running into that danger, and I can't imagine any danger greater than blindness. The risk of harm here was great—it was appreciable and substantial. If we were only to consider only one child out of twelve thousand getting RLF, we would be talking about a substantial risk. We aren't talking about a weird type of risky situation, but even if it were that, it would be substantial enough to change the design of an incubator. The risk of children's getting RLF was substantial, because the design reinforced a medical misconception, a medical untruth. It did nothing but reinforce ignorance. So, based on that awareness, we submit that Issue 1 should be answered "yes."

Issue 2 asks whether or not this was a "producing cause." In other words, did the design of the incubator contribute in some manner to Rusty Smith's blindness? From the evidence, you now know that there can only be one correct answer to that question. If Rusty had not received the oxygen in the concentrations given, he would not, obviously, be blind today from RLF. There is no question that his blindness was caused by the oxygen, despite the implications to the contrary. Dr. Joseph, Dr. Rosenberg, and Dr. Duncan testified that it was, and yes, it was a contributing cause. Issue 2 should be answered "yes."

Issue 3 asks about the negligence and the failure of Aerobator to give any kind of warning. The kind of warning we're talking about was marked as Plaintiff's Exhibit 26, and you will notice the concept of negligence stresses "under the same or similar circumstances." What should a manufacturer have done, for example? You look at the circumstances to determine whether or not something was negligent. These circumstances, you know from the evidence, were that they had a machine that they designed that was based on and incorporated a medical misconception—a medical untruth and misconception that 40 percent oxygen concentration to a premature infant was safe, that it was okay, that it was acceptable. You now know that they were aware even before 1968 and certainly knew by 1970 that infants being placed in their incubators were getting RLF. It was being reported to them, but they did nothing to determine why. They're selling incubators all over the country, big hospitals, little hospitals; general practitioners are using them; obstetricians are using them; pediatricians are using them; people of varying education and abilities are using them. Most importantly, Aerobator knew of the risk of giving routine supplemental oxygen to a premature infant without the clinical need for it. Because if you do that and you do it long enough—certainly eight or nine days is too long—there is an appreciable risk of retrolental fibroplasia.

You will recall that we talked specifically with Mr. Andres, the company's representative, about having a warning and the reasons for having a warning. He admitted it would be cheap to give such a warning. It would bring information to the user. It would probably be adhered to and followed by the user. It would not interfere with the operation of the machine. And then he said, "Well, we had reasons for not giving it." I couldn't help but be reminded of Shakespeare's quotation, that "oftentimes excusing of a fault doth make the fault the worse by the excuse." And that's what this seems like—the excusing of a fault that made the fault worse by the excuse. It wasn't feasible. Well, I guess it became feasible when we drew one up for them—when we printed one out for them like Exhibit 26. We even showed them how to put it on the machine. I don't think feasibility is a very good reason.

Then they said, "Well, we give technical information only." But take a look at the material they furnished. They gave much more than technical information. They had medical recommendations in their letters and in their sales brochures. They wanted to recommend the use of their machine, but now they say it's beyond the province of the manufacturer. That, of course, is another question for you to decide regarding this issue. If that is what you believe and what you want, what you decide to say—that "it is beyond the province of the manufacturer"—then you have the power, by your verdict, to approve this type of thinking.

But what reasoning would lead to that answer? A manufacturer of a medical appliance being used on those frail babies cannot just sit there when it learns of a dangerous medical condition, when it knows the facts; to bury your head in the sand like an ostrich and say we're going to count on doctors' somehow learning it themselves is the ultimate form of hypocrisy. That's the reasoning the defense would have you adopt: think the corporate way, which is, "We're going to sit here with our hands over our eyes and our ears and our mouths like the three monkeys who 'see no evil, hear no evil, speak no evil.' But by the way, in the meantime we're going to do everything we can to sell these incubators, even though we won't advise anyone of the danger." You have to decide whether that excuse makes sense to you. It's the kind of responsibility that we're talking about. It is simply the responsibility of telling what you know or learn about the danger associated with your product.

Issue 4 asks whether the failure to give these warnings is a proximate cause. Certainly. That it causes blindness? Certainly. Was it reasonably foreseeable? Certainly, it was. They knew infants were sustaining retrolental fibroplasia. They knew. Even some of their medical literature tells you that they knew. You now know that even the company's own doctor admitted, "Sure, we knew some people had not gotten the word." Was it reasonably foreseeable that, if the doctors didn't have the word, somebody might use the incubator, give routine oxygen to an infant who didn't need it, and bring about retrolental fibroplasia? Certainly. We say that Issue 4 should also be answered "yes."

Now we come to the hospital's responsibility. Issue 5 asks about the conduct of the hospital. The hospital, like the manufacturer, is measured differently, because it is not an individual, it is many individuals—it is a corporation. The corporate ability to gather and disseminate information is much greater than that of any individual. What are the policies and procedures of the hospital relating to oxygen administration for? What purpose should they serve? Issue 5 asks, "Were they negligent in their policies and procedures?" You now know that we have had a heck of a fight in this case trying to find out what those policies were. But you've heard the evidence as to at least what they knew. You have seen that what was in effect was the wrong thing. It was the WRONG thing.

The purpose of policies and procedures at a hospital is to ensure certain minimum practices. The purpose of policies and procedures is to give guidance and education, to ensure that proper care will be given. Sure, the defense is going to say, "Well, that is left up to the doctor." But not completely. The hospital's role is just as important as the physician's. Their hospital policies did nothing but foster, promote, and lead to the medical misconception. They only nurtured the thought that oxygen in these concentrations is a safe, routine matter for a premature infant who has no need for it. They were drafted and calculated only to bring about retrolental fibroplasia in these infants. What a record for a hospital to brag about. What an achievement. "We had fifty-three children born who died, but only two had retrolental fibroplasia." What a record. Do you think that these policies were promoting anything? They were calculated to produce one thing: retrolental fibroplasia.

"Oxygen concentration"—and I'm quoting the reference that we could find—"oxygen concentration is kept at 40 percent or below unless otherwise specified by the physician." Now isn't that calculated to result in the routine administration of 40 percent or less oxygen to a premature infant whether he needs it or not? Isn't such a procedure reasonably calculated to produce RLF?

In this case the facts, as the law says, will "speak for themselves." What should the procedure have been? Let me remind you of the testimony of their own witness, Dr. Rebecca Swenson. I asked the court reporter to type this short excerpt up because it pretty well summarizes, it seems to me, the necessity of having a proper policy, a safe policy. The question to Dr. Swenson was—and you remember that she was at another hospital at the time—"Let's assume that at the hospital you worked at in 1970 you had an infant who had no clinical signs that indicated he needed supplemental oxygen. Assume that his respiration, his color was all right; didn't your hospital have, for example, as a part of its policies that you did not give supplemental oxygen as a routine measure?" Answer: "That is correct." Question: "And is there not a good reason for having that kind of policy?" Answer: "Yes." Question: "And what is the reason?" Answer: "That the less oxygen the baby is getting, hopefully, the less chance of the baby's getting retrolental fibroplasia."

That is the type of policy that was needed in this case, folks, at General Hospital. And we say that Issue 5 can only be answered "yes."

Issue 6 asks about proximate cause. Again, if General Hospital would have had a policy like the one in effect at the other hospital, this would never have occurred. Rusty would not have been given this oxygen. And so it was a proximate cause and reasonably foreseeable that this would occur.

Now let's talk about the doctors' responsibility. There are two things to keep in mind, it seems to me. The first is that ignorance is not the same thing as negligence. It's hard for a man to admit when he is ignorant of something. These doctors, there is no question about it, were ignorant. They were following the medical misconception. The difference between these physicians, the hospital, and particularly Aerobator is that the corporations were immensely more knowledgeable. They knew what was right. The doctors didn't. If they had known the proper scientific levels of oxygen, I don't think this would have ever happened.

Undoubtedly the defense will make a big argument about the doctors' being negligent, and they will want you to find that the doctors were negligent. You know why? Because some years ago, when this thing first started out, Rusty settled his claim against the doctors for $100,000. And I can tell you something about that which the defense won't—something you will know is only common sense. If there had been a strong indication that the doctors were negligent, if there had been any statements to indicate that what they did was more than mere ignorance, that claim against the doctors would never have been settled for $100,000. But the defense will want to take advantage of that. They will want to tell you it means the doctors were negligent. I think you're too intelligent to fall for that line, and so I think you know the answer is "no," they were not negligent. They were ignorant but not negligent.

And "no," it was not a proximate cause, if you get that far. The reasons are obvious. Dr. Duncan was not even involved in Rusty's care until six or seven days into the case. I don't see how his conduct could have even caused the RLF. Because Rusty had been receiving the oxygen for six or seven days by the time he became involved, how could he have caused it?

So it is crucial, it is critical, not to be misled by any argument about the doctors' being negligent or causing the RLF. You have to tie the knot in your verdict with these answers. It is that important. All the time Rusty was getting the oxygen, the red flag was down. All the time he was getting the oxygen, he was getting percentages that were consistent and expected by the hospital procedures. If we had thought otherwise, if we had suspected negligence, they would still be here. But when they said what they said years ago, we had to let them out for their ignorance and then go against those that were responsible for that ignorance.

You will see that those questions then lead you to the issues on damages. Issue 11 asks about the cost of special care that Rusty needs, and the issue tells you to include in it not only the special care he may get from a tutor but also the special care he will have to receive from his mother. In other words, the fact that she has to be more of a mother, spend more time, do more caring—those are things that should not be used to reduce the damages in Issue 11. We have brought you evidence of what the cost of tutors and special educators would be. And that is just for their services; it does not include anything for his mother. But we submit that a figure of $150,000 based on the evidence would be an appropriate answer to Issue 11.

Issue 12 is broken down into two parts, *a* and *b*. The first part asks you about the mental anguish and physical disfigurement Rusty has sustained in the past, and part *b* asks about the future—those sixty-two or sixty-three years of life expectancy that are left. We believe based on the evidence a figure of $700,000 would be appropriate for Rusty's mental suffering and disfigurement in the past, and the amount of $4 million would be based on the evidence as to his future anguish and disfigurement. You are probably asking yourselves how we arrived at those figures. It's a normal question—one that deserves an answer. So I will tell you that I took the minutes that Rusty has left in his lifetime by the calculation done by Dr. Hudson, the economist, and multiplied it by fourteen cents a minute. I used fourteen cents because that's what a sticker with a warning like the one on Exhibit 26 would have cost. Fourteen cents. The sticker that the manufacturer should have put on the incubator to warn the users of the risk of high oxygen. A fourteen-cent sticker could have saved this child's sight. He has that many minutes of blindness awaiting him.

When you are challenged by these issues, you are going to find, for example, on Issue 12 that the question talks about damages that will "fairly and reasonably compensate." And you're going to find that the only person that this issue even mentions is Rusty Smith. You determine the value of blindness. How do you go about it? Well, I'll tell you one thing not to do. Please don't anyone go back in the jury room and say, "Well, there is just no amount of money that could ever compensate anyone for being blind." The moment anyone says or thinks that, then he or she has disavowed their oath, their job as a juror. I certainly hope that if anyone thinks that way, they were the people who stood up out here some four weeks ago, when we had the voir dire, and said that they could not decide these issues. Because if anyone here now adopts that type of belief, then they have given up on their function, their job, their responsibility.

Yet I really don't think that anyone within the sound of my voice would say that a lifetime of blindness does not deserve substantial damages. But how substantial? How do you evaluate it? I don't know. We live in a time when race horses sell for seven and a half million dollars. Men can make millions of dollars in championship fights and ball games. Investors pay millions of dollars for a painting or a statue. Four, five, six million dollars for a painting. But Rusty—Rusty will never see Secretariat or any horse win a race. He'll never see Muhammad Ali win a boxing match. He'll never see a Super Bowl.

He'll never see a painting or statue that is worth millions of dollars. And if those things are worth so much, the eyes to enjoy them are certainly that valuable.

Issue 13 asks about his damages for loss of earning capacity. As we pointed out on voir dire, each element is to be considered separately. You are instructed to consider each element apart from the others. First the loss of earning capacity. We brought you expert testimony to help you determine this issue. The defendant brought no testimony whatsoever on this significant question. What is Rusty to do? We're talking about loss of the capacity to work and earn a living, and in making our calculations we assume that he will do something. There is an incredible difference between what kind of career he could have had, what type of living he could have earned with his eyes, and what he can earn without them. We brought you, for instance, the information that can be found in a book that has a listing of all the occupations in this country. Fifty thousand jobs. And you can open the book before you, but you will only see two or three hundred that a blind person can do. What can Rusty do? Can he do what you do? Or what about your husband's or wife's job? Could he be a butcher? Could he be a welder? Or terminal foreman, purchaser, truck driver? Sell oilfield equipment? Go down the list. What could he do? We hope that Rusty can meet most of these challenges that are ahead of him that are social, academic, and financial. But we must be realistic when we consider the jobs he even has a chance of occupying.

Then you will reach the issues that inquire about physical incapacity—physical incapacity and inability to care for himself in the future. You know, independence is a funny thing. You can see children begin to—I know I've seen it in mine—begin to be assertive when they are only two or three years old. We try to become independent at a very early age. We want to be able to walk down the street to our friend's house. We want to be able to be with other people. We want to be alone if we want to, by ourselves if we want to be. Come and go when we want to. Shop when we want to. That's a part of being independent. That is what you lose when you are physically incapacitated. Rusty today depends on his mother. But what is he to do when she is gone? The reason we have jurors decide cases like this is because you folks know what life is about, you see. And life is a hard struggle, at best. All of us know that.

You grow up, you marry, you have children, you have people depending on you and, even if you're by yourself and single, still just making and getting through life all by yourself is a hard proposition. That's true for just about any person with two good eyes and a good sound body and the ability to work. How could you do it if you didn't have your eyes? That capacity, that gift that is normally ours, is a very valuable one. The defense will point, I'm sure, with some pride to achievements that blind people have made. We had a very impressive lady in here, Mrs. Miller. I don't know if Rusty can be a Mrs. Miller or not. Because as you have heard from the witness stand, blind people, despite the help, go different ways. Some of them end up at home, as recluses.

Some of them fight it. But we do know this: if Rusty does fight and can somehow cope with this lonely handicap, it will be difficult. But if he does cope with his blindness, that achievement will be his—not Aerobator's and not the hospital's. It will be his and his alone.

Closing Argument

Your Honor, ladies and gentlemen of the jury, I doubt that I can do in the thirty-eight minutes I have left what it took George Patton about a week to do. But Rusty and I feel like General Patton must have felt. In the heat of battle during World War Two, they phoned out to him. He was standing on the battlefield in the midst of the snow, and they asked him to report his position. And I wish I could tell Rusty, because this is Rusty's position. General Patton replied over the phone, "Well, we've got them right where we want them. They have us absolutely surrounded." And that's about the way Rusty is in this case. He's absolutely surrounded. I have never tried a case in my life where I've seen so much distortion. I guess it's because I'm old-fashioned and was brought up a certain way, but I still think there is something such as honor.

What can be the motive for what has happened in this case? Because Mr. Hall, the defense lawyer, is correct. The doctors come in, and one of them, at least, changes his testimony. What can be the motive?

Mrs. Miller, bless her heart, says there are few people who would take advantage of a blind person. Rusty, I've got a surprise for you: there are a bunch of them out there. And they will hand you a five and tell you it's a ten they've given you in change. You won't know until later that someone has done that to you. And they'll do it to you in a lawsuit. When your entire future is on the line. In a minute. In a minute.

Now after we determined what the doctors' position was, that they were ignorant, we filed a lawsuit against Aerobator and the hospital, and we found out that Aerobator knew of these risks and problems. We found out that the hospital was giving oxygen as a routine measure. It wasn't a proper procedure, and we brought Rusty's lawsuit. And then when the lawsuit gets into court and issues are submitted against the doctors who have their judgment—they've settled, they have their legal protection, there's nothing Rusty can do about the doctors—then the doctors come in and start trying to change their testimony. They meet with the hospital and Aerobator. I wonder why. Is that a fair question to ask? I wonder why. The defendants confer freely. They talk to the doctors. The doctors talk to them. They furnish information. Any information Aerobator wants, the hospital will get, even if it means going back ten years to get records. And everything we've done in this lawsuit—it shows from the records—we had to do it the hard way, by court order. By subpoena. It just seems appropriate to me; and I'm not the poet that the guardian ad litem is, but I'll tell you this: Honor is an island rugged and without a beach, and once we have left it it remains beyond our reach. I believe we stand on that island. And I believe the defendants left it a long time ago. They left in three ships: indifference, insincerity, and insensitivity.

They were indifferent to the ignorance of the people who were using their incubators to care for these frail babies. We have proved that they withheld critical medical knowledge from the doctors and nurses using their equipment.

They were insincere in presenting their defense to these serious charges. Their representatives said different things, at different times, in order to escape their responsibility.

Having caused this tragedy, they have been insensitive. They have refused to recognize the magnitude of the tragedy caused by their negligence.

Let me talk with you a little bit about some of the statements that have been made during argument, because Mr. Hall has gone through a bunch of this evidence and I'm not going to go through it in that detail. But I want to recall some of it with you, because it's significant. Let me talk with you if I may about a couple of things, keeping in mind that we are talking about your decision. Your decision is not to determine anything in this case to a certainty. We talk about "reasonable probability." These defendants keep talking about "well, it could have been this, it could have been that." That's not an issue. The question is, What reasonably, probably caused Rusty Smith's blindness? And all the evidence is that it is called redundant oxygen. Giving oxygen when he didn't need it. He had no clinical sign for it. It was given to him because the doctors didn't know better. They thought they were safe.

But what about the manufacturer of the incubator? The one that can't give a warning, the one that couldn't put just a sticker on the front of its incubator. A fourteen-cent sticker. Put it there for someone to see, for someone to know. "Would it have made any difference, doctor?" These are questions to the doctors even though they were trying to do what they could to help these defendants. When you put them to the wall, sometimes they couldn't go all the way. Question: "Doctor, do you consider yourself to be a reasonable man and a reasonable practitioner?" Answer: "Yes." Question: "Are you telling us that if you had seen on the incubator in question the following statement," which was essentially this warning—and I will get to it—that we've used with other witnesses before, "that you would have ignored that, that it wouldn't have brought something to your attention?" And his answer was, "I certainly wouldn't have ignored a message like that." Question: "Certainly not, and you would have either adhered to it or at least looked further into the matter, as a reasonable person?" Answer: "I think I would."

All they needed was the message, and Aerobator had it. Aerobator had the information. Mr. Andres and Dr. Cullen both testified that they knew when they designed this incubator that RLF was caused by oxygen. They knew that infants who were in their incubators from the time they started building them, as of 1960, were getting RLF. They didn't investigate. Why?

They knew as of 1968 that 40 percent was not safe. There's been some suggestion that they never made that statement, and Mr. Hall made it to you, when he said, "We have never told anybody it was safe."

I quote from the deposition from Mr. Grosshodes, which we read to you—Mr. Grosshodes being an employee of Aerobator. Question: "Isn't it true that the reason for the giving of the warning, a red flag being raised at concentrations higher than 40 percent, is to warn of the potential of RLF?" Answer: "I think this has to be inferred, yes." That's from their own man who helped design the machine—from sworn testimony we read you three weeks ago. It's been so long, perhaps a couple of you may have forgotten that. He wouldn't come down here. He wasn't down here to testify, but we have his deposition. We had to go to Pennsylvania to get it, but we have it. That is what their own man said.

We presented interrogatories, as you recall, questions in writing to them that their own man swears to. He was asked, "What was the purpose? Did you investigate RLF?" Their answer is, "We did not investigate the disease, but we designed a system to help in its prevention." And then there comes a time when they knew it wasn't safe. Forty percent wasn't safe, and there was no level that could be considered safe. You only gave it to an infant when he needed it; otherwise you'd give him RLF. And you couldn't give him oxygen for ten or fifteen days, eight days even, without a clinical need, because you would blind him. Remember Dr. Cullen, their medical technologist, as it were; we asked: "Would it be a fair statement to say that this information that we're talking about, the fact that concentrations of oxygen below 40 percent are not necessarily safe, the fact that it is the duration of exposure that is critical, was a significant and important piece of information insofar as it would relate to the care of the premature infant and particularly the avoidance of RLF?" The answer: "Yes."

Did Aerobator know that there were some doctors who believed 40 percent was safe? They say no. They again have forgotten the testimony of their own people that we went to Philadelphia to get on Rusty's behalf. Dr. Cullen in his deposition said, "From 1963 through 1970, Aerobator was aware of the fact that, despite the advances in medical knowledge, in some areas of this country people still believed that as long as you kept oxygen at 40 percent or below, the chances of a child's getting RLF were minimal or nil." And then we asked Dr. Cullen this: "If the hospital had this kind of standing order that we're talking about, wouldn't that indicate that they had that belief?" And he answered, "That's right." We also asked Dr. Cullen whether or not the warning drawn up by Dr. Byman, our expert, would be an accurate one insofar as the medical information is concerned. And Dr. Cullen answered, "That is true."

But they didn't warn anyone, and they didn't tell us. Why? Well, you remember—again, this has been a while—but we asked Mr. Grosshodes, one of their design people, "Why didn't you warn them?" You know what he said? He didn't have three reasons like Mr. Andres did. He said, "We have done it."

Question: "Is it your opinion, then, that the dispensing of information"—this is a direct quotation from his deposition—"regarding RLF with material that would accompany the incubator would not be reasonably calculated to reach people who, by their actions, can affect or bring about RLF?" In other words, dispensing information regarding RLF risks and hazards. Answer: "Of course, it would help." And he goes on, "No harm in telling them." No harm in telling them! And he says, "I think we have done this, too. You ask me if I know of any information we're given these people, but just because I don't know of it does not mean we didn't do it." Their own expert, up in Philadelphia, tried to say they'd done it. But Mr. Andres, when he takes the stand down here, has to admit they didn't do it. And he even gave three reasons why they didn't do it. There's not one single witness, not one single medical expert who has looked at this [*displaying blowup of suggested warning prepared by plaintiff's expert*] and said that that isn't an accurate statement of the risks of RLF as they exist. And they say, "Well, it's not complete; there are other risks." Sure there are! But we're talking about the risk of RLF—mainly we're talking about the risk of doctors' believing that 40 percent oxygen is safe, and the risk of keeping them ignorant, and the risk of not realizing that you don't give premature infants oxygen just for the sake of giving it. You've got to cut the oxygen down and see how the child gets along. That is the way you prevent RLF. That is why they had that policy at other hospitals in 1970. That is the policy that should have been adopted by General Hospital.

You now know, you understand the problems that are faced by one who is outnumbered, as we are in this case, when it comes to developing evidence with appropriate experts. But I think I'd rather have—instead of somebody that has been conferring and working to protect corporate interests—I think I would rather go by what's in the medical journals that are written for the benefit of the doctors. Not for the benefit of a lawsuit, not for the benefit of trying to protect Aerobator or the hospital. But the knowledge that is disseminated throughout the country for the benefit of doctors to look at, that a doctor would stand by, that he would write and put out to help other doctors understand how to protect these babies. Dr. Paul—and this is one of the things that has come to you before in the evidence—in the *American Journal of Ophthalmology* in 1967, he made this statement: "Pediatricians need to have the constant reminder of the dangers of excessive oxygenation beyond clinical needs now, as they did in the 1950s." In other words, he was saying that they still don't realize that you don't give it unless the child needs it, and that just giving him oxygen up to 40 percent is going to cause RLF. Even as recently as 1970, authorities like Dr. Alpind thought that "at the present time the general belief is that oxygen concentrations of 40 percent are innocuous." A fancy way to say harmless. The doctors were told that it was harmless.

Aerobator knew people believed this. Their own medical people knew that doctors believed those words. But they did nothing—nothing to tell people that it was an erroneous belief. They could have sent a letter for the price of a postage stamp. They could have at least spent fourteen cents on a sticker. All the articles that had been written—Paul, Kinsey, Locke, Alpind, Baum, Tizzard, the *British Medical Journal*—they all said, "We studied it." They all said that there is no difference in mortality rates between groups given oxygen routinely and restricting it to clinical needs. And that is what we're talking about, restricting it to when the child needs it.

I'll tell you another erroneous belief, an untruth. The defense says that if I talk to you about Rusty at all, I'm asking for sympathy. How on earth do you decide a case if you don't try to understand what is involved? Yet that is what they suggest you're supposed to do. Close your eyes to Rusty's plight and all that you know, and go back and just do something. Don't even think about Rusty.

That type of philosophy is what brought us here in the first place. Because the manufacturer and the hospital would not consider children like Rusty. They won't face them, and they tell you if you do, then you are being sympathetic. But there is a big difference between sympathy and empathy. Sympathy means that you hurt and I hurt with you. Empathy means you hurt and I understand. That's all we have asked. For people to understand what we are talking about—with blindness—forever.

I've heard that God's most precious gift is sight. And I believe that has been brought to our attention in this case. Sight is important for two reasons that come to my mind. One is for survival. One is for enjoyment. We need sight to survive, and it is the reason God gave all his creatures sight, because it is essential to survive. Survival in this modern world means survival from danger. You know, there aren't many dangers that you might hear. You might hear a car, but it's hard to tell where it is, just listening to it. And as a child, or as an adult, all the things we might run into today, if you think about them, are things we avoid by sight. We need our sight to survive, in order to purchase things for ourselves, to work and earn money and do the things we have to do to survive in this world.

And then we use our sight for enjoyment. I don't know about you, but I don't hear many noises that are pleasurable to me anymore. I go out on a street or even in the country, and only a few sounds are really pleasurable. But really most of the things we do for pleasure are things we see. They are things we use our eyes to see.

What do we know about blindness? I know, for example, in the olden days, in the Bible it talks about if someone had committed a serious sin that they would blind him. That was the most hideous punishment they could think of—blinding. And it's been hundreds of years since any society did that. We don't allow it. If I committed the most heinous crime you could think of, there is no court in our country that would allow that as my punishment—to be blind for life.

We've just passed Christmas time, and I'm blessed with three children, and I know what they got for Christmas. I know that what they got was not what Rusty got. My boys got a telescope. A lot of good a telescope would do for Rusty. They got footballs and helmets. A lot of good that would do for

Rusty. Even an electric train, how would he use it? What could he do with it? Particularly, you know, if you've ever tried to put one of them together, what would he do? I don't know.

The only way it seems to me that you can reasonably evaluate Rusty's blindness is to take a good look at your own lives—for example, your childhood. All of us have memories of a childhood. For most of us they're pleasant memories. There are good things we remember, and there are things that when we want to feel good we remember doing. I bet every one of them was something you did with your eyes, something you saw, something that if you didn't have your eyes you could not have done. As an adolescent growing up, the things you have to see to enjoy doing as a boy: meeting girls, playing sports, and learning to drive a car. I think in my mind of all the things I enjoyed doing growing up as a teenager, and I can run them through my mind. And every one of them I had to see to do. If I couldn't have seen, I couldn't have done them. And if I couldn't have seen, I would not have had the enjoyment.

I think of myself, for example, as a relatively young man. Rusty, whether he goes to college or doesn't go to college as a young man, his time will come. Sometime in the future he will go out and try to earn a livelihood, and even today getting and keeping a job is not the easiest thing to do. You've got to be a solid individual. But how would you like to try to support yourself if you were blind? I'm asking, in a general sense, how would anybody support themselves if they were blind? But you know, the most important thing about life, it seems to me, is not just the work. The work is part of it. But it's the pleasure, too. Because we work to be able to do the things we want to do.

What does it mean to be able to watch a Super Bowl? We're at that time of year. Or the Cotton Bowl? Or go fishing or hunting? It's that time of year. All the things that all of us live for, something special that we want to do. You can think—anyone in the audience can think—what do I like to do when I have the time, I've got my work set aside, and I want to do something for pleasure? Think about it. In almost every instance you have to be able to see.

We ask for nothing but what Rusty is entitled to under the evidence, and under that evidence we ask that you please consider and answer the first six issues "yes." We ask that you answer these issues [*referring to blowup of indicated issues and answers on doctors' responsibility*] "no," and we ask you to award Rusty full damages.

I don't know what full damages are. I know you can get up as the defense did and you can say, "Well, that's too much; it ought to be less." But, you know, anything less than full justice is not justice, it's half justice. And half justice is no justice at all—it's injustice. No one should ever have to settle for less than what is rightfully theirs. You make that decision. You make it as people, though; you make it as people who can use their wisdom to determine what blindness means. That is why we have to have people to decide cases.

I wish that there was some kind of—I can't even wish this, it's so bad—but just for illustrative purposes, I wish there was some way to take a machine so that, instead of having you folks sit here, we could take some people and make them blind for a few days. Or just for a day. Let them try to get around and try to do the things they want to do. So that they could then sit here after we turn the machine off and decide: What is a day of blindness worth?

And they would come up with some figure, whatever, for a day of blindness. Can you imagine what the difference would be—what the figure would be—if we took those same people, we brought them in, and we said, "Now, what is a day of blindness worth?" And they say, "Well, we're going to tell you. Turn the machine off so that we can see." And we turn the machine off, but they still can't see. We say, "Oh, my God, we didn't know. We thought the procedure was acceptable. No one told us. There was no warning on the machine to tell us it was permanent—we thought it was safe." Now what? What is a day of blindness worth? This is a verdict that will speak to a number of issues. It must speak to the responsibility of a manufacturer. It must speak to the responsibility of a hospital. In order to speak where it will be heard, it must reflect the damages that have been proved. If your verdict does not speak to that, the message will never reach those whom it must reach in order for things to change. This is, I think, a very momentous case. It is a verdict that will have significance for a number of reasons. And I know that when you return your verdict it will be one that you will be proud of as a jury. You'll be proud to be able to say, when people ask you about it, "Well, that was the jury I was on. I gave four weeks of my life to decide these critical issues, but I can tell you all about the case."

We appreciate it very much. We will await your deliberations. When you're through, Rusty won't be able to see you, but I know he will want to touch each one of your hands.

29

The Case of the Nurse Who Wasn't Borrowed

A Hospital Liability Argument

THE CAUSE OF ACTION accrued when the plaintiff was administered the wrong medication during routine nasal surgery. The evidence established that the medications nurse in the operating room was instructed by the anesthesiologist to obtain a tranquilizing agent, Inapsine. Instead, the nurse filled the syringe she gave the anesthesiologist with Levophed, a vasoconstrictor. She filled the syringe with the improper medication, labeled it "Inapsine," and handed it to the anesthesiologist. He administered it to the plaintiff, with the result that the plaintiff sustained a heart attack on the operating room table.

The principal problem presented in this case was determining damages. The plaintiff returned to work following a short hospitalization. He worked constantly at the same job after his return. The hospital defended its case on the grounds that the nurse was the borrowed servant of the anesthesiologist and that the damages actually sustained by the plaintiff were minimal. Hence, the challenge presented by this case was to motivate the jury to find significant damages for the plaintiff—in the face of relatively negative diagnostic testing on the plaintiff following his injury as well as a good work record until the time of trial. An offer of $25,000 was rejected, a verdict of $2 million was returned, and justice was served.

Opening Argument

May it please this honorable court, counsel for General Hospital, Dr. Jones, Mr. and Mrs. Smith and members of their family, and the other folks who are interested in this case: I would be remiss, I think, if I did not at the very beginning acknowledge and thank each of you for the time and sacrifice you have made to sit as a juror in this case.

I know that in one juror's situation, a particular sacrifice was made, and sacrifices have been made by all of you. You have taken time from your family and from your work to decide this case for us. We believe we have brought you an important case, an important issue, and I can assure you, as the lawyer

---

Note: The argument in this chapter, with the recitation of facts, was first published in Perdue, *The Law of Texas Medical Malpractice*, 22 HOUS. L. REV. 500-18 (2d ed. 1985).

for Mr. Smith, that if I didn't believe it was important or if I didn't believe this was vital and crucial to this family and he wasn't concerned about the importance of this, we wouldn't have imposed on you to this extent. You are now, as a jury, according to our procedures and according to your oath, about to assume, after you listen to the lawyers, an important responsibility. You are asked to decide issues that will affect one of your neighbors for the rest of his life. The evidence has indicated that is the kind of situation we are talking about.

It is an awesome responsibility. As I have told each of you on voir dire, I have never had the opportunity to sit in those chairs, but I can imagine the responsibility that everyone who has ever taken those chairs in a case like this must feel.

I will note that the court has given you certain instructions that you are obligated to follow, and then the court tells you that you must answer certain questions for the court. Based on your answers to these questions, the court will then render what is called a legal judgment in this case, which sets out the rights and responsibilities of the various parties.

You decide the questions that the court has presented, and the court really has presented to you only five questions. Actually, there are three. One of them happens to be broken down into three parts.

To help you follow—and I am not going to get into this in great detail—but you will see there is a Question 1 that asks whether or not Nurse Green was Dr. Jones's borrowed servant, as has been contended. If you answer Question 1 "no," you don't even have to answer Question 2. Then you go to Question 3, which are the damages that you find have been and will be sustained by Mr. Smith for the rest of his life. His physical pain and mental anguish in the past, his physical pain and mental anguish in the future. His loss of income in the past and future. It is a very simple part of the questions asked you by the court. And, as the court indicated, you can arrive at the verdict with fewer than twelve people, which means to say that if any ten of you decide on all the answers, you agree on the answers, you cannot be kept from reaching a verdict by one or two persons in a case like this. We won't have to try the case over again simply because one person, for whatever reason, cannot understand what has been presented and cannot follow the evidence and cannot follow the court's charge.

During the voir dire examination Mr. Thompson [the defense attorney] referred to me as well traveled. I took no personal offense at that comment, because it is to some extent accurate. I have tried cases in just about every part of this state—a lot of places that are a lot smaller than Victoria, I will tell you, and not as nice as Victoria.

I have represented injured patients throughout this state. I have represented them in the Panhandle, I have represented them in Jasper, I have represented them in the Valley. And there is a reason for that, and you know the reason. It is very difficult when a patient is injured, when someone is injured, to get an attorney in that town to sue the hospital or the doctor in that town. But I feel a responsibility to try to do something about things such as happened to Roque Smith. So I go to Victoria, and I will go to Jasper, and I will go to the Valley.

Now, in my twenty years of practice I can tell you I have seen a lot of things. I have seen doctors who didn't care about their patients. I have seen doctors who were more interested in money than rendering good care. I have seen doctors who tried to shift their responsibility to nurses. I guess I have seen about all of it.

When I have seen it, I have pointed it out. I have criticized it; I have challenged it. I think it is my responsibility to do so.

In this case there is some conduct on the part of this hospital that I will comment on in my argument to you here in the beginning and have further comment on probably, depending on what Mr. Thompson says.

There have been things done by the hospital that I think are reprehensible by both the hospital and their counsel. But in good conscience I have to get up here and as a lawyer and officer of the court who is dedicated and has taken an oath to bring to you what we believe to be true and accurate and to be honest with everybody at all times—whether it be jurors or opposing counsel or witnesses—I have to tell you that all the evidence I have seen that has been presented by any of the parties in this case indicates that Dr. Martin Jones was conscientious toward Mr. Smith. Dr. Jones was concerned about Mr. Smith, was truthful with Mr. Smith and his family, and has been completely candid and honest with you and them about what happened.

I will also tell you that a review of the records has led me to believe that if Dr. Jones had not been honest with Mr. Smith, Mr. Smith probably would never have known what happened.

Now, we initially named Dr. Jones as a defendant, because while our investigation indicated clearly that this was an incident that shouldn't have happened, that was tragic and needless, it certainly was not clear whose responsibility it was. From the very beginning you heard the hospital filing pleadings claiming that Dr. Jones was negligent. And I had to, in representing Mr. Smith, name Dr. Jones in this lawsuit. But I have to tell you in all candor that I don't think he is in the lawsuit.

This attempting to cast responsibility on Dr. Jones by the hospital, I think, is not only unfortunate but also irresponsible. So I must tell you on behalf of Mr. and Mrs. Smith—and I speak for them as though they were standing here talking to you right now because that is what they would tell you if they had the opportunity to speak to you, having heard the evidence and seeing what we have seen—that Dr. Jones should not share any responsibility for this needless tragedy. And he shouldn't share the responsibility under any theory, under any concept or any what has been called technical defense.

Now an interesting thing that you will note, and you can see why—there are no questions now presented to you on the negligence of the hospital, because the court has taken that issue from you. You don't have to decide that.

The evidence is so clear, it is so convincing, it is so overwhelming that no jury needs to pass on that.

This incident happened because the hospital not only was negligent, it was reckless. This was, in the words of Dr. Jones, an unthinkable kind of occurrence. So we go from Questions 1 and 2 to Question 3, which are the damages issues.

Now, our procedure is such that Mr. and Mrs. Smith and I and the Smith family are required to take a position with you about what we believe we have proved by way of damages. That is appropriately so. After we take a position, the defense has an opportunity to respond to that. Then we have an opportunity to answer their response.

It is particularly appropriate in a case like this, where the defense of this case has vacillated, shifted throughout the trial of the case, that we be entitled to take a position, and for one time have the defense take a position clearly where they are and then let us respond to it.

You will note that the question is simply what damages should be found to have been sustained by Roque Smith for his mental anguish and his physical pain in the past, part *a*. For his mental anguish and physical pain in the future, part *b*. And for his loss of earning capacity.

On the voir dire the hospital got up and said, "Well, we believe somebody owes Mr. Smith something; but the issue is who owes it." I submit to you there isn't any question about who owes the money. We began this case, and the hospital's lawyer indicated to you on the voir dire examination—if you will recall, he got up and said to you when you were sitting out where all the folks are now, and I made a careful note of this—that there was absolutely no evidence that Mr. Smith suffered any chest pain or made any complaints of any chest pain until after he had hired a lawyer. Now, that has been over a week ago, and maybe some of you have forgotten that. There are a lot of things that have happened in between, but that was the initial position taken by the hospital.

You recall one of the first things we did with Mr. Smith is point out that the record clearly indicates he was having chest pains in the hospital. He made complaints when he went back to work, and he has continued to have problems, as documented by his coworkers. You will note that when he went over to see the cardiologist in Houston his complaints were shortness of breath, chest pain, and other things that were indicated. The employer's records have also indicated those kinds of problems.

Now, the position of the hospital, as near as I can make it out, seems to be that Mr. Smith has not complained enough and he hasn't gone to the dispensary and said, "I want you to write in the record that I am having chest pain." As you have heard from coworkers, he will have problems on the job and sit down, and he had difficulty doing his work. But since he hasn't gone down and made sure somebody made an entry of it every time, he hasn't complained enough.

There is obviously a reason for that. I would gather from all this, putting it all together, ladies and gentlemen of the jury, that it certainly is fair to say that the defense evidently does not contend that Mr. Smith has exaggerated his complaints. The evidence is that Mr. Smith was given a dangerous drug, a drug in a way and a drug in a dose that has never, to our knowledge, been given to a human being in this manner before. This drug has produced heart damage, and it has probably produced brain damage, and it has probably produced some other damage we may not even know about.

Now the issue to be decided by you, then, when you get to parts *a* and *b* of Question 3 is—and you will see clearly—what damages should be found for the mental anguish that Mr. Smith has experienced in the past and will experience in the future as a result of this incident.

Now when you read that issue you will see the issue is not—and I underline *not*—that some other person might have worried more or that some other person might have been less frightened, might have less anguish, or whatever. That is not the issue.

The issue is what mental anguish has this man experienced. That is what you decide, and that is why we brought you evidence and the court rightfully admitted evidence from his coworkers and his wife and the people who know him about the kind of problems he has had.

The issue isn't that somebody else might have worried less or, as suggested by the defendant, that maybe he ought not to worry as much. The issue is what worry he has experienced and will experience. And I submit to you that the anguish experienced by anyone—the fear, the concern—who experiences a heart attack and recovers from a heart attack is tremendous. It is one of those things that when I was twenty-five I don't think I could understand. When I was thirty, I don't think I could understand. I am now forty-five, and I have been practicing at the pace I am practicing at for about twenty years. As far as I know, I am all right, I am healthy; but I will assure you that when you get up to my age it is a thing that if it were to occur to you it would worry you greatly.

It would be of tremendous concern, because when you have a heart attack, and if you have been around loved ones who have and if you have seen that kind of thing, you know that you look death right square in the face. And not just when it happens, but in the days that follow when you don't know whether you are going to have to look at it again.

It has affected Mr. Smith's ability to sleep. He has developed a stomach ulcer. It has affected his enjoyment of life.

You know, when you start thinking about the mental anguish that Mr. Smith will experience in the future, you must first concern yourself with what period of time we are talking about. He is forty-four years of age. According to the statistics, if he does not die early because of this condition, he has thirty years of life left—10,050 days—262,800 hours.

Now, the defense is going to say, "Well, after all, just a year of worry"; but when you are worrying about the kind of things he has, and when you have trouble sleeping, and when you are worried about providing for your family and you have got these children, you don't experience them in one year just like that. Those things bother you every hour of every day. And when you go to consider the damages for the physical pain and mental anguish in the past as well as those, more importantly, in the future, you have to look at it the way this man has to look at it—by the hour.

I am going to suggest to you that we have proved—realizing that the experience of a heart attack, just the having of a heart attack under that reckless type of circumstances, for the mental anguish and physical pain — that he should be awarded $300,000 for the physical pain. And for mental anguish in the future you should find damages in the amount of $700,000, when you consider that you are talking about 262,000 hours, assuming that he does not find himself, because of the brain hemorrhage and because of the heart problems, not living for that time.

Now, when you consider the issue particularly on future physical pain and mental anguish, you must consider first the period of time we are talking about. I have discussed that, and you must consider what kind of anguish Mr. Smith has had.

We have brought you evidence about what kind of anguish he has had from Mrs. Smith, Emily Smith, coworkers—including Mr. Clark whom you have just heard this morning. They have told you about Mr. Smith's worry, his pain, his difficulties. And I think it is a fair inquiry, since we are opening our argument and since we have suggested and taken a clear, straightforward position with you, to ask these defendants to get up and for once and for all address you and say whether they are suggesting that you should not believe Mrs. Smith, Emily Smith, and these coworkers when they have told you what he has gone through? If that is their position, let them get up and say it, so that everyone can understand that is their position. I think in fairness we are entitled to know that, and I think you are entitled to know that.

You know, a lot of things go into mental anguish, it seems to me. I know in talking to Roque—and there is only one way to represent a client, and that is to really live with him, to get to know him. A lot of things, when you watch somebody on the stand or you hear about it, may not really sink in. But just being around him and seeing what he is going through, you start getting a feel for things that maybe you wouldn't otherwise have.

I can tell you something that would affect me and has affected Roque from the evidence. It is not only that he has got this damage done to his body—that is agonizing enough, that is frightful enough, that is frustrating enough. But to listen and hear how needless this was, how reckless this was, has got to make you even—I can't use the word "angry," but I can sure use the word "anguish." And it has got to make you think, my goodness, how can people condone this kind of thing: of turning a nurse loose in an operating room with the responsibility for medication and not one person ever telling her what she was supposed to do in order to see that those medications were handled safely.

Now there is another thing that I think plays a role in mental anguish in this case. That is the unknown. You know, it is sad that the thing we all fear the most is the unknown. We are concerned and we fear the dark because we don't know what is there.

The defense has pointed out that there are certain things that we haven't established, that we don't know for sure. And I submit to you that the unknown is a thing that frightens Roque and would frighten any reasonable person.

The next issue, the last element of damage deals with earning capacity. You have just heard Mr. Clark testify about the increase in wages at plaintiff's employer over the last ten years, about eight percent a year. Earning capacity is the capacity to earn money, your ability, your capacity to earn and make a living. We all have it; all of us who work and those of us who don't work have a capacity to earn money.

When one is charged with determining the loss of earning capacity, it would seem to me reasonable that you would have to first determine, before you can address yourself to the loss of earning capacity, what was the man's capacity to earn money before this happened. What capacity did he have before he went into General Hospital?

If you take the wages he is making now at Employer, Inc., and you raise them eight percent every year, you will get an idea of what he will be making. I know some of the figures look pretty big, and you say, "My goodness, I can't believe they will be making that much at Employer, Inc., twenty years from now." But Mr. Clark just testified, you know, it is kind of hard to remember when those people were working for ninety-five cents an hour, twenty years ago. It is hard for you to believe back then that you could be making fifteen dollars an hour now. It is hard for us to remember that twenty years ago wages were as small as they were. And it is hard for that reason to imagine that Roque will be making $63,000 a year if he keeps his job, if he just gets the standard raises, no promotions and nothing else.

What I am saying to you is that, if you take Roque's wages and assume he never got another promotion, you assume that you are not even counting what we call the fringe benefits—which are significant—and you are to determine, assuming that Roque works to sixty-five years of age, what his capacity would be before he went into General Hospital, his capacity, his future earning capacity from today was $2 million. In excess of $2 million. That was his capacity before it was damaged.

Now your job is to take that, it seems to me, and say, "All right, now to what extent has that capacity been damaged?" I will tell you from the court's charge that you will see the mere fact that the man continues to work does not mean that his capacity to earn money has not been affected. We have brought you evidence about what would happen if he had to try to get another job. We have brought you evidence about how this is going to affect his ability at the company itself.

If you were, for example, to simply believe that his capacity to earn money, his earning capacity, has been affected by twenty-five percent, that is $500,000, if you believe simply twenty-five percent.

We know that we bring you a difficult task. We know that we bring you an awesome responsibility. But we are satisfied that it is in very good hands.

Thank you very much.

Closing Argument

May it please this court. I do not have the good fortune to live here in Victoria, as has been pointed out. From what I have seen of your city, I wish that I did. It is a fine place.

But it really doesn't matter whether you live in Victoria, or Houston, or wherever. What happened to Roque could happen to any one of us. Life being what it is, some day—it may be next week, it may be next year—I will be in the hospital. I have got three fine sons; one of them will be in the hospital. My wife will be in the hospital. Your brother, your mother, your children could be in the hospital.

I would be scared to death, having heard what I have heard in this case, to be in General Hospital. Did anyone think it was significant at all, or did it mean anything to anyone to realize when something like this happens, unless you have an honest doctor like this man sitting here, you will never know about it?

The medical chart you get when a medication error is made, unless you have an honest doctor like this man sitting over here, who puts it in the record and who goes to Houston with it to try and verify exactly how that error was made—it is not in this medical chart.

So if you lose a son, you lose a daughter, you lose a mother or father or wife or husband or whatever, and you go and you say, "Lawyer, would you get my records for me; something just doesn't seem right." And the lawyer gets the records, and he looks through them and says, "Well, it doesn't seem right to me either, but I can't find any explanation for it in here."

Because, you see, folks, we don't know that when something like this happens and a report is prepared that tells us all the details about what happened, that report is not part of the hospital records. That report goes to the administrative office. That report is put down in a file that you cannot get and that it took us four days of proof before this judge, fighting for it, to get it in so you could see it.

If it does happen to you, something as tragic and needless as this, and you go down to the administrator and you sit down, as this man and his wife did, the administrator's first comment to you is not, as Mr. Thompson indicates, "Gee, we are sorry this happened. We want you to know about this mistake. We want to explain this to you."

The first comment from the administrator is, "Well, what do you think happened?" What do you think happened? This man was lying there on the table. He didn't know what happened. He had no way of knowing what happened.

That statement by the administrator is yet to be denied. Why do you think the administrator asked this man, "What do you think happened?" He wanted to find out; he didn't know that this honest doctor had told this honest man about what had happened, because if he hadn't, do you think this man would have ever known to even ask a lawyer to get the records and take a look at them and pursue it?

Now you heard that actually the culprit in the lawsuit, the reason that you are here, is me. It is not this hospital or anything they have done.

Now, I will tell you that I am subject to some criticism. I am not going to suggest otherwise. I do some things in trying lawsuits, and after I do them I think, "Boy, I wish I had asked this question of that witness. I wish I had been smarter. I wish I had been stronger and done something a little different."

But I'll tell you what I haven't done: I have never sat in a case that I have ever represented anybody on with a report like this and knowing what happened, as this hospital and their lawyers did in April of this year. Having this report to look at and having the report of the doctor as to what happened and getting requests for admissions that I am required to answer under oath and answering them under oath in what we lawyers call verified pleading, the highest kind of pleading that a lawyer can be required to file, and saying, "I don't know anything about it. I don't know how the drugs were stored. I don't know how they got mixed up, if they got mixed up at all."

Yet that is what these lawyers for that hospital did, and I am the one who is subjected to criticism. It is a typical tactic; I see it all over the place. These kinds of tragedies happen at the hospital, and who is at fault? Who is responsible for the jury's having to face these difficult issues? The lawyer who will stand up and represent the patient.

Then they bring Nurse Green in, and she admits that she has told five versions of what happened. And she has met with this lawyer three or four times and admits from the witness stand that the purpose of those conferences was to try and see if they couldn't get up some kind of version. And you know what version they were trying to get up? It wasn't that they didn't make an error; it was what they could get up to pin it on this doctor. It was how they could make her a borrowed servant.

Now you know that we lawyers have ethics, we say, and a lot of folks would doubt that, and rightly so. But I will just ask you this question: Is that kind of conduct of answering questions under oath when you have got information—that kind of conduct of trying to tell a nurse what she ought to say, whether it is true or not—is that the kind of thing that is designed to try to help you folks arrive at a reasonable, fair verdict for this man in this case?

Now it may be that those kinds of things don't bother people anymore, I don't know. I guess I am old-fashioned enough that they still bother me. When a lawyer files a verified pleading and swears to it, it ought to be true.

When a lawyer talks to a witness, he ought to be trying to get the truth out of that witness and not trying to help her with whatever version she can come up with to put it on a man who has been honest.

It did not surprise me, because of that conduct, that it turns out that Mr. Thompson is able to go and sit down with Dr. Oaks, a physician on the staff of General Hospital, and talk to him in detail about Mr. Smith's medical condition without having an authorization from Mr. Smith or a court order to do so. It does not surprise me.

It would frighten me to know that just because a lawyer represents the hospital he can go talk to that doctor and that doctor will tell him anything that that lawyer wants to know.

Now I have no objection to their going out and talking to Dr. Oaks, but we would have asked to have been present. We don't have anything to hide. But I will tell you that I do not have respect for people who don't adhere to the ethics of their profession, whether they are lawyers, or doctors, or whatever.

If you want to put, Mr. Thompson, on your plaque at the hospital, if you want it to read correctly, don't put lofty principles up like a mission to obtain international leadership in the health care field. Those are a bunch of words, because the way you are running that hospital out there, you and some of the members of the staff, it ought to read that the mission of the hospital is to protect the hospital and the investors, as it says later on, at all costs. That is number one. Number two, all others pay cash. And you don't need any other rules.

I don't think this hospital really cares what this jury does. This good doctor has not missed a single minute of testimony. He cares. Have you seen a representative of the hospital sit here during the trial of this case? Have you seen any representatives that you can identify out here?

I am going to tell you, ladies and gentlemen, that the only way you are going to get that hospital's attention is to award full damages in this case. And if you don't do it, it is going to happen again. You can bet on it.

Now, in order for you to perform your job as jurors in answering these damages issues, you have to try to understand how Mr. Smith feels. It is very easy for a lawyer like Mr. Thompson to stand back and say, "Well, why worry, Roque? Just get rid of your lawyer, and you will be all right." That is very easy to say.

You folks who are charged with the responsibility know that your job is to try to understand how he feels and what his problems are and what it would be like to have this kind of thing happen to you with these kinds of problems. But the easiest thing to say is, "Well, don't worry about it."

I can't help but remember this story about Abraham Lincoln. I am an Abraham Lincoln fan, I admit it. I think he was not only a great president but one of the best lawyers who ever lived. But Abraham Lincoln tells about going to New Orleans when they were still flogging people. Back in those days, public flogging was still being done.

They asked him what he thought of the flogging. Abraham Lincoln said, "You know, I can't understand how one human being can take a whip and flog another one. I can't understand that." And as to the crowds that were gathered around there that would stand and watch, he said, "I can't understand those people either that will stand and watch one human being flog another one. But you know, the thing that I really can't understand is the people out in the street that would walk along and see the flogging and turn and continue on their way as though nothing was happening."[1]

Mr. Smith was given a drug that to our knowledge has never been given in that amount in that way to an experimental animal. To a hamster. To a rabbit.

Dr. Jones was honest enough to say it, and Dr. Buckley, the pharmacologist, will tell this man, "You are lucky to be here." But that doesn't mean his damages are any less.

The fact that he has sustained this damage has been confirmed by the medical records and the doctors who have seen him. And there is no—and it is beyond dispute—drug he can take.

You know, Mr. Smith, contrary to Dr. Oaks's testimony, has abnormal EKG findings. It was demonstrated in Houston, but, as you heard, the damage that this drug does is to a part of the heart that doesn't normally show up on an EKG. Yet he has those findings. The extent of that damage, unfortunately, we will never know until the autopsy.

We do know this about the drug. We do know from the pharmacologist that the effects of that drug are progressive, even though we do not know how they progress. Because as you heard the pharmacologist tell you, the effects depend so greatly on when we, in his words, sacrifice the animal and cut the animal open and see what is going on inside.

Mr. Smith has difficulty sleeping, which is verified in the records and by people who have seen him. He has developed a stomach ulcer. I suppose that, according to Mr. Thompson's theory, I have given him a stomach ulcer.

I asked Mr. Thompson if he would get up and say what he believed, and he did. And, if you accept it, then I guess you ought to do what Mr. Thompson suggests, which is not very clear to me at this point. He wouldn't address you on damages and suggest what he thinks is a figure. I wish he had. But he won't get up and say, "No, I only think $200,000 ought to be awarded for future pain and suffering and mental anguish." That is less than a dollar an hour. He won't do that.

You know, when we get to the age of some of us, we begin to wonder what we have accomplished in life. I know I am at that stage. But the longer I am around, the more I realize that life has meaning to you only as long as you

---

1. The originator of this colorful anecdote is Bill Allen, a "well-traveled" Houston trial attorney.

can clearly draw some lines between right and wrong. If you stand up for what is right, you are living. If you pursue what is wrong, you are as dead as a coonskin cap, in the words of Davy Crockett.

Now you have an opportunity, it seems to me, to do something very right and very meaningful by your verdict, or something very wrong. But there is one thing I want you to understand. Regardless of what you do, don't think for one minute, because it is not true, that if you make a mistake this judge will straighten it out or one of the appellate courts will straighten it out. It can't be done. Your verdict is final for all time. I can't come back and say, "Your Honor, for God's sake, give us another trial. Let us have another jury decide the case; they made a mistake." He doesn't have that power, and there isn't a judge in this state who has that power.

We have got to, by your verdict, ladies and gentlemen, send a message to this hospital that when we come into your hospital, be careful with us. And if you give less than adequate damages I will tell you that message will never reach them. And you not only encourage what happened by way of this case, you also encourage what has happened by the manner in which this case has been defended, because it will work. And if it works this time they will try it again.

There is one thing that the defense has not mentioned and did not even discuss during the trial of the case, did not discuss at all with you during argument, particularly on the damage issue. But I think it bears mentioning, and I think it is a very significant issue. There is not one shred of evidence that this man did a single thing to contribute to his injury; that he failed to do anything; that he did do anything that in any way contributed to whatever injury he has. And now your verdict takes a lot of strong people to do what is right in a case like this. And when somebody gets back in the jury room with you and starts saying, "Well, let's do some trading, let's compromise with Mr. Smith," I hope our friends on the jury will ask one simple question: "What can you show me that the man did that means he ought to get less than full damages?" You are absolutely right; it is appropriate for a jury to award less than full damages when the man himself has contributed to his injury. But I hope that when that happens somebody will say, "Tell me one thing that Mr. Smith did wrong other than put his complete confidence in the people who were supposed to be trained to take care of him."

I will tell you that I know this service has been a sacrifice to you, as all the lawyers have indicated. I think that sacrifice will be in vain if your verdict is anything less than the full damages we have proved.

Roque Smith is a good citizen. Mr. Thompson implied otherwise when he made the statements he did. But Roque is a good citizen, and he is a responsible family man. He is a good employee, and he supports his church and his community.

He comes to this courthouse for justice, and he has never before in his life asked twelve people for a thing. And he doesn't ask for anything now except what he is entitled to under the law.

I can't help but ask you—in this day and time it seems we are all concerned about the rights of the criminal; the criminal does this and does that and he has so many rights—and when are we going to start worrying about the victims? When are we going to start looking at the Roque Smiths of the world and say, "It is time we started doing something right by you, sir."

I have heard through this trial, and I have heard from Mr. Thompson again, that, after all, we need not be concerned about Roque because his heart damage is small. His brain hemorrhage is small. His other damages are small. They are all small.

I suppose it is like that story of the doctor who was talking to a patient and said, "Well, we can remove that benign tumor in your neck with a small incision." And the fellow said, "Just where does that incision go to, Doctor?" And the doctor said, "Well, it goes from here to here" [*indicating from ear to ear*]. And the patient said, "Well, Doctor, I guess it depends on which side of the scalpel you are as to what the word *small* means."

I can tell you that it depends on which side of the body you are on when you are talking about this kind of thing. They tell the story about the boy who wanted a toy for Christmas and the family was very poor, but somehow his mother bought the toy. The boy played with the toy Christmas Day, and toward the evening the toy broke and he got upset and carried on and carried on. Finally his mother said, "Son, don't get so upset about small things." And the boy said to his mother, "Mother, what are small things?"

There are things that to some people are small, and there are those things that can be looked at by somebody as being very small and can be very, very serious and very important to someone else.

I can tell you that this is the most important day of Roque's life. You have here in Victoria a very fine courthouse. It is a beautiful courtroom, and it has been my pleasure to try a case before Judge White. I have never been before him until now, but he is a very competent judge, a judge who sits elevated in a robe. We have all these surroundings dedicated to this system that we call the legal system.

But ladies and gentlemen of the jury, all of that doesn't ensure justice for anybody. The only thing that ensures justice is twelve people like yourselves.

This is a difficult task for you, but I ask, if you err in this case—and I hope you will not—I hope the error will be on the side of mercy.

Thank you very much; you have been most attentive.

30

The Case of the Unknown Future

A Hip-Fracture Argument

THE CASE involved a fractured hip sustained by a middle-aged divorced woman. Because the defendant had stipulated liability, the challenge was to obtain full, fair damages for the plaintiff. She had returned to work after a hospital stay of a few weeks and a brief recuperative period. At the time of trial she was earning more money than she earned before the accident. She had continued to be employed in the same capacity at an industrial concern located in Houston. The principal contention advanced by the plaintiff was that the nature of her injury made her susceptible to development of traumatic arthritis in the hip at some later date. Her treating physicians testified by oral deposition that, in their opinion, the development of traumatic arthritis was likely. The defendant called as its expert an orthopedic surgeon who had independently examined the plaintiff and had concluded that the development of traumatic arthritis was not likely in her case. On cross-examination, however, a number of admissions were obtained from that physician about this serious future arthritic complication.

Unfortunately, a transcript of the argument does not reveal the extensive use made of visual aids. Counsel for the plaintiff produced and used a number of visual aids that demonstrated the type of injury she sustained, the manner in which bone heals, and the mechanism of traumatic arthritis.

This argument illustrates the economy of time. The case was tried by the author and his partner, Bob Berry. Bob opened with a fine opening argument, and, in response, the defense argument was quite lengthy, focusing on inconsistencies in the testimony regarding the plaintiff's injuries and limitations.

A jury verdict of just under $500,000 was rendered. This was several times the settlement offer. Before that verdict, the rebuttal went something like this.

Closing Argument

May it please this honorable court, counsel. I heard the other day that the definition of a cynic is one who knows the price of everything but the value of nothing. I think we have just seen an hour of cynicism, and I will tell you that if there are any cynics on this jury who look for the inconsistency where there is none, who like to try to see the bad side of people rather than the good, who would penalize people who try and reward those who won't, you can shut your eyes and ears because I am not going to try to talk to you. But if we have any friends on the jury, I would like to visit with you a little bit about Billie Thomas's case and why she has earned the damages we have proved.

You know, there was a song that was popular a few years ago—a lot of you probably remember it. It went, "Do you need anybody? . . . I'll get by with a little help from my friends." Well, in this case you are Billie Thomas's friends. She cannot get by without your help, and that's why we have the kind of system we do. There is no question that this lady has suffered a significant injury that is going to be progressive in its pain, disability, and medical requirements.

Now I can say without being refuted by any piece of evidence that has come before you that this case has not been proved by a preponderance of the evidence; it has been proved beyond any doubt. Bear in mind what happened. This innocent lady was going to work in a van in the contraflow lane and was hit head-on by an eighteen-wheeler. She was taken to St. Andrew's Hospital, and she sees there an orthopedist by the name of Kelly. She sees him because he is covering the St. Andrew's emergency room that particular day. She doesn't pick him out. I don't pick him out. Mr. Berry doesn't pick him out. He is there as the fellow who, if you were hurt today and you were taken to St. Andrew's with the same kind of injury, you might see Dr. Kelly. He isn't paid $500 an hour.[1] He doesn't work for workers' compensation carriers or come down and present their defenses. He is a treating physician working in a hospital, and Dr. Kelly did what he thinks is appropriate by way of treatment to this lady. Then, at a point in time some nine or ten months after the injury, the question arises, "Well, what is the outlook for this lady? What is her medical prognosis?"

Mr. Jones [*the defense lawyer*] gets up, and he says, "Let me be fair with you. Let me be fair and look at these medical records." This is the record [*referring to blowup of the record*] he has just read from a while ago, and, you know, what he read to you was this sentence right here: "The patient as you know has had an excellent recovery and at this time has no measurable disability"; and he didn't even read any of the rest of it.

Now I would like for you to take a look at the rest of it and ask yourselves as we go along, Is he being fair? He says injuries like this—where the actual force drives the head of the femur into the acetabulum—pose no particular problems or complications if treated properly.

Remember our talking to Dr. Johnson [*the defendant's medical expert*] about that, when the head of the femur is driven into the acetabulum and fractures it, it leads to two possible complications. One is aseptic necrosis. We talked about that. That's bone death where the bone, the hip, just eventually

---

1. The defendant's medical expert had testified that this was his charge per hour for courtroom testimony.

dies. And we have brought you the evidence; we didn't hide it. We brought you the evidence that in her case, thank goodness, that's not a likely complication. It is possible but not likely.

Then Dr. Johnson says the cartilage of the head of the femur, as well as the acetabulum, heals with scar tissue, which can manifest as a late complication in so-called traumatic arthritis of the hip joint and can appear as much as ten years after injury. "This is a serious complication, as it may lead to a long string of conservative measures and possibly even to total hip-replacement osteoplasty if indicated. The incidence of this type of complication in this particular injury is relatively high."

Now, why did he say that? Was he picking it out of the air? Was he making it up? No, because we learned yesterday what happens with this ball and socket that the Good Lord gave us to get around on: when you fracture the acetabulum into segments as hers was fractured and it is displaced, even minimally, you end up with something like this on the inside of your ball and socket on the bone [*referring to blowup*]. Then you remember Dr. Johnson's talking about well, this smooth lining of that socket is torn, too, but when the bone is displaced and torn away, then that smooth lining called the hyaline cartilage is torn, and it doesn't repair itself with the same kind of material. It repairs with scar tissue. You get a rough spot on the inside, and you can't see that on an X ray because that's soft tissue. You get a rough spot over here, and the efficient ball and socket the Good Lord gave us is now as if you took a ball bearing and put a bunch of sand or rocks in it. When it moves it aggravates the joint, and it brings about that initial string or initial insult, which sets up, as inevitably as the sun goes down, traumatic arthritis.

Every single doctor has testified to that effect in this case; even the $500-an-hour expert has said that's why, in this kind of case, this kind of situation, in reasonable probability, "Ms. Thomas, you are going to have traumatic arthritis, and it's going to get worse."

But Dr. Kelly—he wasn't hired by anyone. He is on call at St. Andrew's emergency room; he is asked to give an appraisal of what the future holds for this lady. He hasn't been hired by Mr. Berry. He hasn't been hired by me. He hasn't been hired by Mr. Jones. Dr. Kelly sees her as a doctor attending the emergency room at St. Andrew's Hospital, and he is asked what he thinks would be fair from a medical standpoint by way of disability. And after pointing out that this complication is high, he says therefore he "would assess this patient's high probability of late complication with a 50 percent disability as applied to her left hip for general efficiency."

I will tell you that the biological disability doesn't translate into a 50 percent loss of her capacity. It's probably more than that, because if you have a bad hip and it becomes so painful you can't get around on it, you can't work—that's a total loss of earning capacity. If you have a pickup with a flat tire on it, you might look at it and say, "Well, that pickup truck is 25 percent disabled," but I would like to see you haul a load in it. When you are disabled because you have one bad hip, it translates into a lot more than a 50 percent disability—but that's what he gives her by way of what he calls a biological disability.

One of the issues you have to deal with is how does that injury affect this lady's earning capacity. She is her sole support. She is like a lot of women today. There are those, and I am included, who were raised by a working mother. I know what it is like to have a woman as the head of the household; and when you have got that woman caring for the household, earning capacity is all there is for her. Her children are grown. Is she supposed to—because this reckless defendant ran over her in the contraflow lane—is she supposed to go to her children five years from now and say, "I need you to take care of me"? Is that right? Is that what we ought to do?

If you consider just the figures we have introduced in evidence, this is what Ms. Thomas made [*referring to blowup*]. Does the defense think we have forgotten this evidence? This is what she made her first full year of employment. This is what she made in 1981. You calculate it. You figure it out. You do what you think is right, but I will tell you that the annual increase from 1967 to 1981 was about 14.5 percent. Actually it comes to about 14.8. If you were to then calculate her present earnings up to age sixty-five, you would get an idea of what her earning capacity would be—and it is substantial. That is what her earning capacity would have been if she had not been hurt. And so you have to ask yourselves, "Well, to what extent has that been affected by this injury?" Now, that's loss of earning capacity.

We are not talking about the pain and suffering and the agony. Have we failed somehow to get across with our evidence? Have we as lawyers, Mr. Berry and I, somehow fallen short in conveying what we are talking about?

You know, you use a term *traumatic arthritis*; it's just two words. What happens to these people—because the socket like this begins to be affected—is they have pain. You have heard the testimony. At first the pain is only intermittent. Some days you have it; some days you don't. Some days it's worse than others. It comes and goes. But as this process inevitably sets up, the pain gets worse. It gets more frequent. This poor lady is going to wake up some night and her hip is going to be killing her even on the heating pad. It's going to hurt all the next day. Narcotics will be her only means of relief.

I guess it's because of the things I see representing people like Ms. Thomas, but you could not get me to let one of these fellows put an artificial hip in me. The pain would have to be agonizing before I would let them go to work with their power saws and drills and chisels and polymers that set up chemical processes in your system that can cause anything from death to paralysis, to frozen hips, to whatever. You couldn't get me to do it, and you can't get a lot of people to do it.

You found out yesterday just how straightforward the defense can be, because when the doctor went on the stand and Mr. Jones finished with him, you would have thought that operation was the simplest thing in the world—foolproof, 100 percent effective, the greatest thing since Swiss cheese. But when we got into it, you found out it has a high risk of complications, and the complications are very, very serious. That is why when a person, such as this fine lady, goes to the doctor and the doctor says, "I can do a hip replacement on you," she says, "Well, Doctor, what does it involve?" And he says, "Well, it involves this, but I must tell you, I am required by law to tell you what the risks are." And he goes down those risks just as he said yesterday, "This is what I would do if I were telling any patient to undergo it"—that's why people like Billie Thomas say, "I will go another year in pain if I can. I will try to get by some more before I let you get after me with your power saws and your chisels." That's what we are talking about when we consider what the future holds for this lady in reasonable probability. Excruciating pain, agonizing, progressive pain.

You know, if we had really wanted to put on a show, if this lady were anything other than honest, she would have been limping all over this place. But she has been honest with you in everything she has said and everything she has done; and you folks have watched her, and you have seen that there isn't a false bone in this lady's body other than that bad hip that the defendants brought about. She is an honest lady. She is a truthful lady. She has raised three children. She has been a good citizen. She obeys the city laws. She obeys the state laws. She is a good employee. With all the concern we have these days over the rights of the accused and the rights of criminals, when do we start saying it's time to be concerned about the victims, about the people who obey the laws, the people who are run over on the freeway in the contraflow lane? When do we start saying it's time to look at that? And what happens if we don't?

Mr. Jones, when he was examining Ms. Thomas, asked what I thought was a strange question. He said, "Ms. Thomas, do you object to being your sole support?" She said, "No." No, Mr. Jones, she doesn't object to being her sole support; but she does object, and rightfully so, to having to do it in pain because of a wreck that she didn't do anything to cause. She does object to being deprived of the things she enjoyed, such as golfing and jogging and running around and being able to be independent. Mr. Jones suggests, well, as you get older you don't really need to do that. I am forty-five years old, and my experience is that as you get older, that's when you really start to appreciate being able to do those things. Ms. Thomas does object to the suggestion that this jury ought to gamble with her future, and she really objects to this jury's being asked to gamble with her future by the very people who gambled with her life. This innocent lady could have been killed on that contraflow lane. They gambled with her and everyone in the van. She objects when a defense lawyer gets up to defend a head-on collision on the freeway—and this is all we have been able to bring you about it—and the suggestion is made that it was simply a mistake in judgment. Ms. Thomas objects to the idea that because she has tried—and let's face it, a lot of it is financial necessity—but because she has tried, that somehow her damages should be less than for someone who wouldn't have tried.

When you go back in the jury room, you are going to find that an interesting process happens. I have been talking to jurors for twenty years now, both this way and after the verdict. You are going to find when you get back there, and we have given you what we believe Billie Thomas has earned by way of damages, that there will be one or two jurors who will say, "Yes, the plaintiff proved those damages, but let's compromise. Let's give something a little less. Let's do some trading." When somebody suggests that to you back there and you are, as I indicated, one of our friends, why don't you ask them one question: "Why should I compromise? Why should I do some trading with this lady's future?" It isn't because this senseless wreck was not caused by the flagrant negligence of the defendant. Responsibility has been stipulated, already determined. It isn't because there is any suggestion that this lady did anything to contribute to her own injury. It would be appropriate for you to reduce her damages if she had contributed to her injury, but it is not appropriate to reduce them one penny when she has not. Someone is going to suggest to you, "Well, we ought to do some trading on the damages because the plaintiff could have brought more evidence." I think if anything, we may have been too repetitive with the witnesses, but we wanted you to be able to go back, those people who are our friends, and say "Look, they brought more than one person to verify that. They brought two and three and four and five." We did that so you would have something to work with.

But somebody else might say, "Well, wait a minute. Why didn't the plaintiff bring something from the company over here?" Why don't you ask them this question, "If that was important, if that would have helped the defense, if that would have proved that this lady was entitled to one penny less than what they are asking for, why didn't this defense lawyer bring it?" He has the power to subpoena. Why didn't he bring it? If they had anything they could bring you that would reduce these damages, I can assure you that they would have brought it.

When you come in with your verdict, you will have found the damages that will be administered by His Honor. It's just a verdict. He decides what to do with it, but I will tell you this, he can't add a single penny to it. We have procedures whereby he can reduce it, but he can't add anything to it.

Mr. Jones: Your Honor, I object to Mr. Perdue instructing the jury on the law.

The Court: Overruled.

And you should bear that in mind.

Mr. Jones evidently has some objection to our proving our case with Ms. Thomas's daughter, and son, and neighbor, and good friends, coworkers. He evidently has some objection to our proving this case with Dr. Kelly, who is associated with St. Andrew's Hospital, or with Dr. Travis. He refers to him as the young Dr. Travis. But he has no objection at all to suggesting that perhaps you should decide the case while ignoring all of that and, I guess, basing your decision on the opinions of a $500-an-hour man. I didn't know we had $500-an-hour men. But even if you based your verdict on the defense witnesses, they would support the damages Ms. Thomas has already earned with pain, anguish, and worry, as well as the damages she will earn for the rest of her life.

You know, when he got on the stand, did you notice a difference between the information you had after we asked some questions of him and the information you had when Mr. Jones finished? I take no particular pride in our ability. I am not medically trained, but I can read a medical book. And I have read a lot of medical books—I am not ashamed to admit it—to prepare myself to represent this fine lady just as I would do for any other person in this courtroom who had the same kind of thing happen to him. I will not apologize for Ms. Thomas or for Mr. Berry or for me in proving our case with this lady's friends and relatives and coworkers.

The question of future damages is always troublesome to juries. Bob Berry, in his opening remarks, suggested an analogy to this case that is particularly appropriate. When Abraham Lincoln became President of the United States, he was elected by a plurality—not a majority. He was a despised man, who literally had to sneak into Washington, D.C., to be inaugurated. If one were to write a book, as many have, about this great man, the beginning of the book would paint a depressing picture of a man distrusted by those in power and hated by a great number of Americans. Yet that book, when it was finished, would reveal a man who faced some of this nation's greatest challenges and is responsible for many of the concepts of justice, fair play, and equal rights that we enjoy today.

It is not the first few chapters that are so significant in Ms. Thomas's case. The defense reads those chapters and says to her, "You don't have anything to worry about." It is the chapters that are yet to be written that are so significant to her. According to the statistics and the Good Book, she has thirty chapters left to be written. 10,950 days or pages. It is the pain, the disability, the frustration, the worry, and the torture of those pages that you must concern yourselves about with your verdict.

It is not the brief past of three years that should form the basis for your verdict. The defense says, "Look at history—look at the past." What about the history of that long line of faceless victims who have this injury and have then suffered in the future the pain, the agony and complications that these doctors and the medical books have told us about? Are we to ignore that?

An English poet once wrote, "The Past is like a funeral gone by, / The Future comes like an unwelcome guest."[2]

We would ask that you not gamble with Ms. Thomas's future. The evidence and the law demand that it be compensated, not compromised.

---

2. Edmund Gosse, *May Day, quoted in* J. Bartlett, Familiar Quotations: A Collection of Passages, Phrases, and Proverbs Traced to Their Sources in Ancient and Modern Literature 815b (14th ed. 1968).

31

The Case of the Errant Surgeon

A Surgical Malpractice Argument

THE PLAINTIFF, a young, obese female, submitted to a gastric-stapling procedure by the defendant. The purpose of this procedure is to reduce the size of the stomach, thus producing weight loss. After protracted difficulties, the plaintiff was operated on by another physician, who indicated in his operative report that he removed a staple or staples from the gastroesophageal junction. All the medical witnesses who testified indicated that staples should not be placed in this area. In his original deposition, the subsequent treating physician was fairly helpful in establishing negligence on the part of the defendant. At the time of trial, however, he was less than positive concerning this issue. His testimony may have been influenced by the fact that an attorney who was suing him for a similar incident was in the courtroom taking notes.

The plaintiff's contentions were essentially that the defendant improperly performed the procedure and was negligent in his postoperative care. The defendant countered that there was no showing that the procedure was performed improperly and, further, that the postoperative care was appropriate because the plaintiff's weight loss on each subsequent office and hospital visit was within expected limits. Hence, he contended, the plaintiff could not have been obstructed by the improper placement of staples in the original procedure, because she continued to maintain appropriate weight. The jury verdict found liability on the part of the defendant and awarded substantial damages. And so it went along these lines.

Opening Argument

Ladies and gentlemen, I would be very remiss if I did not, at the outset, on behalf of Paula thank each and every one of you for the attention you have given us during the trial. I don't think I have ever tried a case in which all twelve jurors were as attentive and considerate of the evidence as you have been in this case.

Note: The facts and argument of this case were originally published in Perdue, *The Law of Texas Medical Malpractice*, 22 HOUS. LAW REV. 501, 518–33 (2d ed. 1985).

This is a difficult kind of case for a lawyer to bring on behalf of someone like Paula. It is a difficult thing for Paula to be involved in something like this, but it is a case that I believe you will see—as we discuss what is involved and what the evidence has shown and what has happened in the courtroom—is going to require more than just attentive people to come in with a fair verdict. Just being attentive, just listening, isn't going to do the job. It isn't going to be enough, because you are going to have to use some intelligence and you are going to have to resort to some courage that not all people have. Our system works, and I am not going to wave the flag; I don't think this is an appropriate time for that. But this system that I think we all believe is the finest in the world works because everybody does their job.

This fine judge's job is to rule on the evidence. He applies the law for us. We lawyers don't apply the law; he does. We lawyers each have a job. Our jobs are to bring you the evidence so that you have something to base your verdict on. But the hardest job and the thing that makes the system work is your job, and that is to decide the case. Your verdict, these answers to issues that have been submitted to you by the court, will form the basis for what is called the court's judgment. By that I mean, after you return your verdict, His Honor will look at the answers, and applying the law and some things that may not even be in the record before you, but applying the law and applying your findings, he then comes up with a judgment. In this case there're only two judgments that have been asked for. One is that Paula recover the damages you find, considering such reduction as may be appropriate based on the law and other factors that you should not consider. The other judgment that has been asked for by the defendant is that it doesn't matter what you find by way of damages—Paula shouldn't recover anything. Those are the only two judgments that are involved here, and that is why the court tells you in this charge that every single answer to every issue is important, because if you change one single answer, you change completely the judgment that His Honor will render. You can change night to day or day and light to darkness. That's how important your answers to the issues are.

We told you on the voir dire and Mr. Jackson [the defense attorney] told you that for Paula to recover and for her to have a right to recover, it is our obligation to prove to you by a preponderance of the evidence essentially three things: negligence, proximate cause, and damage. You now see from the issues that have been submitted to you by the court that those are in essence the questions that the court presents to you, for you to find for us, for you to decide for us.

Now the evidentiary standard, or the standard that you use to determine the answer to these questions, is the same for us as it is for the defendant. It is by preponderance of the evidence, the greater weight and degree of the credible evidence. The court says that negligence means failure to use ordinary care. And then the court helps you some more where he says ordinary care means that degree of care that a physician of ordinary prudence treating a surgical patient would use—in other words, the care a surgeon uses under the same or similar circumstances. The court further tells you that, insofar as a doctor is concerned, proximate cause means simply: did the doctor's carelessness cause the problem, and then was it the kind of thing the doctor knew or should have reasonably foreseen that if he did, that if he did it a certain way, it would cause some problems. Those are by way of definition to help you understand the questions that are asked of you.

Issue 1 asks, "Was the doctor negligent in the manner in which he performed the surgery?" We say that we have established by the preponderance of the evidence that the answer to that issue should be "yes."

Issue 2 says, "Was it a proximate cause of damages and injuries to Paula?" We say that by the preponderance of the evidence the answer to that issue should be "yes."

Issue 3 asks whether or not the doctor rendered appropriate postoperative care, and we say that by the preponderance of the evidence the answer to that should be "yes."

[*The various issues are then discussed.*]

Our contention all along is that the doctor did not render appropriate care. The issue as worded says, "Was he negligent in his diagnosis, care, and treatment rendered to Mrs. Paula Jean Brown following the surgery in question?" Of course, when you talk about negligence, care, and treatment, you are talking about, I think, what is called postop care. Those issues all deal with the plaintiff's contentions of what Paula and I said we would prove to you by the preponderance of the evidence.

The issues that follow beginning with Issue 9 deal with damages in this case. All the issues that deal with damages start with some language that is very important, and they say, "What sum of money do you find from a preponderance of the evidence would fairly and reasonably compensate Mrs. Paula Jean Brown?" In other words, what is fair and reasonable to her. The reason for that is, this is the lady who experienced the pain. This is the lady who experienced anguish. This is the lady and her family who incurred the medical bills and expenses. There is no mathematical formula I can give you for determining physical pain and mental anguish. I can point out to you how the issues are presented.

Issue 9 asks about what is called physical pain in the past. Issue 10 is pain in the future. Issue 11 is what is called mental anguish—worry, the agony, the concern—in the past, and then Issue 12 deals with mental anguish in the future. Issue 13 asks about the medical expenses. I don't believe the medical expenses are going to give you any real significant problem. To my knowledge there has been no real issue or attack made on them; it is Plaintiff's Exhibit 13, and it shows a total of $33,018.71.

Paula's agony that she experienced following Dr. Johnson's surgery, her pain and her worry and her concern, were not the same every day. There were some days that her pain and agony were obviously greater than on others. There are some days according to the evidence and according to the records, for example, when Paula wasn't sure whether she was going to live or not.

That to me is a pretty serious type of pain. It's an agony and concern that I personally have never experienced. I feel ill-equipped as a lawyer to get up here and say to you what something like that is worth, and I hope that I never do experience it.

You know there is one thing about trying a case like this, and talking about medicine and hospitals and the possibility of things like this, that comes home to all of us as we hear the evidence. We are all going to die someday. There isn't any *probably* about it; it's absolute. And there is one thing that is deep down in every one of our minds—we say to ourselves that we know that someday death is going to come, but we hope that when it comes it will be quick and it will be peaceful. I know it is my prayer for myself that whenever it comes it will be quick and peaceful and I don't lie up in one of these hospitals agonizing with tubes in every end and that kind of stuff. That kind of concern to me is very substantial. Paula's weight during the time that she was under Dr. James's care got down to 197 pounds. She started at 255 pounds. She lost almost sixty pounds, and that is established by Exhibit 9. I don't think this has been offered to you yet. In fact, there is a good bit of this evidence that we will probably talk to you about during argument, and properly so, that you will have when you go back to the jury room to see and examine for yourselves.

There are some people who question whether there is any hell beyond the grave, but I will tell you one thing—this lady has seen hell on this earth for sure. It is difficult to bring in evidence for you to understand what this lady has gone through. We suggest that for her physical pain in the past she should be awarded the sum of $100,000; that for her physical pain in the future should be found damages in the sum of $50,000; that her mental anguish in the past should be $250,000; and that her mental anguish in the future should be $300,000. Those are our suggested figures; you can believe that more or less should be found. Those damages are peculiarly within your authority to determine. Paula is a young woman; according to the Bible and according to the statistics, she has remaining a life expectancy of somewhere in excess of fifty years. She has a long time to concern herself with any problems and to have any problems that may develop.

Some people have a different approach to people. Some people are taught that you are to be nice to people even if they are heavy, even if they have some physical impairment; but not all people are raised that way. And so, we've got some people on this jury who are very attractive and probably all of their lives have known that they are attractive, and so perhaps it's hard sometimes for those kinds of people to understand. Paula and I know that; I know that, and some of you folks know that, too.

She graduated from high school, she married, she had a son; but she was still self-conscious. Paula was always shy, and she never asserted herself. If Paula had any kind of complaint or grievance, somebody had to assert it for her. In the fall of 1981 she consulted this defendant, inquiring about the benefits of gastric-stapling procedure; they had a brief discussion, and the doctor told her that he would do it. They talked about the cost, but because of the administrative problems you heard about, the surgery was delayed to early 1982.

On January 31, 1982, she checked into St. John's Hospital. She never saw her doctor before the surgery or for three days after she checked in. The surgery was done on February 1, 1982. The initial incision, according to the records, was made at 11:45 a.m. Her abdomen was closed at 12:10 p.m., according to the records. According to the anesthesia record as evidenced before you, this procedure took twenty-five minutes. During the twenty-five-minute procedure, a staple or staples were improperly and carelessly placed into the gastroesophageal junction. Following the surgery, Paula experienced problems with pain and vomiting and spitting up blood. Finally, on the second postoperative day, Paula's stepmother insisted that the nurses get the doctor in. The defendant saw Paula around 10:30 that day. Paula had been throwing up so much that her sheets and her gown had to be changed several times a day, and she continued having problems. According to the nurse's notes, the doctor did not see her again until the day he discharged her, February 6. She went to her stepmother's home in Hawkins, Texas, to recuperate, where she continued to have problems with vomiting and spitting up. On February 12 she saw the defendant in his office to have her stitches removed. Her stepmother was with her. Both ladies tell the defendant that Paula has been throwing up, and the defendant says, "Well, you are stuffing yourself; I know the pattern well." And despite Paula's and her stepmother's assurances that she has been following the doctor's instructions, she is released with no investigation by the defendant as to the problems. Now she goes to her home in Port Neches. She continues to have problems. She's gagging, she has pain in her chest, and she's throwing up. On February 19 a call is made to the defendant's office by Brenda Smith, Paula's best friend; Brenda tells the office staff that Paula can't keep anything down, not even Popsicles. The office staff tells Brenda to take Paula to St. John's emergency room, and Paula is checked into the emergency room at 5:30 p.m.

For two hours she and her husband sit in the emergency room, and finally at 7:30 she is admitted to the hospital, and the defendant sees her for the first time on February 22, 1982. This is following the nurses' being told that Paula was vomiting. This is following Brenda's call to the doctor's office that this patient is vomiting. After seeing Paula, the doctor issued no new orders. His admitting and final diagnosis is nausea and vomiting with dehydration. That is in the record. Paula is found to be her expected weight, and, according to the doctor, since she was at her expected weight, she could have no problems when she is discharged on February 23. Paula returns to her home, and she continues to have problems. She's in pain and vomiting. Her mother-in-law is doing the housework because of Paula's weakened condition. On March 1, Brenda again calls the defendant's office and reports that Paula is nauseated and vomiting and can't keep anything down. She has a burning in her chest, and that's noted in the records. There's no response to the call, no prescription, no suggestion that Paula come in; and, Paula being shy and passive, she waits for her next regularly scheduled office visit. She sees the defendant on March 5. She again tells him that she is vomiting and can't keep her food down. Nothing is done that you have heard from the defense. Her weight loss is acceptable. On March 9 another call is placed to the defendant's office, and a request is made for something for Paula's nerves. Paula is upset and frightened about her physical condition; and her friends see this, and her relatives see this. She continues to have problems and sees the doctor March 25. It's probably on this visit as best we can reconstruct—though Paula couldn't remember the actual date—that Brenda Smith had come with her to the doctor's office. Brenda Smith tells the defendant, "Paula has been throwing up," and Dr. Johnson says to Paula and Brenda, "Well, you are stuffing yourself; I know the pattern well." He is unconcerned.

Paula last sees the defendant on April 19. Again complaints are made and nothing is done by way of investigation or treatment. Paula is worried; she's concerned; she's frustrated; she's frightened; she's scared; all those feelings that all of us would understand when we know that we are not well and the doctor won't listen to us. We can get no answers, and we don't know what the future will hold.

Eleven days later she sees Dr. James and tells the doctor that she has not been able to retain any kind of food whether liquid or semisolid since her surgery. That is Exhibit 19, Dr. James's admitting history. That's exactly what she told him and what he wrote down. Dr. James examines her, and he finds a woman with what he calls fear in her eyes, in his words, a woman who is weak and sick. She's obviously frightened. She is hospitalized, and Dr. James orders certain diagnostic tests to determine the nature of Paula's problems. Because of the type of tests to be done, Paula is put on nothing by mouth the day before the test, April 29. These are copies of the records, and you will have the actual records, and we have paper-clipped the pages. You will see the notation NPO that evening, which means nothing by mouth. They wanted her to have nothing by mouth before they did the upper GI series, but she is given two medications that night in pill form. According to the records it shows the time they are given, 8:50 Dalmane and Tagamet.

You have heard Dr. Johnson describe Tagamet, and most of us know that Dalmane is for sleeping. Tagamet is a large pill. She's taken nothing solid for some time, and 8:50 that evening she is given two large pills. At 8:30 the next morning, an upper GI series was done. Paula was told to swallow the barium. She hopes that she doesn't throw up. She feels like she might, but she doesn't. The doctor says to the technician, "Don't give her the second cup; it's not emptying." The X rays show that there is poor emptying of the esophagus. There is narrowing of the gastroesophageal junction despite the fact that the esophagus is distended and swollen and despite the fact that Paula has had nothing by mouth, even pills, for twelve hours. Two foreign bodies were floating free in the esophagus above the gastroesophageal junction. This is the interpretation by the qualified specialist. She had poor emptying of the esophagus. This is the interpretation before any lawsuit, before any legal proceeding, in a calm, deliberate, scientific environment of the radiologist's office at St. Teresa's Hospital, and that is what he puts in his records.

On May 3 at 9:45 an esophagoscopy is done. Paula is again conscious and fearful as the specialists run down what you have heard is a soft tube to look into Paula's esophagus and stomach. And, again, his interpretation—and it is in evidence before you—is that the gastric stapling is not functioning well and the opening was left high up near the EG junction; and this interpretation is made again before any lawsuit, before there were any legal proceedings, before there's any suggestion about a doctor's being liable for damages. Based on these tests, Dr. James decides to operate, and, again, Paula is exposed to the dangers of anesthesia, bleeding, and all the complications of surgery. She is fearful, she's frightened, and she's worried; but she knows that something has to be done. She knows that she cannot go on living like this. Would anyone undergo surgery unless they were having some kind of problem? Dr. James began the surgery at 9:45 on May 4, and he closed the patient at 10:55. While Dr. Johnson was in Paula's abdomen for twenty-five minutes, Dr. James was in there for one hour and ten minutes.

He finds the obstruction at the gastroesophageal junction that was referred to by the other specialists in their testing. He finds that obstruction was caused by staples being placed in the gastroesophageal junction and this is the cause of her problems. He goes and tells the family what he finds. He walks out of the operating room, and he goes to the family, and he says, "I found a mess in there. They had stapled the gastroesophageal junction." Right then, before any lawsuit, before any claim, before any question that some doctor might be held responsible for those kinds of damages. He immediately dictates his finding into his formal report before any lawsuit, before any pressure can be brought, before considering whether his findings helped or hurt any party to a possible lawsuit. Paula's recovery is slow, but she is discharged on May 9 after eleven days in the hospital. She goes back to her home. On the morning of May 14, she is awakened by a stench that smells like a sewer. She finds that her gown is soaked with pus from the incision, and Brenda takes her to Dr. James's office. The wound is lanced, and she is admitted to the hospital and put in isolation. People who see her—and there are few who do—are gowned and masked. Some nurses don't want to see her. Her son can't see her. She cries; he cries. She develops pneumonia and suffers a collapsed lung. There is a blood clot in her lung. She almost dies. Her doctors say, "Well, we're losing Paula." She is in extreme pain.

She recovers where she can go home, and nineteen days later she is discharged. By this time her hair is falling out. Paula has never been a self-assured person. She has always been shy and self-conscious, and now her hair is falling out. And so she stops going out. She stops going to the store; she stops going to church. Her weight drops to the 190s. And Paula agonizes, and she worries; but, as you have heard, she reaches out and she finds a strength where all of us ultimately have to turn to at times like that, and she begins to deal with her ordeal. She still wonders, and she still worries, and she still suffers. And so I submit to you, ladies and gentlemen, that what we have today is a very shy and withdrawn, bashful lady who trusted this defendant but will never be the same. And when the people visit her at home, as they have, they will tell you Paula is not the same; nor do I think any one of us would be the same if you had gone through what this lady has gone through.

Closing Argument

Ladies and gentlemen, I, like you, have listened to evidence for a week, and I knew that eventually the time would come when the defendant would have to or be forced to get up and give some kind of explanation. You cannot try a case before a jury as intelligent as this, I don't care how clever a lawyer you are or how smart a doctor you are, and hope to get away with inconsistent distortions and statements that go in opposite directions.

When this case began, Mr. Jackson got up, and I could not tell from his opening statement and I could not tell from the presentation of his evidence and the way he questioned witnesses whether the defendant was contending that Paula was vomiting during this period of time or wasn't vomiting. It seems to me it is one or the other. Either the defendant has got to say, "All right, she was not vomiting; she had no problem and therefore when she and her friends say she was throwing up, it just isn't true; don't believe it," or they have to say, "Yes, she was vomiting, she was having problems, but it was because of something else." You see, the problem is they couldn't very well do the second, I suppose, because every doctor testified—and they couldn't get around this—you just don't put staples into the gastroesophageal junction. You can't find that supported by any medical literature anywhere. And they couldn't find anybody to support it. Even Dr. Dewey, who they designated as an expert witness who never testified, never got up here. And you can use your own common sense as to why they didn't bring Dr. Dewey down here to testify after designating him as an expert witness, hiring him a week or two before trial.

I submit to you, ladies and gentlemen, that if you ask yourselves a simple question, you can very quickly begin to head in the right direction toward resolving these issues that the court has submitted to you. And that question is not exactly like the court has worded it, but I think you must answer that question before you can answer the other questions. And that question is, Was Paula Brown obstructed after her surgery by Dr. Johnson? Was she, in fact, obstructed? Now if she was obstructed, that surgery was not done properly. Everybody has admitted, and every doctor has said, that if she was obstructed, then that surgery was not done properly. Now the defense, in their effort to go from side to side and from dark to light, has made contentions that she wasn't losing weight or wasn't vomiting. And we have gone through the record; we have put up the various visits for you; we have produced evidence of witnesses who went with Paula, who were with Paula—

and Paula was having problems. When she saw Dr. James, she said as part of her history, and you can see it in the records, "I haven't been able to hold down liquids or semisolids since the operation."

Now the suggestion is made that, "Well, she saw Dr. James because she didn't want to go back to Dr. Johnson, so she went down to Dr. James and told him, 'I haven't been able to eat anything at all since the surgery.'" And I gather that the defense must also say, to be consistent with the other things they have argued, that that was a lie, that she wasn't telling Dr. James the truth, because that hadn't been happening. And if you believe and if you accept what the defense has argued—that Paula was not obstructed as a result of Dr. Johnson's surgery—then you are going to have to say, "Well, Paula, well, Brenda, you just weren't telling the truth." And I suppose that our friends have all done a lot for us. I don't think Paula's friends, and I don't think any one of you has friends you would ask, and I don't think this woman would ask people to come in and say something other than the truth; and yet that is what has been suggested. You are going to have to believe that this esophagoscopy that was done that shows that the esophagus was inflamed just wasn't there. You are going to have to believe that when she told Dr. James that she had been having all these problems for all this time, she just didn't tell him the truth. She was just making it up. There is no question that one of the things that was found down at St. Teresa's Hospital was a hiatal hernia. And just to give you an idea again how clever lawyers and smart doctoring can mislead you, we have now heard the suggestion, as I understand the argument of Mr. Jackson, that it was her hiatal hernia that was causing her her problems.

Mr. Jackson: No, sir, Your Honor. I never said that. That is a mischaracterization of my argument. I said that the hiatal hernia might be causing the problems she's having right now, but I never said that a hiatal hernia was causing the problems before this.

The Court: All right, you may continue with your remarks.

That is exactly correct, Mr. Jackson, because every expert witness who has testified has been asked that question, and every expert witness, Dr. James and Dr. Johnson have both said, under oath, that the hiatal hernia could not have possibly been the cause of Mrs. Brown's problems. But the hernia was the result of the problems, because those of you who listened to the evidence closely recall how you get a hiatal hernia. She didn't have any indication of it when Dr. Johnson was operating on her, but she had it down there. What causes a hiatal hernia? Pressure from the stomach, which confirms that she was throwing up.

You know, there is a certain aspect that is apparent in this case that is disturbing to me. If Paula Brown had kept going back to Dr. Johnson, don't you think that we can assume that her problems—if she was still living—she'd still have them today? Because if you believe Dr. Johnson, he would have never done anything about it. And if these very tests that were done on her down at St. Teresa's were done here in Beaumont, he would not, if you believe the testimony, ever have done anything about it.

If I understood Dr. Johnson correctly, his testimony was that if Dr. James had followed the usual, customary practice in preparing his operative report, instead of saying what he found—that he found an obstruction in the gastroesophageal junction and freed it—he should have said, he should have put in his report, "I went in, I became disoriented, and I came out." Now that is what has been suggested should have been in that report. I submit that you can draw your own conclusions as to what that indicates, and I would suggest to you that you can draw some other conclusions.

The reason we read Dr. James's deposition to you this morning is to demonstrate something that ought to be pretty clear by now. When Dr. James testified, this lawyer asked, "Well, did the scope go down?" and "Well, I don't know. I think not," and all of that, and he got all confused. But when we took his deposition, he was very straightforward about it and could tell you all about it—where the scope went, how it went, how he formed the basis from that test to do that surgery. But when he gets on the stand, you would think that man was an idiot. Dr. James is no fool. That's a smart doctor. But Dr. James, you see, cannot get around what he found in surgery because that is in writing; he can't say, "Well, that isn't what I found." Now that would look too foolish. So he has to say, "Yes, that's what I found. No question, that's what I found." But then the way you play the game, you see, is, "Well, I will testify in such a way that perhaps this jury will not think so much of my testimony that tends to establish that this procedure was done improperly."

Now Mr. Jackson has argued to you, and it has been suggested to you, that if there were staples in the junction, you ought to be able to see them on the X rays. Now there is one thing that you know from your common sense and from the expert testimony in this case, and that's this—when you are dealing with a contrast medium like barium that blocks out the X-ray film, that dulls it. You will notice, for example, that the staple line that Dr. Johnson pointed to is a line where there is no barium, so there is no obstruction to that part of the staple line. You will also note from the example that obviously is not the complete staple line that is on that X ray. There are some staples unaccounted for. They are there. They are unaccounted for. They are harder to see, because they are in areas where barium exists. Dr. James says he pointed out the gastroesophageal junction for you. But you know where that is; but he refused to look at the films and say where the staples were. Refused to look at those films.

It's no surprise that Dr. Johnson says, "Well, I looked at the film, and I can see that there are no staples in the gastroesophageal junction." But you know something, we have twelve smart folks on the jury with twenty-four eyes. That is all Paula's got, but in this case, that's all she needs. You'll have this back in the jury room—the esophagoscopy that you can look at. And you have a right to get any kind of aid or assistance you need. You can ask for a calculator if you need it; you can ask for a magnifying glass if you need it. And the court, if it's in the court's power to furnish it, will give it to you. And you can look at the X rays.

Some of you folks, I believe from watching your reactions during the trial of this case, are concerned about the quality of care we get today from doctors and the hospitals, and I think rightfully so. And I am probably the world's worst person to be talking to you about this kind of thing because I don't live, as you know and have heard, I don't live in Beaumont. You folks do. Paula lives in Port Neches. The people of this area are the people who have the right to decide what the quality of medical care is that you demand for yourselves and your loved ones. These cases we are talking about, these medical negligence cases—I can tell you, they are hard on people. You have seen what Paula has been through. That is a tough ordeal for her. And they are very expensive. You have seen these records piled up and these depositions piled up. There is a lot of expense and a lot of lawyer time that goes into preparing these cases from both sides to present these cases. There are going to be instances where patients are injured, and, as long as nothing is done about it, it's going to continue. Probably it's going to get worse. As a jury you have to see that a message goes out that it cannot continue.

I would submit to you that you must by your verdict find the defendant responsible and you must by your verdict find the damages that have been proved in this case, because if you don't the message that will be received is that this type of care is all right. It's all right; this type of care is acceptable. You recall the testimony—and I don't expect you to get anything very strong out of any of these witnesses for the reasons that should be apparent—but you recall the testimony from Dr. Johnson when he was on the stand. Question: "Now, is one of the reasons you want to keep staples out of the esophagus the fact that the esophageal junction is considered fairly delicate?" Answer: "It's much more friable and tears easier." Question: "What did you mean by 'more friable'?" Answer: "Like the difference in the strength between a piece of Kleenex and a regular piece of paper. Kleenex with a little pressure would break and tear, and paper won't hold more tension and would not be as pliable." And he was asked about the mucosa, and he said, "It's more subject to scar formation than, say, the stomach would be. In the smaller area, the scars are much more significant there, because every day we do tumor work and various procedures and make incisions in the esophagus, but the scar can be a problem because it is a more confined area than the stomach."

Paula Brown today does not throw up, she does not vomit; but she still has some concern and problems. You know, the amazing thing to me is how the defendant can get up here and argue in this case that, "After Dr. James's work, she didn't throw up anymore," but there wasn't anything wrong with her. What do you think? I hope that we do not hear, and I would ask our friends on the jury if you do hear to think about it. Every now and then somebody gets back on the jury during deliberation and they will say, "No, I wouldn't want a doctor to treat me that way. I wouldn't want that kind of care to be given to me. I don't think it's right. But we just can't find negligence on the part of the doctor." I hope I don't hear that. I hope that, if we have any friends, they will point out that this is the worst form of hypocrisy.

Don't anybody go back and say that we are settling this case. Your decision is not a settlement; it's a verdict. Juries decide cases; lawyers compromise cases. We would not compromise Paula, and I'm not going to do it now. You decide the case. You decide the case on what you think is fair. But I would hope that your verdict on damages will be based on the evidence so that it says we don't want this to happen again. When we come into your hands, please, please be careful with us. Be careful with us. And start with the proposition not that we're not telling you the truth; start with the proposition that we are. Give us the benefit of the doubt. When we come in with a complaint, give us the benefit of the doubt. When we come in with a complaint, give us the benefit of the doubt about out complaint rather than starting off with the idea, well, we're like such and such other patients and they have always told us something that wasn't true.

These are very plain people who have come before you in this case, Paula and her family. But there is a lot of Paula in all of us, I submit. She's a responsible wife and mother. She supports her family. She's a good citizen. And she comes to court, and she asks for justice. And Mr. Jackson, this is right, I'm not going to suggest to you or argue things—and there are probably some things that we could argue—that might get some sympathy, and I hope that we have done nothing that indicates that we are doing that. But to ask for justice, to ask for what we are entitled to and what we have proved. I submit to Mr. Jackson that is not a request for sympathy at all. It's to ask you for full damages. You know, if you give Paula or find damages that are less than what she is entitled to under these facts, that's not justice—it is a half justice, and that's an injustice.

In this day and time we hear so much about the worry and concern for the criminally accused. I can only wonder when we will start being concerned about the rights of the victims like Paula Brown. That, in this case, must be your responsibility. We appreciate very much your attention, and we know that you are going to do the right thing, and we hope and trust that we have brought you the evidence in a way that you have found helpful. Our only hope, as I told you from the very beginning, is twelve intelligent jurors, twelve courageous jurors who will look at what I hope and know you will find to be the truth. Thank you very much.

Bibliography

American Law Institute. *Restatement of the Law, Second: Agency*. Vol. 1. St. Paul, Minn.: American Law Institute Publishers, 1958. Section 267 discusses reliance on care or skill of an apparent servant or other agent. Volume 5 of the Appendix contains citations to the Restatement from January 1954 through June 1983.

______. *Restatement of the Law, Second: Torts*. Vol. 2. St. Paul, Minn.: American Law Institute Publishers, 1965. Section 414 discusses an employer's negligence in exercising control retained by the employer. Several subsequent volumes of the Appendix contain citations to the Restatement.

Bartlett, John. *Familiar Quotations: A Collection of Passages, Phrases, and Proverbs Traced to Their Sources in Ancient and Modern Literature.* 13th ed. Boston and Toronto: Little, Brown & Co., 1955. A valuable source for finding quotations. Indexed by authors' names and principal words in quotations. [Note: The 14th edition, published in 1968, and the 15th edition, published in 1980, include more recent quotations.]

Benham, W. Gurney. *Putnam's Complete Book of Quotations, Proverbs, and Household Words.* New York: G.P. Putnam's Sons, 1926. A comprehensive collection of older quotations and proverbs derived from many sources, including Hebrew, Greek, Latin, and modern languages. Arranged under authors' names and source categories and indexed under subject headings.

Blakely, Newell H. "Article IV: Relevancy and Its Limits." 20 *Houston Law Review* 151-271 (1983). Texas Rules of Evidence Handbook.

Call, John A. "The Psychology of Jury Deliberations." 50 *Texas Bar Journal* 590-95 (1987).

Edwards, Tyron, orig. comp. *The New Dictionary of Thoughts: A Cyclopedia of Quotations.* Revised and enlarged by C.N. Catrevas and others. N.p.: Standard Book Co., 1957. Alphabetically arranged by subjects.

Evans, Bergen, comp. *Dictionary of Quotations.* New York: Delacorte Press, 1968; Avenel Books, reprint 1978, distributed by Crown Publishers. Contains a topical index and an index of authors.

Fadiman, Clifton, ed. *The Little, Brown Book of Anecdotes.* Boston and Toronto: Little, Brown & Co., 1985. Indexed by names and subjects.

Felleman, Hazel, comp. *The Best Loved Poems of the American People.* Garden City, N.Y.: Doubleday & Co. A compilation of familiar poems, arranged by themes.

Gerhard, Eugene C., ed. *The Lawyer's Treasury*. Indianapolis and New York: The Bobbs-Merrill Co., 1956. An anthology of articles appearing during the previous forty-year history of the *American Bar Association Journal* on a wide range of topics.

Guest, Edgar A. *Collected Verse of Edgar A. Guest*. Chicago: The Reilly & Lee Co. (now Contemporary Books, Inc.), 1934.

Hamlin, Sonya. *What Makes Juries Listen*. New York and Washington, D.C.: Harcourt Brace Jovanovich, Law & Business, 1985. A discussion of principles involved in the communication process in the courtroom from voir doir through final argument. Includes a chapter on visual aids.

Hittner, David. "A Judge's View of Jury Service: A Personal Perspective." 47 *Texas Bar Journal* 227-34 (1984).

Ingersoll, Robert G. "Liberty." In *Prose—Poems and Selections from the Writings and Sayings of Robert G. Ingersoll*. 3d ed., rev. and enl. New York: C.P. Farrell, 1888.

Jones, Merritt B. *Speak, Listen, Communicate!* New York: D. Van Nostrand Co., Litton Educational Publishing, 1978. A basic speech and communications textbook.

Jordan, Walter E. "Expert Testimony—Cause of Present Physical Condition." 29 *Texas Bar Journal* 805-06, 843-48 (1966).

Kelly, Patrick D. *Blashfield Automobile Law and Practice*. 16 vols. Rev. 3d ed. St. Paul, Minn.: West Publishing Co., 1965-79. Supplemented. Volumes 11 and 12 cover trial evidence in the automobile case.

Kornblitt, Herbert, ed. *The Dictionary of Persuasive Phrases for Lawyers*. Miami: Marby Publications, 1962. Arranged alphabetically by legal subject headings.

Kramer, Charles. *Medical Malpractice*. Rev. ed. N.p.: Practising Law Institute, 1965. Includes an appendix with examples of medical briefs for various medical complications.

Levine, Moe. *Structure and Function in Advocacy*. Belleville, Ill.: Trial Lawyers Service Co., 1968. Covers injuries to the body and the mind, with commentary by medical doctors. Contains medical illustrations.

______. *Summations: The Best of Moe*. Washington, D.C.: Trial Lawyers Service Co., 1967. A collection of speeches and summations covering a wide range of topics, e.g., precepts of persuasion, damages, impairment of intellect of child, evaluation of pain, economic replacement for loss of mother, impairment of enjoyment of life, and the "whole-man" thesis.

______. *Surgical Malpractice: Surgical Errors and Accidents and Professional Liability to the Injured*. Washington, D.C.: Trial Lawyers Service Co., 1970. Presents physicians' views on problems and complications in particular areas of practice: anesthesiology, general surgery, orthopedic surgery, neurosurgery, cardiac and thoracic surgery, obstetrics, and gynecology. Also discusses the various stages of the malpractice trial, from voir dire to final argument.

McKenzie, E.C. *14,000 Quips & Quotes for Writers & Speakers*. New York: Greenwich House, reprint 1984; distributed by Crown Publishers. Originally published in 1980 by Baker Book House Co., Grand Rapids, Mich., as *Mac's Giant Book of Quips & Quotes*. A collection of quotations without attribution under alphabetically arranged subject headings.

Perdue, Jim M. *The Law of Texas Medical Malpractice*. 2d ed. Houston: Houston Law Review, 1985, vol. 22, nos. 1 and 2. A comprehensive treatment of prosecuting and defending a Texas medical malpractice case.

Philo, Harry M. *Lawyers Desk Reference*. 7th ed. Vol. 1. Rochester, N.Y.: The Lawyers Co-operative Publishing Co., 1987. Chapter 6 discusses automobile accident investigations and lists additional resource material.

Smith, Lawrence J. *Art of Advocacy: Summation*. New York: Matthew Bender & Co., 1987. Outlines structure and function of summation techniques and applies techniques to cases involving specific accidents and injuries, e.g., cervical sprain, quadriplegia, loss of worker's leg, ruptured lumbar disc, and burns. Includes chapters on product and premises liability and psychiatric malpractice.

______, and Malandro, Loretta A. *Courtroom Communication Strategies*. Kluwer Litigation Library. New York: Kluwer Law Book Publishers, 1985. A comprehensive treatment of courtroom strategy, including communication principles and techniques involved in impression formation, persuasion, credibility, and the decision-making process of jurors.

State Bar of Texas, Committee on Pattern Jury Charges. *Texas Pattern Jury Charges*. Vol. 1. 2d ed. Austin: State Bar of Texas, 1987. Supplement 1989. Covers motor vehicles and damages.

______. *Texas Pattern Jury Charges*. Vol. 2. 2d ed. Austin: State Bar of Texas, forthcoming. Covers workers' compensation and damages.

______. *Texas Pattern Jury Charges*. Vol. 3. Austin: State Bar of Texas, 1982. Supplement 1984. Covers medical malpractice, nonmedical professional malpractice, product and premises liability, and damages.

Stone, Irving. *Clarence Darrow for the Defense*. New York: The New American Library, Signet, 1971 reprint. A biography of Clarence Darrow, with examples of Darrow's summations.

Stevenson, Burton. *The Home Book of Quotations*. 10th ed. New York: Dodd, Mead & Co., 1967. Alphabetically arranged by subject. Indexed by authors' names and principal words in quotations.

Texas Jurisprudence. 3d ed. Vol. 6, s.v. "Appellate Review," §§ 767-769. Vol. 8, s.v. "Automobiles," §§ 318-322, 398-403. San Francisco: Bancroft-Whitney Co., 1980. Supplemented annually. The sections in volume 6 discuss the "Golden Rule" argument; in volume 8, the rights and duties of pedestrians and drivers.

Tottenham, Terry O., "Current Hospital Liability." 28 *South Texas Law Review* 1-36 (1987).

U.S. Public Health Service. National Center for Health Statistics. *Vital Statistics of the United States, 1980*. Vol. 2, § 6, "Life Tables." DHHS Pub. No. (PHS) 84-1104. Washington, D.C.: Government Printing Office, 1984. See the most recent publication for current life expectancy tables.

Vehicle Speed and Stopping Computer. Del Mar, Cal.: Lawyers & Judges Publishing Co., 1986. Instructions for determining stopping distances at a given speed for a specific vehicle.

Wellborn, Olin Guy, III. "Article VIII: Hearsay." 20 *Houston Law Review* 477-550 (1983). Texas Rules of Evidence Handbook.

Index

E

L

M

O

P

A NOTE ON PRODUCTION

Text composed at the State Bar of Texas, Austin, Texas, on the ZSI-565 (Zeta Systems International) system in Compugraphic Paladium (11/13 x 30). Cover and jacket composed by G&S Typesetters, Austin, in Garamond and Helvetica Condensed.

Text printed on 60-lb. Congressional opaque natural vellum and jacket printed on 100-lb. Lustro Offset Enamel (LOE) by Hart Graphics, Austin.

Bound in Roxite series A vellum by Universal Book Binders, San Antonio.

Cover and jacket designed by Karen Crowther, Austin.